MW00774010

The Battle of Ezra Church

=== AND THE ===

Struggle for Atlanta

◆ CIVIL WAR AMERICA ◆
Peter S. Carmichael, Caroline E. Janney,
and Aaron Sheehan-Dean, *editors*

This landmark series interprets broadly the history and culture of the
Civil War era through the long nineteenth century and beyond. Drawing
on diverse approaches and methods, the series publishes historical works
that explore all aspects of the war, biographies of leading commanders, and
tactical and campaign studies, along with select editions of primary sources.
Together, these books shed new light on an era that remains central
to our understanding of American and world history.

THE BATTLE OF

Ezra Church

═══ AND THE ═══

Struggle for Atlanta

EARL J. HESS

The University of North Carolina Press

CHAPEL HILL

Designed and set in Miller by Rebecca Evans. Manufactured
in the United States of America. The paper in this book meets
the guidelines for permanence and durability of the Committee
on Production Guidelines for Book Longevity of the Council on
Library Resources. The University of North Carolina Press has
been a member of the Green Press Initiative since 2003.

Jacket illustration: Martin's brigade line firing at Sharp's
first attack (*Harper's Weekly*, August 27, 1864).

Complete cataloging information for this title is
available from the Library of Congress.
ISBN 978-1-4696-2241-5 (cloth: alk. paper)
ISBN 978-1-4696-2242-2 (ebook)

Dedicated to

MY WIFE PRATIBHA,

for all she is

Contents

Preface xi

═ CHAPTER ONE ═

A Delicate Movement

Maneuver, Battle, and Logistics

1

═ CHAPTER TWO ═

They Are Sherman's Flankers

July 27

26

═ CHAPTER THREE ═

General Hood Will Attack Me Here!

Morning, July 28

42

═ CHAPTER FOUR ═

That Shrill, Terrifying Yell

Brantley's Brigade

58

═ CHAPTER FIVE ═

A Scene of Absolute Horror

Sharp's Brigade and Johnston's Brigade

73

═ CHAPTER SIX ═

The Biggest Kinde of a Rot

Clayton's Division and Manigault's Brigade

94

═ CHAPTER SEVEN ═

The Blood-Stained Path
Walthall's Division
114

═ CHAPTER EIGHT ═

Nerve and Persistency
Along the Line on July 28
132

═ CHAPTER NINE ═

The Bloody Effects of That Half Day's Work
The Battlefield
148

═ CHAPTER TEN ═

Enough for One or Two More Killings
Evaluating Ezra Church
162

═ CHAPTER ELEVEN ═

Our True Move
July 29 to August 3
178

Conclusion
194

Order of Battle 209
Notes 215
Bibliography 253
Index 267

Illustrations

William T. Sherman 3

John Bell Hood 5

Area of Operations around Atlanta 7

Oliver O. Howard 15

Stephen D. Lee 20

John A. Logan 29

Developing Union Line 35

Ezra Church in *Battles and Leaders* 45

Ezra Church in *Harper's Weekly* 47

Union and Confederate Skirmish Lines 52

Brantley's Brigade Begins Attack 60

Brantley's Brigade at High Tide 66

Sharp's Brigade Attacks 75

Firing Line of Martin's Brigade 76

Dead Brook 77

George D. Johnston 79

Johnston's Brigade Attacks 81

Logan's Line 84

Charles C. Walcutt 88

Randall L. Gibson 95

Clayton's Division Attacks 97

Capturing a Confederate Flag 101

Henry D. Clayton 107

Manigault's Brigade Attacks 109

Alexander P. Stewart 115

O'Neal's Brigade and Reynolds's Brigade Attack 118

Quarles's Brigade Attacks 125

Morgan's Division Marches 139

Union Advances after Ezra Church 188

Union Line in Mid-August, 1864 190

Preface

Heavy musketry suddenly erupted near Ezra Church a short distance west of Atlanta at noon on July 28, 1864. The sound signaled the beginning of the third battle fought for Atlanta since Gen. John Bell Hood took command of the Army of Tennessee only ten days before. Pressed to the gates of Atlanta after conducting a fighting retreat from Dalton since early May, the Confederates were desperate to stop Maj. Gen. William T. Sherman's army group from entering the city. They failed to gain an advantage over the Federals at Peachtree Creek on July 20 but nearly crushed Sherman's left, held by the Union Army of the Tennessee, on July 22. That large battle, however, resulted in a defensive victory for Sherman's men even though Maj. Gen. James B. McPherson was killed.

Those two battles did not derail Sherman's strategic plan. Rather than waste men in frontal attacks against the strong City Line of Atlanta, he pursued a strategy of snipping the railroads that fed Hood's army in the city. The last one now remaining entered Atlanta from the south. Under its new commander, Maj. Gen. Oliver O. Howard, the Army of the Tennessee moved from east of Atlanta to the west of the city on July 27. The next day, it deployed a line extending the Union presence southward, aiming at the rail link south of Atlanta. Hood moved three divisions of his army to meet Howard and placed Lieut. Gen. Stephen D. Lee in charge of an effort to block the move and set up a flank attack on Howard the next day. Having taken his command only the day before, Lee was young, inexperienced, and new to the Army of Tennessee. He made a snap decision on reaching the area late on the morning of July 28; he would immediately attack Howard instead of just blocking him.

Thus began one of the most intense battles of the Civil War, dominated almost completely by small arms fire delivered by veteran Union troops against determined but uncoordinated Confederate attacks. For about five hours those attacks kept coming across a shallow valley between the opposing lines, desperately urged on by Lee in an effort to justify his decision to disobey Hood's orders and initiate the third battle for Atlanta. In the end, when the firing slowly died down that evening, at least 3,000 Confederates lay dead and injured on the field, more than one-fourth of those who participated in the series of disjointed assaults. In startling contrast, only 632 Union soldiers were counted among the fallen out of a number nearly equal to the attacking force.

This book is an effort not only to detail the course of the battle of Ezra Church but to make sense of what happened there. It also assesses the role played by this phase of the Atlanta campaign in the overall history of Sherman's effort to capture the city. This study is based on thorough research in published primary sources and archival material. It takes its place alongside my previous book, *Kennesaw Mountain: Sherman, Johnston, and the Atlanta Campaign*, as another installment in a series of battle studies detailing the individual engagements of Sherman's drive toward Atlanta. The campaign has already been given a great deal of attention by historians as a campaign. My intent in this series is to devote a great deal of attention to the battles as battles—to study these engagements down to small tactical levels, as well as to assess each engagement within the larger operational course of the campaign.

Ezra Church has often been seen as an example of tragic loss on the Confederate side, easy victory on the Union side, the failure of Hood's effort to save Atlanta by taking aggressive action, and the success of Sherman's effort to capture the city by maneuver rather than by fighting. It is true that Sherman and Hood were responsible for setting the larger strategic course of this phase of the Atlanta campaign, but the grand tactical context was set by Howard and Lee. These two young and promising officers were new to their commands, and both knew each other from their West Point days. They were given a great deal of latitude to conduct the Ezra Church phase of the Atlanta campaign as they saw fit. Lee was eager to prove himself with offensive action, while Howard was keenly aware of the need to protect flanks after his near disaster at Chancellorsville on May 2, 1863, when Stonewall Jackson crushed his Eleventh Corps and nearly won the battle in one stroke. Howard knew that Sherman's decision to give him command of his and Grant's old field army was controversial, and he was alert to handle his units to ensure success.

While the strategic and grand tactical context was under the influence of the generals, the primary tactical context was the domain of division, brigade, and regimental commanders. The rank and file in gray made the attacks, and the rank and file in blue repelled them. When everything else was considered, the battle of Ezra Church centered on whether Southern men had the courage to cross that shallow valley and close in on the line of spitting muskets that faced them, and whether Northern men had the grit to stand their ground on the top of a narrow, crooked ridge and fire coolly at the approaching gray mass. The Confederates nearly overwhelmed the Union right flank, they engaged in hand-to-hand combat at the Union center, and they put so much pressure on the Union left that the Federals massed several regiments there to hold an important angle in Howard's line.

In other words, the battle of Ezra Church was not an easy victory for Howard and his men, contrary to popular impressions based on the huge disparity of losses. The Confederates threw all they had into those attacks. The fact that they failed and lost nearly five men for every Union casualty is not an indication that they had no chance of winning the battle. The Fifteenth Corps, which bore the brunt of those assaults, barely held on to its position on the ridge. Some regiments in the corps were stressed nearly to the breaking point, and many regiments from the Sixteenth and Seventeenth Corps had to be called up to help their struggling comrades. The Confederates came closer to victory at Ezra Church than they had a right to expect, given the breakdown in coordination among the brigades of the three divisions that conducted the battle. Only a comparatively thin blue line prevented Lee from rolling up Sherman's right flank during the course of that hot afternoon of July 28.

The experience of battle at Ezra Church was shaped by many factors of a long and short character. The string of impressive victories achieved by Federal forces in the Western Theater from Shiloh on created an enormous well of self-confidence in most Union soldiers who participated in the Atlanta campaign. They had undiluted faith in Sherman and were certain Atlanta would fall. These Federals had also honed their campaigning skills and battle stamina in numerous movements and engagements over the past three years. In contrast, soldiers in the Confederate Army of Tennessee had a long history of failed campaigns and lost battles, even though they often fought with spirit and determination. In fact, that field army had won impressive tactical success on the first day at Shiloh, at the battle of Perryville, the first day at Stones River, and the second day at Chickamauga. But its commanders were not able to translate tactical success into strategic victory. As a result, the Army of Tennessee struggled with everything from periodically low morale to material shortages and a persistent problem with coordinating attacks from the division level on up.

The Atlanta campaign accentuated both the strengths and weaknesses of Union and Confederate armies because it was conducted on the principle of continuous contact over the long haul. Under General-in-Chief Ulysses S. Grant's direction, Federal armies were to engage their enemy and continue pressing home the advance in order to shorten the war and deteriorate Rebel military resources. In the end, only the operations in Virginia (personally directed by Grant) and those in Georgia under Sherman proceeded in this fashion.

In the Atlanta campaign, Grant's new policy meant that the opposing armies would be in nearly constant touch with each other for months at a time. The Federals endured this strain better than the Confederates. Their administrative and logistical system was far more robust. They effectively used field fortifications to support the tactical offensive, digging in upon each new advance to secure even small additions of ground on contested battlefields. While the Confederates also learned to dig in effectively, they consistently used fieldworks merely as defensive tools to hold well-selected positions. With more men, Sherman was able to outflank these defensive positions time after time during the course of the campaign. Maneuver mixed with battle when necessary was Sherman's modus operandi. Under Gen. Joseph E. Johnston, the Army of Tennessee acted mostly in the passive defensive mode of operations, and that led to Johnston's dismissal from command on July 18. Hood took active defensive measures by striking out at Sherman, meeting the Federals on battlefields that often had little if any elements of field fortifications.

The Unionists had also honed their skirmishing skills during the long course of the Atlanta campaign. With the armies locked for weeks in continuous contact, there was ample time to engage in the mini-battles that often took place between the lines when opposing forces were within striking distance of each other. Backed by high morale and often led by brigade commanders who wanted to shine in these small fights, the Federals normally outperformed their gray-clad opponents on the skirmish line in Georgia. By late July, Confederate skirmishing had been so unsuccessful as to become a concern for worried commanders.

The battle of Ezra Church took place within this context of successful Union movements and battlefield victories and declining Confederate effectiveness. Rebel success was not doomed to failure; if an effective plan for catching the Yankees unprepared while moving to or just after they assumed a new position could be managed, there was still enough fight left in the average Confederate soldier to offer a serious threat to Sherman's progress.

What happened at Ezra Church deserves more attention than it has previously received because of all these elements in its story. Similar things could be said about other battles during the Atlanta campaign; they are among the more important, interesting, and instructive engagements of the Civil War that have not yet been treated in detail by historians.

I am very grateful to the staff at all the archives listed in the bibliography, and to several graduate students at various universities who have helped me to gather material for this study. I also wish to thank the two anonymous readers of the manuscript recruited by the University of North Carolina Press for offering significant suggestions and additional primary source material useful in the last round of revision.

Most of all, I owe a huge debt to my wife, Pratibha, for sharing her life with me. She and I also are responsible for the maps that appear in this volume.

CHAPTER ONE

A Delicate Movement
Maneuver, Battle, and Logistics

During the first half of his campaign toward Atlanta in the summer of 1864, Maj. Gen. William T. Sherman relied on a combination of maneuver and fighting to deal with each fortified Confederate position from Dalton down to the Chattahoochee River. There was hard fighting at Resaca, New Hope Church, Pickett's Mill, and Kennesaw Mountain, but the key to Union progress had always been Sherman's ability to pin the Confederates in their works and move part of his army group to flank each position. He thereby compelled enemy forces to retreat or risk losing their line of communications. From the first week in May until July 9, when Gen. Joseph E. Johnston evacuated the Chattahoochee River Line and crossed to the south side of the stream, Sherman advanced ninety miles into northwest Georgia and now was only ten miles short of Atlanta. The Federals lost about 21,000 men, reducing the initial force of some 100,000 troops but by no means incapacitating Sherman's ability to continue advancing. Johnston's Fabian tactics conserved Confederate manpower; only about 9,000 Rebel troops were lost out of the 65,000 men available from the start of the campaign until June 6. There are no reliable estimates of total Confederate casualties after that date.[1]

The Atlanta campaign entered a new phase when the Federals crossed the Chattahoochee River on July 17. The long advance from Dalton was then transformed into a short march toward a fortified city within striking distance of the enemy, if Johnston chose to attack. Sherman had no intention of assaulting the heavy earthworks that made up the Atlanta City Line. Begun the summer before, this ring of earthen redoubts and connecting infantry trenches was well sited and built. As early as June 30 Sherman had written his wife that he would avoid the earthworks and cut

1

the rail lines leading into the city. To Henry W. Halleck, the chief of staff in Washington, D.C., Sherman explained his views with clarity. Rather than "attacking Atlanta direct, or any of its forts, I propose to make a circuit, destroying all its railroads. This is a delicate movement and must be done with caution."[2]

By this stage of the Atlanta campaign, Sherman had perfected the operational art of clinging to his railroad while maneuvering so as to compel his opponent to abandon one strongly fortified position after another. In fact, he had done so eleven times since Dalton. His normal mode was to extend the Union line as much as possible to bypass a Confederate flank but maintain a continuous front that was linked with the railroad. On two occasions, Sherman deviated from that routine by loading wagons with several days' rations and breaking contact with the rail line temporarily in order to conduct a more sweeping flank movement if merely extending the line was not successful. He had done so when crossing the Etowah River in order to avoid the rugged country around Allatoona Station on May 23, regaining contact with the railroad two weeks later several miles south of Allatoona. Once again, Sherman prepared a similar flank maneuver to bypass Kennesaw Mountain on July 2, but Johnston detected the movement and retired before it was consummated.[3]

Sherman hoped he would not have to plan a risky, detached maneuver to reach the railroads near Atlanta. The Georgia Railroad, extending eastward from the city toward Augusta, was within his reach by extending the Union line from the Western and Atlantic Railroad. The only other rail route, the Atlanta and West Point Railroad, lay south of the embattled city. It would be a stretch to extend the Union army all the way to reach it because Sherman wanted to keep his left flank within striking distance of the Georgia Railroad to prevent his enemy from reconstructing and using that route.

For the Confederates, the key to retaining Atlanta lay in their ability to protect these railroads. Johnston's strategy lay in a passive defense dependent on maneuvering to block Union moves and the construction of field fortifications to secure key positions. It is easy to argue that Johnston's strategy was excessively defensive; he rarely attempted to launch counterstrikes and thus allowed Sherman more latitude for maneuver. He had largely done the same thing when defending Richmond during the Peninsula campaign and Jackson, Mississippi, right after the fall of Vicksburg. In the first case he was severely wounded during the only offensive strike he conducted (which failed to stop the Federals), and in the second instance he evacuated Jackson without a significant battle.[4]

◆ WILLIAM T. SHERMAN ◆
(Library of Congress, LC-DIG-cwpb-07315)

What Sherman intended for Atlanta was not a siege, even though many observers and historians have noted the siege-like characteristics of what developed around Atlanta. But the heavy earthworks within close range of the enemy and the bombardment of the civilian population did not alone make a siege. There was no possibility of a Union investment of Atlanta, for Sherman had too few troops. He never considered conducting siege approaches. Sherman wisely sought success in maneuver and offering battle when circumstances favored fighting. The Confederates needed to operate with a similar balance of options and not just rely on fortifications to stop Sherman, but Johnston did not seem keen on balancing his options.[5]

Sherman initiated his move against the Georgia Railroad on July 17. Maj. Gen. George H. Thomas's Army of the Cumberland anchored the move by extending east from near the junction of Peach Tree Creek and the Chattahoochee River, covering the area north of Atlanta. Maj. Gen. James B. McPherson's Army of the Tennessee was detached to march toward the area of Decatur, about five miles east of Atlanta on the Georgia Railroad, to tear up tracks. Maj. Gen. John M. Schofield's Army of the Ohio moved between McPherson and Thomas directly on Decatur.[6]

While the Federals were feeling their way through unknown territory north and east of the city, Confederate president Jefferson Davis made a difficult decision. He had become frustrated and alarmed that Johnston had given up so much territory without attempting a general engagement with the invader. Gen. Braxton Bragg, former commander of the Army of Tennessee and currently serving as Davis's chief military adviser, visited Atlanta to see if Johnston had any plans to take the offensive. It seemed to Bragg as if he did not. When Davis pressed Johnston to share his plans, the general vaguely talked about watching for an opportunity to strike at the enemy if one presented itself. This was the last straw for Davis, who issued orders for the replacement of Johnston by one of his corps commanders, Lieut. Gen. John Bell Hood on July 17. Although a severe critic of Johnston in letters to the president and Bragg, Hood was taken by surprise by his sudden elevation to command the army. He initially tried to persuade the president to postpone the appointment, but Davis would hear none of it. Hood reluctantly assumed command on July 18 in the midst of Sherman's move toward the Georgia Railroad. Hood was well aware that he had been named Johnston's successor because he had repeatedly urged offensive action as the best course to deal with Sherman and he immediately began to plan a strike against the Federals.[7]

Sherman found out about the Rebel change of commanders on July 18.

✦ JOHN BELL HOOD ✦
(Library of Congress, LC-DIG-cwpb-07468)

Later that day, Schofield's and McPherson's troops hit the Georgia Railroad at and near Decatur and began the work of destruction. On July 19, both armies turned west and began to move toward Atlanta, skirmishing with Confederate cavalry. Thomas's men also moved closer to the city on July 19, crossing Peach Tree Creek and lodging at various points on the south side only a short distance north of Atlanta. Sherman fully expected a major battle on July 20, but he anticipated that Hood would strike Schofield and McPherson to regain control of his railroad. Instead, Hood struck at Thomas north of the city, hoping to catch the Army of the Cumberland as it was in the act of completing its crossing of Peach Tree Creek. Because of the need to maneuver the Army of Tennessee so as to cover Thomas's front and the developing front east of Atlanta as well, the attack had to be delayed. Finally, at midafternoon of July 20, two of Hood's corps, commanded by Lieut. Gen. Alexander P. Stewart and Lieut. Gen. William J. Hardee, struck Thomas. On some parts of the line, notably where Maj. Gen. Joseph Hooker's Twentieth Corps had not fully taken position, the attack caught the Federals at a disadvantage. But the troops reacted quickly, advanced uphill against the enemy, and secured the most advantageous ground needed for a stout defense. On other parts of the line, the Federals repelled Hood's men as well. By dark, the Confederates lost 2,500 troops while Thomas lost about 1,900 men. Hood's first battle at Atlanta was a failure.[8]

While moving toward the city with Schofield's army, Sherman received word of the battle at Peach Tree Creek and pondered his next move. With the Georgia Railroad already cut, the tracks leading into Atlanta from the south were the next target. The Atlanta and West Point Railroad met the Macon and Western Railroad at a place called East Point about six miles south of Atlanta before the combined lines entered the city. "If we cannot break in, we must move by the right flank and interpose between the river and Atlanta, and operate against the road south," Sherman informed Thomas on the night of July 20. "If you can advance your whole line, say to within three miles of Atlanta, I can throw a force around your rear to East Point."[9]

Before committing himself to a move around the north and west of the city's perimeter, Sherman continued to press Schofield and McPherson up to the outer line of Confederate earthworks. This outer line ran west to east, between Peach Tree Creek and the city, and then abruptly turned south to cover the eastern approaches to Atlanta as well. McPherson's troops skirmished heavily to capture a high hill south of the Georgia Railroad on

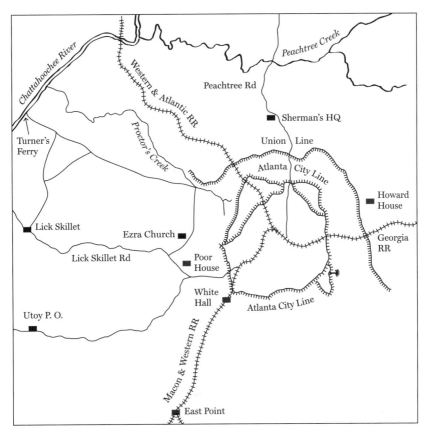

Area of Operations around Atlanta
(Earl J. Hess and Pratibha A. Dabholkar)

July 21, compelling the Confederates to abandon a long segment of this outer line. But the Rebels held firm along the rest of the position fronting Thomas and Schofield. Maj. Gen. Oliver Otis Howard's Fourth Corps, Army of the Cumberland, tried to maintain a link between Hooker's corps and Schofield's army in the center of the Union position where the Confederate line angled south. He had known Hood from West Point and had been impressed by the lesson of July 20 to anticipate that the new Confederate commander would repeat his offensive efforts. "Hood is great for attacking," Howard wrote in an effort to explain to Schofield why he could not send his only reserve force to strengthen the Army of the Ohio, "and I feel that it is necessary for safety to retain this brigade in a movable condition."[10]

On the morning of July 22, Sherman's mind was fully on the next move against East Point and the difficulties of reaching out so far from his line of communications, the Western and Atlantic Railroad that linked his army group with Chattanooga. It was imperative that he maintain firm control of the railroad bridge across the Chattahoochee River and cover the sector north of Atlanta with Thomas's army. "If the enemy holds on to Atlanta," Sherman wrote Thomas at 11:00 A.M. on July 22, "I wish you to press down close from the north and use artillery freely, converging in the town. I will then throw McPherson again on your right to break the Macon road." Sherman contemplated letting his cavalry try to break that road, but he had little confidence in its ability to do so. Only the infantry could do the job well.[11]

But Hood had other plans. Noting that McPherson allowed his left flank to remain unprotected, Hood evacuated the rest of the Outer Line north of Atlanta and fell back to the City Line. Then he marched Hardee's Corps all during the night of July 21–22 to flank the Federals. When Hardee struck at about noon, the Army of the Tennessee was taken by surprise. Fortunately Maj. Gen. Grenville M. Dodge's Left Wing of the Sixteenth Corps had paused on high ground near that exposed flank, while marching to assume a position to cover it, and was ready to stop the most serious Rebel attempt to turn Sherman's line. Moreover, troops of Maj. Gen. Francis P. Blair's Seventeenth Corps fought magnificently when Hardee's men attacked them from three different directions. None of these assaults took place simultaneously, allowing the Federals to fight from both sides of their slim earthworks as needed. An Iowa brigade was decimated, but the rest of Blair's line held against great odds. Hood's Corps, temporarily under the command of Maj. Gen. Benjamin F. Cheatham, attacked McPherson's front and captured a battery along with a segment of Maj. Gen. John A. Logan's Fifteenth Corps line, but counterattacks soon reclaimed the ground and the guns. McPherson was killed by Confederate skirmishers early in what came to be known as the battle of Atlanta, or the battle of July 22, and Logan took charge of the army for the duration of the engagement. He had full reason to be proud of his men for turning a near catastrophe into a magnificent victory. With Confederate losses of 5,500 men and Union casualties of 3,722, July 22 was the costliest engagement of the Atlanta campaign.[12]

Sherman deeply grieved for McPherson, his friend and subordinate, but he soon occupied himself with planning the projected move toward East Point. The plan was to detach the Army of the Tennessee from Schofield's line and move it behind the Federal position around the north and to the west side of Atlanta. Sherman's chief engineer, Capt. Orlando M. Poe, and the chief engineer of the Army of the Tennessee, Capt. Chauncey B. Reese, scouted the terrain on July 23 to select a new line of earthworks running toward the rear and from the left of Schofield's position. It would be a refused line to protect Sherman's left flank after the Army of the Tennessee pulled out. The angle of the line was located at the Howard House about half a mile north of the Georgia Railroad. The Federals dug this new position from July 23 to 26, the work performed by troops detailed from the line and supervised by the chief engineers of the Fifteenth, the Left Wing of the Sixteenth, and the Seventeenth Corps. Meanwhile, Reese scouted all the available roads in the area and then showed them to staff members of each corps so the troops would know their exact routes.[13]

Logan's men spent many hours digging this new line and strengthening their older works facing the Confederates in Atlanta. A shortage of entrenching tools hampered the work somewhat, but the surprise and near disaster of July 22 taught the Army of the Tennessee a lesson. The men had become rather complacent because of Johnston's defensive policy during the campaign and had operated under the assumption that the Rebels would evacuate Atlanta soon. Now they knew that Hood had inaugurated a new policy and were alert for another strike. They erected abatis and chevaux-de-frise before the works and dug the trench deeper, enlarging the parapet before placing head logs on the top. "We are diging up the whole Sunny south in Breast work," commented John C. Brown of the 9th Iowa in his diary. After four days of digging, Logan's men felt ready to receive another attack from Hood. "We changed sides of our works 4 times so as to front the Rebs" on July 22, wrote Edward W. Allen of the 16th Wisconsin, "now they can come from any point & find us at home."[14]

The Army of the Tennessee remained wary even after securing its position. Allen's regiment was called to arms on the night of July 25 upon the report that the enemy was about to mount an attack. "We watched & waited, every minute expecting to see them emerge from the woods," he reported. But there was no advance; the Confederates sent up rockets for some reason, and Allen could "plainly hear them hollow & yell" every time one went up into the air. "I guess they were wise in not coming for we are *ready* & prepared for them this time."[15]

The Federals all along Sherman's extended line improved the earthworks they constructed when taking position near the main Rebel earthworks protecting Atlanta. When Poe inspected Logan's earthworks, he was satisfied that the Army of the Tennessee had done all it could to hold its position. Members of Schofield's Army of the Ohio improved their works as Howard's Fourth Corps erected abatis and other obstructions in front of its position. Hooker's Twentieth Corps dug new lines a bit closer to the Confederates and constructed secondary lines behind its forward position. By the night of July 26, Sherman reported to Halleck that his troops were well protected on a line stretching from the Georgia Railroad east of the city around to Proctor's Creek on the northwest side of Atlanta.[16]

At the same time that the Federals dug in, Sherman wanted Logan to make sure the Georgia Railroad could never be used by Hood. He urged Logan not to worry about another attack, but to keep out a strong skirmish line, finish his entrenchments, and send work details to tear up all remaining track between his position and Decatur. Sherman particularly wanted Logan to heat and twist the iron rails so they could not easily be used again. Logan assigned Brig. Gen. Charles R. Woods's First Division of the Fifteenth Corps the task, supplemented by Brig. Gen. John W. Sprague's Second Brigade of Brig. Gen. John W. Fuller's Fourth Division, Left Wing, Sixteenth Corps.[17]

Logan's army also completed the melancholy task of cleaning up the battlefield of July 22 and taking care of its wounded. Musicians and details of men from the ranks buried the dead on July 23 and 24, in addition to improving the earthworks when they had any spare time. Surg. John Moore, Logan's medical director, moved the army's field hospitals from their location near the battlefield toward the Western and Atlantic Railroad. It was not easy; Moore even called the move "annoying, as well as injurious to many of the wounded." He transported them by ambulances to Marietta, a distance of twenty miles, and loaded them on cars for transport to Rome, Georgia, where the Army of the Tennessee had established hospitals. The entire process of moving several hundred injured men took several days.[18]

In preparing for the move to the west of Atlanta, Sherman relocated his headquarters. He had stayed at the Howard House, located on a prominent hill where the right flank of the Army of the Tennessee joined the left flank of Schofield's Army of the Ohio. From there Sherman had witnessed the fierce battle of July 22 and had seen McPherson's body after it had been recovered from the field. Now he shifted headquarters to a large white house located behind Howard's Fourth Corps line on the Peach Tree Road that ran north from Atlanta to Buck Head. The house stood near the Confederate Outer Line works and was quite close to the battlefield of Peach Tree Creek. From there Sherman would direct the move west.[19]

Sherman probably felt some apprehension about embarking on a risky maneuver with a general new to his command. He spent much time instructing and encouraging Logan, telling him that he need not worry about another Confederate attack. Hood had tried it against the Army of the Tennessee once and was severely beaten; he would not "again attempt it, but will await our action," Sherman assured Logan. When asked whether he should continue drawing supplies by wagon from Roswell, far up the Chattahoochee River where the Army of the Tennessee had crossed on July 17, Sherman told Logan to shift his supply arrangements so as to draw directly from the trains where the Western and Atlantic Railroad crossed the river.[20]

Logan also received instructions from Sherman about a cavalry raid by Brig. Gen. Kenner Garrard, who commanded a division of horsemen attached to the Army of the Cumberland. Sherman had sent Garrard out to Covington twenty-five miles southeast of Decatur to tear up more track. Sherman wanted Logan to demonstrate along his line and send out infantry to the east to support Garrard's return. Logan dispatched Woods's division for that task. Garrard returned on the afternoon of July 24, having burned two bridges, a locomotive, and some cars, in addition to wrecking forty miles of the Georgia Railroad. "As soon as my cavalry rests," Sherman told Halleck, "I propose to swing the Army of the Tennessee round by the right rapidly and interpose between Atlanta and Macon, the only line open to the enemy."[21]

On the same day that Garrard returned, Sherman felt the need to buck up Logan's spirit. "Act with confidence," he told his subordinate. "Know that the enemy cannot budge you from your present ground, and act offensively to show him that you dare him to the encounter. You can understand that being on the defensive he cannot afford to sally unless at great peril." Sherman thought that after two failed attempts Hood would revert to Johnston's policy of blocking Federal moves. His main concern was in organizing the logistics of shifting 30,000 men to the west of the city, not in steeling himself for another attack. Logan was not only new to his enlarged responsibilities but had been deeply involved in repelling the surprise attack on July 22. He apparently was having some difficulty adjusting in the days after that terrible battle.[22]

Sherman issued orders for the move west on July 25. In simple language, the document spelled out the process for extricating Logan's Army of the Tennessee from the Union left and Schofield's preparations for protecting that flank after it was gone. The Federals were giving up the Georgia Railroad, but it was in no condition to be used by the Confederates, and Schofield's men were located only a half mile north of the track as well. Sherman also outlined in these orders his plan for another assault on Hood's supply line, unleashing his cavalry to ride deep behind enemy lines and tear up track on the railroad south of Atlanta. Logan was to pull out of his position, and the cavalry would set out on its mission at the same time, during the early morning hours of July 27.[23]

This double approach to striking Confederate logistics understandably created a sense of confidence in Sherman's thinking. In his orders outlining the plan, Sherman included instructions for how his subordinates should follow up if the enemy suddenly evacuated Atlanta. After issuing these orders, Sherman wrote to Lieut. Gen. Ulysses S. Grant, general-in-chief of the U.S. Army, expressing his feeling that the campaign could end very soon. "None remains to him but the Macon road," Sherman wrote of Hood, "and I think I will have that soon." The scale of the coming move, involving the entire Army of the Tennessee and most of Sherman's cavalry, seemed to justify his optimism. John C. Van Duzer, a telegraph operator with Sherman's army group who fed daily reports to Washington, was impressed by preparations for the move. "Tomorrow hope to have news for you, as movement to destroy railroad south of Atlanta starts at daylight—very strong."[24]

The cavalry aspect of Sherman's master plan was more risky than moving Logan's infantry. Union and Confederate commanders had tried repeatedly throughout the war to use their mounted troops on long-range strike missions to disrupt enemy communications, with greatly mixed results. The planned raid against the Atlanta and West Point Railroad would be the biggest effort Sherman had yet made to use his mounted arm against Rebel logistics in the campaign. Maj. Gen. George Stoneman took charge of his division (which was attached to the Army of the Ohio) and Garrard's division to have a total force of about 5,000 troopers. Sherman directed Stoneman to ride east of Atlanta toward the rail line south of the city. Brig. Gen. Edward M. McCook took charge of his division (which was attached to the Army of the Cumberland) and a division of cavalrymen under Col. Thomas J. Harrison (which had just reached Sherman after raiding through central Alabama from Tennessee). McCook commanded about 4,000 men and would start from the Chattahoochee River and ride west of Atlanta. Sherman hoped the two mounted columns could meet near Lovejoy's Station by the night of July 28, about fifteen miles south of Atlanta. While preparing the strike, Stoneman asked Sherman for permission to rescue Union prisoners of war in Macon and at Andersonville after tearing up the railroad. Sherman had serious doubts that he could do this but reluctantly authorized him to try it. If Stoneman could bring home even a few prisoners, he would earn "the love and admiration of the whole country," Sherman thought.[25]

Both of the Federal mounted columns would have to ride past Confederate cavalry on their way to the railroad south of Atlanta. Maj. Gen. Joseph Wheeler's Cavalry Corps, Army of Tennessee, had troops on Hood's right flank east of the city while Brig. Gen. William H. Jackson's division covered Hood's left flank and the area west of Atlanta. Jackson's division had formerly been attached to the Army of Mississippi, that collection of regiments brought from the Department of Mississippi and East Louisiana by Lieut. Gen. Leonidas Polk to reinforce the Army of Tennessee in May. Polk had been killed at Pine Mountain on June 14 and eventually was replaced by Lieut. Gen. Alexander P. Stewart. Moreover, the Army of Mississippi was incorporated into the Army of Tennessee administrative structure and renamed Stewart's Corps on July 26, the day before the Federals began their major offensive. At that point, Jackson's cavalry division was also incorporated into Wheeler's Cavalry Corps.[26]

McCook's Federal troopers had probed south of the Chattahoochee River for several days in the area west of Atlanta, which would soon become the scene of operations for Logan's Army of the Tennessee. Jackson had worked hard to contain their activities as close to the river as possible and screen the entire area from curious Yankees. Brig. Gen. Lawrence S. Ross's Texas Cavalry brigade established its base at a small town called Lick Skillet about six miles west of Atlanta. Green's and Howell's Ferry was located on the Chattahoochee River another two miles west of Lick Skillet, while Mason's and Turner's Ferry was located two miles upriver from Green's and about the same distance due north of Lick Skillet. Ross had skirmished with the Federals along the road leading from Lick Skillet to Turner's Ferry since July 22. Two days later, when McCook's men crossed the river in some force to establish a permanent presence on the south side, Ross warned Jackson that the enemy "intend crossing with a formidable force to strike the road below Atlanta."[27]

In fact, Jackson's men put up such a strong show of resistance that McCook came to the conclusion he could not break through the screen on his projected ride to the railroad. Sherman ordered the laying of a pontoon bridge at Turner's Ferry, but he also conceded to McCook's judgment and allowed the cavalry commander to move the bulk of his men farther downstream from the ferry to bypass Jackson's division.[28]

Sherman had another important issue to settle before starting the next phase of his campaign for Atlanta. "The sudden loss of McPherson was a heavy blow to me," Sherman wrote to Halleck. "I can hardly replace him, but must have a successor." It was not entirely his decision, for the appointment had to be approved by higher authorities, but Sherman's choice would bear great weight in the process of finding a replacement for the slain officer.[29]

The natural course would have been to recommend Logan as permanent commander of the Department and Army of the Tennessee, but Thomas put a stop to it. Sherman told Grenville Dodge the details of that story many years after the war. Logan had foolishly made an enemy of Thomas well before the Atlanta campaign began. The Army of the Tennessee was operating outside the limits of its department, which was located along the east side of the Mississippi River, and had to rely on transportation facilities within Thomas's Department of the Cumberland. As early as March 1864 Logan had complained to Sherman that Thomas restricted his use of the railroads by requiring passes and orders to be approved by the provost marshal or any local commander in the Department of the Cumberland. When Sherman told Thomas of this complaint and urged him to moderate his system, Thomas complained of Logan as a troublesome fellow. He "said that he was hard to get along with," in Dodge's words. Throughout the early part of the Atlanta campaign, Thomas and Logan displayed further evidence of disliking each other. Therefore, when Sherman asked Thomas about a permanent replacement for McPherson, Thomas told him bluntly that he would resign if Logan retained the position. Sherman pressed him further on this point until Thomas felt guilty about letting him down in the middle of the campaign and withdrew his threat, but Sherman understood his feelings and decided not to recommend Logan.[30]

Thomas urged Sherman to appoint Oliver Otis Howard instead, and Sherman readily liked the idea. A graduate of Bowdoin College in Brunswick, Maine, and of the West Point class of 1854, Howard was one of the most accomplished and dependable corps commanders in Sherman's army group. He had taught mathematics at the academy before the war began and had held commands on every echelon from a regiment to a corps in the Army of the Potomac and the Army of the Cumberland. Howard lost his right arm because of wounds suffered at the battle of Fair Oaks on June 1, 1862, but this serious injury kept him out of the field only until the following August. His worst day, however, was May 2, 1863, when his Eleventh Corps was outflanked and smashed by Stonewall Jackson's famous attack at Chancellorsville. Howard managed to survive that fiasco and commanded

◆ OLIVER O. HOWARD ◆

(Library of Congress, LC-DIG-cwpbh-03097)

competently under trying circumstances on the first day at Gettysburg. Maj. Gen. Joseph Hooker, commander of the Army of the Potomac at Chancellorsville, supported his young subordinate in the wake of the battle and also commanded him again when the Eleventh and Twelfth Corps were detached under Hooker's direction and sent to Tennessee in the wake of the Union defeat at Chickamauga in late September.

Howard's career soared in the West. He came under Sherman's orders during the Chattanooga campaign and the relief march to Knoxville. The two admired each other and worked well together from the start. When the Eleventh and Twelfth Corps were consolidated into the Twentieth Corps, Sherman appointed Howard commander of the Fourth Corps of Thomas's army. Howard directed its movements very effectively. The only bad decision he made during the campaign was to launch an unwise attack at Pickett's Mill on May 27. Given the charge of finding and turning the developing enemy line, his men stumbled through the wooded, largely unknown terrain until they thought they had reached their goal, and then Howard and his subordinates threw one brigade at a time against a stout line of Rebel infantrymen who shot them down by the hundreds. The slaughter at Pickett's Mill accomplished nothing and could have been avoided, but Sherman hardly paid attention to it in his reports and memoirs.[31]

Every commander, Sherman included, committed a mistake or two for every success he achieved in the war, and Howard was no exception. Overall he was a superb choice for army commander. Howard remembered that on either July 24 or 25 Sherman surprised him while the two were reconnoitering on the Fourth Corps front northeast of Atlanta. Sherman suddenly asked, "How would you like McPherson's Army to command?" Howard was modest almost to a fault, and his first response was "I have a good corps and am satisfied, and as General Hooker is senior to me in rank he might be deeply offended." Sherman told him that he had consulted with Thomas, and both agreed that Howard would be a better choice. Howard must have known that Sherman and Hooker had not gotten along well during the campaign, a situation that mostly resulted from Hooker's unbridled ego and sensitivity about being demoted from command of the Army of the Potomac to that of a corps under a western general. Howard tried to assure Sherman that "Hooker is a good commander, and I believe will be really truer to you than you think." That was Sherman's opportunity to be blunt. "Hooker has not the moral qualities that I want—not those adequate to the command; but if you don't want promotion, there are plenty who do." Now it was time for Howard to be frank. "General Sherman, you misunderstand me; I am grateful for your confidence and that of General Thomas, and will undertake anything."[32]

After that conversation, Sherman submitted Howard's name for the command, and Grant approved it by the afternoon of July 26. The general-in-chief was not enthusiastic, but he trusted Sherman's judgment. "No one can tell so well as one immediately in command the disposition that should be made of the material on hand," he told Secretary of War Edwin Stanton. Halleck telegraphed Sherman only two hours after Grant's approval that he had authorization to place Howard in charge of the Department and Army of the Tennessee. Halleck's telegram was sent at 4:00 P.M., July 26, only a few hours before Logan was due to start that army on its move to the west of Atlanta. While Sherman told Howard the news, he waited until the next morning before informing Logan of the change and placing Howard in his stead.[33]

Howard had a few hours to privately contemplate this important step in his career. He would assume the most responsible position of his war service, commanding one of the three armies in Sherman's army group, and the force that Grant had molded into one of the most successful armies of the Civil War. It also was the force that Sherman had commanded as well. Howard had personally known McPherson, making his replacement of the respected martyr of July 22 both poignant and meaningful. In fact, Howard was keenly aware that McPherson was one year ahead of him at West Point and that Howard had succeeded him as cadet quartermaster sergeant in his second year, as president of the Dialectic Society, and as cadet quartermaster in his senior year. Howard thought of McPherson as "so young, so noble, so promising," and mourned his death. Moreover, Howard was aware that Hood had been a member of McPherson's West Point class, and he knew a bit about Hood's personality. "He is a stupid fellow," Howard had written his wife after the battle of July 22, "but a hard fighter, does very unexpected things."[34]

The replacement of Logan with Howard was not entirely based on Thomas's feelings; Sherman later explained that he had doubts about Logan's administrative abilities. Logan was a politician at heart, without a West Point training or any other military education of any kind. He had learned how to be an effective soldier, successfully commanding a regiment, a brigade, a division, and a corps. But Logan was largely an inspirational leader who had learned enough administrative skills to succeed up to corps level. Sherman did not believe he was capable of commanding an army. The position entailed not only command of the Army of the Tennessee but control over the large geographic Department of the Tennessee. Stretching from Cairo down the eastern side of the Mississippi River to Natchez, that department's most important task was protection of commerce and the towns that supported it along the river. The department embraced 110,000 troops along the Mississippi, which Logan would have had to direct from a distance of hundreds of miles at the same time that he mastered the movements of 30,000 men in the Fifteenth, the Left Wing of the Sixteenth, and the Seventeenth Corps in Georgia. Sherman thought he did not have the training or aptitude for the job. Whether he devised this explanation after the fact as a rationalization for his decision or sincerely believed it from the beginning, we will never know. What is certain is that Howard had all the qualifications for handling both the administrative and the operational tasks associated with the command. Logan, Dodge, and Blair had no military training, and it was completely understandable that Sherman wanted a West Pointer to lead the Army of the Tennessee.[35]

In his memoirs Sherman asserted, "I . . . needed commanders who were purely and technically soldiers, men who would obey orders and execute them promptly and on time; for I knew that we would have to execute some most delicate manoeuvres, requiring the utmost skill, nicety, and precision." Still, Sherman knew that Logan would be hurt and the Army of the Tennessee would not really understand why a stranger supplanted one of their own. Moreover, the change in commanders would take place exactly at the start of this delicate movement. Howard's steadiness and skill would be put to the ultimate test on July 27 and 28 as he was asked to take over an army of strangers and move them into harm's way west of Atlanta.[36]

Sherman's faith in him and Thomas's recommendation were the steadying elements in Howard's mind as he received word at 10:00 P.M. of July 26 that his promotion had been approved. "I want you to-morrow to assume command and give directions to the Army as it goes into position," Sherman wrote. "If you will come to my headquarters [in the morning] I will ride with you and explain my wishes." Sherman also wanted to put Logan back in his Fifteenth Corps command before the movement challenged a Confederate response. After Howard read Special Field Orders No. 44, written by Sherman's staff and officially placing him in command, he also wrote a farewell message to his troops in the Fourth Corps that night. He had grown to admire these western men, whose steadiness, self-confidence, and aggressiveness seemed like a contrast to the men he had commanded in the East. "Believing from my heart that our cause is right and just before God, as I take leave of you I commend you to His blessing, and trust He will assist our armies to complete the work which He has enabled them so gloriously to bring to the present stage of success." After penning his farewell, Howard tried to sleep before dawn compelled him to assume a new, far more responsible role in the war.[37]

A dozen miles from Howard's tent, behind the Atlanta City Line, John Bell Hood also made an important decision about personnel within the Army of Tennessee. "I need a commander for my old corps," he informed Secretary of War James A. Seddon on July 19. "I have no major-general in that corps whom I deem suitable for the position." Hardee thought one of his division commanders, Benjamin F. Cheatham, was the best qualified, and Hood had temporarily appointed him to the post even though Cheatham "did not desire it." Cheatham's lackluster performance on July 22 demonstrated that he left a good deal to be desired as a corps commander. Hood suggested Maj. Gen. Mansfield Lovell, whose competency was shadowed by the fact that he was in charge of the defenses of New Orleans when the city fell to a combined Union naval and land force in April 1862. Hood also liked Maj. Gen. Wade Hampton, who was a cavalry commander in Virginia. Last, Hood suggested Lieut. Gen. Stephen D. Lee, who had replaced Polk as commander of the Department of Mississippi and East Louisiana.[38]

The authorities in Richmond quickly chose Lee. Born in Charleston, South Carolina, in 1833, three years later than Howard's birth in Maine, Lee also graduated in the same West Point class as Howard in 1854. In fact, the two served together in Florida three years later. Lee commanded artillery in Virginia during 1862, fighting at Second Bull Run and Antietam, but he became a successful general of infantry during the long campaign to defend Vicksburg against Ulysses S. Grant. Lee commanded a small force that defeated Sherman's attempt to take the city in late December 1862 in what came to be called the battle of Chickasaw Bluffs. He was one of the best brigade commanders in Lieut. Gen. John C. Pemberton's Army of Mississippi and East Louisiana during the remainder of the Vicksburg campaign and siege, earning recognition and a chance at higher command responsibilities.[39]

Lee received that advancement in 1864 when he replaced Polk in Mississippi. Faced with the job of defending the eastern part of the state with minimal resources against a series of Union thrusts out of Memphis, Vicksburg, and other occupied towns along the Mississippi River, Lee performed competently as the administrator of a significant department accorded second-rate status by Richmond. But disturbing signs began to appear

◆ STEPHEN D. LEE ◆
(Library of Congress, LC-DIG-cwpb-05330)

regarding Lee's ability to handle large bodies of troops on the battlefield. In dealing with one of the most threatening Union offensives in Mississippi, designed like the others to keep the Confederates so busy they could not send cavalry forces under Maj. Gen. Nathan Bedford Forrest to raid Sherman's supply lines, Lee and Forrest confronted Maj. Gen. Andrew Jackson Smith in battle near Tupelo on July 14. Both Lee and Forrest agreed to launch an attack on Smith's 14,000 men, who were partially fortified with rail breastworks, but the assault degenerated into an uncoordinated rush that the Federals had no difficulty repelling. For three hours the attacks were pushed with little sign that anyone was in control of them and Lee lost 1,326 of the 10,000 men involved while Smith lost only 674 troops. Despite this victory, Smith retired to Tennessee but the battle of Tupelo was an eerie foreshadowing of what was to come at Ezra Church. The Richmond authorities either did not know the details of the battle or ignored them while ordering Lee to the Army of Tennessee less than two weeks after the engagement.[40]

Lee's career shadowed that of Hood in the Civil War. Both were young men of promise and potential, but potential only went so far with them. Both men did well when under good direction from a superior officer or, in Lee's case, when administering a department. Both men tended to be aggressive when it came to making tactical decisions on the battlefield, but neither had the innate ability to smoothly execute those tactical plans with large numbers of men. That was essentially an administrative function demanding brainpower. Both men were being shoved into positions for which they were, at the least, not prepared and, at the worst, ill-suited to fill.

Hood had already demonstrated his inadequacy in handling his corps command during the first half of the Atlanta campaign. The most notable example had been the battle of Kolb's Farm on June 22, when he unwisely launched an attack on Sherman's right wing west of Marietta without authorization from Johnston and without scouting the terrain or the Union position. Moreover, the attack was disjointed with little coordination between divisions. The result was a blunt repulse that cost Hood 1,000 casualties. He did block the further advance of Hooker and Schofield toward Marietta, but he could have done that merely by fortifying his corps in their path without the loss of a single man.[41]

When Jefferson Davis decided to relieve Johnston and replace him with Hood, he was justified in his dissatisfaction with Johnston. But there was little cause for elevating Hood to the position. It was done because of Hood's personal relationship with Davis and Bragg's strong liking for the young general. On Hood's urging, Davis approved the appointment of Lee to take over Hood's Corps a week later. The president had already been impressed by Lee's performance in Mississippi. The young general was expected to reach Atlanta on July 26, the day before Sherman began his delicate movement to the west of the city.[42]

Lee was a complete stranger not only to his corps but to the entire Army of Tennessee and would have only a few hours to become acquainted with the men and the topography of the region before being thrust into an important mission to stop that westward movement. On two occasions when corps commands came open in the Army of Tennessee in 1864, they were filled with outsiders (Hood and Lee). Davis seems to have had a prejudice against the division commanders in that army, probably because of the virulent criticism leveled by many of them against their longtime commander, Braxton Bragg. Davis had been compelled to visit the army twice to quell disturbances among the Bragg dissidents. Perhaps that is why he preferred to bring new blood into the army rather than reward successful division leaders like Patrick Cleburne with corps commands. Only once did a corps job go to an insider, when Stewart replaced Polk.[43]

The appointment of Lee to the Army of Tennessee was a gamble, as was the appointment of Hood to lead that army. Most Confederates were still willing to give Hood a chance to prove himself, and Lee genuinely seemed a good choice if one were ignorant of the details surrounding the failed assault at Tupelo. Sherman also was taking something of a risk by appointing Howard to the Army of the Tennessee on the eve of his move west, but Howard at least had a long history of command responsibilities on many levels in different field armies. He also had proved himself during nearly three months of campaigning thus far in Georgia (except for the mistake made at Pickett's Mill). Howard was far better prepared for what was to come than Lee.

While both sides waited, the Confederates continued to improve their fortifications around Atlanta. They placed abatis and other obstructions in front of the City Line at night until the ring of earthworks became layered with defensive features. The citizens of Atlanta endured Union bombardment, which had begun as early as July 20. Shells falling into the city "scared the women and children and *some* of the *men* pretty badly," recorded Samuel P. Richards in his diary.[44]

Those troops stationed near the July 22 battlefield could still smell rotting bodies four days later, emanating from remains that had been overlooked by burial details. But the smell could not deter the Federals from continuing their preparations for the move. Once again, Chauncey Reese led staff members from the Army of the Tennessee in a ride to show them the roads their commands would have to take in that move, while details improved the roads all day of July 26.[45]

Detailed instructions for the movement were issued in Special Field Orders No. 79 from Logan's headquarters. Still unaware of the decision to replace him, Logan spelled out the process of evacuating his works. Woods's division was to pull back at 4:00 P.M. on July 26 to occupy the new refused line of works stretching east from the Howard House. Dodge was to pull out and lead the way west with his Left Wing, Sixteenth Corps, while Blair would follow Dodge. Then Maj. Gen. Morgan L. Smith, who took over the Fifteenth Corps when Logan replaced McPherson, would bring up the rear of the army, Woods to leave last. The artillery would be pulled out soon after dusk on July 26, the gunners wrapping gunnysacks around the wheels to muffle the noise. The army was to reduce its transportation to the minimum. Logan allowed only one ammunition wagon to accompany each regiment and battery, while the other wagons were to be parked near the center of Sherman's line. Corps headquarters repeated these instructions and emphasized that the movement out of the works should be conducted as quietly as possible, with all instructions given "in a very low tone of voice."[46]

Sherman wanted cooperative movements from Thomas and Schofield. Thomas was to send out a regiment from each division to press the Confederate pickets and draw attention from Logan's movement. Thomas's right flank was held by Maj. Gen. Jefferson C. Davis's Second Division of Maj. Gen. John M. Palmer's Fourteenth Corps. Davis had dug in along Proctor's Creek when the Army of the Cumberland moved forward to confront the City Line on July 22. Davis protected Sherman's right flank by occupying a long refused line along the north bank of Proctor's Creek, which drained from a point northwest of Atlanta toward the Chattahoochee River. Davis's command would become a reserve as soon as Dodge marched past Proctor's Creek. This allowed Davis to send a brigade out to reconnoiter southward from the creek on July 27, just before Dodge arrived in the area. Sherman wanted that brigade to head toward "the old village of White Hall, about two miles and a half [southwest of] Atlanta," and draw as much attention from the Confederates as possible. "These demonstrations should proceed slowly and deliberately, and last all day," Sherman told Thomas, and "should be as bold and provoking to the enemy as possible, tempting him to sally out and test our present lines."[47]

Schofield had a more complex task because he had to adjust his army's line to accommodate Logan's pullout. He prepared to make Sherman's left flank a bastion nearly impregnable to assault. Schofield saw to it that the new refused line of works connected with an abandoned Confederate line that faced east and was located well to the rear of his own position. He ordered a long stretch of this Confederate work to be refurbished for his use so that he would have protection on three sides, creating a pocket within which he could park his trains and field hospitals. One of his divisions would hold the refused line facing south, while the other would hold the abandoned Confederate line facing east. Howard was to shift two brigades of the Fourth Corps to the abandoned Confederate works as well as extend his main line south to the point where the new refused line joined it. "The present movements are expected to be decisive," Schofield warned his subordinates. "The enemy is desperate and consequently bold."[48]

Sherman was ready. He wrote to Halleck on the night of July 26 that he intended to move the entire Army of the Tennessee to threaten East Point that night. Sherman hoped to compel Hood "to abandon Atlanta or allow us, at small cost, to occupy the railroad south of the town." He was convinced this was the right strategy, writing his wife that "I must gradually destroy the Roads which make Atlanta a place worth having."[49]

Sometime on July 26, Stephen D. Lee arrived at Atlanta by a train using the very line that was the target of Sherman's move. Braxton Bragg was in the city that day and reported that Lee was "most favorably received." Hood was busy with other administrative changes that day as well. He issued an order incorporating the Army of Mississippi into the Army of Tennessee as Stewart's Corps, instructing Jackson's cavalry division from now on to report to Wheeler's corps headquarters. He also replaced his chief of staff, Brig. Gen. William Whann Mackall, with Brig. Gen. Francis A. Shoup. Mackall, a close friend of Johnston, was unable to work with Hood and requested to be relieved of his responsibilities. Shoup had served as Johnston's chief of artillery, so Hood now appointed Col. Robert F. Beckham to be the army's new artillery chief. Within the space of one day, Hood had one brand new corps commander, another corps commander who had lost his independent status, a new chief of staff, and a new chief of artillery. And Hood himself had been in command of the army for only eight days.[50]

The day before all these changes, on July 25, Hood had issued a general field order to the Army of Tennessee with the intention of instilling an aggressive spirit in the men. "Experience has proved to you that safety in time of battle consists in getting into close quarters with your enemy. Guns and colors are the only unerring indications of victory. . . . If your enemy be allowed to continue the operation of flanking you out of position, our cause is in great peril. You have but to will it, and God will grant us the victory your commander and your country expect." As a young commander, new to his trust and grateful to Hood for the increased responsibilities, Lee must have taken the sentiments of Hood's order very much to heart.[51]

CHAPTER TWO

They Are Sherman's Flankers
July 27

Completely unaware that his command of the Army of the Tennessee was soon to end, Logan issued orders for his men to leave their works east of Atlanta on July 26. The movement was to begin at midnight. While some men tore up blankets to wrap around the wheels of guns and limbers, ordnance officers distributed 100 rounds of small arms ammunition per man in preparation for the move.[1]

The Second Division of Dodge's Left Wing, Sixteenth Corps, commanded by Brig. Gen. John M. Corse, led the way that night. Corse had taken charge of the division only a few hours before the move on July 26. He had previously served as acting inspectoar general on Sherman's staff but was tapped to replace Brig. Gen. Thomas W. Sweeny, a tempestuous one-armed Irishman. Sweeny insulted Brig. Gen. John W. Fuller, Dodge's other division commander, for actions during the battle of July 22. In an unusual confrontation, Sweeny started a physical scuffle with Dodge during the heated exchange of views on the issue. Sweeny was arrested and now awaited trial. Corse was a talented, energetic commander, so the division was in good hands. His officers gave their instructions in whispers as they maneuvered their regiments and brigades out of the trenches and into the dark night.[2]

Fuller, who also was involved in the scuffle with Sweeny, led the Fourth Division out of the works. He left Brig. Gen. John W. Sprague's Second Brigade in the trenches near the angle formed by the meeting of the new refused line and the older main line. Sprague's job was to cover the pullout of the corps. Another brigade commander in Fuller's division was told "to vacate the whole line quietly, to allow no fires, and to have no talking above a whisper."[3]

The Seventeenth Corps pulled out next, but Blair's artillery preceded the movement of his infantry. Gunners muffled their wheels with gunnysacks and placed leather washers at moving parts to reduce noise before leaving their works at 11:00 P.M. At about the same time the Confederates opposite Blair's position sent up several signal rockets, "which were of various colors and were a splendid sight a free exhibition to our brigade," wrote William Fultz of the 11th Iowa. Blair's infantrymen left their works at about the same time as Dodge's, but they took place in the developing column of march behind the Sixteenth Corps troops.[4]

As the Seventeenth Corps men formed in the dark along crude military roads only recently cut through the woods, no one knew where they were going. The darkness was stifling. "Stumps, roots and logs made a very rough road to pass over," according to L. D. Hord of the 32nd Ohio. If someone had a tin cup, he hung it from his belt and behind his back "so his file leader could have some little guide."[5]

Company I of the 32nd Ohio had been detailed to picket duty at 6:00 P.M. on July 26. It remained on the picket line only 150 yards from the enemy all night as the Seventeenth Corps pulled out and began to move slowly away. Corp. Charles E. Smith could hear the Rebels "talk and sing till late at night." His company was on the battlefield of July 22, and the men slowly began to realize that many bodies had been overlooked by burial details because the stench became "almost unendurable." The smell from many rotting bodies of horses, which the burial details had not the time or strength to inter, added to their misery. The company finally gave up the picket line just before dawn and rushed to rejoin its regiment.[6]

The Sixteenth and Seventeenth Corps marched slowly past the new refused line of works held mostly by Woods's division of the Fifteenth Corps, which had the assignment of covering the pull out for the entire army. When the other troops were gone, the rest of Morgan L. Smith's Fifteenth Corps also evacuated its works and marched past Woods's position. Then Woods pulled out and allowed Schofield's Army of the Ohio to fill the refused line. Smith's Second Division must have caused some alarm among Confederate pickets when it left the works, for Rebel artillery fired a few shells in its direction. The rounds were short because most of the men were away from their trenches by that time, and no one was hurt.[7]

"The Army of the Tennessee is moving to the right of the army," wrote Oscar L. Jackson of the 63rd Ohio in his diary that morning. "They are Sherman's flankers, having made every one of his great flank movements in the campaign." Logan was "in the saddle all night," he remembered years later, "and with my staff personally supervised the movement of every corps." His trains moved to safe positions north of the Chattahoochee River so the army could travel light and with only minimal food but plenty of ammunition.[8]

As the dark night gave way to dawn, Logan was in for the shock of his life. He rode to Sherman's headquarters at the White House on Peach Tree Road, the main route linking Atlanta with Buck Head due north of the city and quite close to the Peach Tree Creek battlefield. There he was informed for the first time that Howard would take over permanent command of the Army of the Tennessee. Howard was already there to assume the position. He issued an order after taking over to inform the army of the change in commanders. Howard assured the men that "I fully realize the delicate nature of my responsibility. Your late beloved commander was my personal friend, and while I unite with you in profound sympathy and regret for his irreparable loss, it shall be my constant aim to emulate his noble example."[9]

When the head of Corse's division neared the Peach Tree Road on the morning of July 27, Dodge rode ahead to Sherman's headquarters and found Logan sitting on the porch "of a log building," with Sherman inside the structure. Dodge spoke to Logan and learned of the change of commanders. He then walked in to implore Sherman to keep Logan in his place. Sherman's only response was that "it was alright; that he would tell me the reasons some time." All Dodge could do was to console Logan for a few minutes on the porch. He believed Logan heard what Sherman said because the door remained open during his brief conversation with the general. There were tears in Logan's eyes. "I spoke to him very cordially," Dodge recalled, "and said to him that I was greatly disappointed at the change, but I hoped it would end alright. He, like a good soldier, said it would, but he said it was pretty hard on him."[10]

Dodge's disappointment at the change of commanders had nothing to do with Howard personally, but with the fact that an outsider had replaced a man who had fought in the Army of the Tennessee since the beginning of the war. Dodge believed this feeling was universal among his colleagues and subordinates. "They felt that an army that followed Grant, Sherman, McPherson, and Logan . . . had material enough in it to command it."[11]

Dodge could not stay at Sherman's headquarters long. As Corse's division crossed the Peach Tree Road, leading the army westward, Dodge mounted and rode along with it. Howard now took his rightful place at the head of the column, riding along with Dodge. Sherman also came along with a few staff members, and the trio rode together as the army's long

◆ JOHN A. LOGAN ◆
(Library of Congress, LC-DIG-cwpbh-03223)

column made its way in a circular route behind Thomas's Army of the Cumberland.[12]

But Logan did not ride with them. Sherman wanted him to resume command of the Fifteenth Corps, but he was devastated by the turn of events and needed time to absorb it. Sherman understood. He wrote a quick note before leaving the White House to authorize a break for Logan. "Take a good rest," Sherman told him. "I know you are worn out with mental & physical work. . . . After you have rested come down to Davis's position and thence to the new position of your Corps. Assume command of it and things will move along harmoniously & well." Concluding with a sentence that confirmed the new state of things, Sherman told Logan, "Gen. Howard & I will go off to the Right to Survey the New Field and prepare the way for the troops."[13]

Late that night, after the day's work had been done, Sherman informed Washington of Logan's reaction. The disappointed officer believed "he ought to have been allowed the command of the army in the field until the end of the campaign; but I explained to him that a permanent department commander had to be appointed at once, as discharges, furloughs, and much detailed business could alone be done by a department commander." Apparently Sherman did not fully explain to Logan why he did not want him to fill that important role, leaving Logan confused as well as disappointed and increasingly bitter by the hour.[14]

Meanwhile, the Army of the Tennessee continued moving forward. Corse's division had rested for a bit and ate a hurried breakfast earlier that morning at about 6:00 A.M., behind Schofield's line. Then it started again at about 9:00 or 10:00 A.M. and reached the Peach Tree Road soon after, when the little drama associated with Logan's demotion took place. It continued marching behind Thomas's army, crossing the Western and Atlantic Railroad, until reaching the right of Palmer's Fourteenth Corps near the headwaters of Proctor's Creek late in the afternoon of July 27.[15]

Blair's Seventeenth Corps stopped for breakfast behind the line of the Fourth Corps and heard a heavy artillery fire by Union guns as the Rebel skirmish line mounted a push against the Federal skirmishers to find out what was going on. "The artillery fire was very rapid and heavy and made the woods and hills echo," remembered Charles E. Smith of the 32nd Ohio. Blair's men rested until 9:00 A.M., and meanwhile anyone with a relative or friend in a Fourth Corps unit tried to find him for a brief visit. Sometimes the meetings lasted but a few seconds before the Seventeenth Corps column resumed marching. The Fifteenth Corps also stopped for breakfast behind the line of the Fourth Corps and received three days rations in addition to its meal.[16]

The weather on July 27 was changeable, but it did not seriously hamper Sherman's move. It rained off and on during the course of the day, although some members of the Army of the Tennessee recalled that the rain was quite heavy. The historian of the 70th Ohio asserted that the men "were compelled to march hard all day through wet and mud, as it rained the greater part of the day." The exertion after lying in trenches for a while was tiring. Everyone reported that the sky was cloudy, but more often than not all that fell was "a drizzling rain for a while." At times the drizzle turned into a heavy shower that lasted a short time.[17]

Davis's division of Palmer's Fourteenth Corps held the extreme right of Sherman's line. Two of Davis's brigades had dug in securely on the north side of Proctor's Creek, which drained toward the northwest from an area relatively close to the Atlanta defenses, while the third brigade rested in a reserve position to the rear. Davis's right was, as Sherman expressed it, "strongly refused." South of Proctor's Creek was no-man's land, an area not yet traversed by Federal troops and patrolled by Confederate cavalry. When Sherman, Howard, and Dodge reached Davis's headquarters ahead of Corse's division, Sherman reported his progress to Schofield and outlined his intentions. The Army of the Tennessee would pass Davis's position and head south so that, by facing to the left, it could take position on a slight ridge extending in that direction. This would pose "a strong threat to East Point." Sherman assumed the enemy would extend his line to match this development, but at least he would be able to "make him extend till he is out of Atlanta."[18]

Sherman took Howard to a hill near Davis's headquarters where he could point out the location of the wooded ridge and the line of Rebel earthworks. He instructed the new commander of his favorite army to align along the ridge as soon as Corse appeared. Sherman also told Howard there was little to fear from Hood. He could continue south in marching column of fours down the road heading south and to the west of the ridge, a road that led directly toward a small chapel called Ezra Church.[19]

But Howard surveyed the terrain and had different ideas. Having survived a devastating flank attack by Stonewall Jackson at Chancellorsville and vividly aware of what Hood had done at Peach Tree Creek and on July 22, he had no intention of taking any risks. The road was narrow, and there were woods to the east of it. If Hood launched a surprise attack on his marching column, he would not have time to close up and form line in a good position to receive him. Howard was also well aware that his appointment had caused controversy and that Sherman was taking something of a chance supporting him as commander of the Army of the Tennessee. He was determined not to fail.[20]

Howard then told Sherman of his views and asked permission to deploy from marching column onto the ridge differently. "Instead of pushing out my right into the air," he wrote after the war, "I would carefully unfold by having the divisions take their places on Thomas' right, moving up in succession, so that each successive division would protect the flank of the preceding." Sherman listened and repeated his idea that Hood would not bother him. But he also had no objection to Howard's handling his army in any way he thought best. Sherman then left Howard to his task. By this simple action Sherman demonstrated his confidence in Howard's ability and allowed him to begin his long tenure as commander of the Army of the Tennessee. This incident also demonstrates that Howard had a more accurate assessment of what was to come than Sherman.[21]

Howard's caution was reinforced by the fact that he was moving into contested territory with no cavalry to screen his infantry or to gather information about the enemy. Howard had a small mounted escort attached to army headquarters, but that was inadequate for these tasks. Signal officers tried to find out what they could of Rebel positions but offered little useful information.[22]

Davis helped Corse to deploy when the Sixteenth Corps division appeared near Proctor's Creek. The 10th Illinois and four other regiments deployed as skirmishers in front of Davis's position. When the head of Corse's division appeared, these regiments advanced and drove Confederate skirmishers from their pits and toward the defenses of Atlanta. Corse continued to march to the rear of the Fourteenth Corps regiments as he directed his division to turn south along the road previously scouted by Sherman and Howard.[23]

Howard instructed Dodge to place his command in two lines on the ridge, and Dodge relayed those instructions to Corse when the division leader stopped at the hill near Davis's headquarters (already referred to as "the Jeff. C. Davis hill"). Howard personally consulted with Corse, impressing on him the need to be prepared for anything as he went south. Corse's division began to cross Proctor's Creek at 3:00 P.M., deploying each brigade successively and wheeling them left, his left flank resting on the creek so as to come into position on the wooded ridge connecting to the right flank of Absalom Baird's Fourteenth Corps division. Corse also deployed a skirmish line to precede his command. In a heavy shower, the division advanced through the woods, tree branches already wet with the rain, until resting securely on the wooded ridge. Then Corse's men began to dig entrenchments, placing a work for six guns on a prominent knoll of the ridge with a fine view of Atlanta some 2,000 yards away. They had marched fifteen miles since the night before to reach their new position northwest of Atlanta and facing east.[24]

Howard was frustrated that Fuller's division had experienced some delay and was not immediately ready to follow Corse into position. This caused a small rift between Howard and Dodge, an unfortunate start to their association. When Howard complained about the delay, Dodge reassured him that Fuller's division, which had been delayed by a break to eat a meal, would be up soon. "He rather hesitated and doubted it," Dodge recalled. But Fuller appeared soon after that interchange. Dodge reported the arrival to Howard. "This astonished him and he was much more" cordial in his conversation with Dodge as a result. But the incident "did not make a favorable impression upon me." Dodge did not realize how tense Howard was that day about ensuring that no surprise should befall his new command.[25]

Fuller crossed Proctor's Creek by 4:00 P.M. and deployed skirmishers. He then proceeded in the same way that Corse had moved into position, by deploying each brigade successively and wheeling to the left. It took longer because Fuller had a longer distance to traverse, but his men pushed enemy skirmishers ahead as they wheeled up to the ridge. By this time dusk was fast approaching, and Blair's Seventeenth Corps troops were not yet in position to deploy. Howard decided that Blair should bivouac for the night. Fuller therefore had to refuse his right flank to guard against a surprise in the night.[26]

Blair reported that wagons and artillery had impeded his march along the roads, thus accounting for his delay. Brig. Gen. Mortimer D. Leggett's Third Division tried to deploy in the darkness and wet underbrush but was delayed by Rebel skirmishers and more so by the fast-falling darkness. Blair halted Leggett before he had closed up on Fuller but was near enough to be within easy supporting distance. Brig. Gen. Giles A. Smith (the younger brother of Morgan L. Smith, who still commanded the Fifteenth Corps while Logan rested) brought Blair's Fourth Division up to a point so that he could rest his left flank just behind Leggett's right wing at dusk. Smith also swung his line back to form nearly a right angle with Leggett's line and cover the rear of the Seventeenth Corps position.[27]

Morgan L. Smith's Fifteenth Corps brought up the rear, and there was no chance for it to take position before night. The men had a tiring march that day, drenched by showers and baking in the hot sun whenever it shone through the cloud cover. When halting for rest, many men fell instantly asleep and had to be awakened by their comrades when the order to continue arrived. As the historian of the 55th Illinois put it after the war, "the tiresomely slow tramp, tramp, hour after hour, seemed as though it never would end. Occasionally the shells from Atlanta burst over us, always harmlessly." Thomas W. Connelly of the 70th Ohio asserted that his comrades had no difficulty sleeping "in any position—standing, sitting, lying down; or we could sleep while marching." By the time they halted that night, they had been on the move for twenty hours.[28]

The Fifteenth Corps bivouacked in front of Davis's division and to the rear of Dodge's and Blair's commands for the night. Different units of the corps ended their weary march anywhere from 10:00 P.M. to midnight, but all members of the corps were able to get some sleep that night. Morgan L. Smith arrayed his corps across the space behind Howard's developing position west of Atlanta. Woods's division, for example, bivouacked behind Blair's Seventeenth Corps troops so that Morgan L. Smith's men covered the entire rear of the Army of the Tennessee. Howard was taking no chances even in the dark.[29]

While the Army of the Tennessee moved west on July 27, news that Howard had replaced Logan filtered through Sherman's army group. Logan was not the only man who was offended by the turn of events. When Joseph Hooker learned that his former subordinate had been elevated above him to this choice assignment, he became indignant and angry. Hooker wrote to Thomas's chief of staff asking that he be relieved from any duty in Sherman's army group. "Justice and self-respect alike require my removal from an army in which rank and service are ignored," he concluded. Hooker was the ranking subordinate among Sherman's generals, and he had commanded the Army of the Potomac for five months. Moreover, he had supported Howard in the wake of the fiasco at Chancellorsville and contributed to the saving of the young man's career.[30]

George W. Balloch, Hooker's chief commissary, pinpointed the exact problem. "If any of the Generals of the Army of the Tenn had been assigned to the command Gen. Hooker would not have said a word although they are all junior to him: but to come into the Dept Cumberland & take a junior officer it was more than the old Genl could stand."[31]

But it was also true that Sherman and Hooker did not get along well together. Trouble had been simmering since the start of the campaign, mainly

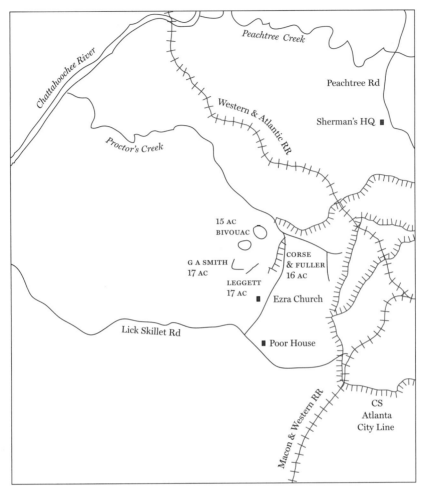

Developing Union Line
(Earl J. Hess and Pratibha A. Dabholkar)

fueled by Hooker's unbridled egoism and Sherman's inability to brook a
subordinate who did not know his place. The battle of Kolb's Farm provided
the clash that brought things into the open. Although his Twentieth Corps
held back the sudden attack by Hood's Corps and inflicted heavy casualties
on the Confederates, Hooker sent a hasty dispatch that the entire Army
of Tennessee confronted him. Neither Thomas nor Sherman believed this
was literally true. Sherman berated Hooker the next day in a face-to-face
confrontation. He told him bluntly not to send intemperate messages with
exaggerated claims gathered mostly from the word of Confederate prisoners. A mini–cold war existed between the two men ever since June 22.[32]

"Make Hooker resign his post as commander of the Twentieth Corps," Sherman told Thomas upon learning of the man's request to be relieved, so "that he cannot claim it and occasion delay in filling the vacancy." Thomas must have felt the same way about Hooker; he made no effort to calm the angry corps leader and did exactly what Sherman instructed. In fact Sherman mentioned in his memoirs that Thomas "*heartily*" approved of Hooker's resignation.[33]

Sherman explained to Halleck at 8:30 P.M. that evening that "Hooker is offended because he thinks he is entitled to the command. I must be honest and say he is not qualified or suited to it. He talks of quitting. . . . I shall not object. He is not indispensable to our success. He is welcome to my place if the President awards it, but I cannot name him to so important a command as the Army of the Tennessee." Later that night Sherman passed on word to Halleck that Thomas wanted to replace Hooker as Twentieth Corps commander with Maj. Gen. Henry W. Slocum, who had led the Twelfth Corps before Hooker had been placed in charge of that command and the Eleventh Corps for the trip to Tennessee in the fall of 1863. Slocum had no desire to serve again under Hooker and was then reassigned. Now he was happy to return to his old comrades. Until Slocum arrived from his current post in Mississippi, division commander Alpheus S. Williams temporarily led the corps. In addition, Thomas wanted to appoint Maj. Gen. David S. Stanley to replace Howard as Fourth Corps commander. Sherman approved all these recommendations.[34]

While the high command was happy to see Hooker leave, the rank and file of the Twentieth Corps was overwhelmingly disappointed. The soldiers loved Hooker with a passion and believed he was the most successful general in Sherman's army group. Even so, most of the men supported Hooker's reason for leaving. He "has put up with more than I should had I been in his place," wrote John R. Comfort of the 137th New York to his father. "To my notion he is as smart a Genl as the U.S. affords. . . . Other Genls would not work with him because they knew him to be more able than they were." While a lot of eastern soldiers such as Comfort liked Hooker, the general's biggest fan club existed in William Ward's Third Division, which consisted mostly of western troops who had not experienced Hooker's disastrous battle of Chancellorsville. John H. Roberts of the 22nd Wisconsin thought him "an excellent commander" who was not, as most people believed, rash or headstrong. "He always went ahead and examined the position before he sent his men there . . . while other Generals were back in the rear."[35]

As word of Hooker's resignation filtered through the ranks on July 27, word also circulated that their hero would take one last ride along the corps line to say goodbye. Those men who were not on duty lined up along a road to see him, but they stood for a long while without catching a glimpse of their former commander. Hooker believed his ride might draw too much attention from the Confederates and lead to an unnecessary exchange of artillery fire, so he canceled it.[36]

There had been a blizzard of new appointments to many command and staff positions in both armies fighting for Atlanta since July 18, only ten days since. These command changes occurred on the army level for the Confederates and for the Federals, on the corps level, on the division level, and among Hood's staff. The shake-ups in blue and gray were now over just hours before the battle of Ezra Church began.

Sherman assessed the progress of Howard's march to the west on the night of July 27, informing Halleck that "I think to-morrow must develop something." Sherman believed the Federals could force Hood "to extend and choose between Atlanta and East Point. I don't think the enemy can hold both." Howard had arranged his new command to prevent any surprises in the night.[37]

Orders for the next day went out on the night of July 27. Schofield was to mount a major demonstration on the far Union left to divert enemy attention. Not only was the Twenty-third Corps skirmish line supposed to press forward vigorously, but Schofield was to send out a reconnaissance in force, supported by cavalry, to locate the Confederate right flank and see if it had moved. Sherman also wanted to use Davis's division, which now was behind the Union line and available to support the operation on the right. He gave orders for Davis "to march down toward Turner's Ferry," he recalled in his memoirs, "and then to take a road laid down on our maps which led from there toward East Point, ready to engage any enemy that might attack our general right flank." That order was filtered through Thomas's and Palmer's headquarters.[38]

Logan rested all day until riding out to join the Fifteenth Corps after dark on July 27. He relieved Morgan L. Smith, who returned to command of the Second Division. Logan issued orders for the movement of his corps the next morning, instructing the division leaders to form their men long before dawn so Woods's First Division could go into line to Blair's right, to be followed by Brig. Gen. William Harrow's Fourth Division, then Smith's Second Division. Each division was to refuse its right flank to protect against an enemy thrust while the movement was underway. Logan wanted his subordinates to make sure that their men had 100 rounds of ammunition before starting as well.[39]

Howard's men settled down for rest and refreshment on the night of July 27–28. They established pickets while the command bivouacked mostly in wooded terrain. The troops ate pork and hardtack without the aid of fires. When any Federals lit a campfire, it drew the attention of Confederate artillerists who compelled them to stamp it out with a few well-aimed shots. The troops slept on rails if they could find any, but Charles E. Smith of the 32nd Ohio reported that his clothes were still soaked with a combination of rain and sweat. He became cold while standing picket, even though nights in Georgia during late July usually were quite warm.[40]

Cloud cover obscured the moon most of the night of July 27–28, but the sky cleared by about 3:00 A.M. Logan restlessly urged his men to begin their redeployment in preparation for rolling into line south of the Seventeenth Corps at dawn. Woods began this deployment by rousing his men and moving them into position to Blair's right, followed by the other divisions. As Howard remembered it, Logan "deployed nearly his entire corps during the night." Although Logan was careful not to mention Howard's name in any of his reports concerning the operations around Ezra Church, he must have consulted with his new commander about the manner of his deployment because it was consistent with the way in which Dodge and Blair had moved into position. Logan must have understood Howard's desire to make sure no surprises came upon the Army of the Tennessee during the movement because he took every precaution against such a chance.[41]

Confederate observers reported the Federal move west of Atlanta to Hood's headquarters soon after it began. Joseph Wheeler, whose cavalry held the far right of the Rebel line, advanced skirmishers at dawn to a point 100 yards north of the Georgia Railroad. Hood's staff informed Wheeler that he and Hardee were to hold the right wing securely because the enemy planned to strike the far left of the Rebel line. Wheeler's scouts provided the earliest warning that McCook and Stoneman had set out on a major raid to the south of Atlanta. Hood therefore ordered Wheeler at 11:00 A.M. to detach some of his troopers and give pursuit. Early in the afternoon Hood sent part of William H. Jackson's cavalry division in pursuit as well. By the night of July 27, Hood was willing to part with Wheeler personally so he could manage the operations against the Union raiders. But Francis Shoup, Hood's new chief of staff, warned Wheeler that he should take only enough men along that were needed to protect the army's supply line.[42]

Stephen D. Lee formally took command of Hood's old corps on July 27 as the Federals were marching around the northern perimeter of Atlanta. Benjamin F. Cheatham, who had led the troops since July 18, now went back to his division in Hardee's Corps. Lee's new command lay in the City Line east and northeast of Atlanta when he took charge of it. He made a little speech to a group of men, appealing "to our patriotism and referred with pride to the record that the troops composing the corps had made," according to one who remembered his words.[43]

Lee had no time to get to know his command, for orders soon arrived from Hood's headquarters to move two divisions out of the works. Brig. Gen. John C. Brown and Maj. Gen. Henry D. Clayton were to move to the area between the Peach Tree Road and the wagon road toward Marietta to rest and receive extra ammunition so that every man had sixty rounds. Lee was to keep the portion of Maj. Gen. Carter L. Stevenson's Division that lay west of the Peach Tree Road in place for the time being and report personally at Hood's headquarters. Lee issued the necessary orders to start this movement and rode to consult Hood, who told him to move immediately toward the west, beyond the existing left flank of the Confederate line opposite Baird's division of Palmer's Fourteenth Corps. Hood identified the road linking the village of Lick Skillet with Atlanta as the focal point of coming operations, and he wanted Lee to position two divisions there that night.[44]

Hardee was responsible for taking over the lines evacuated by Brown and Clayton. Patrick Cleburne's Division replaced Brown with his right resting on the Georgia Railroad and his command stretching one and a half miles north. Cheatham's Division replaced Clayton by midafternoon. Brown was just beginning to place his division between the Peach Tree Road and the Marietta Road near sundown when he received Lee's order to move west. The Confederates arrived at the Lick Skillet Road well after dark and bivouacked for the night, followed soon after by Clayton's Division. Hardee's Corps now held the Confederate right from the Georgia Railroad to the Peach Tree Road with Stevenson's Division of Lee's Corps and Stewart's Corps holding the rest of the line north and northwest of Atlanta.[45]

By 4:00 P.M., when Brown and Clayton were moving west, Shoup instructed Stewart to extend his left a bit as soon as Brown and Clayton reached the general area of the Lick Skillet Road. Hood had already alerted Stewart to have sixty rounds of ammunition issued to each man and be ready to move if called on to do so. Lee was instructed to send help to Stewart if the Federals suddenly struck at his corps.[46]

The vulnerable left flank of Hood's line was strengthened upon word that the Federals were on their way. Brig. Gen. Daniel H. Reynolds's Arkansas brigade of Maj. Gen. Edward C. Walthall's Division already anchored the extreme left of the line, his brigade's left flank resting on the Lick Skillet Road. Reynolds had extended his command down to that point on the afternoon of July 26, before the Federals began their move to the west of Atlanta. Only Confederate cavalry was positioned farther south than Reynolds's Brigade. When word arrived late on the afternoon of July 27 that the enemy was approaching the area, Reynolds got busy and fortified his skirmish line. Reynolds led a small brigade; when a battalion of 150 workers from the Confederate government works at Columbus and Macon reported for duty in Atlanta on July 26, Hood assigned them to Walthall's Division, and Walthall gave them to Reynolds. Major Youngblood's Battalion had no experience in the field and was a dubious addition to Reynolds's force. But Reynolds also received more troops on July 28 in the form of Gholson's Brigade of dismounted cavalry, which was then led by Col. John McGuirk. It just arrived from Mississippi and added 450 more men to Reynolds's depleted brigade.[47]

Committed to staying at his headquarters in Atlanta, located at the house of L. Windsor Smith on the southwestern edge of the city, Hood became more worried as the day progressed. He well knew that "the holding of Atlanta . . . depended upon our ability to hold intact the road to Macon," as he expressed it after the war. There was time to act before the Federals reached their goal. At 6:40 P.M., Shoup sent word for Stewart and Lee to meet at Hood's headquarters for a conference.[48]

The army commander intended to strike at Sherman before the Federals could reach the vital rail link between Atlanta and Macon. The Lick Skillet Road became the focal point of his planning. That road marked the end of the current Confederate line. It left the city and veered northwest, intersecting the north-south road that ran past Ezra Church about three miles from Atlanta and on northward toward Proctor's Creek. Howard already was beginning to deploy the Army of the Tennessee southward along that road to form his line facing the city. Hood reasoned that if his troops could secure the intersection before the enemy reached that point, he could block any further progress south. Lee was assigned the task of moving out to secure the junction on the morning of July 28. He was to merely hold Sherman at bay, not attack him that day. Stewart meanwhile would move two of his divisions (Walthall's and Maj. Gen. William W. Loring's) out along the Lick Skillet Road and set up to attack the Union flank and rear on the morning of July 29.[49]

Hood put together a promising plan to deal with Sherman's effort to reach the railroad to Macon. It was reminiscent of his effort on July 22, designed not only to stop the forward movement of his enemy but to damage him considerably if all went well. Hood's plans contrasted favorably with Johnston's passive defensive measures because they combined elements of both defense and offense. In planning the move, however, Hood ignored his most experienced corps commander. Hardee had been dissatisfied by Hood's appointment to command the Army of Tennessee and had tried to be relieved of his position as a result. Davis, however, convinced him to stay. Hardee had not done well at Peach Tree Creek on July 20, and he had failed to capitalize on his successful flanking movement on July 22. Hood instead relied on his next most experienced corps leader, Stewart, to conduct the risky flank attack while trusting to his newest corps commander to merely block and hold the Federals in place. Given the circumstances it probably was the best plan open to Hood, but all plans are dependent on the players and the decisions they make at critical junctures in the flow of events. The next day would prove whether Hood's handiwork would succeed or fail.[50]

=== CHAPTER THREE ===

General Hood Will Attack Me Here!

Morning, July 28

The cloudy, rainy conditions of July 27 gave way to clear skies and warm temperatures the next day. To at least one member of the Twentieth Corps, it was "indeed a most beautiful morning, every thing looks green and lively."[1]

The Federals were in motion at daylight. Fuller's division of the Sixteenth Corps had taken post in the woods after dark, and now dawn revealed ways unit commanders could improve their positions. Some went forward only 150 yards, while others moved closer to the enemy by half a mile. Blair's Seventeenth Corps had halted in darkness while advancing toward the ridge. In the early gray light, some of his units continued to advance half a mile to reach their assigned location on the high ground. Confederate skirmishers offered stiffer resistance this morning than the day before. Seventeenth Corps skirmishers had a lively time of it, trading volleys with their opponents before driving them back as the main line moved swiftly up to the ridge. Once there, the Federals began to dig in, gathering tree branches, logs, and fence rails for the purpose of making a breastwork and throwing dirt over it. After the Seventeenth Corps settled in along the ridge, Blair's right flank rested a quarter of a mile north of Ezra Church.[2]

Logan took control of the Fifteenth Corps when it began to move early on the morning of July 28. Woods's division formed battle line between 3:00 A.M. and dawn, the men throwing up a few logs as a breastwork and then cooking their breakfast while they waited. As soon as Giles A. Smith's Seventeenth Corps division set out, Woods also moved south through thick woods. He met little opposition as yet from Rebel skirmishers. The division marched as much as a mile and a half in this way before wheeling so as

42

to face east along the ridge and connect with Giles A. Smith's command. Woods's line went past Ezra Church and curved eastward to conform to the configuration of the ridge. His brigade commanders formed two lines for better defense.[3]

The left end of Harrow's division maintained connection with Woods's right flank during the difficult move south. Harrow also advanced through the trees and then wheeled into position to Woods's right. Harrow's division faced entirely south, taking advantage of the fact that the ridge curved west for some distance. This offered Logan the opportunity to post his corps as a long refused line to Howard's new position. Harrow's men exchanged a few rounds with Confederate skirmishers along the way, but there was no serious opposition to his advance. Maj. William B. Brown's 70th Ohio held the extreme left of Harrow's line. An interval of about 100 yards had developed between Brown's left and the right end of Woods's line, and the two divisions occupied positions nearly at right angles to each other. The skirmish lines of the two divisions also were not connected anymore because of the wheeling movement through the trees, so Brown sent out an extra company to reconnect them. Col. Hugo Wangelin, whose brigade occupied the extreme right of Woods's line, moved the 29th Missouri and the 17th Missouri (Battalion) from his second line to fill the 100-yard gap between the two divisions.[4]

As the rest of Harrow's line settled in along the irregular ridge stretching west, it received more scattered skirmish fire. "We swung in about two miles over the hills and through the hollows and over fences and through thick woods," recalled Andrew J. Clayton of the 99th Indiana. The division was firmly in place by about midmorning.[5]

Morgan L. Smith resumed command of the Second Division when Logan took charge of the corps that morning. Smith's men had the assignment of holding the extreme end of Sherman's long line at Atlanta. They moved south in conjunction with Harrow's division, skirmishing and marching through heavy timber for two miles before approaching the slightly timbered ridge that Logan had identified as the resting place of the new line. Smith's skirmishers drove the Rebel skirmishers from the shallow height to be followed by Smith's main line. It was now about 10:00 A.M. As the Federals began to prepare defenses, Smith's skirmishers continued across the shallow swale just south of the ridge toward the next rise of ground against resistance by the Confederate skirmishers.[6]

Howard kept close watch on Logan's deployment. He was riding with his staff members and a small mounted escort through the heavy timber and within sight of the Fifteenth Corps troops when Sherman rode up to join him. As they talked, the skirmish fire in front of Logan began to pick up and artillery rounds fired from guns located in the Atlanta defenses sailed through the treetops. "We both felt that the enemy was becoming more obstinate," Howard recalled years later. "I said: — 'General Hood will attack me here!' 'I guess not; he will hardly try it again,' Sherman replied." Howard then reminded Sherman that he had studied for three years with Hood at West Point and knew that he was "indomitable in heart."[7]

Sherman's brief stop with Howard was but one episode in a full day for the commanding general. He was keen to observe the Army of the Tennessee complete its deployment. "I want to watch the effect on that flank," he wrote to Schofield. Sherman had visited Dodge and Corse before continuing to ride south along the road Howard was using as the axis of his advance, the road that led to Ezra Church. Confederate artillery rounds sailed over the area from an unidentified Confederate battery probably located on the Lick Skillet Road, supporting the Rebel skirmishers. A projectile "passed over my shoulder and killed the horse of an orderly behind," recalled Sherman. This prompted him to leave the road and ride toward the southwest across country. He finally came up with Howard and Logan just behind Smith's division line. Sherman dismounted and talked with both of them, especially with Howard, downplaying the possibility of another attack. He also walked close to the line with Morgan L. Smith and tried with the division commander to locate the battery on the Lick Skillet Road that had just annoyed him. He made it clear that Smith should arrange for some method of neutralizing its fire.[8]

Sherman felt convinced that Hood would not dare another attack on his flank as he had done on July 22. There seemed to him no indications of a large force in front of Logan. To calm apprehensions, Sherman told Howard of his plan to have Davis's division reconnoiter toward Turner's Ferry and then move south to arrive at a point where it could protect Howard's right flank. All seemed to be working smoothly, so Sherman left Howard and rode back toward the north. "Thus he permitted me to conduct my first battle alone," Howard gratefully recalled in his memoirs. But the new commander of Sherman's old army was still convinced there likely would be trouble.[9]

As Smith's skirmishers contended for the next rise of ground south, all of Logan's main line secured its position on the shallow ridge. This ground would become a bloody battlefield in a couple of hours, and Ezra Church was the most prominent landmark on it. The building was referred to as

Ezra Church in *Battles and Leaders*. This postwar depiction shows the Union line in action on the opposite side of the church structure and a column of reserves approaching to offer support. (Johnson and Buel, *Battles and Leaders*, 4:321)

Mount Ezra Church or Ezra Chapel. Everyone agreed it was a small, unpretentious, and old building. In fact, the Prussian John Henry Otto of the Fourteenth Corps derisively wrote of it as "a little log meeting house where the darkies used to congregate and sing their 'Hallelujahs.'"[10]

Jacob Cox, who commanded a division in the Twenty-third Corps, made an intensive study of the geography surrounding many phases of the Atlanta campaign. He noted that the road Howard had used as the axis of his advance southward linked Elliott's Mill on the north with Ezra Church on the south. Just south of the church this road was intersected "by a more important one," Cox wrote "leaving the southwest suburb of Atlanta near the race-course, and running west to a village near the Chattahoochee, bearing the cacophonous name of Lickskillet." While the railroad from Atlanta to East Point ran along the major watershed that drained northwest, forming Proctor's Creek and other watercourses, the Lick Skillet Road ran along the minor watershed between Proctor's Creek on the north and Utoy Creek to the south.[11]

The battlefield held many advantages for the Federals. They were well established on a ridge that admittedly was not very high. It resembled the rise of ground one finds in an undulating landscape. But this feature, slight as it was, happened to be placed exactly where Howard's army needed it, allowing Logan's corps to extend a long refused line west of the main, east-facing position of the other corps. For the most part, an open field lay in front of Logan's line, and a shallow swale a few feet deep ran roughly parallel to it. The next undulation south was about half a mile away, and it was apparent that the Confederate skirmishers were located there. On the right wing of Woods's division, the land in front of Wangelin's brigade was covered with "a thick growth of small trees." But most of Logan's men had open and rolling country before their position, and the irregular ridge had scattered trees on its top. Even in front of Blair's and Dodge's lines, the ground was largely open and undulating toward the east with the Confederate City Line located on high ground around Atlanta.[12]

Logan thought his corps held a very good position. It "was one of the most favorable that could have been chosen by us, it being the crest of a continuous ridge, in front of the greatest portion of which a good and extensive fire line was opened." Engineer officer Poe agreed with Logan, calling his position "a most admirable one." But both Logan and Poe ignored one disadvantage; the ridgeline was not straight. It jigged and jagged in an odd way, forcing the Federals to adjust their line to its eccentricities. James P. Snell, a clerk on Corse's division staff, carefully examined the ground after the battle and noted that Logan's line was "like the contortions of a wounded snake." These sudden little changes in the direction of the line would cause some difficulty for brigade and regimental commanders who had to deal with them under tremendous pressure from attacking Confederates. But it also must be noted that these sudden turns allowed the Federals to obtain enfilade fire on the attackers at some locations along the line.[13]

Howard ordered Logan's men to fortify the ridge as soon as possible, but the Federals needed no urging. They had long been in the habit of throwing together some sort of protection for every new position taken up since the start of the campaign. Soon the Fifteenth Corps troops were gathering rails, logs, and stumps from a partially cleared field just to the north of the ridge. Howard recalled with pleasure the sight of them running back and forth with "logs and rails in their arms and on their shoulders." The Confederates had captured many entrenching tools belonging to the Army of the Tennessee in the battle of July 22, so the troops now simply piled up anything they could find to make a breastwork on the surface of the ground rather than digging a trench. Sixteenth Corps troops did the same thing, utilizing what few tools were available to dig battery emplacements. In the Seventeenth Corps, the Federals found stones to add to their breastworks and cut canteens in half as crude substitutes for shovels, piling up some

Ezra Church in *Harper's Weekly*. This contemporary print was based on a
field sketch by Theodore R. Davis and shows the Union line in waiting
before the battle. (*Harper's Weekly*, August 27, 1864, 557)

dirt over the linear arrangements of rails, logs, rocks, and even knapsacks.
Some enterprising Yankees used pocketknives to cut saplings before their
line to serve as an obstruction.[14]

In the Fifteenth Corps, orders to fortify emanated not only from Howard
but from division commanders as well. Brigade leaders reinforced the sense
of urgency, and the men generally went to work with energy and will. Like
their Seventeenth Corps comrades, Logan's men used knapsacks if nothing
else was available.[15]

In Wangelin's brigade, holding the far right of Woods's division at the
angle in the Federal line, there were no tools of any kind available. The men
scrambled to find usable material, and Ezra Church offered them an opportunity. "Benches were taken out of the church and filled with knapsacks
to serve as breast-works," Wangelin reported, "and doubtless did better
service than ever before." The men also found a fence nearby and tore it
down to use the rails. They recalled in their memoirs finding at least one
small building in the area, reportedly an old schoolhouse. In half an hour,
they tore it apart and used the logs to serve as the base of their breastworks.

"Whatever was at hand, was used," recalled John T. Buegel of the 3rd Missouri. They even threw the window frames of the building onto the pile.[16]

In Harrow's division, to Wangelin's right along the south-facing ridge, every brigade commander ordered and encouraged his men to make breastworks as fast as they could. The result was a collection of miscellaneous articles that at best rose knee high, but it was better than nothing. No tools were available in the division, so the men loosened dirt with their bayonets and threw it onto the pile with their bare hands. The result was what Lieut. Col. Robert A. Gillmore of the 26th Illinois called "a thin line of works." Lieut. Col. James Harrison Goodnow of the 12th Indiana, however, reported that his men were able to create "a pretty good defense against pieces of bursting Shells and musket balls."[17]

Two of Harrow's brigade commanders, Col. John M. Oliver and Col. Reuben Williams, sent details to the rear to search for entrenching tools. After some time they returned with a few shovels and axes that they had scrounged up somewhere. The tools, however, arrived just as the battle was starting and were hardly used before the men had to throw them down and handle their muskets in more deadly work.[18]

Similar efforts to fortify took place along the line held by Morgan L. Smith's division, completing a nearly continuous line of hasty works fronting the Fifteenth Corps position. Lieut. Col. Samuel R. Mott of the 57th Ohio reported that his works were "only eighteen to twenty inches high." Howard keenly observed the process of making these defenses and agreed with Mott's assessment. "The shelter at best was but little," he admitted, "but was a fair one to men when kneeling and better when lying down." The profile of the ridge itself offered a good deal of protection for reserve units positioned behind Logan's line.[19]

The Federals were indeed fortunate that the course of the campaign had taught them the value of throwing together any kind of protection as fast as possible. Even Grant, who had nothing to do with the operations west of Atlanta, noted in his memoirs how important it was for Logan to construct even a slight pile of logs to protect his position. Sherman also understood the timeliness of this act, referring to the Federals "throwing up the accustomed pile of rails and logs, which after a while assumed the form of a parapet," in his report of the campaign. "The skill and rapidity with which our men construct these is wonderful and is something new in the art of war."[20]

Another distinctive feature of the Atlanta campaign was the intense level of skirmishing that had developed ever since Sherman crossed the

Etowah River two months before. Locked for lengthy periods of time within a few hundred yards of each other, both sides resorted to skirmishing as a way to wear down their opponent on a daily scale between major moves and engagements. Over the course of time, the Federals generally proved more aggressively active on the skirmish line. They were bolstered by high morale, plenty of ammunition, and a confident faith in themselves and their commanders. Federal officers did not hesitate to reinforce the skirmish line beyond the two-company-per-regiment regulations, at times raising skirmishes almost to the level of small pitched battles between the lines. As previously, the Yankees proved to be the better skirmishers during Howard's deployment west of Atlanta on July 28.[21]

Ever since Logan began his movement toward the ridge early on the morning of July 28, he had been opposed by a brigade of Mississippi cavalry under Brig. Gen. Frank C. Armstrong, belonging to William H. Jackson's division. Jackson had already committed his other two brigades to different areas. Lawrence S. Ross's Texas cavalry brigade was spread out farther west to screen McCook's Federal horsemen near the Chattahoochee River, while Brig. Gen. Samuel W. Ferguson's Alabama and Mississippi brigade was positioned on the Confederate right flank east of Atlanta.[22]

Frank A. Montgomery's 1st Mississippi Cavalry took position early on the morning of July 28. He then relieved a Georgia regiment on picket north of the Lick Skillet Road. The Georgia officer reported no Federals in the area, but when Montgomery advanced his picket line across an open field, the Yankees opened fire when the Rebels were only halfway across. This was the start of a spirited skirmish as Logan began his move south to complete the deployment of the Army of the Tennessee. By the time Montgomery's picket line retired to the tree cover on the south side of the open field, he could see the Federal skirmish line extending beyond sight to right and left. Montgomery also sensed that a large force of infantry was moving up behind those blue-coated skirmishers. He sent word a short distance to the rear so that Armstrong would know the enemy was on the move in force.[23]

"I soon found that I had an army to contend with," Montgomery recalled. The men in his regiment fell back while still mounted on their horses and stopped periodically to fire from the cover of the thin woods through which they retired. Fortunately for the harried Rebels, the Federals advanced cautiously. Montgomery fell back to a cleared area lying north of the Lick Skillet Road that was dotted with a handful of buildings. The field and the structures were situated atop the next rise of ground in this undulating terrain, the one immediately south of the line that Logan's infantrymen were already beginning to occupy as their main position. The Federal skirmishers were approaching across the swale between the two ridges. Montgomery dismounted his regiment and sent the horses to the south side of the Lick Skillet Road, about 250 to 300 yards to his rear, to seek shelter in another patch of woods. Then he arranged his command to take whatever shelter the landscape afforded. A Federal skirmisher who saw the position later described how the dismounted Rebel troopers used "stone piles, log house, blacksmith shop, corn-crib and rail fence" as ready fortifications.[24]

By now Armstrong had brought up the rest of his brigade and arranged the 2nd Mississippi, 28th Mississippi, and Ballentine's Mississippi Regiment to the right of Montgomery's position. The men also did what Montgomery's troopers had done, seek any shelter they could along the line. Armstrong dismounted to survey the situation. For the next two hours, the Federal skirmishers made three tentative advances against this fairly strong position, cautious not to lose men unnecessarily. Armstrong had no difficulty resisting pushes such as this. He sent word to Hood about the situation and received an answer to hold on at all hazards to delay the Unionists until Lee's infantrymen could reach the field. Armstrong was determined to stay where he was until compelled to fall back.[25]

On the northern side of the swale from Armstrong's men, Logan's main line was securing its position on the slender ridge leading westward from the area of Ezra Church. It is probable that a battery had accompanied Armstrong's brigade, because several Federals other than Sherman reported receiving artillery fire from the south. Sherman consulted with Smith about how to deal with the Rebel artillery. Howard and Logan also offered their advice until Smith issued orders for two regiments to advance and help the skirmishers take the next rise of ground south. As Smith reported, his objective was "to drive in the enemy's skirmishers and compel him to fall back or develop his intentions and fight." But the decision to push any Rebel artillery away from the Lick Skillet Road also was an objective in this skirmish advance.[26]

Smith filtered the order down to his rightmost brigade, commanded by Brig. Gen. Joseph A. J. Lightburn. Born in Pennsylvania but having grown up in the western mountains of Virginia, Lightburn threw his lot in with the loyalists of that region upon the outbreak of the war. He led the 4th West Virginia and commanded a brigade in the Vicksburg siege, the Chattanooga campaign, and the drive toward Atlanta. His men had taken a prominent part in the failed assault at Kennesaw Mountain on June 27.[27]

At about 11:30 A.M., Lightburn sent forward Col. Wells S. Jones's 53rd Ohio on the far right of his line. When Jones advanced part way, he realized help was needed, so Lightburn prompted Maj. Thomas T. Taylor to send assistance from his 47th Ohio. Taylor advanced Companies B, D, and K toward a point to connect with Jones's left flank. Jones then saw that Armstrong's cavalry line extended farther west than his own regiment, so he again asked Lightburn for help. The brigade leader sent the rest of Taylor's 47th Ohio off toward Jones's right flank. Howard kept a close watch on developments and intervened in the process to give a verbal order to Maj. Charles Hipp to advance his 37th Ohio of Lightburn's brigade to help cover Jones's right. Hipp placed six of his companies between the skirmish line and the main Union position to act as a reserve for the vulnerable flank. He also sent two other companies on picket duty along some small roads that led toward Logan's right flank.[28]

Morgan L. Smith's artillery chief now brought some guns into action to support Jones's effort to take the next ridge. Capt. Francis DeGress personally directed two pieces of Lieut. George Echte's Battery A, 1st Illinois Light Artillery as they advanced between the main line and the Union skirmishers. Echte managed to fire at least twenty rounds in the effort. One section of the 4th Ohio Battery also was placed between the main position and the skirmish line on the sector held by Col. James S. Martin's brigade.[29]

The reinforced Union skirmish line began to increase pressure on the Confederate cavalry holding the ridge just north of Lick Skillet Road after 10:30 A.M. Armstrong positioned himself mounted behind Montgomery's 1st Mississippi Cavalry, about where Jones and Taylor were pressing forward, to observe events and encourage the troops. The pressure soon became too much. Two companies on the left of the regiment began to give way. Armstrong rode toward those men but his horse was shot thirty steps short of the place where they were falling back. Armstrong demonstrated aplomb by jumping off just before the steed hit the ground and walked quickly to the commander of one company, demanding to know why he was falling back. When told his men were out of ammunition, Armstrong yelled, "It don't make a d—m'd bit of difference, I'll have you plenty of ammunition here in a minute." The general then stayed with these men until the extra rounds arrived, and they stuck to their position. A member of the 28th Mississippi offered Armstrong his own mount, and the brigade leader jumped on and rode away.[30]

But Armstrong's heroics could not hold his brigade on the ridge forever. Soon his men were compelled to give way to the reinforced Union skirmish

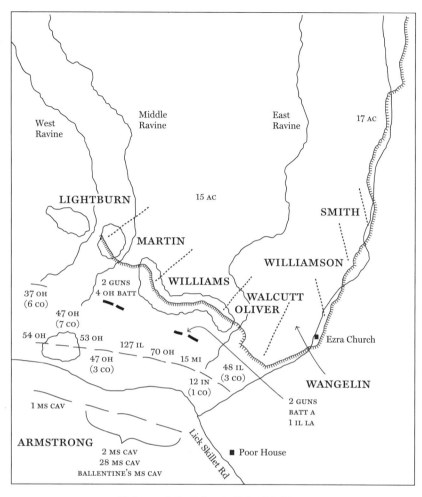

West
Ravine

Middle
Ravine

East
Ravine

17 AC

15 AC

LIGHTBURN

SMITH

MARTIN

WILLIAMSON

37 OH
(6 co)

2 GUNS
4 OH BATT

WILLIAMS

WALCUTT
OLIVER

47 OH
(7 co)

54 OH   53 OH

127 IL   70 OH

Ezra Church

47 OH
(3 co)

15 MI

48 IL
(3 co)

12 IN
(1 co)

WANGELIN

1 MS CAV

2 GUNS
BATT A
1 IL LA

ARMSTRONG

2 MS CAV
28 MS CAV
BALLENTINE'S MS CAV

Lick Skillet Rd

Poor House

Union and Confederate Skirmish Lines
(Earl J. Hess and Pratibha A. Dabholkar)

line. They fell back across the open field from the line of buildings and crossed to the south side of Lick Skillet Road. The Federals followed up yelling "hip, hip, hurrah!" according to a man in the 1st Mississippi Cavalry, who thought it was "very unlike a real manly exultant yell." Montgomery fell back into the woods south of the road where his horses had been tended, but he lost contact with the rest of Armstrong's brigade to the right. Nevertheless he remounted his regiment and then wondered what to do next. Just then, he heard the noise of many feet off to the right; it was the van of Lee's infantry column finally arriving near the scene of action.[31]

The Federal skirmish line settled in on the ridge which ran at a slant compared to the course of the Lick Skillet Road. On the Union right, Jones and Taylor occupied a hill that was part of the ridge feature and which lay so close to the road that the Confederates declared their enemy had possession of it. But the ridge diverged from the road considerably as one surveyed the landscape toward the Union left. Jones and Taylor worked fast to consolidate their position on the slight hill, calling on Lightburn for more troops. While Jones's 53rd Ohio formed the anchor of the position, Taylor's 47th Ohio had companies to the left and right of Jones. Soon Maj. Israel T. Moore's 54th Ohio was moving up to take position to Taylor's right, making it the rightmost Union regiment of Sherman's long line.[32]

Armstrong lost at least sixty men in the heavy skirmish his brigade endured on the morning of July 28. "We had a pretty tight time of it," reported Angus M. Martin of the 28th Mississippi Cavalry. His regiment lost twenty-four men. Angus's brother John Martin was slightly injured when a Federal ball "struck his gun and tore the stock to pieces. Some of the splinters or a fragment of the ball cut his thumb gust [sic] enough to make him have a pretty sore finger for a few days."[33]

Units from other divisions in the Fifteenth Corps contributed to the general skirmish line that had taken the next rise of ground to the south of Logan's position. From Col. James S. Martin's brigade of Smith's division, the 127th Illinois added its weight to the skirmish line. Col. John M. Oliver contributed the 70th Ohio from his brigade of Harrow's division. In fact, Oliver reported that the Federal skirmishers captured forty of Armstrong's troopers when they took the ridge. Members of the 70th Ohio also stepped on the "hard gravel" pavement of the Lick Skillet Road for a time before falling back to a better position. The sun already was burning the flinty roadbed and making it hot for anyone who stood on it. The 15th Michigan of Col. Reuben Williams's brigade of Harrow's division also contributed to the skirmish force and advanced toward the spot where the elusive Rebel battery was firing canister. James Harrison Goodnow sent Company D, 12th Indiana, to reinforce the skirmishers from Williams's brigade, while Col. Lucien Greathouse sent three companies of his 48th Illinois from Oliver's brigade.[34]

The course of the skirmishing near Ezra Church demonstrated once again that the Federals were willing to commit substantial manpower to the mini-battles that developed between the lines. Armstrong's four regiments were significantly outnumbered by the six and a half Federal regiments that opposed them. Moreover, the Yankees were armed with long-barreled infantry weapons, while Armstrong's troopers carried short-barreled guns.

To keep the enemy from the Lick Skillet Road, Armstrong needed substantial infantry reinforcements, but Hood failed to provide them.

Predictably, the outcome of the skirmishing along Lick Skillet Road was in favor of the Federals, but soon the tide seemed to turn. Increasing signs of a large Confederate infantry force assembling on the other side of the captured ridge became apparent to many Union skirmishers just before noon. On Woods's front, wounded skirmishers who came back into the main line for treatment told their comrades who were still setting up breastworks, "Hurry up, boys; the Johnnies will soon be after your scalps."[35]

On the far Union right, where Jones, Taylor, and Moore held the little knoll on the skirmish line very close to Lick Skillet Road, the signs were even more evident. Jones and Moore had their regiments (the 53rd and 54th Ohio) stretched out as skirmish lines to cover as much front as possible. From their positions, the men could see glimpses of Confederate infantry forming 400 yards away at the edge of some trees. They directed their fire at the developing formations but did comparatively little damage at that range. "Far as the eye could reach to the right and left stood that mingled line of yellow and gray," recalled Edwin W. Smith of the 54th Ohio.[36]

Ever since 9:30 A.M. Hood had been encouraging Jackson to hold the enemy back from the Lick Skillet Road "to the best of your power," in Shoup's words. Jackson impressed that directive on Armstrong who urged his Mississippi cavalrymen to do their best. Hood hoped to free Carter L. Stevenson's division of Lee's Corps from trench duty and use it on the left flank. But initial plans to have the Georgia Militia extend its line to the right and relieve Stevenson west of Peach Tree Road failed to materialize that morning. Shoup therefore urged Hardee to bend every effort to extend his corps line to the left and take over Stevenson's sector. As late as 10:30 that morning Hardee still had not been able to do so, and Stevenson remained where he was rather than reinforce Lee's other two divisions on the Lick Skillet Road.[37]

Lee received Hood's order to move west along that road at 11:00 A.M. In Lee's words, his objective was to "check the enemy, who was then moving to our left, as it was desirable to hold that road, to be used for a contemplated movement." Shoup explained to Hardee precisely what Hood's intentions were in this movement. "General Lee is directed to prevent the enemy from gaining the Lick Skillet road, and not to attack unless the enemy exposes himself in attacking us." Hood fully expected a Union assault somewhere that day or the next and wanted Hardee to be ready for it.[38]

There was no explanation why Hood waited so long to send Lee out. Perhaps he was waiting for Stevenson to join him first. By that late hour, 11:00 A.M., the Federals had already begun establishing their defensive position along the ridge, and their skirmishers were pushing forward in a move that would take them onto sections of the Lick Skillet Road. Armstrong's hard-pressed men were beginning to wear out. Hood set Lee in motion in the nick of time, but there was no real need for the delay. If Brown and Clayton had started at the crack of dawn, they could have arrived much earlier. Both divisions would have then been able to confront the Fifteenth Corps with a reinforced skirmish line supported by ample reserves that could have held its own well north of the Lick Skillet Road. Alternatively, if Hood had detached an infantry brigade to help Armstrong's cavalrymen, the Confederates might have held Logan's skirmishers north of that road all morning before Lee's divisions arrived.

As it turned out, John C. Brown received orders to go "with the utmost dispatch" along Lick Skillet Road to the vicinity of the Poor House, about a mile from the Atlanta City Line, where Armstrong's cavalry was contending with the enemy. Brown was relatively new to his division. A native of Tennessee and a graduate of Jackson College in Columbia, he had served as colonel of the 3rd Tennessee and endured months of prison life after his regiment was included in the surrender of Fort Donelson. Promoted to brigadier general in August 1862, Brown led a brigade in the Army of Tennessee until replacing Maj. Gen. Thomas C. Hindman as commander of the division in July 1864.[39]

Before receiving the order to move out, Brown's men had taken a leisurely pace that morning. Isaac Gaillard Foster of the 10th Mississippi enjoyed a breakfast of "light bread biscuits, irish potatoes ham & pickles." The men were told to relax after that but not to stray too far away from their weapons as a movement was anticipated. But they had ample time for repose before ordered into ranks again for the move west.[40]

Henry D. Clayton's division followed Brown's men. A native of Georgia and a graduate of Emory and Henry College in southwest Virginia, Clayton was a lawyer in Eufaula, Alabama, and a legislator before accepting the command of the 1st Alabama at the outbreak of war. He later raised the 39th Alabama and commanded it in the Kentucky campaign and at Murfreesboro where he was badly wounded. Promoted to brigadier general in the spring of 1863 and commanding a brigade from that time, he received a commission as major general in early July 1864 when he took over Alexander P. Stewart's division. Stewart had been promoted to lieutenant general and command of the Army of Mississippi (soon after renamed

Stewart's Corps). Clayton had left one of his brigades commanded by Brig. Gen. Marcellus Stovall in the works and now brought three others toward the Poor House.[41]

As Lee approached the area, he immediately learned that Armstrong's cavalry brigade was hard pressed and falling back. There was some truth in Lee's report of the situation written six months later. "I soon found that the enemy had gained the road, and was gradually driving back our cavalry." He ordered Brown and Clayton to form a battle line south of the Lick Skillet Road due south of the Fifteenth Corps position.[42]

Were the Federals actually in control of the Lick Skillet Road? While there was a kernel of truth to the idea, it was not entirely accurate. At best, some parts of the Federal skirmish line were so close to the road or actually on it for a time, that it would not have been feasible for Stewart's men to use the roadway to assault Howard's flank on July 29, which was Hood's intended plan of action west of Atlanta. But that tentative Union "possession" of the road could easily have been dealt with by deploying a heavy skirmish line from Brown's division and pushing it forward. That would have freed up the road for Stewart's movement and fulfilled Hood's plan to the letter with minimal Rebel casualties. But this is not what Stephen D. Lee did during the late morning of July 28 near the Poor House. He made a snap decision to launch a major attack on the Federals and drive them away.[43]

In every way this was a tragic mistake. Lee chose not to wait until Stewart could come up to help him. He had scant information about the main Union position and did not know the terrain. He did not even know his own troops, and he did not bother to inform Hood of his decision, much less ask his advice about the matter. The youngest lieutenant general in the Confederate army, who had just taken command of his corps the day before, failed to obey his orders and exercised far too much latitude in taking a course of action that would kill and wound thousands of his men in a battlefield endeavor with dubious prospects. It is true that if Hood had been on the field instead of at his headquarters in Atlanta, this might not have happened. In contrast, Sherman rode around all along his own line to personally observe developments and offer advice to his subordinates. This was not Hood's style during the Atlanta campaign, and he deserves a good deal of criticism for providing no on-site guidance by his presence or supervision by his staff officers. But that does not absolve Lee of the full responsibility for starting the battle of Ezra Church in a way that Hood did not want, and when there were promising alternatives to deal with the Federal presence on and near the Lick Skillet Road.

The last word on Lee's mission from army headquarters came from Francis Shoup, who wrote a dispatch addressed to the corps commander at noon. "If the enemy should make an assault upon our left the general directs you to strike him in flank." By then the trigger had been pulled, and Brown and Clayton were already rolling forward across the shallow swale that separated Lee from Logan. Yet Lee's attack could not be justified by this message, which he received at 1:05 P.M., more than an hour after the battle started. There was no evidence that the Federals intended to attack him with their main line, and he was not striking their flank. Because Logan's Fifteenth Corps had formed a long refused line to that of the Seventeenth Corps, Lee actually was conducting a direct frontal assault on the enemy. If he had deployed a heavy skirmish line, he might have learned that important fact before launching his main force in what was a massive reconnaissance in force with scant information about what lay ahead.[44]

As the drama north of Lick Skillet Road took shape, Hood continued to urge Hardee to find men to replace Stevenson west of Peach Tree Road and free up his men for operations west of Atlanta. Cheatham tried to see if he could spare a brigade for the purpose, and Cleburne was instructed to form his division in only one rank to facilitate the stretching of Hardee's Corps line.[45]

Lee's actions in the vicinity of the Poor House became evident to the enemy. Union signal officers had set up observation posts and detected the movement of large numbers of Rebel infantry along Lick Skillet Road. Lieut. John H. Weirick reported the movement to Logan, as did Lieut. Isaiah C. Worley. In short, the Federals had sufficient warning of trouble to be ready for it.[46]

Arthur M. Manigault, who commanded a brigade in Brown's division, later estimated that Lee brought 9,000 men into action on July 28 to attack as many as 18,000 Federals. The estimates of modern historians as to numbers involved in the engagement vary considerably. But Lieut. Col. Harry T. Toulmin reported that Johnston's brigade of Brown's division took 1,143 men into action on July 28. If that number can be taken as average for all units, then the ten Confederate brigades that took part in the battle of Ezra Church totaled 11,430 men. By the same estimate, the Federals, who had the equivalent of eight brigades involved in the fight, totaled 9,144 men. It is possible that Union troop strength might have been a bit higher on average than that of Confederate units. A safe conclusion is that both sides were about as equal as they could be in the coming battle.[47]

CHAPTER FOUR

That Shrill, Terrifying Yell

Brantley's Brigade

Lee operated under a sense of desperation when he chose to attack the Federals late on the morning of July 28. John C. Brown's division, the first to near the scene of action, began the battle as soon as it arrived. Brown rode ahead of his men as they marched along Lick Skillet Road until he encountered William H. Jackson near the Poor House. Jackson had ridden to the area on reports that Armstrong's brigade was engaged in heavy skirmishing. He told Brown that his men were being pressed hard but that the Federals had only a "small" infantry force on the field. He must have given the same report to Lee and thereby influenced the new corps commander to go on the offensive. By the time the van of Brown's Division reached the vicinity of the Poor House, Lee showed up from his brief reconnaissance of the area. He told Brown "to form rapidly in rear of a commanding position in the road in advance of the Poor-House." Brown straddled the Lick Skillet Road by placing Sharp's Brigade in the center and south of the road. Brantley's Brigade took position to Sharp's left while Johnston's Brigade aligned to Sharp's right, north of the road. Brown held Manigault's Brigade in reserve. Lee made his intention very clear. "I was directed to attack and drive the enemy to Ezra Church and hold that position," the division commander reported.[1]

William Felix Brantley's Brigade of Mississippi troops constituted the far left element of Lee's line. Born in Alabama but nearly a lifelong resident of Mississippi, Brantley practiced law and helped to vote the state out of the union at the secession convention. He commanded the 29th Mississippi in many bloody battles of the Army of Tennessee until his brigade commander was mortally wounded on July 22. Brantley was commissioned brigadier general on July 26 and now was leading the brigade into battle for the first time.[2]

Brantley arrived on the scene following Sharp's Brigade in the line of march along Lick Skillet Road. As Sharp took position to the left of the road, Brantley marched behind his men to take his place on the far left of the line. Under Brown's instruction, Brantley bent his left wing back a little to protect against a possible approach by the Federal skirmishers against his flank. Lieut. Col. James M. Johnson, who commanded the consolidated 29th and 30th Mississippi on the left, sent out twenty men as flankers according to Brantley's instructions. Johnson also deployed forty men and three officers as a skirmish line under Capt. William McCulloch of the 30th Mississippi. Brantley placed Capt. T. S. Hubbard's 34th Mississippi to the right of Johnson's consolidated regiment and Col. Robert P. McKelvaine's 24th and 27th Mississippi on his right.[3]

Most observers place the time of Brown's attack at noon, but other men who were on the field gave widely varying timings for the onset of the battle at Ezra Church. Those timings ranged from 10 o'clock to 12:30 and resulted from the fact that the men did not synchronize their watches. The majority of testimony settled on the noon hour, indicating that Lee wasted little time in starting his offensive, hoping to catch the Federals before they had a chance to properly fortify their new position.[4]

Brantley's Brigade not only held down Lee's left flank but also achieved initial success and came rather close to turning the Union right early in the battle. Brown gave Brantley the word to move forward by guiding to his right so as to keep connection with Sharp's Brigade while also being wary of enemy movement to his left. When the Mississippians began, they immediately drove the Union skirmishers in their path back north and cleared the Lick Skillet Road. Brantley stopped on the road to re-form his line as Brown instructed him to "swing my left around" so as to make his brigade line straight and consistent with the rest of the division. Brantley made this adjustment while re-forming. According to one regimental commander, the brigade spent fifteen minutes adjusting its line on the Lick Skillet Road. The Federals could see the Rebels in plain view. Some of them thought it was an awe-inspiring sight as the gray line dressed itself before pushing north.[5]

When Brantley's men continued their advance north of Lick Skillet Road, they realized that the Federals had several regiments on the little knoll that lay not more than a quarter mile from the roadbed. These were

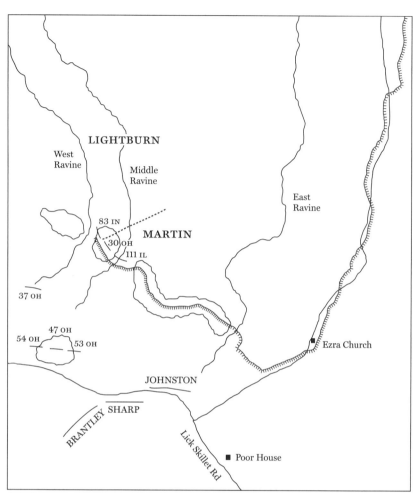

Brantley's Brigade Begins Attack

(Earl J. Hess and Pratibha A. Dabholkar)

Jones's 53rd Ohio, Taylor's 47th Ohio, and Moore's 54th Ohio. Jones and Taylor had advanced their men a bit to form a skirmish line while Moore continued to occupy the knoll. Brantley had no difficulty pushing Jones and Taylor back to the height, but the three regiments made a brief effort to hold the knoll even though they were isolated in a forward position with no immediate supports.[6]

Jones, Taylor, and Moore held their men on the knoll and opened heavy fire. They stopped the Confederates in their front for a time but then an officer called Taylor's attention to the fact that gray-clad troops were working around both flanks to bypass the knoll. They were attempting to enter a wooded hollow that lay just to the rear of the Union position. Spreading the word, all three regimental commanders realized they had to evacuate the place or be trapped. By the time orders were given, Brantley's men were only fifty yards from the front of the three Union regiments and there was no more than a gap of 200 to 300 yards behind the Federals. They gave up their position and raced through the gap, although some Unionists had their fighting spirit at a high pitch and refused to leave. Henry Bumfoeder, the acting adjutant of the 47th Ohio, stayed to fire his revolver and had to be dragged away just before it was too late. Another man in the regiment, a German American soldier in Company G, "also had to be pulled away," according to the regimental historian.[7]

It may well be true, as John K. Duke of the 53rd Ohio put it, that "we held our position longer than we should have done." But Duke felt there was a good reason to do so. "If we fell back without making a stubborn resistance the army would be surprised and possibly defeated." As it was, the retreat was chaotic because it was undertaken under duress. At least 20 Federals were taken prisoner, and most of those who escaped were unable to rejoin Logan's main line because the Confederates who were encircling the knoll blocked their most direct line of retreat toward Logan's right flank. After falling back 500 or 600 yards from the knoll, they took position some distance from that flank, detached from the Fifteenth Corps line and on a continuation of the ridge a bit farther west of the flank.[8]

Along the way during their retreat, the men of Jones, Taylor, and Moore encountered Maj. Charles Hipp's 37th Ohio, occupying an advanced post between the main line and the knoll to cover Logan's right flank. It was posted on "nearly an open field on a [tolerably] nice Raise witch give us Some Advantage," thought Capt. Henry Schmidt. Hipp had already sent out six companies to extend the Union skirmish line west and used other troops to cover roads leading to the Federal flank. When Hipp asked Wells S. Jones what he should do to help the retreating units, Jones replied, "Fight like the devil—there is nothing else to be done here." A minute or two later Hipp was shot in the arm just above the elbow, which broke the bone. He was seriously injured in the side as well. Serg. Ernst Torgler later received a Congressional Medal of Honor for carrying the major off the field. Capt. Carl Moritz now took charge of the 37th Ohio, or rather of the minority who remained with the regiment minus those earlier sent out as skirmishers and flankers. The men held long enough for Schmidt to see how their fire affected the Mississippians. They "Came Study the dead and wounded just faling by Scores and dit not Seem to mind it but Some Fled." Moritz then ordered the men to fall back to the ridge as best they could.[9]

Most of the Federals who occupied forward positions managed to escape Brantley's advance. They quickly took new positions on the ridgeline, but they were not connected with Logan's right flank. The gap between the rest of Lightburn's line and the 53rd, 47th, 54th, and 37th Ohio was about 200 yards, and thin woods occupied the part of the ridge where those four regiments now had established their line. The West Ravine, one of three ravines that intersected the battlefield, separated those regiments from the remainder of the brigade. Lightburn had the 83rd Indiana on the right of his continuous line, its right flank resting at the brush-filled West Ravine, with the 30th Ohio and then the 111th Illinois to the left. This gap presented an opportunity to the Confederates if they could find it and exploit the cover of the vegetation that filled the West Ravine.[10]

By now the battle had raged long enough to be noticed by everyone within long earshot of the muskets. W. C. Smith, a trooper of Montgomery's 1st Mississippi Cavalry, heard the "manly cheering of our Southern troops, so different from the affected" yelling of the Federals as Brantley's Brigade commenced its advance. He then heard the musketry, which "was very terrific for a while and sounded to us who stood in the edge of the woods out of sight of both sides, just like some monstrous machine grinding." Soon after that, Smith noticed a "long string of wounded men" passing by, seeking medical help in the rear.[11]

Thousands of Union soldiers along the Sixteenth and Seventeenth Corps line also heard musketry off on Logan's front and were impressed by it. His comrades in the Fifteenth Corps "opened with a murderous volley of musketry which made the very heavens ring," recalled Charles E. Smith of the 32nd Ohio in Blair's corps. "The roar was similar to the roar of thunder and increased along the line to the left for nearly half a mile for some time."[12]

Howard also was aware that a battle had started, for he had established a command post only 200 paces behind the center of Logan's line. He remembered for the rest of his long life the sound and fury of the engagement, describing the Confederate attack as a sudden burst of violence hurled upon the Federals. "That shrill, terrifying yell," he wrote after the war while attempting to convey the spirit with which the enemy launched the initial phase of the battle at Ezra Church.[13]

Logan was very near Howard when the battle began, and the new army commander had his first chance to observe his demeanor under fire. Howard later wrote that Logan had a tendency "to be in a somewhat depressed mood," basing that observation solely on how the corps leader had reacted to his demotion from command of the Army of the Tennessee. But, as soon as the first shot was fired, Logan became a changed man. Then "he fired up, became cheery, animated & active." Howard watched as Logan rode after a handful of men who broke from the ranks and forced the stragglers back to their line "manifesting a fierceness that few men were willing to encounter."[14]

Many other Federals observed Logan's demeanor that day as the battle lengthened. He rode about behind his corps line to encourage the men, shouting orders to stand fast and fire low. Rumor had it that Logan was seen personally carrying cartridges to the line to replenish supplies of ammunition. Another rumor put words in Logan's mouth; when the subject of reinforcements for the Fifteenth Corps came up, Logan reputedly said "that he could hold the ground 'till hell froze over.'" Another report expressed Logan's fighting spirit. It portrayed the corps leader as telling a subordinate, "You have no reserves, everything is in line! Hold your lines at all hazards, and if your guns can't be discharged, use your bayonets! Bayonet every Rebel that dares come over your works, and every man that attempts to leave the ranks while this fight lasts."[15]

Despite the powder smoke, the noise, and the confusion of the battle, many Federals believed they caught glimpses of the Confederate commander. Howard knew Lee personally from their days as cadets at the U.S. Military Academy. He received reports that Lee appeared very close to the action to urge the Confederates forward. While Howard never personally saw Lee, he believed these reports. In fact, Edwin W. Smith of the 54th Ohio saw a Confederate officer on a white horse and tried several times to shoot him but failed. It is not known what type of horse Lee rode, and this may well have been another Confederate officer, but several Confederate officers reported that Lee vigorously exposed himself to enemy fire in order to inspire his men on the battlefield that afternoon.[16]

Sherman had left Howard's side just before the attack began, allowing his new army commander to conduct the battle on his own. One of the first tasks facing Howard was to secure his right flank, which certainly was weak and vulnerable. His primary way of dealing with that problem was to rush reinforcements to the western end of Logan's line. Sending out staff officers, Howard began almost immediately the task of drawing more troops to the Fifteenth Corps from the other two corps in his army, which were not yet threatened by the Confederates. This process of reinforcement took place during almost the entire course of the battle and brought eleven regiments, the equivalent of two additional brigades, to Logan's aid.[17]

Col. George E. Bryant heard the sound of battle as soon as Brantley's Brigade encountered the three Federal regiments on the knoll. He quickly formed the two reserve regiments of his First Brigade, Third Division of the Seventeenth Corps, and got them ready for action. Soon after forming them, word arrived from Howard to send the regiments to Logan's assistance. Lieut. Col. James K. Proudfit's 12th Wisconsin took the lead, followed by Lieut. Col. Robert N. Pearson's 31st Illinois. Both regiments moved on the double-quick for more than one mile toward the right of Logan's line. The heat was intense during the noon hour, and many of the men became overheated by the exertion. Hosea Rood of the 12th Wisconsin remembered two men who "never fully recovered" from that experience and claimed that James H. Clement died a week later "because of over-exertion" in the hot, humid atmosphere.[18]

While these reinforcements were on the way, Brantley's men came very close to crushing Logan's right flank. Jones's 53rd Ohio, Taylor's 47th Ohio, Moore's 54th Ohio, and part of Moritz's 37th Ohio occupied a position on the ridge, detached from the rest of Lightburn's brigade with a gap of 200 yards between, and the brush-filled West Ravine as well. The Confederates quickly sized up the situation and began to penetrate the gap, threatening to isolate and swallow the detached Federals, while pressing forward on their front and threatening to circle round their right as well. For the second time the Unionists had to fall back from an untenable position, but this time there was no line to the rear for them to fall back on. Instead, the men of these four regiments retired about thirty yards until they reached the foot of the shallow ridge, where they had an opportunity to re-form their lines as the Southerners occupied the ridgetop.[19]

The Confederates who entered the gap also came close to turning and crushing the rest of Lightburn's brigade. The 83rd Indiana, which held the right end of Lightburn's continuous line just east of the brush-filled ravine, gave way under the pressure. Lieut. Col. George H. Hildt reacted quickly to that fallback by refusing the right wing of the 30th Ohio, immediately to the left of the faltering Indianans, so as to deliver fire on the Rebels in the gap. This gave time for Capt. George H. Scott to re-form the 83rd Indiana in position so the men also could fire into the gap. "We slaughtered them terribly," reported a member of the 83rd Indiana. Wayne Johnson Jacobs of the 30th Ohio reported that a handful of Confederates "gained our works but instantly fell dead, one of them pierced by 39 balls." Other

Rebels lay prone within short range of the Union line and tried to protect themselves by gathering chunks of wood and dirt clods lying nearby. Such slim measures failed to shield them from the rain of fire, and they retired. The right flank of Lightburn's brigade, and of Morgan L. Smith's division, and of Logan's Fifteenth Corps held firm.[20]

This was the first crisis of the battle at Ezra Church. Logan's right flank—indeed, Sherman's right flank—held on by a thread. Brantley did not have enough men to keep the Federals occupied in their front while he tried to flank their right at the same time. Moreover, only half of Lightburn's brigade was isolated—the rest of the brigade held firmly on the east side of the West Ravine. More importantly, Howard was well aware of the danger and was rushing reinforcements to the flank as fast as possible.

The tide of battle on the far right flank quickly reverted to the Federals' favor. Jones, Taylor, Moore, and Moritz re-formed their men at the foot of the ridge and counterattacked. The troops yelled lustily on the way up the shallow slope. The 54th Ohio was on the right, the 37th Ohio next to the left, the 47th Ohio and then the 53rd Ohio on the far left, with Wells S. Jones commanding the entire force. According to Taylor, the Federals drove Brantley's men from the ridgetop "more by noise than numbers."[21]

The reinforcements arrived in time to participate in this counterattack, although members of Jones's group of four regiments never gave credit to them. It is possible, given the wide gap between the four regiments and the rest of Lightburn's brigade, that there was plenty of room for additional troops to participate in reclaiming the right flank. Perhaps the hard-pressed men of Jones's demi-brigade honestly did not notice the additional troops.

Members of the 30th Ohio, which occupied a position just east of the brush-filled ravine, saw the reinforcements arrive. They had also seen the Confederates ascend the ridge and enter the woods that covered it, chasing away Jones's men. A. B. Crummel told his adjutant of this, and the adjutant replied "You will see the 'Dutch' give them h—l directly." Actually, the adjutant was referring to the German 37th Ohio because he knew it was operating in that area. But, of course, the 37th Ohio completely failed to give anyone hell under the circumstances it found itself in and was part of the group that was giving up the ridgetop.[22]

Right after that moment, Crummel saw two new regiments approach led by Capt. Frederick W. Gilbreth, one of Howard's aides-de-camp. As soon as the 12th Wisconsin neared the gap that existed to the right of the 83rd Indiana, Proudfit formed it in the West Ravine and advanced up the

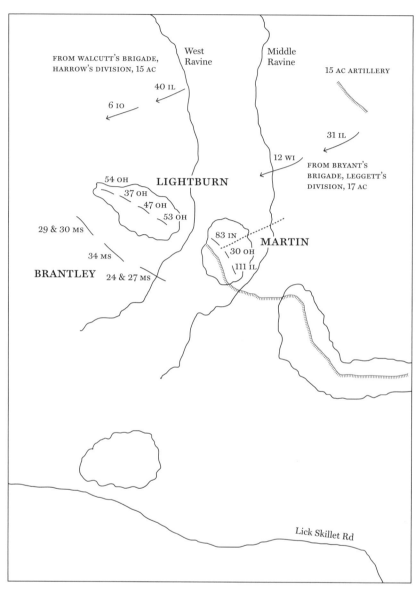

Brantley's Brigade at High Tide

(Earl J. Hess and Pratibha A. Dabholkar)

ridge slope toward the spot recently vacated by Jones's demi-brigade. He advanced about the same time that Jones launched his own counterattack. The combined weight of this thrust sent the Rebels back. "We ran to them and drove them. It was awfull," reported Alonzo Miller of the 12th Wisconsin. Pearson's 31st Illinois was too late to take part in the counterattack. It took up a reserve position to bolster the defenses of the restored right flank but was not engaged during the course of the day.[23]

The 12th Wisconsin and 31st Illinois were not the only reinforcements rushing to secure the right flank. Logan had taken the initiative to bring help to the threatened spot at the same time that Howard arranged for Seventeenth Corps troops to come up. Brig. Gen. Charles C. Walcutt's brigade acted as a reserve for Harrow's division. Walcutt dispatched his staff member, Capt. Samuel H. Watson, to lead the 6th Iowa and 40th Illinois to the right, but Logan rode up to assist Watson in pushing the reinforcements as fast as possible. The combined strength of the two regiments did not exceed 400 men.[24]

The troops moved at the double-quick in the heat, led by Maj. Thomas J. Ennis's 6th Iowa, and both regiments marched by the flank. Innis moved round the position of Jones's demi-brigade to extend the Union line farther west and confront those Confederates who had already begun to work around Jones's right. The 6th Iowa halted only thirty yards from Brantley's men and faced to the left to form line once again. Just as the Iowans were in the process of doing it, the Confederates fired a terrific volley at them. Innis was shot off his horse, and Capt. William H. Clune took control of the regiment. The Iowans managed to form line and open fire through the trees before advancing up the ridge slope to the right of Jones's command, which by now had either begun or finished its counterattack up the ridge. At this point the shallow ridge was littered with "tangled brush and briars," which had helped to shield Brantley's men when Innis initially halted and re-formed his regiment. Maj. Hiram W. Hall's 40th Illinois soon followed the 6th Iowa, but Hall was badly wounded when his men reached the crest of the ridge. Capt. Michael Galvin took charge of the regiment.[25]

The loss of Innis hit many men hard because he was a popular and widely admired officer. Shot in the abdomen, he lay dying for eight hours. The bullet entered from the loins and coursed through the abdomen, producing a wound from which a good deal of omentum protruded. The surgeons could only apply simple dressing and try to make him comfortable. John Corse, who had commanded the 6th Iowa earlier in the war, took time from his division duties to visit Innis before he passed away at age twenty-four. His fellow officers thought of him as "noble, gallant and chivalric," while Walcutt believed his death was "a great loss to his regiment and country. He possessed every quality of a good soldier." At the same time that Innis was shot, Capt. Thomas J. Elrick of Company D, 6th Iowa, also suffered a very similar wound and died later that day.[26]

Members of the 6th Iowa pursued Brantley's fleeing men a short distance south of the ridge crest when the Federals drove them away, but they soon returned to their line. The Unionists gathered fence rails and other material to construct a breastwork on the crest with the 6th Iowa holding down the far right and the 40th Illinois next to it. Jones's demi-brigade occupied the area just east of those two regiments, and the 12th Wisconsin was to its left. The gap apparently was not filled by Federal troops even now, but at least there were enough men on the ridge crest west of it to offer stronger resistance if the enemy reappeared. Clune also sent out three companies from the 6th Iowa to cover his right flank. The Union line thus formed west of the gap was not perfect. Taylor reported that "many gaps intervened between regiments," but unit commanders tried to see that "every inch of the ground in our front" was covered by oblique fire if not direct fire. Jones placed Moritz's hard-hit 37th Ohio a short distance to the rear to act as a reserve.[27]

The first major crisis of the battle for the Federals had been met and averted. Little more than grit and determination on the part of Jones's demi-brigade and the timely arrival of four fresh regiments staved off disaster. Howard proudly recalled that his extreme right gave way only about thirty yards before recovering its ground. John C. Brown reported that his men carried the Union position "in many places," which was an exaggeration built upon on a small success. The Confederates did not seem to have understood how close they came to a larger victory on this part of the battlefield. Their possession of the ridge crest was limited in extent and brief in duration, and of course they occupied only a detached portion of the Union line.[28]

Although Federal officers did not report it, they apparently sent out a skirmish line after reclaiming their position on the ridge crest. Brantley and his regimental leaders clearly report that the brigade fell back from its high tide to the knoll previously taken from Jones's demi-brigade and re-formed on it and to the east of the rise of ground. They just as clearly report being attacked by the Yankees in this position. It must have been skirmishers, for there is no indication that the main Union line advanced. Alternatively, it might have been those members of the 6th Iowa who advanced some distance south of the ridge crest before returning to the main Union position.[29]

At any rate, whatever Union force confronted Brantley at the knoll did not represent a major thrust against the Confederates, but the Rebel brigade quickly retired from its position anyway. By this time, McKelvaine had been wounded and was succeeded in command of the consolidated 24th and 27th Mississippi by Lieut. Col. William L. Lyles. The regiment fell back in some confusion because the Federals struck just when Lyles was in the process of moving it by the right flank to close up the brigade line. Lyles fell back fifty or sixty yards before he could re-form his men. Hubbard's 34th Mississippi stood and fought for ten or fifteen minutes before retiring. On the far left of Brantley's line, Johnson's consolidated 29th and 30th Mississippi fell back because the rest of the troops to his right retired.[30]

Brantley re-formed his brigade about 50 or 60 yards south of the knoll, but the Federals did not pursue. After a short while, Brown sent instructions for him to fall back an additional 300 yards to near the starting point of the attack. Brantley later explained the rather precipitous withdrawal from the knoll in the face of a Union skirmish line by noting that his brigade had been greatly weakened by losses thus far in the battle. He also cited "innumerable cases of utter exhaustion among the best men" of the brigade, as well as "the absence of a goodly number who had no legitimate excuse."[31]

Not long after resuming his original place at the starting point of the attack, Brantley received orders from Brown (undoubtedly urged on by Lee) to attack again. The steam had already been taken out of the brigade, but Brantley obeyed the order. His Mississippians moved forward along the same line of advance at about 2:00 P.M., two hours after the start of the first effort. They made it to a point about sixty yards south of the knoll, which still was held by a Union skirmish line. Here, at a point where the brigade had temporarily fallen back while retreating from the first attack, the Mississippi men stopped and traded fire with the Union skirmishers for as long as an hour. By this time reports filtered in that indicated the Federals were fighting the same division that had captured a section of the Fifteenth Corps line on July 22 before being driven back by a counterattack. It gave the harried members of Lightburn's brigade some solace to know they "did their best to repay them for the heavy loss which was inflicted upon us by them on that occasion," according to Thomas Taylor.[32]

When Brantley retired from the second attempt, he fell back to the slight ridge just north of the Lick Skillet Road to secure possession of the roadway. His men gathered rails to make a breastwork. They remained there until the arrival of Stewart's Corps on the field sometime after 3:30 P.M. and then retired farther south.[33]

Brown was satisfied with the performance of Brantley's men, referring to their "great gallantry" in the attacks. The division leader blamed overwhelming numbers of Federals for the failure, arguing that the Confederates engaged four corps of Sherman's army group that afternoon. Regimental officers also praised their men. Hubbard noted that Serg. Andrew J. Hamilton of the 34th Mississippi advanced ahead of the line to fire at the Federals and killed a Yankee officer who was trying to rally his troops. Eddie Evans, described as "a mere boy," asked permission to carry the colors of the 24th Mississippi and did so in a way "to elicit the admiration of all," according to Lyles. Evans advanced the flag in the open until only fifty yards from the Federals and waved them "defiantly, and called upon his comrades to rally to the flag."[34]

Brantley compiled statistics about his casualties at Ezra Church. He lost a total of 126 men, but did not report how many were engaged. The consolidated 24th and 27th Mississippi suffered the most, 77 out of 430 men engaged, while holding down the right wing of the brigade. That represented a loss rate of 17.9 percent. The consolidated 29th and 30th Mississippi, occupying the left wing, suffered 31 casualties out of 277 men engaged (70 of those men were on the skirmish line to screen Brantley's left). That amounted to a loss ratio of 11.1 percent. The 34th Mississippi in the center lost 18 troops. The percentage of brigade men who were listed as severely wounded as opposed to slightly injured was unusually high. In all regiments, the severely wounded accounted for 60 percent of the total wounded, while the slightly wounded accounted for about 27 percent. The dangerously and mortally wounded made up the rest.[35]

The loss of prominent individuals, officers and enlisted men alike, made an impression on their comrades. Thomas Jefferson Newberry's friend, William Brown, was killed in the ranks of the 29th Mississippi that day. "He was shot through the head above the right eye with a minnie ball," explained Newberry. "He fell dead I don't think he hardly knowed he was struck."[36]

Brantley, reporting on the first battle in which he led the brigade, tried very hard to explain away the failure of its attacks. "The extreme heat, the scarcity of water, and the hurried manner in which we went into the engagement, caused a great many to fall out of the ranks." No officer could do much about the heat and shortage of water, but Lee was responsible for the haste with which the offensive was conducted.[37]

There was very little artillery firing on either side during the battle of Ezra Church, although exactly how many and which guns were involved remained rather murky. Logan reported that the Confederates employed one battery, but he used none at all. As noted in a previous chapter, two sections of Union guns were deployed just before the attack to support the heavy skirmishing by Logan's infantrymen, but both of them were pulled out of action as soon as the first Confederate attack came rolling across the valley from the south. DeGress had placed two guns of Lieut. George Echte's Battery A, 1st Illinois Light Artillery, between the main line and the skirmishers when Jones and Taylor advanced to take the knoll near Lick Skillet Road. Echte fired at least twenty rounds before Brantley's first attack forced him back behind the main Union position. On Martin's brigade front, just to the left of Lightburn's brigade, a section of the 4th Ohio Battery had also been run forward of the main line to support Union skirmishers before Brown launched his assault. It too had to be hauled back hastily upon the appearance of Sharp's brigade at about the same time that Brantley advanced.[38]

Federal artillery played a very small role in repelling Lee's attacks at Ezra Church. According to Logan's chief of artillery, Maj. Thomas Davies Maurice, this was because "the nature of the grounds" offered little opportunity for the guns to deploy properly. The ridgetop was narrow and winding and often covered with trees. There essentially was room only for the Union infantrymen. It was not advisable for the guns to be placed behind the troops and fire over their heads because misfires could endanger them. Those men positioned along the Sixteenth, Seventeenth, and at least a portion of Woods's division of the Fifteenth Corps, facing east rather than south, did receive Confederate artillery fire that often amounted to an intense bombardment during the course of the day. This fire mostly came from the Confederate City Line protecting Atlanta's western perimeter. But the battle of Ezra Church was fought with very little fire from the big guns. It was, as a newspaper correspondent accurately phrased it, a fight that "was almost entirely one of musketry."[39]

But Howard was prepared to use massed artillery to support his threatened right flank. The Fifteenth Corps had twenty-seven guns available, and Howard gave instructions for all but one of them to be assembled so as to fire on any Confederate attempt to turn Smith's division. Howard recalled "some remarkable experiences on other fields," so he wanted to make victory "doubly sure." Presumably he was referring to Hardee's successful effort to flank McPherson's left on July 22. At any rate, the guns were positioned a bit to the rear and right of Lightburn's brigade and sited to cover the entire area around his right flank. Some breastworks of rails were made for at least some of the pieces, and pioneers not only helped make those works but could support the artillery with their muskets if called on to do so. Capt. Andrew Hickenlooper, Howard's chief of artillery, arranged this massive concentration of firepower. In the end, it was not necessary to unleash the guns because the Confederates never made a large-scale effort to turn Logan's flank after the first attempt to do so by Brantley.[40]

The attack and repulse of Brantley's Mississippi troops was but the first episode in Lee's effort to drive the Federals away from the Lick Skillet Road. Brantley opened the conflict by coming close to crushing Logan's right flank. If Lee had given the situation more thought and made efforts to shift troops westward to flank the end of the Union line, the chance for a Rebel victory would have increased. Even so, the Confederate assault loomed large in the minds of Logan's harried troops. It was "the most persistent and bloody attempt to dislodge us from our position and turn our right that I have ever witnessed," wrote Morgan L. Smith.[41]

Some two miles to the north, Sherman had ridden as far as the headquarters of Absalom Baird's division of the Fourteenth Corps, positioned just north of Proctor's Creek along Thomas's Army of the Cumberland line. While chatting with Baird, the sound of heavy musketry suddenly could be heard in Howard's direction. "Logan is feeling for them and I guess he has found them," remarked Sherman. Soon after that a staff officer arrived from Howard bringing news that a major assault was under way. "'Good' said Sherman, 'that is fine' 'just what I wanted' 'just what I wanted, tell Howard to invite them to attack, it will save us trouble, save us trouble, they'll only beat their own brains out, beat their own brains out.'" According to Baird's staff officer, Maj. James A. Connolly, Sherman continued speaking in this vein in a confident and happy way, "while his boys in blue were reaping the terrible harvest of death."[42]

CHAPTER FIVE

A Scene of Absolute Horror

Sharp's Brigade and Johnston's Brigade

Two other units of Brown's division moved forward at noon, about the same time that Brantley began his attack that day. Sharp's Mississippi brigade occupied the center of Brown's line while Johnston's Alabama brigade held down the right wing. Both units conducted their attack with enough spirit and determination to challenge the opposing Federal line and pressed three Union brigades and part of a fourth.

Jacob Hunter Sharp was a native of Alabama but grew up in Mississippi. He attended the University of Alabama and entered the profession of law in his adopted state. Enlisting as a private, he soon was commissioned and fought in the great Western battles from Shiloh on before becoming colonel of the 44th Mississippi in the summer of 1863. Sharp replaced his brigade commander and was promoted to brigadier general two days before leading the Mississippians into battle at Ezra Church.[1]

Sharp formed his brigade immediately south of the Lick Skillet Road with Brantley to the left, Johnston to the right, and Manigault to the rear as a reserve. He sent the 9th Mississippi Battalion Sharpshooters out as skirmishers. When it became apparent that the battalion was too small to cover the brigade front, he dispatched a company each from the 10th Mississippi and the 41st Mississippi to supplement the sharpshooters. Lieut. J. B. Downing took charge of the skirmish line and posted it 200 yards in front of the brigade.[2]

When the order came for Brantley, Sharp, and Johnston to advance, Downing advanced his line and found the Federal skirmishers only 250 yards ahead. They already were protected by a slight breastwork of fence rails and had a section of artillery supplied by the 4th Ohio Battery "posted a short distance in their rear," as Downing reported. The Rebel skirmishers moved across an open field "in a most gallant style" and took the rail works, losing only six men. Downing then waited at this position until Sharp's main line approached, when he moved his skirmishers to the rear to "keep up stragglers." Downing could not explain why the company assigned to him from the 41st Mississippi failed to take part in the advance; it did not appear until after the brigade had reached and then passed the location he took from the Union skirmishers.[3]

Sharp had his main line formed with the 41st Mississippi on the left, then the 9th Mississippi, the 7th Mississippi, the 10th Mississippi, and his 44th Mississippi on the far right. While Downing gave the impression his sharpshooters alone took the Union skirmish position, several reports emanating from the main line indicate that many of Sharp's units contributed to that feat. The 41st and 9th Mississippi on the left initially moved through a small patch of dense woods and across an open field where they stopped to dress their lines. Then the two regiments continued across a cornfield and through another dense patch of woods and undergrowth that was 400 yards deep. Emerging from the trees, they found an open field 150 yards across with the Federal skirmishers sheltering behind rail piles on the other side. Without mentioning Downing's skirmishers, regimental commanders reported driving the Yankees away, the eruption of hand-to-hand fighting as some of the Federals stubbornly refused to yield, and the capture of several prisoners.[4]

A member of Company I, 127th Illinois, which occupied the Union skirmish line opposing Sharp, testified that the short contest for the rail piles was intense. "Pretty soon we saw them come," wrote Andrew McCormack to a friend, "and gave them the best we had in the wheelhouse, but still they came." In fact, Sharp's line nearly grabbed the entire complement of Company I. McCormack was determined to get away and "started as fast as Jim Shank's horses could travel. The rebels kept hollering, 'Halt, you son-of-a-bitch,' but I could not see it."[5]

The two guns of the 4th Ohio Battery also had to skedaddle. Maj. Clemens Landgraeber, the artillery chief of Woods's First Division, had sent it to a position about 100 yards in front of Martin's brigade, Morgan L. Smith's division, between the main Union line and the skirmishers. Capt. George Froehlich commanded the battery, but no one reported who led the section. The guns fired shell and spherical case shot at the Confederate battery that had annoyed Sherman and other high-ranking officers in blue late that morning. The Federal gunners managed to pull back in time to

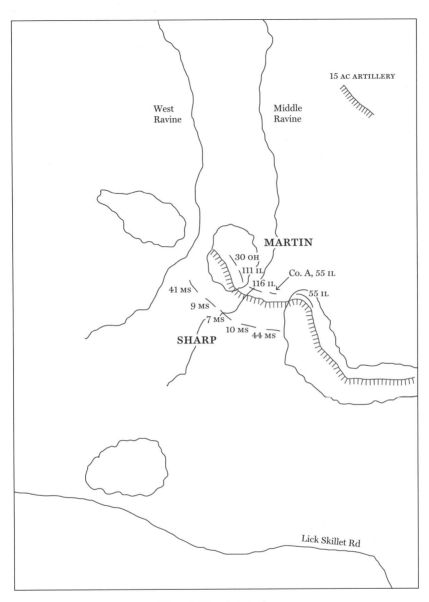

15 AC ARTILLERY

West
Ravine

Middle
Ravine

MARTIN

30 OH

111 IL

Co. A, 55 IL

116 IL

41 MS

55 IL

9 MS

7 MS

10 MS   44 MS

SHARP

Lick Skillet Rd

Sharp's Brigade Attacks
(Earl J. Hess and Pratibha A. Dabholkar)

Firing Line of Martin's Brigade. A dramatic and accurate depiction of Martin's brigade line firing at Sharp's first attack. (*Harper's Weekly*, August 27, 1864, 556)

avoid Sharp's heavy attack, dragging their weapons across a low point in the breastworks to rejoin the battery behind the main line.[6]

Sharp followed up his initial success in taking the enemy skirmish line but soon found difficulties complicating his way. Upon resuming the forward movement, the 41st and 9th Mississippi on the left discovered that a gap was developing between the right flank of the 9th and the left flank of the 7th Mississippi, a gap that grew wider as the brigade continued forward. Sharp reported that the 41st Mississippi itself began to scatter and lose cohesion with each forward step. After moving about half a mile from the starting point of the attack, Sharp's men began to ascend the wooded slope of the ridge upon which Logan had established his line, and there they encountered further difficulties. Because of the doglegs in the Union position, the Federals could obtain an enfilade fire on Sharp's right wing.[7]

In this way, the irregularities of the topography favored the Unionists. Lieut. Col. R. G. Kelsey's 44th Mississippi, occupying the extreme right of Sharp's brigade, received the worst of the enfilading fire. Just in front of Kelsey's regiment, "a large hollow" (the Middle Ravine) intersected the Union line. He received so much "destructive fire" that his ranks were too thinned for him to carry the enemy works.[8]

Dead Brook. This contemporary print was based on a field sketch by
Theodore R. Davis. The brook drained the swale that lay between the opposing lines
and ran northward along Middle Ravine through the Union position. (*Harper's
Weekly*, August 27, 1864, 557)

The Federals were well aware of their advantage. The 55th Illinois occupied the part of the line that was intersected by the hollow. Its Company A
was positioned in the depression, and the assistant surgeon and attendants
had set up a field hospital in the valley. West of the hollow, Martin held the
116th Illinois and 57th Ohio on the continuation of the high ground. Open
fields covered with stumps lay before the skirt of trees in which these two
regiments had formed. A small brook lined with a rail fence crossed that
open area and drained along the Middle Ravine. Martin had an almost
ideal position to defend.[9]

From the perspective of the 116th Illinois, it was "a grand sight" as
Sharp's battle line approached the ridge across the open ground. Elijah
Coombe of Company C could see an officer mounted on a white horse
giving directions to the Confederates, and "as he turned to give an order,
down went their guns, and here they come at a double-quick with a yell!"
William McCulloch Newell of the 57th Ohio described the experience of
meeting Sharp's men as "a moment of terrible suspense. We let them come

up within forty steps of us and then we arose and gave them one of the most terrible & withering fires it was ever my lot to witness, but still on they come & some of them got almost up to us, but only to die."[10]

The 55th Illinois had begun to fire when the enemy was some distance away, dropping a few men as the gray line advanced. Logan walked about in the rear of the regiment yelling, "Hold them! steady, boys, we've got them now." Most members of the regiment were able to fire obliquely along Sharp's line and enfiladed the right wing with terrible effect. Still Sharp's Mississippians made it as close as fifty yards, according to some Union accounts, before they stopped and broke for the rear in retreat. When they fell back, "a line of battle of dead Rebles lay before us stiff & dead," according to William McCulloch Newell.[11]

Sharp's retreat was a disjointed movement because the gap between the 7th and 9th Mississippi had already divided his command into two wings. Lieut. Col. Benjamin F. Johns of the 9th Mississippi could not see the rest of the brigade to his right, but he understood that the order had been given for everyone to retreat, so he pulled his men back to the cornfield. Col. J. Byrd Williams admitted that his 41st Mississippi had gotten considerably scattered in the advance because of the cluttered terrain it traversed. But he insisted that the men held for half an hour exchanging rounds with the enemy before falling back. Sharp, however, reported the 41st was so scattered that "it was impossible to handle it as an organization. The fire on the right was too severe to be withstood."[12]

On the far right of the brigade line, Sharp found that the 44th Mississippi had suffered enormously from the raging enfilade fire delivered by the 55th Illinois. The 10th Mississippi to its left had lost nearly as many men plus five color-bearers. The 7th Mississippi in the center of the brigade received virtually all the destructive fire it endured from the right, from the ridgeline occupied by the 55th Illinois. In contrast, Sharp reported that losses in the 9th and 41st Mississippi on the far left were comparatively light.[13]

Federal fire stopped Sharp's brigade at fairly close range, but George D. Johnston's brigade achieved somewhat more success. Born in North Carolina but raised in Alabama, Johnston graduated from Cumberland University in Lebanon, Tennessee, and set up a law practice in Marion, Alabama. He also served as mayor and state legislator. Johnston was a lieutenant in the 4th Alabama at First Manassas before being commissioned major of the 25th Alabama and thereafter colonel of the regiment. He fought in

◆ GEORGE D. JOHNSTON ◆
(Library of Congress, LC-USZ62-83412)

all the major campaigns and battles in the West before his promotion to brigadier general on July 26, 1864, the same date of Sharp's commission.[14]

Johnston had formed to the right of Sharp, his left resting at Lick Skillet Road. The brigade then moved forward through thick woods before entering an open field where it received heavy fire from the Union skirmish line. The combination of moving through woods, over several fences, and dealing with this fire disorganized the line so much that Johnston halted to reform after advancing 350 yards. The men lay down as soon as they had rectified the line in order to avoid the minie balls. Much of that fire was delivered by three companies of the 48th Illinois, which had been sent from Oliver's brigade of Harrow's division to the skirmish line. These companies, led by Capt. Stephen F. Grimes, fired at relatively close range to disarrange Johnston's formation and compel the Confederates to pause and reform.[15]

The Illinois skirmishers caused more trouble for the Confederates than they realized. Johnston was struck by a bullet and severely wounded in the leg. Col. John G. Coltart of the 50th Alabama took command of the brigade, but he was felled almost immediately by another bullet. Now Col. Benjamin R. Hart of the 22nd Alabama took charge, only to be hit so quickly that he could not make his presence felt. Finally, Lieut. Col. Harry T. Toulmin of the 19th Alabama took over and retained command of the brigade. By some accounts, the Alabamans had halted within easy range of the Union skirmish line for twenty to forty-five minutes before the command structure could be firmed up and the men restarted. But, as Capt. Isaac M. Whitney of the 22nd Alabama pointed out, it was with "only a very light line" because of the casualties suffered during that time.[16]

Johnston would not continue with his men. He had been wounded by a shell fragment on his thigh at the battle of Stones River a year and a half before, and now a bullet fractured a bone in his leg. He had received his commission as brigadier general literally while marching along Lick Skillet Road that morning toward the pending battlefield. Thomas T. Smith, who belonged to the 43rd Mississippi in Loring's Division, happened to see Johnston being carried away from the scene of action on a litter as his command was moving toward the battlefield. Smith had known Johnston before the war, and "being a large fleshy man he looked like a small elephant as he lay on the stretcher."[17]

When the brigade resumed its advance, the Union skirmishers scampered back to their main line, and the Confederates easily took the breastworks that had protected them. Like Sharp's men, Toulmin's command was compelled to traverse patches of thick woods that slowed and further disorganized the formation. Capt. Napoleon B. Rouse of the 25th Alabama described some of these patches as so thickly braced with underbrush that they were "almost an abatis by nature." The Alabamans crossed "an old field" and struggled across a fence into a thin patch of woods that fronted the Union position on the ridge. Different parts of the extended line halted at different distances from the enemy. While the 39th Alabama stopped about eighty yards short of the crest, the 25th Alabama surged forward until fifty yards from the Yankees.[18]

The attacks by Sharp and Johnston covered a surprisingly wide extent of the battlefield. In part it was because the Confederate line became extended a great deal. The brigades lost connection with each other quite rapidly, and no reports indicate that Sharp's flank ever touched Brantley's to the left or Johnston's to the right. Johnston's halt near the Union skirmish line further

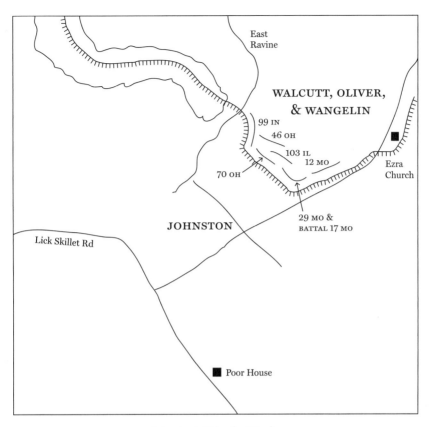

East
Ravine

WALCUTT, OLIVER,
& WANGELIN

99 IN

46 OH

103 IL

12 MO

70 OH

Ezra
Church

JOHNSTON

29 MO &
BATTAL 17 MO

Lick Skillet Rd

Poor House

Johnston's Brigade Attacks
(Earl J. Hess and Pratibha A. Dabholkar)

distanced his command from Sharp's. As a result, Brown's three brigades attacked in piecemeal fashion with no support to right or left, and they all advanced spread out more than usual. Moreover, the Fifteenth Corps line was not straight; the doglegs in it constricted Logan's front more than normal for a corps line. This combination of a gray line that was unusually extended and a blue line that was unusually constricted meant that Brown's Confederate division nearly covered the front of an entire Union corps. This circumstance greatly favored the Federals as they could pack more men per linear yard of front than the Confederates could throw at them. More importantly, the Federals had the opportunity of obtaining crossfires on some parts of the Rebel line.

Brig. Gen. William Harrow had barely formed his Fourth Division along the snakelike ridge before Toulmin's brigade appeared in his front. He had placed Col. John M. Oliver's Third Brigade on the left, connecting with Woods's division at a rather sharp angle in the line. Col. Reuben Williams's First Brigade, on the right, connected with Martin's brigade of Smith's division. While Williams occupied a section of continuous ridgetop, Oliver's brigade line was bisected by the East Ravine and a stream draining northward toward Proctor's Creek. It was one of three such ravines that ran through the irregular Union line. Brig. Gen. Charles C. Walcutt's Second Brigade was held in reserve along the stream in the East Ravine.[19]

Williams managed to place a small reserve for his brigade too. An officer of much and varied experience, he had formerly commanded the 12th Indiana and now relied on that regiment to provide reserve power for his brigade. Lieut. Col. James Goodnow currently commanded the 12th Indiana, which occupied a spot just behind the 26th Illinois. Soon after the Confederates drove in the Union skirmishers, Goodnow moved Companies G and K under Maj. Elbert D. Baldwin to reinforce the line just to the left of the 26th Illinois. Later he also sent Companies C and H but held the other six companies in their reserve post for the time. The Alabama troops approached Williams's position with loud yells, reinforced by the sharp crack of musketry echoing through the thin woods fronting much of the Union line. Goodnow was impressed by his enemy's determination and drive. In fact, he noted that many Confederates made it to a point only thirty paces from the blazing Union rifles.[20]

Along Oliver's brigade line, retiring Union skirmishers brought back a warning. "Boys, get ready, for they are coming in force." Soon after, as Thomas W. Connelly of the 70th Ohio put it, "the cornbread yelp was heard in our front." Lieut. Col. Frederick S. Hutchinson ordered the 15th Michigan to open fire as soon as the skirmishers cleared the front, yet the Confederates managed to surge forward until within fifty paces of his regiment. The view in front of the 70th Ohio was obscured by fairly dense underbrush which allowed Toulmin's men to get quite close to the Federals before suffering the full effect of their fire. The Alabama troops were already about forty or fifty paces away when they became visible targets, and the 70th Ohio finally opened fire. Toulmin's troops managed to advance farther until, according to Federal accounts, the weight of the fire forced them to stop twenty to thirty paces from the blazing muzzles.[21]

The attack by Johnston's brigade overlapped Harrow's division and pressed against the far right wing of Woods's division as well. The two divisions joined at an angle; that circumstance, plus the thick underbrush fronting the line, rendered this one of the more vulnerable spots of Logan's position. Maj. William B. Brown's 70th Ohio held the far left of Oliver's brigade, and Lieut. Col. Jacob Kaercher's 12th Missouri held the extreme right of Wangelin's brigade, Woods's division. Before the Rebel attack, Wangelin had filled a gap between his command and the 70th Ohio by moving reserves into it. Thus Lieut. Col. Joseph F. Gage's 29th Missouri and a small battalion of Maj. Francis Romer's 17th Missouri now were on line. These four regiments were responsible for holding the angle in Logan's position under grueling pressure all afternoon, and Toulmin's advance was the first of several attacks facing them.[22]

The Rebel approach was particularly ominous for Wangelin's men. Their own skirmishers came back with warnings that the enemy was on the way, but Wangelin did not necessarily credit them. Born in Germany and formerly colonel of the 12th Missouri, Wangelin had lost an arm owing to a serious wound received at the battle of Ringgold the previous November. He took command of a brigade after recovering and led it capably during the Atlanta campaign. There was "some apprehension," Wangelin later wrote, "that the report was exaggerated, as usual in such cases." But then the Confederates could be detected by the sound they made while moving through the undergrowth. "The cracking of brush announced the approach of the enemy," reported an adjutant's clerk named David Allan Jr. in the 29th Missouri. "When they were within three or four rods of our works they became visible." In other words, the Alabama troops suddenly appeared in full form only sixteen to twenty-two yards away; only then did the Missouri Yankees open fire. Gage had already told his men in the 29th "to keep cool, take good aim, and when the order was given, to fire by will and aim low." Now they put his words into effect as fast as they could. The result was "such a terrific fire . . . that no mortal could stand," in Wangelin's words. As the Rebels continued to move forward, "cheering and yelling like demons," thought Gage, the Federals rested their rifle barrels on the pile of rails and other material that sheltered them. The heavy fire issuing from hundreds of muskets stopped Toulmin's command. According to one Federal, the heaviest firing lasted fifteen minutes before signs became apparent that the enemy had retired into the underbrush, but the Yankees continued firing into the smoke anyway just in case they were mistaken.[23]

To the left of Wangelin, Col. James A. Williamson's Iowa brigade was a witness to this fierce encounter, but it was not involved in the firing. John C. Arbuckle, who had joined the 4th Iowa only the previous March, stared in awe at the Rebel formation as it emerged from the brush and thought "it was the most imposing and invincible battle line" he had ever seen. He

Logan's Line. A contemporary print based on a field sketch.
(*Frank Leslie's Illustrated Newspaper*, August 27, 1864, 364)

worried about Wangelin's men, whether they would be able to repel the onslaught behind their frail breastworks. Arbuckle could catch glimpses to tell what happened when the first Union fire erupted; "the enemy lines went down as if the earth had opened to swallow them up." For some time the field was too enshrouded in smoke for anyone to see much, but as soon as the firing stopped one could tell that "it was a scene of absolute horror."[24]

The first attack conducted by Sharp's and Johnston's brigades failed. The Rebels fronting Oliver and Wangelin slipped away under cover of the battle smoke, while those fronting Williams dropped back, as many Rebels took shelter behind trees to fire at the Unionists. James Goodnow told his wife that the Federals did not suffer much from this first attack on Williams's brigade, for the enemy "fired up hill at us, and over our little breastworks, and the most of the bullets went over our heads." The 99th Indiana in Williams's command sent men forward to clear the ridge slope of these snipers, and they captured a few of them in the process. By this time, a handful of shovels had been brought forward to Wangelin's brigade, and eager hands used them to dig in front of the breastwork and add some dirt to raise its height.[25]

Sharp's men fronting Martin's brigade of Morgan L. Smith's division also fell back; in fact, they had fallen back before Johnston's brigade gave up its position at high tide. Some members of Martin's brigade also followed up the Rebel retirement by moving forward to clear the ground of lingering Confederates. At least one Federal, Willis Hasty of the 55th Illinois, was killed while doing this. The rest stayed in position and quickly gathered more rails, old logs, and stumps from the partially cleared field behind the Union line in order to increase the height of the breastwork.[26]

Near the angle in Logan's line, Oliver ordered skirmishers to follow up the enemy withdrawal. Brown sent Company E of the 70th Ohio as a contribution to the force of this line while the rest of his men worked hard on their breastwork. Before long the skirmishers came bounding in again, yelling, "Boys, get ready; they are coming." Sharp and Toulmin were launching a second attack.[27]

Sharp reformed his command as soon as the men had fallen back from their failed first assault. His second attempt fared less well than the first. His left wing moved forward until it received oblique fire from the right, probably from the 55th Illinois occupying the high ground just east of the

Middle Ravine. The left wing stopped there for a while trading shots to no avail. J. Byrd Williams also noted that the men of his 41st Mississippi, on the far left of Sharp's formation, were exhausted by this stage of the battle. Their "jaded" condition contributed to their inability to stand the fire, and Williams fell back a second time with the rest of the brigade. Observers in the 55th Illinois on the ridge also noted that Sharp's second assault "visibly lacked the verve and tenacity of the first." Sharp's right wing was unable to advance even as far as it had gone during the first attack. Thus the left wing had no support to its right and many members of the 9th, 10th, and 41st Mississippi used that as another explanation for why their second attack failed.[28]

In fact, Sharp's Brigade as a whole had no support to the right because Toulmin's brigade launched its second attack later than Sharp did. Toulmin had retired to the Lick Skillet Road and made a temporary breastwork of rails after the first repulse. The troops stayed there only a few minutes, however, before Toulmin set them off again. In fact, the brigade broke apart on the way north. The 25th and 39th Alabama went only as far as the former Union skirmish line, where Johnston and several other high-ranking officers had been shot in a static firefight during the first attack. Here they stayed and fired at the Union skirmish line just ahead for fifteen or twenty minutes before retiring. But the 19th, 22nd, and 50th Alabama did not stop there. They continued moving northward, driving back the Union skirmishers until they hit the main Union line again.[29]

This time the Confederates made a big impression. The three Alabama regiments moved without stopping until they touched the frail breastworks on top of the ridge. The colors of the 19th Alabama and the 50th Alabama were planted on the works, and at least a portion of the 50th managed to take possession of a section of the barricade for a short time.[30]

Reuben Williams's brigade barely held back this second attack. Williams noticed at the height of the action that a part of his line began to waver, and he called on his only reserve regiment for help. James Harrison Goodnow had already dispatched four companies of the 12th Indiana to fill the line left of the 26th Illinois; now he sent Companies A, D, F, and I forward. Williams not only used these companies to bolster the line but ordered three of them to move forward to the left of Toulmin's three regiments, where they opened an enfilading fire on the Confederate flank. The 26th Illinois was hard pressed and badly needed this assistance. Many of its members had fired so often by this stage of the battle that their muskets were fouled. As they retired to the rear to clean the barrels, Goodnow's men held the line for them. At some point in the fierce battle, a Confederate color-bearer was so close to the Federals that he reportedly killed a man in the 26th Illinois by stabbing at him with the spear head that adorned the top of his flag staff. That color-bearer was in turn shot in the head by another Federal soldier. Williams reported that Capt. Sam Boughton was able to take a Rebel officer prisoner by grabbing his collar and pulling him over the breastworks. The Confederate was so angry that he "showered the most vindictive curses upon us one and all" for half an hour afterward.[31]

Oliver's brigade was pressed equally hard to Williams's left. The 19th Alabama came close to breaking through the line. The Confederates "charged Rite in to our Ranks," reported Jonathan Blair of the 48th Illinois on the far right of Oliver's command. "So that we puled them through our lines & Captured them." The colors of the 19th Alabama fell into the hands of willing members of the 48th Illinois as well.[32]

On the far left of Oliver's brigade, members of the 70th Ohio confirmed that this second attack came onto them "with greater fury" than the first, and "the fighting became most terrific." While the Confederates did not touch the breastworks held by the 70th, they applied so much pressure that the Federals could barely hold their position. The gray line halted about twenty-five yards from the Unionists, a color-bearer planted his flag in the ground, and the line stood there firing rapidly at the Yankees. The return fire at first was so great that the Rebels fell back about fifty yards. At some point in the pullback their color-bearer was shot, and the flag fell to the ground, but the gray line halted and resumed firing at the enemy. At this range, seventy-five yards, both sides settled into a long firefight in which neither could obtain an advantage over the other. Smoke crowded the intervening space, and men on both sides fell dead and wounded in a standoff between the opposing sides. As Capt. Louis Love of the 70th Ohio put it, his men "kept pouring a murderous fire into the enemy, which kept them from advancing, although they attempted it several times."[33]

The Federals needed additional firepower to force the Confederates back, and they received it in the form of reinforcements from Walcutt's brigade. Charles C. Walcutt was another stalwart brigade leader in Logan's corps who, though an Ohioan by birth, had graduated from Kentucky Military Institute. A severe wound received at Shiloh did not stop him from gaining valuable experience at Vicksburg, Chattanooga, and during the Atlanta campaign. Walcutt had been holding his regiments in columns within the East Ravine that bisected Harrow's division. From this spot he had already sent the 6th Iowa and 40th Illinois to strengthen Logan's

◆ CHARLES C. WALCUTT ◆
(Library of Congress, LC-DIG-cwpb-05912)

right flank. About the time that Sharp and Toulmin hit Harrow the first time, orders arrived for Walcutt to send troops to support Harrow's other brigades. He began to move the 103rd Illinois, 46th Ohio, and 97th Indiana forward. These regiments took position about the time that the second attack reached its high tide and were able to play a role in repelling it.[34]

The 103rd Illinois was the first to arrive. It took position covering the junction between Oliver's brigade and Wangelin's brigade, where the angle of Logan's line continued to worry commanders. Capt. Franklin C. Post settled the 103rd Illinois just behind the Union line, its right wing overlapping the left wing of the 70th Ohio and the left wing of the Illinois unit overlapping the 29th Missouri and the 17th Missouri Battalion. Post's men fired over the heads of those in front of them.[35]

Not long after the 103rd Illinois took position, the 46th Ohio arrived near the front line. At first, Lieut. Col. Isaac N. Alexander placed the regiment some distance behind the right wing of the 70th Ohio and the left wing of the 99th Indiana. The men set to work making temporary breastworks by gathering "rails and such material as we could hastily throw together." But soon an order arrived to move closer to the line. Alexander simply advanced straight ahead through the trees, but then he was told that the Federals holding the angle to the left needed assistance. He ordered his men to march left oblique until the right wing of the 46th Ohio covered the right wing of the 70th Ohio. This also placed the left wing of the 46th behind the right wing of the 103rd Illinois. The vulnerable angle in Logan's line now had ample manpower.[36]

Moreover, the 46th Ohio was armed with Spencer repeating rifles, capable of holding seven rounds in a spring-fed magazine with rapid unloading and reloading by moving the trigger guard. The men fired these weapons over the heads of comrades in front—for some it meant firing over the heads of both the 103rd Illinois and the 29th Missouri. It was difficult to aim under conditions such as this, and the Ohio riflemen just lay down a curtain of fire in the general direction of the static gray line seventy-five yards away. The effect of this Spencer fire, added to that of Springfield and Enfield rifle muskets worked by the other four regiments, impressed observers. As one Federal put it, his comrades "rose up and began 'pumping death' at them." Whether this fire actually took down a greater number of Confederates than normal is questionable, but at least it gave a boost of confidence to the harried defenders of the angle. Members of the 70th Ohio were deeply grateful to the 103rd Illinois and the 46th Ohio for the way in which they relieved "our exhausted ranks" that afternoon, endearing "those regiments to us as long as memory exists."[37]

Once again, not only the 29th Missouri and the 17th Missouri (Battalion) were hit by the Rebels but the 12th Missouri as well. Once again, smoke covered the intervening space between the opposing lines, obscuring the view but not smothering the fierce yells of the Confederates, which could be heard along with the sound of musketry. Wangelin hurried forward his last reserve, the 3rd Missouri, and distributed its men to all points of his right wing that seemed vulnerable.[38]

The 29th Missouri felt the pressure more than any other regiment in Wangelin's brigade. When the Confederates neared the 70th Ohio, that regiment wavered a bit, threatening the right flank of the 29th Missouri. Maj. Philip H. Murphy stepped toward Col. Joseph S. Gage to consult with him about the danger when a bullet tore into his chest, passed through the lungs, and came out between the shoulder blades. As Murphy dropped to the ground, Gage called for a stretcher, and the major was taken to the rear. Soon after, Walcutt's reinforcements arrived to steady both the 70th Ohio and the 29th Missouri. J. R. Tisdale, who was among the number carrying Murphy to the rear, noted that the bullets seemed to increase in volume as the party stumbled back from the front line. Murphy survived his horrible wound. The twenty-six year old officer had helped to organize the 29th Missouri and had been absolved of charges of drunkenness on duty by a court-martial in March 1863 during the Vicksburg campaign. Regimental clerk David Allan informed his family that the unit's "greatest misfortune" at Ezra Church was that Murphy had been disabled for further service.[39]

Despite the pressure exerted on the angle, Toulmin's men failed to break through the Union line during their second attack. To the left, Sharp's brigade failed to make a dent in the Federal position. After some time, both brigades fell back, Toulmin's three regiments retiring much later than either Sharp or the rest of his own command. The Mississippians of Sharp's command were by now overheated and thirsty. Many of them suffered enormously from the lack of drinking water as their tongues "were swollen so as to protrude from our mouths," remembered a lieutenant. Eventually all of Toulmin's brigade retired to Lick Skillet Road and reformed, then moved forward a bit to the slight ridge just north of the road to lie down and await orders. The physical condition and the spirit necessary for further fighting had evaporated among Sharp's and Toulmin's men.[40]

In their effort to evaluate the performance of these two brigades, officers tried to put the best face on circumstances. Brown argued that at least Brantley and Sharp had "acted with great gallantry" in conducting their attacks. Kelsey of the 44th Mississippi pointed out that the casualties alone proved his men had tried their best against difficult odds. Brown thought "the major portion" of Johnston's brigade "behaved well," but he also criticized the behavior of a good part of the unit as "behaving badly, its demoralization was so great it could not be made effective." Brown referred to the 25th and 39th Alabama, which had stopped and retired at the Union skirmish line during the second attack.[41]

Sharp lost a considerable number of men on July 28, even though there are no reports of brigade-level casualties. The 10th Mississippi suffered seventy-nine losses, including eleven out of eighteen officers. The shooting of prominent individuals struck home for many in the brigade. Capt. George W. Braden of Company I, 9th Mississippi, died as the result of a bullet smashing into his cheek bone. He had enlisted as a private and was wounded in the thigh at the battle of Munfordville during the Kentucky campaign. Pvt. Cyrus A. Johnson had been detailed to commissary work ever since early 1862. He could not resist the temptation to go into battle with his comrades of the 9th Mississippi and was shot in the shoulder in a way so that the bullet traversed his entire body. Johnson died soon after receiving that injury.[42]

The total casualties for Toulmin's command also are not available, but the loss of prominent individuals led to mention of their names in official reports. Color-bearer William R. Leary of the 22nd Alabama moved the regiment forward by keeping the flag well ahead of the line during the brigade's second attack. He "gallantly bore forward the colors of his regiment, [and] fell with the folds covering his body."[43]

With the pressure off, the Federals in Williams's and Oliver's brigades could not only breathe more easily but also tend to needed business. The 48th Illinois, occupying the far right of Oliver's brigade, had by now run out of ammunition for its Smith and Wesson rifles and could not find more within easy reach. Oliver sent a message to Williams asking for assistance, and Williams dispatched the 90th Illinois to replace the 48th in line. William H. Odell bragged in a letter to his nephew that, before the 48th Illinois was relieved, it had "whipt them a gain wors than ever." Details now brought up some entrenching tools and distributed them along the line of Oliver's brigade, giving a few to each company. The men set to work with a will, throwing dirt onto the rail breastwork. It proved to be "of the greatest advantage" in the rest of the action that day, according to Oliver. While most of the members of both Williams's and Oliver's brigades worked on their defenses, a Union skirmish line again went forward to follow up the second Rebel retirement from the front.[44]

Stephen D. Lee was satisfied with Brown's handling of his division, despite the lack of success in breaking the main Union line. His troops had thus far driven back the Federal skirmishers (although not by any means on a permanent basis) and cleared the Lick Skillet Road for Confederate use. In that sense, Lee had already accomplished the primary part that he had to play in Hood's overall plan. But he had accomplished this in an unnecessarily bloody fashion. Lee complained that portions of the division failed to rally properly and failed to support their comrades on the second attempt against Logan's line. He blamed much of the failure and the heavy losses on lack of coordination due to demoralization among some regiments, although he did not see this as Brown's fault. In fact, Brown suffered a slight wound at one point in the fighting but continued to exercise command of the division.[45]

On the Union side, many observers could justly feel proud of their performance thus far in the battle. Along the Fifteenth Corps line, the machine-like noise of the small arms fire imparted a sense of awe. Logan's men "fired *such* volleys they cannot be described," wrote the quartermaster of the 55th Illinois. Jesse Dozer of the 26th Illinois mentioned the "constant roaring of musketry" and the "perfect Clouds of smoke in the Air."[46]

Long after the war, Howard characterized the fighting along Smith's, Harrow's, and part of Woods's sector as heavy, but he also wrote proudly of the "rapid and well directed firing" by his new command. "Nothing could stand against it, and the most of the Confederates either fell to the earth, or turned and fled protecting themselves as best they could by the trees and the incidents of the ground." Jacob Cox, whose division held a part of Schofield's Twenty-third Corps line, wrote in his history of the Atlanta campaign that Howard's position "was never seriously in danger."[47]

But the men involved in repelling two attacks by Brown's determined Confederates never painted their battle as easy. While a newspaper correspondent who wrote under the acronym Q.P.F. exaggerated when he said that the enemy forces "were sometimes killed in the very act of vaulting over" the Union breastworks, the truth was that some of Toulmin's men did capture or trod on those works during the height of their second attack. Q.P.F accurately wrote of the enlisted men's view when he asserted that "for a time it was not absolutely certain that they would be able to maintain themselves. A timely reinforcement of a single regiment, judiciously distributed, quickly determined the question." That was true not only of Williams, Oliver, and Wangelin but of Lightburn as well. The Fifteenth Corps line was thin enough to demand help at critical moments, but fortunately reserves were available and moved toward the threatened points just in time to make a large difference in determining victory or defeat.[48]

CHAPTER SIX

The Bigest Kinde of a Rot

Clayton's Division and Manigault's Brigade

An hour ticked by between the start of Brown's attack on the afternoon of July 28 and the arrival of Henry D. Clayton's Division on the scene, forcing Brown to fight without support. Moreover, Clayton brought only three of his brigades to the battlefield, leaving the one commanded by Brig. Gen. Marcellus A. Stovall in the Atlanta defenses. Clayton's Division moved out along Lick Skillet Road and toward the sound of combat, arriving about 1:00 P.M. As the division hastily formed to the right of Brown's command, pioneer Hiram Smith Williams was stunned by the scene of confusion, the noise of the firing, and the scurrying of slightly wounded Confederates seeking safety in the rear. R. F. Eddins of the 19th Louisiana did not like the looks of things. "We began to smell the bigest kinde of a rot," he reported to his sister.[1]

Clayton placed two of his brigades in line immediately north of and almost parallel to the Lick Skillet Road while keeping one in reserve. Brig. Gen. Randall L. Gibson commanded the lead brigade and took position first. Although born in Kentucky, Gibson grew up in the plantation aristocracy of Louisiana and graduated from Yale University in 1853. A lawyer and for a time attaché at the American Embassy to Spain, Gibson commanded the 13th Louisiana in many battles of the Western Theater and won promotion to brigadier general early in 1864. He placed his Louisiana troops as ordered, but the ground just north of the road at this point was "covered with a remarkably dense undergrowth." The 16th and 25th Louisiana held the right of the brigade line, followed toward the left by the 4th Louisiana Battalion, 19th Louisiana, 20th Louisiana, and the 13th Louisiana, which held the left. Gibson then sent Maj. John E. Austin's Louisiana Battalion Sharpshooters forward to skirmish and report on what lay ahead of his

◆ RANDALL L. GIBSON ◆

(Library of Congress, LC-DIG-cwpb-04007)

brigade. Then Gibson rode over to the right to see if Clayton had any special instructions.[2]

Clayton was just then supervising the placement of Brig. Gen. James T. Holtzclaw's Alabama brigade to Gibson's right, having ordered his third unit, Brig. Gen. Alpheus Baker's Alabama brigade, to take position to the south of the road as a reserve. When riding back to his command, Gibson was stunned to see it already moving forward "without any order from me or notice to me." He later learned that Lieut. Col. Ed. H. Cunningham, the assistant inspector general on Lee's Corps staff, had taken it upon himself to order the brigade forward. Cunningham spoke to Col. Leon von Zinken of the 20th Louisiana, who was in charge of the left wing, and von Zinken repeated the order so that the entire brigade obeyed it. Gibson was careful in his report to explain that von Zinken was not in charge of the entire brigade and should have communicated Cunningham's instructions to him before moving the men. Even Clayton was unaware that a part of his division was on the move. Lee was ultimately responsible for this mixup that sent Clayton's Division into the attack in piecemeal fashion. He had told Cunningham to bring up Clayton's men as fast as possible, and Cunningham cut corners to do so. As a result, Clayton was robbed of the opportunity to conduct a coordinated assault, for neither Holtzclaw nor Baker was ready to join Gibson when the Louisiana brigade went forward.[3]

Gibson spurred his horse as he saw his brigade disappear into the thick vegetation, but he made little progress. The brush was so thick "I could see but a few paces," and his horse had to pick its way carefully through the tangle. The brigade aimed at the angle in Logan's line, held jointly by the left of Oliver's brigade and the right of Wangelin's troops. At first the Confederate infantrymen had difficulty plowing through the brush; it was "so thick one could scarsely get along," reported R. F. Eddins. But they made it through and easily pressed the Union skirmish line back. From here the ground was open—too open in some ways for the safety of the Louisiana troops. At least the left wing of Gibson's Brigade and, at times, the entire line marched across open fields at quickstep as they closed on the Union position. Gibson finally caught up with his men about this time.[4]

As the brigade neared the fringe of woods lining the Union position on top of the ridge, it received heavy fire. Slowing and then stopping in the increasing cloud of powder smoke, the Louisiana men made it anywhere from thirty to eighty yards from the Union position before reaching their high tide. Here they went to ground and returned the fire from prone positions for some time. "We fought the enemy in a thick woods and they

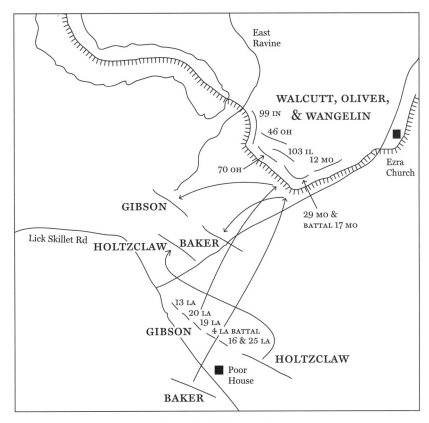

East
Ravine

WALCUTT, OLIVER,
99 IN & WANGELIN

46 OH

103 IL
12 MO

70 OH

GIBSON

29 MO &
BATTAL 17 MO

Ezra
Church

Lick Skillet Rd   HOLTZCLAW   BAKER

13 LA
20 LA
19 LA
4 LA BATTAL
16 & 25 LA

GIBSON

HOLTZCLAW

Poor
House

BAKER

Clayton's Division Attacks
(Earl J. Hess and Pratibha A. Dabholkar)

behind breast works," wrote Lieut. Emmett Ross of the 20th Louisiana to
his fiancée Mary; "they mowed us down like grass."[5]

From the perspective of the Union line, it seemed as if Gibson's men
came forward only a short time after the repulse of Toulmin's second attack.
While a newspaper correspondent claimed that half an hour had elapsed
between the assaults, John Oliver thought the "short interval" between
them "did not amount to a cessation of the battle." Before long, Oliver saw
that some color-bearer had planted a Rebel flag only twenty paces from his
brigade line. From the standpoint of Lieut. Colonel Gage's 29th Missouri,
it seemed that Kaercher's 12th Missouri opened fire first on the Louisiana
troops. Before the powder smoke obscured no-man's land, Gage "could
see the rebel lines melt away before their volleys." Then Gage told his own
Missourians to open fire. His men "knelt, rested their pieces on the works,"

and blazed away. The 46th Ohio added fire from its repeating rifles, aiming over the heads of Gage's men, and "together they sent forth a sheet of lead which mowed down their front line."[6]

There was no possibility of Gibson pushing his men any farther. As he later reported, they hit "an overwhelming force in a position splendidly adapted for defense and difficult of assault." Clayton agreed with Gibson and began to make arrangements for his reserve unit, Baker's Brigade, to go in as well.[7]

But Gibson could not hold his men close to the Union line and wait for Baker for more than about fifteen minutes. As Oliver aptly described the effect of the Union fire, the Rebel "lines were broken up by deadly musketry, their columns staggered, halted, and after vainly endeavoring to stand, gave back some distance." Gibson retired to a ravine where the men re-formed ranks. Then he moved the restored line forward a short distance to the crest of the ravine slope where it stayed about 400 yards from the Union position with some degree of natural cover. A rail fence provided a ready place to align the brigade, which rested here for the next hour, exchanging long-range fire with the Federals.[8]

Gibson's Brigade suffered heavily during its first and only attack at Ezra Church. Col. Thomas Shields held the beautiful flag of his 30th Louisiana aloft when he fell close to the Union works, and the regiment also lost Maj. Charles J. Bell, killed at about the same time. Shields represented an anomaly in the Confederate army. Born in Ohio and acquainted with Charles Walcutt, he had moved south before the war and committed himself to the Confederate cause. Reportedly, his 30th Louisiana had many upper-crust members of New Orleans society in its ranks.[9]

Lieut. Emmett Ross had joined the 20th Louisiana only two months before and now was severely wounded in Gibson's attack. "I was struck in the left Knee by a minie ball," he informed Mary, "causing a very painful and ugly wound." Ross lay on the battlefield for an hour after the brigade fell back from its high tide until he "concluded to crawl to the rear and avoid being Captured." He managed to get off the field and into the hands of the regimental surgeon. Ross reported that the 20th Louisiana lost eight out of eleven officers in the battle, and thirty-eight out of fifty-four men. If Ross's figures were accurate, the regiment had but nineteen troops available for duty by the end of the day.[10]

In a battle like this, the only units that escaped heavy losses were those suddenly detached to other duty before the attack. Company D of the 4th Louisiana Battalion, known as the National Guards and commanded by

Capt. David Devall, had been separated from the battalion for reasons that were not reported. The troops watched the attack from the thin shelter of some charred tree trunks. At least two men were injured by stray bullets in this position, but Devall had no idea what if anything he was supposed to do. By the time Gibson pulled his men back to the ravine and then up to the crest to settle in for long-range firing, Devall found his battalion commander and received orders to rejoin the parent unit. His men had escaped the worst of the fight at Ezra Church.[11]

The units forced into the assault suffered terribly. Capt. S. A. Hightower's Company C, 19th Louisiana, lost 27 men out of 44 engaged, or 61.3 percent of its strength. Hightower's company contained about 10 percent of the manpower in the 19th Louisiana but suffered 21.7 percent of the 124 men lost by the regiment. Lieut. Michael H. Loveless was hit by three balls, one of which "passed half through his bible the bible saving him a sever wound perhaps his life," according to Lieut. Col. Hyder A. Kennedy who himself was hit on the wrist and suffered a painfully broken bone. Kennedy's brother John came up missing. He was last seen firing his weapon in line, but no one could account for his whereabouts after the battle. Kennedy told their father of his hope that John would show up in a list of prisoners taken by the Federals, but even as late as August 15 there was no sign of him. It saddened Kennedy to think of the losses in his old company of the 19th Louisiana, "bereft as it is of almost two thirds of its members at one Stroke."[12]

The battle at Ezra Church seared the memory of survivors in Gibson's Brigade. Someone memorialized it in a crudely written poem aping Alfred Lord Tennyson's "Charge of the Light Brigade" and published it in the *Mobile Register and Advertiser*. Entitled "Charge of the Louisiana Brigade, July 28th, 1864," it proclaimed:

> Onward thro' shell and shot,
> Onward and wavering not,
> Onward thro' tempest hot
> Of lead and fire,
> Marched on th' undaunted flag,
> And not a foot did lag,
> As went the glorious rag
> To the foe nigher.

The anonymous author found in the Crimean War experience of the English Light Brigade a fit model with which to compare the futile attack of Gibson's Brigade. Southern newspapers had printed dozens of soldier poems that conveyed a confident and heroic vision of battle for the cause early in the war. But by the midpoint of the conflict, the number had dwindled owing to war-weariness, or perhaps weariness with the poor quality of poetic voice to be found in these pieces. This anonymous poet and the editor of the Mobile newspaper countered the trend by treating readers with yet another view of heroic battle that failed to convey the fruitless and tragic nature of the fight at Ezra Church.[13]

Just as they had done after the first and second attacks by Johnston's Brigade, the Federals now sent skirmishers into no-man's land following Gibson's assault. They reported the enemy had taken shelter not far away and also brought back the flag that Shields had been carrying when he was shot. In fact, Pvt. Harry Davis of Company G, 46th Ohio, was credited with the "Capture of flag of 30th Louisiana Infantry at Atlanta, Ga.," in an official list of "Medals of Honor awarded for distinguished services." Of course, there was no opportunity for Davis to "capture" the flag, he merely picked it up off the ground on the way back to the main Union line. Isaac N. Alexander, his regimental commander, forwarded the flag to Walcutt's brigade headquarters with credit to Davis. According to Walcutt, Logan later decided to give the flag to Davis along with "a very complimentary letter," indicating that Davis may have spun quite a story about how he obtained the flag. A little more than a week later, Capt. Louis Love reported that Shields was shot on the sector held by his 70th Ohio, but he knew that Davis of the 46th Ohio had obtained the colors and, "I understand, still retains them."[14]

Perhaps Davis received so much attention because the flag of the 30th Louisiana was a magnificent banner that impressed everyone who saw it. "The border is of buff moire antique," reported a correspondent for the *Cincinnati Commercial*, "the ground work of beautifully fine, red worsted, and the diagonal bars of blue silk, edged with white, and dotted their entire length with stars. For several minutes our men hesitated to fire upon it, thinking it was the national colors." In fact, reports about the flag were published in several newspapers, including *Harper's Weekly*. When the *Commercial* story appeared, a report was printed in the *Vicksburg Daily Herald* that the flag had been issued by the Confederate Department of Alabama, Mississippi, and East Louisiana. The flag apparently found its way back to Southern hands sometime after the war. One of the colors on display at the Confederate Memorial Hall Museum in New Orleans is identified as the one Shields carried at Ezra Church.[15]

Capturing a Confederate Flag. This contemporary print dramatically depicts the taking of a flag from a dying Confederate color-bearer. It accompanied news reports of the battle at Ezra Church and came to be associated with Harry Davis's recovery of the 30th Louisiana flag. (*Harper's Weekly*, September 17, 1864, 593)

After Gibson's men fell back to the ravine, Joseph Gage wanted to take a quick look at the lay of the ground in front of the 29th Missouri in order to better direct his fire. He and a small group of Federals sallied over the breastworks and went no more than forty yards before they encountered a lone Confederate hiding behind a stump who fired at Gage. The Federal officer had a very close call. He "felt the ball pass through my whiskers, burning my cheek." While Gage drew a revolver and shouted at the man to drop his weapon, several of his privates opened fire and killed the Rebel. Gage quickly eyed the terrain from this spot, and the group went back to the line where other Federals were quickly improving the rail breastworks by working on the outside of the fortification.[16]

From the perspective of units uninvolved in repelling Gibson, the gray effort seemed to be hopeless. John C. Arbuckle of the 4th Iowa was utterly amazed that the Confederates were still trying to break Logan's line. As with the other attacks, a good deal of enemy fire sailed over the breastworks and landed some distance behind the Union line, where Yankee reserve troops often were hit. "I saw brave men in reserve in that field digging holes with their bayonets to shield their heads," wrote H. M. Brandle of the 3rd Missouri. Col. David Carskaddon of the 9th Iowa was shot in the head that afternoon, even though his regiment lay in a supporting position and was never directly involved in the fight.[17]

If the Federals were amazed that Gibson had attacked, they must have been even more astonished that yet another gray unit was on its way. Henry Clayton rode over to Gibson's Brigade soon after it re-formed in the ravine to find that it needed help. Brown's Division to the left offered no support, and there was nothing to Gibson's right. Clayton now decided to send in Alpheus Baker's Brigade, his reserve unit. Gibson regretted that Baker was not ready to attack in conjunction with his own effort, but he had only Cunningham and von Zinken to blame for that.[18]

Little was recorded of Baker's attack, but the brigade aimed at the angle in the Union line, the exact spot that Gibson had just failed to break. As the Alabamans marched forward, they encountered dozens of bodies and wounded men who had fallen in the attack by the Louisiana brigade. In fact, "the ground was literally covered with their dead and wounded," recalled William Sprott of the 40th Alabama. The brigade landed up quite close to the enemy before grinding to a halt. According to Sprott, Lieut. Col. Alexander A. Greene of the 37th Alabama was killed only twenty or thirty paces from the Union line, and other parts of Baker's command also "got with a few yards" of the target.[19]

Joseph Gage verified that Baker's Brigade came within thirty yards of the 12th Missouri before halting. He credited "the constant fire" of that regiment and the 46th Ohio for stopping the Alabama brigade. The Ohioans especially "did some very effective work at long range," meaning that they continued to fire over the heads of their comrades and obliquely in places to strike Baker's Brigade.[20]

Baker's effort was "a terrible charge" in the words of a survivor named Elbert Decatur Willett in the 40th Alabama, but it was over faster than Gibson's assault. In fact, Clayton argued that it failed "in much less time [than Gibson] was repulsed," while Grant Taylor of the 40th Alabama reported to his wife and children that Baker was repulsed "in a few minutes." Baker launched a serious effort, but the men fell back more quickly than Gibson's troops.[21]

Just as he had attacked exactly where Gibson had tried to break the Union line, now Baker fell back to the same place as Gibson. The Alabama troops took position to Gibson's right along the fence that lined the top of the ravine slope and opened long-range fire at the Yankees. Now Clayton began to worry that the Federals, emboldened by their success, might attack Gibson and Baker. He ordered Holtzclaw to move forward from his staging area just north of the Lick Skillet Road and take position in supporting distance of the other two brigades. Holtzclaw did so, moving his command by the left flank and trying to keep it from view of the enemy as much as possible.[22]

Baker's men settled down in a comparatively safe place behind the fence and opened a scattering fire. After a while, some of the men calmed down enough to notice ordinary things around them. J. H. Curry and Serg. Walter Mims Gilkey saw a rabbit suddenly appear from the brush and head toward the Union line 400 yards away. Acting on a youthful impulse, Curry ran after it, slapping his hands on his knees and the frightened rabbit darted away. The sergeant was amused. "Suppose our people at home should see us playing with this rabbit during this battle, they would think we had lost our senses," said Gilkey.[23]

In the end, Clayton used only two of the three brigades available to him in an effort to fulfill Lee's urge to push the enemy back, and the cost was indeed high. The left wing of Gibson's Brigade suffered more heavily than the right wing. While Gibson never reported his losses, subordinates offered estimates of brigade casualties that ranged from 400 to 540 men. Thomas B. Mackall, one of Clayton's staff officers, placed Gibson's losses at 500 while historian Stuart Salling notes in his history of the brigade that troop strength dropped by 352 men from July 18 to July 29. Salling also tallies a loss ratio of 58.6 percent in the 20th Louisiana (34 men out of 58). John Irwin Kendall, then serving on a brigade staff in another division, noted that the 4th Louisiana (his old regiment) lost 82 men out of 240 engaged for a loss ratio of 34.1 percent. Losses in Baker's Brigade were much lower. Mackall counted it at about 100 men, amounting to 600 casualties for Clayton's Division at Ezra Church.[24]

The retirement of Baker's Brigade led to an extended period of relative calm for the Federals who held the angle in Logan's position. They sent out another skirmish line, which scooped up a few prisoners and established itself between the ravine and the Union position. Protected by the skirmishers, several men now wandered out onto the battlefield for various purposes, often spurred on by curiosity. David Allan Jr. of the 29th Missouri walked onto the field, and "there seen a sight I never beheld before. Along the front of our battalion lay the dead Rebels in piles of three and four. We found one Colonel, one Lt Col, two Majors and several line officers besides any quantity of enlisted men. It beat all the sights I have ever seen, even that of the 22d inst on our right."[25]

Along the sector held by the 29th Missouri, J. R. Tisdale darted onto the battlefield in search of a knapsack. He had put his own knapsack down to help the wounded Major Murphy to the rear, and someone had stolen it. Tisdale's brief survey of the field haunted him for the rest of his life. "What a sight of dead men I beheld there," he remembered in 1888, "they lay in windrows, as though cut down like grass before a scythe. The carnage was awful indeed." The wounded among the bodies called out for help, but Tisdale was unable to do anything, for he could catch glimpses of activity away to the south indicating the Confederates might be mounting another attempt. On the way back to his own line, Tisdale spotted a good knapsack lying next to what he believed was the body of a sergeant belonging to the 19th Louisiana. "I hastily cut a strap" and took it back to the line. He later found close to ten dollars in gold and silver coins, some Confederate printed currency, and two "fine woolen blankets." He considered it was indeed "a good outfit" for his trouble.[26]

Allan and Tisdale saw proof of an important fact. Despite the heavy pressure exerted by three Rebel brigades on the angle, the Confederates had failed to break the Union line and had suffered severe losses. They were "butchered at every point," wrote Maj. Abraham J. Seay of the 32nd Missouri in his diary. "The work was hot and heavy, but the 15 A.C. did it all well and effectually." Wangelin boasted that his men "felt sorry that no further attacks were made on them, as they felt invincible in their position, and would have proved it."[27]

Wangelin's losses were comparatively light. Those regiments not directly engaged lost a handful—for example, the 32nd Missouri suffered only two casualties, while the 31st Missouri lost no one. Even the 12th Missouri lost only twenty-one men, protected as it was by the breastwork. But the loss of officers in the 12th was high compared to the loss of enlisted men, indicating that the officers felt compelled to expose themselves more than usual to direct and inspire their men. Within the history of the regiment, the lowest ratio of officer-to-enlisted-man casualties (one to thirteen) occurred during the Vicksburg campaign. At Ezra Church, the ratio was one to four. Lieut. Col. Jacob Kaercher, commander of the regiment, was shot in the abdomen. Capt. Albert Affleck of Company A was severely wounded in the left thigh very close to the hip and suffered a great deal for hours afterward. Ironically, this was the last battle of the 12th Missouri. It had not reenlisted for the war, and its three-year term of service ended in August 1864.[28]

For the rest of Woods's division, the battle of Ezra Church consisted of waiting for an attack that never came or moving reserve units about to support those troops who were attacked. Col. Milo Smith's First Brigade held the far left of Woods's line, connecting with the Seventeenth Corps to the left. Smith shifted the 76th Ohio southward to support Wangelin. The regiment stood up in an open field with bayonets fixed only fifty yards behind the front line. At least seven men were hit by stray bullets in this place until Smith allowed the regiment to lie prone on the ground to reduce casualties. The intense sunshine also stressed the men, causing symptoms of sunstroke among them.[29]

Wangelin's men fired thousands of rounds while repulsing four attacks, creating a magnificent show of musketry for the reserve troops watching only a short distance to the rear. "The dense growth of young timber in front of our lines," recalled William Royal Oake of the 26th Iowa, "seemed to melt as snow before a hot sun, as it was mowed down by that cyclone of lead." The constant firing created calls for more ammunition among the troops. H. M. Brandle of the 3rd Missouri received orders to obtain more cartridges, and he found four ammunition wagons within range of the battlefield; but Confederate rounds that overshot the mark found them too. Five mules were killed at one wagon. The driver of another wagon became frightened and turned too sharply, overturning it. A third wagon suffered the same fate, while the African American driver of the fourth wagon "ran way." At least the ammunition was left behind and was carried forward by men detailed for the purpose. Lieut. Cary M. Marriott, one of Woods's aides-de-camp, carried boxes of ammunition up to the line on his horse, exposing himself greatly all the while.[30]

Reuben Williams worried that his men were expending ammunition so rapidly he would be unable to resupply them in time. Just when his brigade was down to only six boxes, someone saw the ordnance train of the Sixteenth Corps appear half a mile to the north. Williams sent a staff officer to get two of the dozen wagons in that train, but the officer in charge refused to help. Williams then went personally and was determined to succeed, even if he had to take the cartridges by force. Fortunately, the officer relented and let him have two wagons. They were driven close to the line and sheltered in a "patch of shrubbery," where men detailed from Williams's regiments came to carry box after box forward. For one soldier the exertion proved too much. Williams described him as a "very large and rugged man," but he died while carrying a box of 1,000 cartridges that weighed 100 pounds on his shoulder through the hot, humid air.[31]

Other men found comparative safety, or at least an escape from the hottest part of the battle, in the rear areas. William Charles Pfeffer had been detailed as a teamster from the ranks of the 29th Missouri. He "went back to the rear when the fighting commenced to be out of the way," even though his regiment fought the toughest fight of its war service that afternoon. Pfeffer took refuge in a hollow where he made some coffee, but Confederate artillery rounds began sailing into the ravine. He retired two miles away "to a safe place" where he could cook a meal without interference.[32]

Woods's men could feel justly proud of their accomplishment on the afternoon of July 28. "The old Fifteenth Corps was there as a stone wall," boasted J. R. Tisdale of the 29th Missouri. During his effort to find more ammunition for Wangelin, H. M. Brandle briefly spoke with Logan, who also asked him to see if Woods needed anything else to hold his position. Brandle made his way to Woods's command post, where the general bluntly told him to inform Logan that he needed nothing. Moreover, "he would hang every rebel on the bayonets that crossed the rail piles."[33]

Though Clayton's Division had tried, it accomplished nothing. Only Gibson and Baker made concerted efforts to strike the enemy, and Clayton went to some pains to explain why Holtzclaw did not do so. He was under instructions from Lee not to extend his line farther to the right than a branch that had been pointed out to him. In short, Clayton was told not to attack the east facing part of Howard's long line. In order to obey that instruction, Holtzclaw would have had to attack by veering much to the

◆ HENRY D. CLAYTON ◆
(Library of Congress, LC-DIG-cwpbh-00512)

left and across an open field, exposing his men to enemy fire. Moreover, after the bloody repulse of both Gibson and Baker, Clayton wisely decided not to waste any more manpower. He simply moved Holtzclaw into a supporting position rather than throw him into another unsupported assault. This method of attacking in small, successive waves failed to achieve any results for the Confederates.[34]

Soon after Clayton suspended further attacks against the angle in the Union line, Lee prompted a renewal of action by a part of Brown's Division farther west. Brig. Gen. Arthur M. Manigault's Alabama and South Carolina brigade had been waiting in a reserve position all this while, and now Lee wanted the men to try their luck against the formidable Union position. Born in South Carolina, Manigault became a businessman and served as a volunteer officer in the Mexican War. He commanded the 10th South Carolina early in the Civil War and served in the West since the late spring of 1862. He received a commission as brigadier general in April 1863.[35]

Manigault had formed his men in a reserve position to the rear of the line formed by Brantley, Sharp, and Johnston. When the forward line of three brigades moved on to attack, Manigault also moved his brigade forward about a quarter of a mile and halted to await orders. There his command was shielded from the enemy by a belt of thick woods.[36]

After some time had elapsed, Manigault received instructions to try his hand. He clearly recalled the scene with Lee and Brown both giving him instructions and encouragement. Brown told him how to align his brigade so as to be parallel with the Union line and pointed out where he was to strike at "the highest portion" of the ridge that Logan occupied. This was a long continuous segment of the ridgeline between the East Ravine and the Middle Ravine, a portion occupied primarily by Williams's brigade of Harrow's division. The right end of Oliver's brigade line also was targeted. From Manigault's perspective, it seemed that this part of the ridge "for the distance of 300 yards" was higher by fifteen to twenty feet than any other segment of the Federal position.[37]

After telling Manigault where to strike, Brown tried to encourage him with the prospects. His brigade would have no trouble taking the ridge, Brown assured Manigault, "as the enemy were not in force, and only held it with a few light troops. General Brown also remarked by way of encouragement, I suppose, to myself, and the line near which we were standing, that General Sharp with his brigade had found no difficulty in executing a like order." Manigault did not question this assertion because the belt of trees had shielded his view from the results of Sharp's attack. Yet Sharp sat

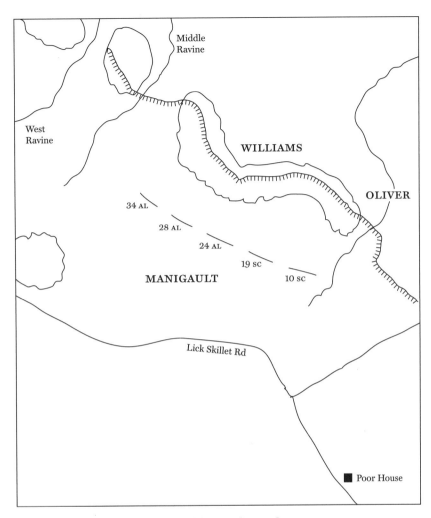

Manigault's Brigade Attacks
(Earl J. Hess and Pratibha A. Dabholkar)

on his horse not far from Manigault and did not dispute what Brown said. "No suspicions whatever arose in my mind as to what was really the true state of affairs," Manigault wrote in his memoirs. But after the fact, he was stunned that Brown gave him such an inaccurate picture of the course of the battle thus far. "I never yet have been able to explain to myself how it was that those officers so unblushingly made such a statement, known, as they must have done, that it was totally incorrect."[38]

Assuming the best, Manigault pushed his troops forward. He had the 34th Alabama on the left, then the 28th Alabama, 24th Alabama, 19th

South Carolina, and the 10th South Carolina on the far right. Initially the men marched through the belt of woods that had shielded them from the combat playing out a few hundred yards away. Then they entered an open field and stopped "for a minute or two to correct the alignment," in Manigault's words. Farther on was another skirt of wooded ground, with an open field on the other side of it. There, in the cleared area, the men encountered a deep ravine, and the ground rose beyond the ravine toward the ridge crest occupied by the enemy, with additional tree cover on the upward slope of the ridge. The ravine they crossed was a continuation of the ravine that Gibson, Baker, and Holtzclaw occupied farther to the right.[39]

The brigade moved onward with no support to right or left, traversing woods and field alike, receiving heavy enfilade fire on both flanks in addition to fire directly from the front. Many men dropped along the way. While passing over an open space, Lieut. Col. C. Irvine Walker of the 10th South Carolina kept special watch on a man who had reportedly acted badly during the battle of July 22. Walker was pleased to see that he kept up with the rest, even though he held a frying pan in front of his head to calm his nerves.[40]

Manigault's men continued forward, pressing back the Union skirmishers. They entered the skirt of trees covering the ridge slope and now, about seventy-five yards from the enemy, could see glimpses of Union troops crouching behind their breastworks. On the far left, the 34th Alabama managed to get to a point fifty or sixty yards from the Federals before coming to a halt, suffering from enfilade fire from the left. The 24th Alabama near the center of the brigade line made it to a point about thirty to forty paces short of the Federals and received heavy enfilade fire from the right. To the left of the 24th, the 28th Alabama lay down at this point for cover but only for five minutes, according to Lieut. Col. William L. Butler. Soon it became evident that different parts of the brigade line were falling back, so every regiment retired several hundred yards in some confusion. Stunned by the experience, Maj. John N. Slaughter of the 34th Alabama reported that his men had never endured such destructive fire in the war.[41]

Manigault assembled his brigade in the same field where it had briefly stopped to realign, after passing through the first skirt of timber on its advance. Many men were already exhausted by their experience and the increasing heat of the afternoon. Within the ranks of Slaughter's 34th Alabama, quite a few troops wandered off to find water and sit in the shade a few minutes before returning to the line.[42]

While most members of the brigade busied themselves with reforming ranks, C. Irvine Walker decided to take advantage of a strip of woods that seemed to extend toward the Union position. He and Capt. Robert Z. Harllee led a group of men forward through the tree cover. "It was an exceedingly foolish move, but I was a boy, only 22 years of age," Walker recalled much later. Reaching a point where the Union line was visible, Walker told the captain that they should form a column, and then he looked to the rear. To his surprise the men had already left. He and the captain were quite alone and too near the enemy for comfort. The officers quietly walked back, but Walker decided to leave the tree cover at one point and enter a field where he suddenly came across a Union skirmish line only thirty yards away. "Surrender, you damn Rebels!" the Federals shouted, but Walker and his captain ran as fast as they could for 500 yards across the open ground and escaped. Harllee lost two fingers in this foolish escapade, but Walker got away unscathed.[43]

Walker returned to his regiment, which by now had re-formed, as Harllee sought attention for his injured hand. Soon Stephen D. Lee rode along the brigade line. Walker was surprised to see that he carried the regimental flag of the 10th South Carolina. "I was mad and rushed for him and took away the colors," Walker remembered. "General Lee, you cannot take that flag, sir, I am the Lieut. Col. of that Regt., give it to me, and I will go where you want them to go." Lee was impressed by his spirit and gave up the colors. "Move the 10th. S.C. to the front and make your regiment form on you there," he told the impetuous youth. Walker did as instructed but was soon wounded for his trouble and taken off the field.[44]

Lee was desperate to keep the pressure on Logan that afternoon. His personal exertions prompted Manigault's Brigade forward once again. In Manigault's mind, it seemed as if only ten minutes had passed since the end of the first attack before Lee urged him on. The brigade advanced toward the same high section of the Union ridgeline it had struck before and with even more dismal results. Butler's 28th Alabama made it to a point 150 yards from the Union position before "determined" fire, probably by Union skirmishers, who were well in advance of the main line, forced it to retreat. The 19th South Carolina also stopped much farther from the target before retreating. On the far left of the brigade line, the 34th Alabama became separated from the rest of Manigault's men and stopped some distance from the Unionists to fire from behind stumps and logs for a while before falling back.[45]

This second attempt by Manigault's command was conducted with much less spirit and coordination within the brigade than the previous attempt, but it also was unsupported to right or left. Soon the men fell back to another rally point where they held for a while before Manigault retired another 100 yards to an unidentified road that ran west to east. It was partially dug into a slope, and thus the road cut provided shelter from stray bullets.[46]

Not more than twenty minutes after falling back to this road, Manigault received an order from Brown to conduct yet a third assault. "I could scarcely credit my senses," the astonished brigade commander later wrote. "I had made my report as to the cause of our failure, and the position and strength of the enemy, and I thought the corps and Division commanders had seen enough for themselves to give assurance of the utter impracticability of obtaining any success."[47]

Yet Manigault dutifully gave the order for his men to prepare for another try and rode to consult with Brown before leading them forward. The division commander "almost immediately replied to my remarks that the order was not his own. He disapproved of it, and was satisfied that the brigade had done all that it was possible for them to do, and that we had just ground for regarding ourselves as being unjustly and ungenerously dealt with. Such were the orders given him by General Lee, which he could not do otherwise than extend." After this interchange, Manigault felt he had no recourse but to conduct the attack and suffer the consequences. Brown "seemed much annoyed and excited as I turned to leave him." But fortunately Manigault heard his name being called before he reached the brigade. It was Brown, riding hard to catch up with him to let him know he had made a decision. "He intended to disobey General Lee's order, and would abide the consequences, at the same time withdrawing the instructions that he had previously sent me."[48]

The brigade's work was done. At this point in the course of events, the van of Walthall's Division began arriving on the field to take up the Confederate cause, so Manigault merely held the brigade in place and awaited orders. His men made a breastwork for protection, and one regiment, the 28th Alabama, was detached to arrest stragglers in the rear until dark. All that was left was to eulogize the fallen in these two failed attempts to break the Union line. Serg. Major W. J. Tinsley of the 34th Alabama was killed near the enemy's position. "A young man of splendid mind, finished education, and heroic courage, his loss fills the regiment with gloom," reported Maj. Slaughter. Capt. Starke H. Oliver mourned the loss of promising officers in the 24th Alabama, a regiment that had already lost all of its field officers and was now commanded by the senior captain. During a critical point in the battle, Manigault was left "temporarily without any assistance" because his last two staff officers were badly wounded.[49]

Regimental leaders strove to put the best face on this fiasco they could. John Slaughter argued that the overwhelming majority of his men in the 34th Alabama did "their whole duty." They "behaved admirably, and advancing with promptness, and not falling back at any time without orders, and rallying readily at the command." But John C. Brown did not agree. He reported that "the greater portion of Manigault's Brigade behaved badly."[50]

This compelled Manigault to defend his men. "For the failure of the command to carry the point that they were ordered against I can scarcely blame either officers or men," he wrote in his report. "They fought as gallantly as I have ever seen them do." Manigault blamed the defeat on the enemy. The Federals outnumbered him and held a position that was naturally very strong, "and rendered doubly so by their engineering skill."[51]

John Slaughter added more points to explain the 34th Alabama's defeat on July 28. "The regiment was nearly out of water, not having time to fill their canteens before going into action. They had marched two or three miles without resting. They marched at a rapid pace during the time of the whole of its movements previous to coming into action, and then the great sultriness of the day, all conspired against their strength and vigor for the lost effort." All this so exhausted the officers and men that little could be expected of them after the failure of the first assault. Slaughter also noted that this was not an isolated incident. Many times before in the campaign higher-level officers in the division had handled the men poorly just before a major engagement.[52]

By late afternoon, both Brown and Clayton had failed in their efforts to break the Union position. It was now up to Walthall's Division of Stewart's Corps to provide the last hope for Lee's ill-considered offensive.

CHAPTER SEVEN

The Blood-Stained Path

Walthall's Division

The Confederates who fought at Ezra Church arrived on the field in stages. First Brown came at nearly noon, and then Clayton at nearly 1:00 P.M. Alexander P. Stewart brought one division of his corps to the scene of action by about the time Brown fought his division to a point of exhaustion. Stewart did not expect to find a battle in progress; his instructions were to prepare for a flank attack on Howard's army the next day, after Lee had secured possession of the Lick Skillet Road. Instead, Stewart was assailed by desperate pleas for help in pursuing the offensive Lee had started, an offensive he had no hand in starting. Moreover, Stewart had only one division to throw into the fray; his other available division was still moving toward the battlefield.[1]

In short, Stewart found himself in a difficult situation. Born in East Tennessee, he had graduated from West Point in 1842 but had resigned from the U.S. Army soon after to teach at Cumberland University in Lebanon, Tennessee, and later at Nashville University. He received a commission as brigadier general early in the war and rose in rank and command responsibilities owing to his reliable performance in the field. Stewart deserved promotion to lieutenant general and command of Polk's Army of Mississippi (which was incorporated into the administrative structure of the Army of Tennessee as Stewart's Corps). Assuming command on July 7, 1864, Stewart led it capably in the battle of Peachtree Creek on July 20. Now, eight days later, he was about to enter his second engagement as corps leader.[2]

Lee strongly suggested that Stewart throw his leading division under Maj. Gen. Edward C. Walthall into battle by attacking the part of the Union line just assaulted by Brown's division. "The enemy was still within easy range of the Lick Skillet road," Lee reported, "and I believed that he would

◆ ALEXANDER P. STEWART ◆
(Library of Congress, LC-DIG-ppmsca-20282)

yield before a vigorous attack." Stewart did not hesitate to help Lee because
he "was found to be engaged and in need of assistance."[3]

Stewart's latest biographer has rightly pointed out that the lieutenant
general did not have to go along with Lee's suggestion. The circumstances
of the field and the battle thus far were unknown to Stewart, and he would
have been well advised to hesitate in the face of Lee's admitted failure to
break the Union line. It is true that Lee imparted a sense of urgency and
fading opportunity to Stewart, who quickly decided to join in. It is also true
that Stewart was generally known to have favored offensive action against
Sherman ever since he took control of the corps. He easily bought into
Lee's offensive spirit and decided to ignore Hood's instructions in favor of
taking advantage of an avenue that might result in tactical success. Moreover, neither commander outranked the other because their commissions
as lieutenant general were dated the same day, June 23, 1864. Hood had
not authorized either one to give orders to the other. Their relationship on

the battlefield depended on mutual cooperation, and Stewart was willing to cooperate.[4]

Walthall's Division, which had been resting in a supporting position since July 25, had moved out of the trenches on the morning of July 28 and marched along the Lick Skillet Road. Commanded by a stalwart officer from Mississippi, the division was one of the best in Stewart's Corps. Walthall had been a lawyer before the war and held commissions in the 15th Mississippi and the 29th Mississippi. He fought in many Western battles, rising to brigade and then division command. Stewart had ridden ahead to the battlefield and now sent word for Walthall to march quickly toward the area of the Poor House where Lee's Corps was fighting. Col. Edward A. O'Neal led the first brigade, which still was officially designated Cantey's Brigade after an earlier commander. His men were already becoming heated and tired from their first march in three days. O'Neal deployed his command to the left of Lick Skillet Road. Brig. Gen. Daniel Harris Reynolds's Brigade formed to the right of O'Neal and along the road itself, while Brig. Gen. William A. Quarles's Brigade took up a reserve position behind O'Neal.[5]

The men of Brown's Division were ready to be relieved. They fell back as soon as Walthall took position in order to recuperate from their failed efforts that afternoon. Toulmin, for example, retired some distance south of the Lick Skillet Road where he sought sources of fresh ammunition as his men rested. Still later, his brigade moved by the right flank for half a mile where the troops stacked weapons and spent the evening.[6]

From what little Walthall could learn of the enemy position, it seemed to be "a line of great natural strength," bolstered by "temporary works." O'Neal and Reynolds moved out to attack about 2:00 P.M., providing only a short interval between the end of previous action and the initiation of this new effort. Born in Alabama, a college graduate and lawyer before the war, O'Neal had served in the Army of Northern Virginia before winding up with a command in the West and led Cantey's Brigade well at Peachtree Creek on July 20.[7]

O'Neal reported that his men "moved forward in perfect order through an open field," encountering the dead and wounded of Brown's assault because the brigade aimed roughly at the part of the Union line previously hit by Brantley. In addition to threatening Lightburn's brigade, O'Neal also confronted a portion of Martin's brigade. O'Neal had his sharpshooter battalion in line holding down the extreme left of the brigade formation, with the 29th Alabama to the right, then the 26th Alabama, the 17th Alabama, and the 37th Mississippi anchoring the right flank. Receiving fire early on, the brigade moved across the shallow swale between this open field and the Union position. Here "the fire became so hot and galling the men sought shelter behind a fence" and opened fire. Unfortunately for Lee's plans, the brigade stayed there without resuming its advance. There is no indication of the exact distance from Lightburn's brigade, but O'Neal's men planted themselves fairly close to the blazing Union muskets. The right wing of the 17th Alabama had become "somewhat detached" from the rest of the regiment because of the tree cover and the severe wounding of Maj. Thomas J. Burnett, but the brigade remained in a relatively stable line.[8]

O'Neal blamed Reynolds for his failure, noting that he lost connection with the other brigade in Walthall's formation early in the advance and never saw it afterward. Actually O'Neal veered off to the left to hit the extreme right of Logan's line, while Reynolds moved right at the same time. As a result, Walthall's attack spanned a surprisingly wide sector of the battlefield. O'Neal argued that his men, "with some exceptions," conducted themselves with bravery and steadiness "worthy of the highest admiration" as they continued to take cover and fire at the enemy.[9]

The renewal of attacks on Logan's right flank prompted more efforts to bring up reinforcements from other, less threatened parts of the Union line. Howard sent to Dodge for two Sixteenth Corps regiments and asked Sherman if Thomas could spare some troops. Sherman told Howard that Davis's Fourteenth Corps division was supposed to be on its way to cover Logan's flank. But a second appeal from Howard led Sherman to order a brigade from another Fourteenth Corps division on its way.[10]

Dodge was able to send help much faster than Sherman could, and he dispatched the 12th Illinois, 66th Illinois, and 81st Ohio from Lieut. Col. Jesse J. Phillips's brigade of Corse's Second Division. Essentially these were all the units currently available to Phillips, so he personally led the contingent toward Logan's flank. Soon after doing this, Dodge decided he could spare more troops now that there were no signs of action on his front. He also sent the 64th Illinois (from Lieut. Col. Henry T. McDowell's brigade) and the 35th New Jersey (from Brig. Gen. John W. Sprague's brigade) of Fuller's Fourth Division. Col. John J. Cladek of the 35th New Jersey was placed in charge of both regiments for the move to the right. The 64th and 66th Illinois were armed with Henry repeating rifles.[11]

By the time these Sixteenth Corps troops traversed the ground between Howard's left wing and his extreme right, the danger posed by O'Neal had passed. There would be another gray wave surging forward later in the

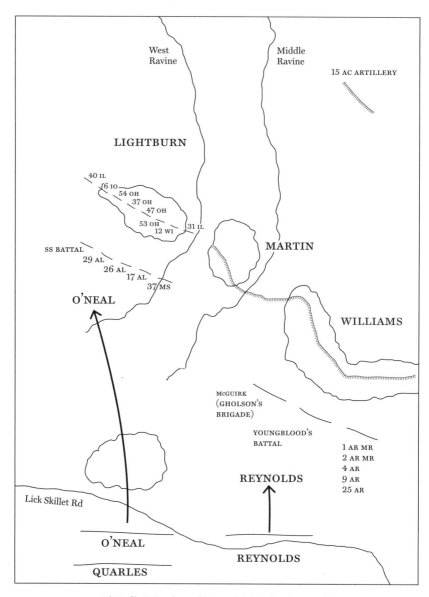

West
Ravine

Middle
Ravine

15 AC ARTILLERY

LIGHTBURN

40 IL
6 IO
54 OH
37 OH
47 OH
53 OH
12 WI
31 IL

MARTIN

SS BATTAL
29 AL
26 AL
17 AL
37 MS

O'NEAL

WILLIAMS

McGUIRK
(GHOLSON'S
BRIGADE)

YOUNGBLOOD'S
BATTAL

1 AR MR
2 AR MR
4 AR
9 AR
25 AR

REYNOLDS

Lick Skillet Rd

O'NEAL

REYNOLDS

QUARLES

O'Neal's Brigade and Reynolds's Brigade Attack
(Earl J. Hess and Pratibha A. Dabholkar)

afternoon, so Howard's effort to provide more troops to bolster the end of his line would still pay dividends. But for the time being, O'Neal's Alabama troops remained stuck in their prone position about where the shallow swale merged into the ridge slope.

Off to the east of O'Neal's static position, Reynolds drove his men toward the right. He had a good but small brigade of Arkansas troops at his command. Two days earlier, Youngblood's battalion of government workers from Columbus and Macon had added 150 men to the brigade. Then at noon on July 28, Brig. Gen. Samuel J. Gholson's Brigade (under Col. John McGuirk) added 450 troops to Reynolds. Youngblood's men had no combat experience of any kind, but McGuirk's command was regularly organized and had some experience in the field. Despite the fact that McGuirk joined Reynolds literally on the way to the battlefield, he brought a hefty addition to the 400 Arkansas troops. In fact, the size of Reynolds's command more than doubled with the addition of Youngblood and McGuirk. Even so, only 1,000 Confederates were ready to go in under Reynolds's command that afternoon. McGuirk held the left of the brigade line, while Youngblood occupied the center and Reynolds's Arkansas men constituted the right wing.[12]

When Reynolds set out about 2:00 P.M. his men marched across an open field for 200 yards and drove away the Union skirmish line. On the way, Youngblood's Battalion "got in some confusion," according to Reynolds, "and many of them left the field, though a number of them acted very well." After driving off the skirmishers, Reynolds continued moving forward into the skirt of tree cover on the ridge slope, aiming at Williams's brigade and Oliver's brigade of Harrow's division. His line did not extend far enough to affect the right flank of Wangelin's brigade. Capt. John W. Lavender of Company F, 4th Arkansas, remembered advancing under the extreme heat until the main Federal line opened a raging fire when the Confederates were still about 300 yards away. The Arkansas men refrained from firing and kept pressing forward as "rapidly as possable," Lavender wrote. The Rebels fired a volley at about 150 yards from the enemy; then Reynolds ordered them forward on the double-quick. They managed to surge forward before momentum failed some thirty to forty yards short of the slim breastworks. The combined firepower of Reynolds's command now was directed on the Union position, although John Lavender did not believe the Yankees suffered much, protected as they were by breastworks. The return fire "was literally mowing our men Down," he recalled.[13]

Reynolds had gotten much closer to the enemy than had O'Neal, but he could not stay there for long. He began to receive a devastating flank fire from the right because no friendly troops were off in that direction to offer assistance. Reynolds then retired about fifty yards until he could find some shelter behind fence rails and trees farther down the ridge slope. Here his men held for some time, returning the fire issuing from behind the fortification about 100 yards away. John McGuirk demonstrated considerable initiative by ordering his brigade forward on a second attack, but because he did not consult Reynolds, it was impossible for anyone to support the effort. McGuirk suffered "considerable loss" and fell back a second time to the brigade position. His unauthorized attack was the fifth time that Confederate troops approached the position held by Harrow's division that afternoon. Reynolds praised McGuirk's men for "great gallantry," but he could not do the same for Youngblood's command. Although he recognized that some of the government workers tried to share the dangers of the battlefield, most of them "did not behave with the coolness and courage of veterans."[14]

The Confederates drove vigorously up to their high tide, producing an equally vigorous musketry from the blue-clad troops that was described as a roar by all who heard it. The 26th Illinois of Williams's brigade reportedly fired a total of 40,000 rounds of ammunition during the course of the afternoon, a good deal of it in repelling this last assault, and the regiment lost forty men altogether during the battle.[15]

In Oliver's brigade, just to the left of Williams's command, the Federals were equally vigorous in dealing with the repeated Rebel assaults. The sound of musketry ebbed and flowed according to the successive waves of gray rolling in from the south. "The firing was incessant," wrote a newspaper correspondent, "swelling out, as the rebels charged, into a fierce and steady roar, and again dying away as they receded, to a fitful rattling." Company commanders in the 70th Ohio detailed two or three men to make sure that additional cartridges as well as fresh water were available to the regiment. Martin Palmer of Company G was too ill to fight but well enough to bring up ammunition and canteens to the front line, exposing himself to enemy fire in the process. Members of the 15th Michigan in Oliver's brigade found that their muskets became fouled because of the steady firing. These weapons had to be cleaned out after twenty-five rounds or so, and the men were compelled to walk to the rear a bit to find a brook where they could swab out the barrels; then they returned to the firing line and continued their deadly work.[16]

Despite the breastworks, some of Reynolds's fire found targets in Oliver's brigade. Thomas Connelly was standing two feet from Capt. James F. Summers of Company B, 70th Ohio, when the officer was "shot through the breast" as he pointed toward the Rebels. Summers had been encouraging his men. "There they come! Pour it into them!" he shouted when the ball slammed into his body. At least one man was killed while carrying Summers to the rear. The captain died three hours later after imploring those around him to, "Tell my friends that I died at my post."[17]

At one point in Reynolds's attack a staff officer tried to encourage the 70th Ohio to move forward and drive the Rebels away. Capt. Henry L. Philips, who was serving on detached duty from the regiment as Oliver's adjutant general, told his colleagues, "Boys, it is our time to make a charge. You must cross over the works and go for them. It is hard, I know, but we must do it." The right wing crossed the breastworks, and the left wing was in the process of doing so when Philips changed his mind and told everyone to fall back behind the works again. It is unclear why he canceled the advance. Thomas Connelly reported long after the war that an order could be heard from a loud-voiced Confederate officer to charge the Yankees as they emerged from their works, but it is difficult to understand how anyone could be heard from such a distance in the midst of rifle fire. Likely Philips changed his mind because he quickly saw how many men were hit as they left the protection of the breastworks. Several members of the 70th Ohio were lost in this short, ill-advised move by Philips.[18]

Oliver received reinforcements from the Seventeenth Corps near the end of the battle, and Howard was responsible for it. Although he did not specifically mention calling on Blair to send help, Howard was a bit confused about this issue. He consistently referred to Seventeenth Corps regiments that came to Morgan L. Smith's aid as being armed with Henry repeaters, but those repeater units really came from the Sixteenth Corps. Moreover, some of the fresh regiments that Blair sent went to Harrow's division and others to Morgan L. Smith's division, further confusing the commanding general decades later when he penned several accounts of the battle at Ezra Church.[19]

Howard sent his call for troops to Blair at about 2:00 P.M. Blair told Brig. Gen. Giles A. Smith to send two regiments to Logan from his division, and Smith dispatched the 3rd Iowa and 13th Iowa, placing both under Col. John Shane of the latter regiment. The men moved on the double-quick close to half a mile to reach the line held by Oliver. There they found the Fifteenth Corps troops worn out by constant firing all afternoon, many of their weapons too foul to be of much use, and Reynolds still holding on only about 100 yards away. Shane put both regiments on the line, replacing the 97th Indiana and the 99th Indiana. With fresh troops and clean musket barrels, the volume of fire was too much for Reynolds. He pulled his men back a short distance to obtain better cover. The Confederate fire lessened considerably but continued for some time afterward. The Rebel balls generally sailed over the Union line but perforated the flag of the 13th Iowa.[20]

The worst part of the battle at Ezra Church was over for Williams and Oliver. This segment of the Union line had been pressured repeatedly during the course of the afternoon but had with difficulty held its position. Oliver gave enormous praise to the 70th Ohio, which received the heaviest pressure in his view, for maintaining its post. The regiment suffered thirty losses that day, and as soon as Reynolds fell back a little and the Rebel fire lessened, it sent out a skirmish line and strengthened the breastworks.[21]

These Federal skirmishers from the 70th Ohio and other regiments of Oliver's brigade probably encountered a skirmish line that Reynolds sent out, not to his front but to his right. Reynolds realized that, after spending a short time in his static position 100 yards from the Federals, no supporting troops lay beyond his right flank. He sent out two companies to extend a skirmish line off toward the right, and that line eventually connected with the left end of a skirmish line that Clayton had established to screen the three brigades of his division. By 5:00 P.M., Reynolds received an order to fall back from the battlefield. Leaving his skirmish line in place, he ordered his men to retire to Lick Skillet Road. From there they moved 400 yards to the left and began to build breastworks. Reynolds held his men there until 10:30 P.M. when he was ordered back to the Atlanta defenses.[22]

Reynolds's Brigade suffered considerable losses in its assault that afternoon, especially among the officers. Pvt. John W. Leeper of the 2nd Arkansas Mounted Rifles (dismounted) wrote that "many of our best men were killed." Col. Henry G. Bunn of the 4th Arkansas suffered a broken arm when a ball hit it, and he also was struck in both thighs. Bunn, however, recovered from his triple injury. Reynolds suffered 320 casualties out of 1,000 engaged, a ratio of 32 percent. Youngblood's Battalion lost 9 out of 150, while Gholson's Brigade lost 144 out of 450. Reynolds's Arkansas troops lost 167 men of 400 who were engaged.[23]

In addition to the heavy loss of manpower, Reynolds's horse was shot in the head during the attack. The ball entered about three inches above his left nostril but the steed, affectionately named Robert, continued to carry Reynolds throughout the engagement. "I have ridden him at Richmond, Kentucky; Jackson, Mississippi; Chickamauga, Moore's Mill [on July 19,

1864] and Peachtree Creek," Reynolds noted in his diary, "and this is his first wound." After the surgeons had a chance to care for the men, Reynolds sent Robert to the field hospital so they could cut the ball out of his head.[24]

While O'Neal and Reynolds had been active in pressing forward the Confederate effort, William A. Quarles's Brigade remained in reserve. Born in Virginia but raised in Kentucky, Quarles attended the University of Virginia and practiced law in Clarkesville, Tennessee, while dabbling in politics. He commanded the 42nd Tennessee, was captured at Fort Donelson, and led a brigade in Mississippi and later in the Army of Tennessee. When Walthall told him to look well to the left from his reserve position at the Lick Skillet Road, Quarles sent a skirmish line and scouting parties in that direction. He received from them fairly accurate information about the location of Logan's right flank. Walthall also was concerned about the fact that his division had no immediate support to the right. He told Lee of his worry and sent a staff officer to inform Stewart as well, receiving assurance that other troops would see that his right was not threatened.[25]

Walthall therefore felt comfortable moving Quarles up a bit closer to the action. He also told Quarles to detach the 42nd Tennessee and 49th Tennessee to support Capt. James H. Yates's Mississippi Battery of Preston's Battalion, Stewart's Corps. Col. William F. Young of the 49th Tennessee took charge of both regiments as Walthall personally supervised their placement to help the only battery he had available. Young's troops carried fence rails so they could use them to form a breastwork in their supporting position. Yates's Battery had difficulty reaching the battlefield because the Lick Skillet Road was filled with columns of marching troops (Walthall's men and, behind them, Loring's Division). But as soon as it reached a suitable place to deploy, the battery opened fire only to suffer heavily at the hand of Federal skirmishers. Thus Young's effort to make breastworks was a wise precaution, but his men suffered considerable casualties before they secured their position with rails.[26]

When O'Neal called on Walthall for help, the division commander ordered Quarles to move forward. As Young led his men off on a divergent mission, the rest of Quarles's brigade readied for action. Quarles assigned officers to lead wings of his brigade, putting his assistant adjutant general, G. Thomas Cox, in charge of the right wing. His assistant inspector general, Capt. Stephen Cowley, later claimed that Quarles assigned him to control the left wing, but Quarles made no mention of such an assignment in his report.[27]

It was about 4:00 P.M. when the Alabama and Tennessee brigade started the last Confederate attack of the day, aiming at roughly the same part of the Union line that the first attack had targeted. To duplicate O'Neal's path, Quarles moved left oblique for a while until he crossed an open field and then redirected so as to move forward again. As he advanced, Union fire began to descend on his command, growing hotter with each passing yard. Cowley thought the troops "marched beautifully" despite the fire. "I pushed them forward in perfect order," he later bragged to a friend; "it was the happiest moment of my life, to see them charge with such a 'yell.'" Quarles's men passed over the prone members of O'Neal's Brigade and continued toward the Union line.[28]

Quarles went farther in his attack than had O'Neal, and his men paid the price for it. The left wing ground to a halt about thirty yards from the Federals. Here, as Stephen Cowley phrased it, "the beauty of the advance transformed itself into reality, men were falling like grains before the Reaper." Parts of the brigade line wound up even closer, twenty paces or so, from the blazing Union muskets. At this close range someone shouted for the men to fall to the ground for cover, and they did so, reducing casualties by that move. According to E. W. Mebane of the 55th Tennessee, the men lay for at least half an hour firing back at the enemy. Caught up in battle spirit, Billy Adams shouted, "Give it to them, boys" before he was shot in the side of the head and killed in the ranks of the 55th Tennessee.[29]

This last Confederate attack on Morgan L. Smith's division was almost too much for the exhausted Federals. Between assaults they had worked to improve their breastworks and relished the opportunity "to take breath," as George Hildt of the 30th Ohio put it. A few daring individuals even ventured onto the battlefield looking for tobacco among the fallen Rebels. A. B. Crummel found "long plugs of old Virginia natural leaf" which he shared with his comrades of the 30th Ohio. Crummel also carried a wounded Confederate to the breastwork by letting him climb up on his back as he crawled on his hands and knees.[30]

The strength of Quarles's assault impressed the Federals. Many muskets in Lightburn's brigade were becoming so fouled as to be nearly useless, and several men blistered their hands because the gun barrels had become so hot from rapid firing. William Weber of Company F, 47th Ohio, injured his hand while ramming a load down because the hot barrel caused a premature discharge of the musket. The men lessened the pace of their firing and, when possible, poured water from canteens down the barrel to cool the weapons. They had plenty of ammunition, for officers detailed a few men to bring up ample supplies. In the 54th Ohio, ordnance boxes were dropped

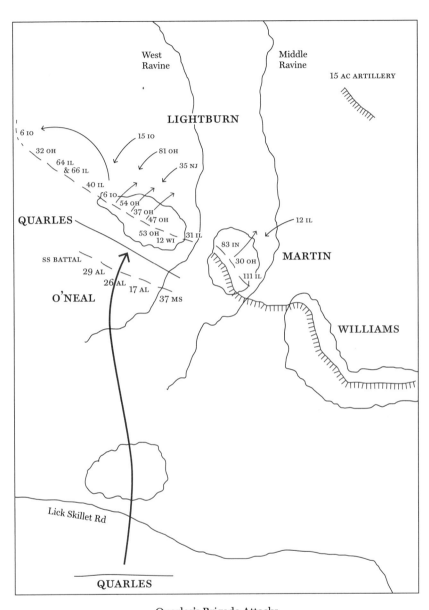

West
Ravine

Middle
Ravine

15 AC ARTILLERY

LIGHTBURN

6 IO

32 OH

64 IL
& 66 IL

15 IO

81 OH

35 NJ

40 IL

6 IO
54 OH
37 OH
47 OH

12 IL

QUARLES

53 OH
12 WI

31 IL

83 IN

SS BATTAL

29 AL

30 OH

MARTIN

26 AL
17 AL

111 IL

O'NEAL

37 MS

WILLIAMS

Lick Skillet Rd

QUARLES

Quarles's Brigade Attacks
(Earl J. Hess and Pratibha A. Dabholkar)

on the ground along the regimental line and broken open. Cartridges soon were strewn along the ground for the men to pick up when needed. It was a wasteful method of ammunition supply but deemed expedient given the emergency.[31]

The firing by Quarles's men had an effect on the Federals. One of the Seventeenth Corps units that had rushed to Lightburn's aid early in the battle engaged in a fierce fight with the Tennesseans and Alabamans. Daniel Titus of the 12th Wisconsin got into a heated discussion with two comrades as to who had shot a Confederate that everyone had seen fall. Someone told Titus he should take better cover, as the heat of the argument caused him to become careless. When Titus turned "to smile at the kindly suggestion" he was hit by a ball that "cut across his temple killing him instantly." Titus was among the twenty regimental members who fell while giving aid to the Fifteenth Corps that day.[32]

Lightburn's brigade needed additional relief and fortunately it came at the right time. Howard's effort to bring Sixteenth Corps troops to the endangered right flank paid off with the arrival of several fresh regiments. Morgan L. Smith's staff officer, Gordon Lofland, put it accurately, even though he embellished the situation, when he reported the condition of Lightburn's men at this point in the battle. "They were completely exhausted, the muskets so heated that they could no longer be fired, and hope had almost died within them, when the timely arrival of other troops encouraged them to hold on until the enemy retreated."[33]

After receiving word at about 2:00 P.M., five Sixteenth Corps regiments moved as quickly as the heat of the afternoon permitted from near the left of Howard's line to the extreme right. Lieut. Col. William K. Strong, Howard's inspector general, gave directions to the 64th Illinois and 66th Illinois, both of which were armed with Henry repeating rifles, and told them to extend the line farther west and to the right of the 6th Iowa and 40th Illinois.[34]

These Sixteenth Corps men mostly took over the responsibility for returning fire at Quarles's men from the members of Lightburn's brigade. When the Henry repeaters went into action, everyone on the Union side took notice of them. Howard wrote in awe of these "fearful weapons" after the war, referring to the "fire that never stops till the ammunition is exhausted." He exaggerated the effect by writing that "in less than five minutes the whole flank was clear of enemies, the ground was strewn with the slain, and the living found shelter only among the trees to their rear." Other observers also were impressed by the rapid firing that issued from the

Henry rifles, but there is no reason to believe it brought down an enormous number of targets. Quarles's and O'Neal's men were already lying prone some distance away and undoubtedly were protected from the worst of the fire erupting from the two Illinois regiments.[35]

Fresh units now took the place of tired men in the line. Lieut. Col. Robert N. Adams led the 81st Ohio into position, helped in finding his way by a member of Morgan L. Smith's staff. He moved his men through the ranks of Jones's demi-brigade on the ridgetop that represented the end of Logan's line. At least two of Jones's regiments, the 54th Ohio and 47th Ohio, took this as an opportunity to retire. Most likely, the depleted 37th Ohio did the same when Cladek's 35th New Jersey came forward to align with the 81st Ohio. In essence, these two fresh regiments took over defense of this sector from Lightburn's tired men. While the New Jersey regiment had mostly clear ground in its front, the 81st Ohio troops found thick undergrowth in front of their position. The Ohioans therefore waited until their comrades to the left opened fire, and then they began shooting into the brush, knowing that the Confederates were still positioned a relatively short distance away. "The musketry-fire at different times was terrific," recalled Charles Wright of the 81st Ohio. Lieut. Col. Henry Van Sellar's 12th Illinois appeared next and was directed farther to the left, on the other side of the West Ravine, to relieve the 30th Ohio.[36]

For many members of Lightburn's command, these fresh troops came in the nick of time. "Our guns were so heated as to be difficult to hold and dangerous to load," reported Wayne Johnson Jacobs of the 30th Ohio. "Many of the boys' guns were so dirty as to be useless. A gloom pervaded each mind as he looked in the face of his comrades and saw the failing energies of his comrades." They let out "a long, loud cheer" when the reinforcements arrived.[37]

Joseph Saunier also recalled that his comrades in the 47th Ohio were exhausted and their weapons almost useless by this stage of the fight. Maj. Thomas Taylor told everyone to use the bayonet if necessary to hold the ridge. Suddenly the Federals heard cheering to the rear and saw the 81st Ohio move up the slope toward their line. "Never was relief more acceptable," Saunier put it. The fresh men passed through the ranks of the 47th Ohio, and then Saunier and his comrades fell back behind the ridge. For at least an hour the members of the 47th Ohio rested. They cleaned their gun barrels "by urinating & pouring water into them & shooting it out," according to Taylor. The regiment moved back up to the line to stand as a ready reserve by about 5:00 P.M. Although largely replaced by troops from other divisions, Lightburn's men justly felt proud of their achievement on the afternoon of July 28. They had withstood four attacks, at least two of them very heavy and dangerous, and had refused to be driven from the main Union position.[38]

Yet another contingent of reinforcing troops arrived soon after the Sixteenth Corps men showed up, and it came from Blair's Seventeenth Corps. Howard had asked Blair for more help, and Blair had ordered Giles A. Smith to send two regiments to Logan's assistance at about 2:00 P.M. Smith selected the 15th Iowa and 32nd Ohio, placing the two under Col. William W. Belknap of the former regiment. The 15th Iowa belonged to Col. William Hall's Third Brigade, and the 32nd Ohio was part of Col. Benjamin F. Potts's First Brigade.[39]

When Belknap reached the area held by Lightburn, he placed both regiments in line just at the foot of the ridge and waited for orders. Very soon word arrived for help, and Belknap sent the 32nd Ohio off to the far right of the line in order to extend it still farther west. While passing by immediately to the rear of the line, Corp. Charles E. Smith of the 32nd Ohio could hear the Federals yell "Fort Pillow Fort Pillow" in the excitement of combat. That yell represented a note of revenge for the killing of unarmed black Union soldiers the previous April in western Tennessee. Another member of the regiment recalled seeing Logan sitting on his black horse watching the battle, as "calm as though on dress parade." The regiment took position and quickly assembled a breastwork, but it was not attacked for the rest of the day. "We saw more rocks than rebels" on the narrow ridgetop, according to L. D. Hord, but the stones made good protection against the stray shots that constantly sailed toward the regiment.[40]

Soon after sending off the 32nd Ohio, Belknap received a request to relieve the 6th Iowa on line. He quickly moved the 15th Iowa up to accomplish that task. The 6th Iowa fell back for rest and to clean its weapons, and then it went farther right to create a skirmish line extending westward from the position of the 32nd Ohio.[41]

By the end of the battle at Ezra Church, a total of eleven regiments came to Logan's assistance, five from the Sixteenth Corps and six from the Seventeenth Corps. They played an enormously important role in Howard's success. Morgan L. Smith went out of his way to express his gratitude for the assistance. The battle was indeed a prime example of the spirit of cooperation that characterized relations between different commands in the army that Grant had created.[42]

With so many fresh troops pouring into the sector held by Lightburn's brigade, Logan's right flank finally was secure. Just to the east, on the other side of West Ravine, Martin's brigade felt the pressure as the right wing of Quarles's Brigade poured in fire from its prone position close to the Union line. At the height of this contest, an unidentified Union officer walked behind the rear of the line and told everyone to "Fall back, fall back! They are flanking us!" Although a few regimental officers in the 116th Illinois repeated the order, no one obeyed it. "The boys could not see it," recalled Elijah Coombe, "and held their ground." After the battle, no one could identify the officer who had given such bad advice. Martin reported some confusion among at least one regiment caused by the mistaken impression that the line was being flanked, but it was soon rectified. Most of Martin's officers performed in a steady and determined manner and held the men to their task of loading and firing as quickly as possible. The musket barrels of many troops in the 116th Illinois became so fouled that they had to pour water from canteens to clean them out. Regimental officers detailed men to bring up more cartridges.[43]

Quarles gamely held his brigade anywhere from twenty-five to fifty paces from the Union position, according to his own estimate, in a hope that something would come of it. The men lay prone and returned fire for some time as the Sixteenth and Seventeenth Corps reinforcements moved up to bolster the opposing line. Confederate prospects dimmed with each passing minute. Quarles's command was "attenuated by casualties to a mere line of skirmishers," and it was obvious that, even if he could break the Federal position, it "would have been barren of results" because there were no supporting troops nearby to exploit the advantage. Quarles sent word for help, but none was available. He reluctantly gave the order to retire.[44]

Both Walthall and Stewart supported the decision to fall back. The division leader argued that Quarles had "made a bold and bloody assault, but his command was checked by the strong force in his front." In fact, Walthall believed that even if his entire division was doubled in numbers he would not have had enough men to succeed against the Fifteenth Corps position. He sent a staff officer to inform Stewart of his opinion and received word to hold on until Loring's Division arrived, when he could fall back to Loring's rear. Stewart had nothing but praise for Walthall's attack, calling it a "desperate fight" attended with heavy casualties.[45]

Not only Quarles but O'Neal fell back at about 5 or 6 o'clock that afternoon to end the series of Confederate assaults. Two men fell dead or mortally wounded in O'Neal's Brigade while bringing the colors of the 37th Mississippi off the field. Washington Bryan Crumpton, who also served in the 37th Mississippi, had been slightly injured in one of his legs and had some difficulty retiring. Once started, however, Crumpton was able to make "good time getting away. Bullets from three directions plowed the ground like great worms in the earth." In fact one of those spent balls badly bruised him. "For ten days my body was sore from the passage of bullets, some through my clothing, and some that made my clothes threadbare as they passed, leaving a sore place on the flesh as if scorched by fire. My case knife turned off two bullets and my tube wrench and screw driver in my cartridge box were broken by another."[46]

Capt. Thomas H. Smith, a member of Quarles's staff, counted a crushing loss ratio for the brigade. Out of 913 men taken into action, the brigade lost 495. Of that number, 400 were wounded, 76 were killed, and 19 were counted as missing. That amounted to 54 percent casualties in one fierce assault. Stephen Cowley provided different numbers, claiming that Quarles took 1,100 men into action and lost 595 of them, but the loss ratio was the same as Smith's estimate, 54 percent.[47]

The number of prominent officers who fell in Quarles's brigade was legion. "I cannot mention ½ the officers Killed and wounded," admitted Cowley in a letter to his friend. He reported that seven regimental commanders were shot down in half an hour and that the 1st Alabama emerged from the trial with only three commissioned officers left. At least two of the brigade's staff officers had their horses shot and volunteered to help Yates man his guns. Quarles mourned the loss of an aide-de-camp named Ashton Johnson, "a high-toned gentleman" from St. Louis who was killed. "Exiled from his home on account of his adherence to our cause, though a mere boy he entered our service with all the ardor of his age." Cowley provided a long list of officers killed and wounded in the brigade, noted the loss of Johnson as well, and reported that Quarles's "fine bay horse was Killed under him." "I was only hit on the foot with a spent ball & my stirrup broke with piece of shell," he reported.[48]

In the left wing of the brigade, the 1st Alabama lost a very effective officer in Maj. Samuel L. Knox. He had skillfully commanded a skirmish line that held its ground against great odds in the Union attack at Kennesaw Mountain on June 27, but he was dangerously wounded early in the battle of Ezra Church. The 53rd Tennessee reportedly lost ninety-seven men in the assault; its Col. John R. White was killed, and the successor, Maj. William C. Richardson, was mortally wounded while taking the regiment back to the Lick Skillet Road.[49]

Sometime after the battle, E. W. Mebane informed his brother in Huntingdon, Tennessee, of the enormity of loss in the 55th Tennessee. "George W. Joyner is also numbered with the dead, and his brother Jo Joyner. George Joyner was shot through the head, and his body lost. John Leak was shot dead on the field. Jo Joyner was shot in the thigh, but his worst wound was in his left arm, which was shattered to pieces." Joyner "could not stand" the use of chloroform so his arm was not amputated. It became "mortified" and caused his death three days later. "John Shankle, Parson Mack, and I made him a coffin and buried him as well as circumstances would permit." The list of sufferers continued with James B. Hamilton, who "was shot about the face; is supposed to be dead; fell into the hands of the enemy." In the middle of this sad account, Mebane took time to inform his brother that James Hemphill had displayed bravery and pluck. When the regimental color-bearer was shot, "James picked it up immediately." "Brother George, I know you will shudder to hear me relate the sufferings of our poor boys, those in whom you and I prided in so much, and hoped to live with and cherish after the war. I loved them for their firmness and their honour."[50]

Nearly every survivor in Quarles's brigade felt the weight of the event and the consequences. "This was the hottest contest we engaged in during the war," argued Joseph Love of the 48th Tennessee. Others believed that only the battle of Franklin produced heavier casualties for the brigade. The flag of the 49th Tennessee was perforated by thirty-two holes, and two or three bullets marked the staff as well. Col. William F. Young of the 49th Tennessee lost his right arm as the result of a wound at Ezra Church. Lieut. Joseph Hurt was killed on July 28, prompting a sad remembrance on the part of his friend James Madison Brannock, surgeon of the consolidated 4th and 5th Tennessee in Hardee's Corps. "He was a brave & good man. He talked a great deal about home lately, & I think had a settled conviction that he would never see his family again."[51]

As the brigade retired to a less exposed position near the Lick Skillet Road, it was time to care for the injured and put the ranks back into shape again. Quarles was impressed by the actions of J. H. McNeilly, chaplain of the 49th Tennessee, who "exhibited the qualities of the Christian soldier. Following the blood-stained path of his regiment, he was everywhere to be seen ministering to the physical and spiritual comfort of the dying and the wounded." Quarles could well have added that, at this point in the day, there was little else to be done.[52]

CHAPTER EIGHT

Nerve and Persistency

Along the Line on July 28

One more division became available to both Stewart and Lee by the time Walthall's Division had spent its energy in the last Confederate attacks of the day. Commanded by William W. Loring, it followed Walthall and arrived on the field to form line along the Lick Skillet Road. Born in North Carolina but raised in Florida, Loring had extensive military experience. He fought the Seminoles, lost an arm in the Mexican War, and held significant commands from western Virginia to the Vicksburg campaign. Loring temporarily replaced Leonidas Polk as commander of the Army of Mississippi after the bishop general was killed on June 14, but Stewart was chosen as the permanent replacement. Loring swallowed his disappointment and returned to his division.[1]

Any plans to use Loring's men to continue the attacks that evening quickly fell apart. Just as the division began to form, an aggressive line of Federal skirmishers appeared within striking distance and began to lay down fire on the assembly area. Loring was hit in the left part of the chest and injured enough to incapacitate him for the rest of the day. Brig. Gen. Winfield Scott Featherston took command of the division. He had led it during the time when Loring commanded the Army of Mississippi. Surg. P. F. Whitehead, Loring's medical director, reported that his chief suffered a flesh wound, but it kept him out of action until September 10. Featherston finished the task of assembling the division along and just south of Lick Skillet Road. He placed Brig. Gen. John Adams's Brigade on the right, Brig. Gen. Thomas M. Scott's Brigade on the left, and his own brigade, now under Col. Robert Lowry, in the center.[2]

Ironically, Stewart also was hit by the Federal skirmish fire before Featherston finished forming the division. Stewart exposed himself by riding into an open field in view of the enemy when a spent ball struck his forehead. It created a curiously shaped mark in the form of a V. The wound produced a good deal of blood which blinded the general, and the blow itself dazed Stewart as well. Aristide Hopkins, a member of his staff, led him off the field. Surgeon Whitehead was delighted to learn that the injury was not dangerous despite early reports. Stewart was out of action until August 7.[3]

Edward C. Walthall now took command of Stewart's Corps, while William A. Quarles took charge of Walthall's Division. Col. Robert A. Owens of the 46th and 55th Tennessee assumed command of Quarles's Brigade. The spent troops needed relief, and Walthall pursued the course Stewart had already laid out, placing Walthall's Division to the rear of Loring's fresh line. But Walthall amended that plan by telling Quarles to extend the division to the left of Loring's command, not behind it.[4]

The troops of Loring's Division were also pelted with Union skirmish fire. They protected themselves somewhat by lying down and taking advantage of folds in the ground. The 35th Alabama, among other regiments, lost several men. Thomas T. Smith in the 43rd Mississippi felt something flow down his leg and believed he had been wounded. Upon closer examination, it was only water. A ball had punctured his canteen and caused a flow to begin that initially frightened and worried him. Loring had brought at least two artillery units to the battlefield, Cowan's Mississippi Battery and Wade's Missouri Battery. Both units suffered casualties but offered little if any supporting fire for the Confederate infantry.[5]

There was no need to endure this suffering. It could have been avoided if the Confederates had established a good skirmish line on this part of the field, but they failed to do so. Ironically, Lee's task was to secure the Lick Skillet Road. After five hours of repeated attacks, the Confederates still had not fully done so, at least in this area. Loring, Stewart, and dozens of the rank and file were hurt while standing on or near that road late in the afternoon. The Federals had skirmished aggressively all during the Atlanta campaign, usually outfighting their gray-clad opponents between the lines. Now, as on many other battlefields, the Confederates were paying a heavy price for their lack of attention to effective skirmishing.

While awaiting orders in their reserve position, the men of Loring's Division not only dodged Union bullets but now and then recognized friends in other units. Mathew Andrew Dunn of the 33rd Mississippi in Featherston's Brigade noticed his friend Clem lying on the side of the Lick Skillet Road with a bullet in his leg. Clem belonged to a regiment that had previously participated in the battle. Dunn left the ranks to talk with him. Clem did not think the injury was too severe, but surgeons later amputated the leg.[6]

Neither Dunn nor his colleagues could know whether they would be called on to advance and suffer the same fate as Clem. Stewart had not indicated before his injury that he intended to throw Loring into the fight, and Walthall displayed no enthusiasm for the idea. Lee seems to have lost his desire to continue the battle as well. There is no evidence that he urged Walthall to prolong the effort, so the fighting dwindled to the level of light skirmishing that evening.

John Bell Hood remained at his headquarters all day on July 28, largely unaware of what was happening near the Poor House and Ezra Church. As early as 2:20 P.M. Francis Shoup urged Lee to "hold the enemy in check. The object is to prevent him from gaining the Lick Skillet road." An hour later, Hood's headquarters became aware that an engagement of some kind was taking place. Shoup told Stewart "not to do more fighting than necessary, unless you should get a decided advantage." Not until 3:30 P.M. did anyone at Hood's headquarters reveal an awareness of a heavy battle taking place west of Atlanta. That led to another message informing Lee he should not allow the enemy "to gain upon you any more than possible."[7]

Samuel G. French, who commanded Stewart's other division, spent the day riding about in anticipation of active service. He felt that a battle of some sort was pending west of the city and heard the heavy musketry erupt when Lee launched his initial attack at noon. Late in the afternoon, in response to a note from Walthall, French sent Ector's Brigade (under Col. William H. Young) and Guibor's Missouri Battery to his assistance. Young arrived after the fighting was over and took position in echelon to the left and rear of Walthall's Division, anchoring the extreme left of the Confederate line. Even so, several members of Guibor's battery were wounded by Union skirmishers.[8]

Hood decided to remain at his headquarters despite indications that a major action was taking place near Ezra Church. He sent a flurry of dispatches in an effort to manage affairs. Hood also sent a note calling on Hardee to consult with him as soon as possible. On the way, Hardee received a second, urgent note calling him to headquarters. "He told me that Lee and Stewart were fighting the enemy on the Lick Skillet road," Hardee informed his wife two days later, "and he wished me to go out there and look after matters. While I was with him news came that Stewart and Loring were wounded." Hardee made his way out the Lick Skillet

Road only to find that the battle had already ended. The Confederates "had been severely handled," he reported, and "Lee was acting strictly on the defensive." Hardee had authority to take command of all the troops on the battlefield but found it unnecessary to do so. Hood also sent word for Benjamin F. Cheatham to come to his headquarters, apparently intending that he replace Stewart temporarily in command of Stewart's Corps.[9]

In brief dispatches to the Richmond authorities, Hood began to interpret the events of July 28 in a comforting way. He noted that the Federals completed their deployment that morning by driving back the cavalry skirmishers, and "a sharp engagement ensued" when Lee's and Stewart's troops arrived on the scene. He reported the result as accruing "no decided advantage to either side" but noted that Lee still held the Lick Skillet Road at the end of the day.[10]

News of the fight filtered along the opposing lines near Atlanta as the afternoon progressed. Troops on the far Confederate right, northeast of the city, could hear the sound of musketry and artillery. Closer to the action, officers in the Sixteenth and Seventeenth Corps were watchful in case gray-clad troops suddenly threw themselves on their lines as well. The Federals in Dodge's and Blair's commands improved their breastworks and endured heavy artillery fire from the defenses of Atlanta. Some of the fire also came from the south as scattered batteries belonging to Lee and Stewart established positions from which they enfiladed the Seventeenth Corps line. So many solid shots rolled along the ground behind the line held by Elisha Stockwell's 14th Wisconsin that "it was a sight to see them. They came bounding along so thick one couldn't count a quarter of them."[11]

Sixteenth Corps men also put up with a considerable amount of shelling during the course of July 28. Enfilade fire compelled many of Dodge's troops to leave their works and take shelter wherever the parapets happened to be placed so as to shield them from projectiles. Much of this enfilade fire from the south and direct fire from the east seemed to be aimed at various Union batteries along the Sixteenth Corps line, but nearby infantry units took the brunt of it. While some of Dodge's batteries could not return the fire, others tried to counter it as best they could.[12]

From his command post near the scene of action, Sherman began to reason that Hood might have weakened his line somewhere to throw so much weight against Howard. He therefore told Thomas and Schofield to see if any weak spots existed in their sectors. Fourteenth Corps troops made a demonstration that brought on heavy artillery fire well into the evening hours. Twentieth Corps officers advanced heavy skirmishers, who found that the Rebel works were still fully manned. One such Union line got close enough so that the men could overhear Confederate officers tell their troops to hold fire until the bluecoats came very close. The 13th New Jersey captured thirty-six Confederates in aggressive skirmishing that afternoon. David S. Stanley's Fourth Corps, to the northeast of Atlanta, also pushed forward a strong skirmish force in fulfillment of Sherman's directive. It captured several prisoners but found the Confederate position strongly manned. "I think any attack upon their main line, excepting by a regular well managed assaulting column, must have failed," reported Stanley.[13]

Schofield left no stone unturned in his effort to find a weak spot in the enemy position opposite the Twenty-third Corps. He anchored Sherman's left flank with a long refused line that faced south and which had been constructed just before Logan pulled away from the July 22 battlefield less than forty-eight hours before. Long before Sherman's directive to test the Confederate position arrived, Schofield had urged Maj. Gen. Jacob D. Cox to explore what lay ahead of his position. On the morning of July 28, Col. Daniel Cameron responded to Cox's order and sent the 63rd Indiana and 65th Illinois out from his brigade sector on that refused line to skirmish forward. The two regiments traversed the ground evacuated by Logan and came to rest in the old Fifteenth Corps skirmish pits that faced west and which were near some burned dwellings, probably the Augustus Hurt House near the Georgia Railroad. Those regiments had pushed Confederate skirmishers back in their swinging advance to this old line. In the afternoon, after Sherman's directive arrived, Cameron sent the 24th Kentucky and 103rd Ohio to reinforce the 63rd Indiana and 65th Illinois. The reinforced skirmishers advanced westward until within 250 yards of the Atlanta City Line, sparking a good deal of firing along the sector held by the Twenty-third Corps.[14]

Sherman urged Schofield to do more as the fighting at Ezra Church heated up. "General Howard is being hard pressed on our right," he wrote his subordinate, "and I desire that you press the enemy with vigor in your front, and, if practical, break their lines, which must be lightly held." But Schofield was convinced that the main Rebel works were still fully manned and confessed in a dispatch to Thomas that "I have very little hope of being able to carry any point of the enemy's works." Schofield told Sherman frankly that "it seems to be impossible to carry any point of the enemy's line without going beyond the defenses of the town, which would take me far from the rest of the army."[15]

With this message, and with the realization that Howard had weathered the storm and produced a stunning success, Sherman admitted that he had little hope of Twenty-third Corps troops breaking Hood's line. He explained his earlier message by writing that "the attack on General Howard was so persistent that I did not know but that Hood had actually stripped his line of all but the militia." Sherman went on to relay developing news of the battle to Schofield, characterizing Howard's fight as "splendid" and believing it "must go far toward determining a speedy evacuation of Atlanta."[16]

Sherman, of course, was overly optimistic about the results of the bloody fight at Ezra Church. In fact, he tended to be overly optimistic during the entire course of the campaign. Sherman also found it difficult to coordinate a promising troop movement that could have spelled disaster for Lee if it had worked as planned. During the early morning hours of July 28, he had ordered Thomas to send Davis's division of Palmer's corps along a route that would take it to Howard's right flank. Sherman wanted Davis to "move to Turner's Ferry, and then, by road leading to East Point, to feel forward for Howard's right. I want to connect Howard's right, back with some known point of Turner's Ferry . . . and want to reach out as far as possible." Sherman also hoped that Davis could "catch the attacking force in flank or rear at an unexpected moment" if the Rebels tried to turn Howard's right flank. When Howard found out about this move he instructed Dodge to send the 9th Illinois (mounted) to cooperate with Davis. As Howard later reported, his understanding was that Davis would protect his communications by covering the roads to the right and rear of the Army of the Tennessee and provide support for his right flank if needed. Dodge sent Capt. Samuel T. Hughes's 9th Illinois "to picket all roads leading to our right and rear."[17]

Sherman's order to Thomas was copied and sent on to Palmer and then to Davis, but Davis replied that he was too ill to lead the division on July 28. "I regret being sick," he told Palmer, "am too weak to sit on my horse. Perhaps I will be better by this afternoon; hope so." Brig. Gen. James D. Morgan, a capable brigade commander, took charge of the division that day. He studied the copy of Sherman's dispatch to Thomas and planned to execute the directive exactly as indicated. Morgan took command of the division at 9:00 A.M. and marched west along the road to Turner's Ferry an hour later.[18]

The morning hours ticked by as Howard completed his deployment with heavy skirmishing, and signs seemed to indicate a battle in the offing. Sherman rode to Palmer's headquarters after leaving Howard because, as he put it, "I attached great importance to the movement" of Davis's command. There he learned that Davis was too ill to lead the division and that Morgan was in charge. Sherman became worried. He had known Davis since the division had constituted part of a large relief force Sherman commanded to lift the siege of Knoxville the previous December, and he trusted Davis. Sherman and Palmer now rode to Davis's headquarters and reached the place just as the sound of musketry could be heard to the south, opening the battle of Ezra Church. David R. Waters, a volunteer aide on Davis's staff, remembered what happened next. Sherman nervously exclaimed, "I wish to God Davis was in command of his division to-day." Davis overheard this remark and forced himself out of bed, dressed, and told his staff to mount. His black servant helped the general into the saddle, but Davis "fainted and would have fallen had he not been caught. He was carried back to his bed."[19]

Morgan had been making rather leisurely progress thus far, moving at a measured pace toward Turner's Ferry. Two hours after starting out, the sound of heavy musketry indicated a battle had begun on Howard's refused wing. Back at Davis's headquarters, Sherman told Davis to send one of his staff officers to find Morgan and hurry him to Howard's support. By the time the officer found Morgan, the division was in the vicinity of the Chattahoochee River taking a break for lunch. Upon nearing this point, Morgan came across elements of the 9th Illinois and found that many of the roads in the area had been barricaded by Confederate cavalry. Davis's staff officer communicated Sherman's desire that the division make itself available for Howard's use, and it needed to be there immediately. Morgan turned the head of the column around and began making his way toward the southeast along a network of small roads only dimly known to the Federals, in comparison to the major road directly linking Davis's position with Turner's Ferry.[20]

This move was the start of a frustrating afternoon for the men of Davis's division. Morgan had no accurate map of the area and no local guides to help him on his way. As a result the division was compelled to march by instinct as much as by knowledge, and it soon encountered resistance in the form of Confederate cavalrymen. These came from Brig. Gen. Lawrence S. Ross's Texas cavalry brigade of Brig. Gen. William H. Jackson's Division. Jackson had dispatched Ross early that morning to help the troopers of Brig. Gen. William Y. C. Humes's Division to cover the network of roads in the area. After talking with area residents, Morgan moved a mile from the Chattahoochee and turned right off the Turner's Ferry Road onto a road that generally ran toward East Point. Soon after moving toward the southeast, the van of his division came upon Ross's troopers "well posted

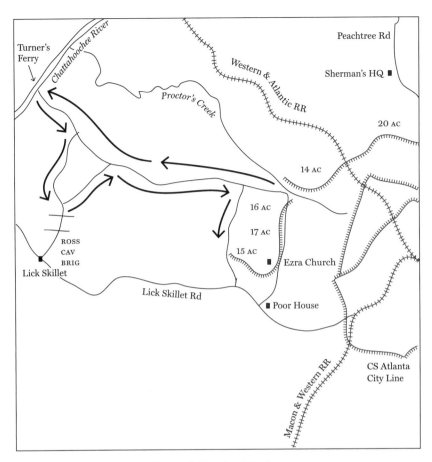

Morgan's Division Marches
(Earl J. Hess and Pratibha A. Dabholkar)

and in good numbers." Morgan deployed a regiment to skirmish forward and push them back.[21]

Ross's Texans put up stiff resistance. They took advantage of every feature in the landscape and delayed the Union march as much as possible. "From one position the enemy was driven," recalled Henry J. Aten of the 85th Illinois, "only to be found in another." Meanwhile the sound of musketry near Ezra Church was ever present as Morgan's men slowly made their way along the route they hoped would take them to the battlefield.[22]

Meanwhile, Howard became more anxious for reinforcements. He hesitated to take too many regiments from Dodge and Blair, fearing that the Rebels might threaten them from the east, and worried "that by continually

throwing in fresh troops" the Confederates "might at last succeed in breaking our line." So Howard sent a message to Sherman for at least a brigade
from Thomas's army. Sherman replied that Morgan was on his way and
Howard should wait for him. Of course, Howard knew that the division
was operating off to the right and rear of his line, and he liked the idea of it
coming to battle at the right time and place, "something as Blucher did on
Wellington's left at Waterloo," he wrote in his autobiography. At 1:45 P.M.,
Palmer informed Thomas's headquarters of Howard's request and reported
that he had no troops to spare other than Morgan's division. Word of Morgan's march filtered through the ranks of Howard's army that afternoon.
It "made our hearts glad for we were in great danger of being outflanked
and crushed," recalled Charles E. Smith of the 32nd Ohio.[23]

But all hopes for Morgan's timely arrival proved to be false. The division slowly pushed its way along the obscure roads that Ross blocked and
was taking a long and frustrating time to make its appearance. Davis sent
another staff officer to find the men and hurry them along. The officer came
across Morgan after the division had advanced only one and a half miles
along the small road branching off from the Turner's Ferry Road. It had
managed in that amount of time, much of the afternoon, to push Ross's
troopers back only a little more than one mile. The staff officer told Morgan
that Howard was hard pressed and the division should get to the scene of
action as quickly as possible. It was decided the best course was to return
to the Turner's Ferry Road, which was completely clear of Rebel troops.
From there the men could move to the scene of action by roads well known.
It would mean a longer journey in terms of distance but without impedi-
ments. Because his van was then engaged in particularly heavy skirmishing,
Morgan decided to continue pushing forward on the obscure road until he
reached a crossroad leading off to the left that could take him back to the
Turner's Ferry Road, necessitating a bit more delay. Meanwhile, the sound
of the musketry at Ezra Church seemed never to stop.[24]

Morgan pushed his command along his chosen course before turning
left onto a crossroad. He then returned to the Turner's Ferry Road. There
the troops made haste along a familiar route. But by the time Morgan's men
neared the vicinity of Howard's flank, the battle was over. Moreover, as dusk
was settling, his men entered a swampy area and got bogged down in muck
and darkness. "We were a set of tiared [sic] boys," complained John Hill
Ferguson of the 10th Illinois. "The day being very hot, quite a number were
sun struck." Henry Aten was furious at the turn of events during this long

day. "The men were mad, tired and hungry, and they came straggling in, making the night air streaked with the most lurid profanity. They did not know who had caused the eccentric movement of the day, nor on whom to fix their curse. So they consigned every one from the commanding general down who might be suspected of having any connection with that day's march . . . to the sulpherous flames of a Hadean future."[25] The swamp into which the division marched at dusk made the mood of the men far worse. It took hours to sort out bivouac areas, and once assigned, the ground proved to be anything but comfortable. "It was as dark as hell when we got into camp, and the confusion was great," remarked Matthew Jamison of the 10th Illinois. Officers stood by with torches in their hands to light the way as men filtered in as late as the early morning hours of July 29 to find a place to sleep. Most of them were too tired to fix a meal.[26]

Sherman was disappointed that his plans for Morgan's division failed to produce dividends, but he blamed the delay on the dimly known road system of the area. He further complained to Halleck that "many of the roads laid down on our maps did not exist at all," thereby relieving Morgan of blame for the failure of his movement. Nevertheless, the missed opportunity frustrated Sherman for the rest of his life. He had no fear of disaster to the Army of the Tennessee but wanted Morgan to reap a more complete victory by turning the battle into "a disastrous rout [of] the enemy." If in the right place and at the right time, and under an aggressive commander, the division certainly could have taken the offensive and severely damaged Lee's spent troops at the end of the day. But it was not to be. "I cannot attribute the failure to want of energy or intelligence," Sherman told Halleck in his official report, "and must charge it, like many other things in the campaign, to the peculiar, tangled nature of the forests and absence of roads that would admit the rapid movement of troops." But in his memoirs, Sherman wrote more petulantly that "the woods were dense, the roads obscure, and as usual this division got on the wrong road." Howard, however, correctly noted that in addition to faulty maps and bad roads the spirited resistance of Ross's troopers derailed Sherman's plan.[27]

The officers and men of Morgan's division were keenly aware of what had happened (and what had failed to happen) during their march on July 28. "This was a most damnable performance," complained Matthew Jamison. "We earnestly desired to get into this mix-up with Hood's army." A member of Battery I, 2nd Illinois Light Artillery, summed it up well when he wrote that "the division went farther than was needful, and it took too long to get back to the flank." Morgan also summed up the day's work when he reported that it was "a late start, an excessively hot day, a long and hard march (fourteen miles), and a late and very dark camp."[28]

Members of the division sought an answer to the questions posed by the day's miscues. David R. Waters claimed that a clue was provided in a conversation between Sherman and Palmer at Davis's headquarters. "Gen. Sherman was excited and very impatient," Waters believed. In comparing copies of his instructions, Sherman realized that a clerk at Palmer's headquarters had written directions for Morgan to march "to" Turner's Ferry rather than "toward" that spot. Instead of finding the obscure roads leading toward East Point early in his march, Morgan assumed he was to do so only after reaching the Chattahoochee River. Palmer defended his staff and refused to admit any mistake, thus starting a rift between the two officers that contributed to Palmer's resignation from Fourteenth Corps command a couple of weeks later. Other veterans of the division later investigated the incident and supported this explanation for the events of the day.[29]

There is little doubt that a clerk's error confused Morgan about the purpose of his march on July 28, but several other factors contributed to the failure of his division to play a role in the battle of Ezra Church. He started the division at 10:00 A.M., a delay mostly caused by Davis's illness and the need to shift commanders before starting. Morgan moved slowly after he started and displayed little awareness that he had anything important to do that day, even though it was clear that he was to support Howard's flank and the sound of gunfire could clearly be heard in that direction from the head of his division. He further allowed a small force of Rebel cavalry to delay his division of infantry. Members of the division resented Sherman's slur, written in his memoirs, that the division always was slow, but in truth Morgan did not handle his command well that day. His actions reinforced Sherman's tendency to view the Fourteenth Corps as habitually sluggish in its movements. The only Fourteenth Corps general he trusted was Davis.[30]

Howard waited impatiently for Morgan to appear all afternoon, only to be disappointed. In late afternoon, while the firing continued on Logan's front, Howard gave up waiting for the division and sent his brother and staff member, Charles H. Howard, to ask Sherman for more troops. This time the chief readily assented. He sent instructions to Thomas who managed to get Palmer to release a brigade. Col. Marshall F. Moore's Third Brigade of Brig. Gen. Richard W. Johnson's First Division, Fourteenth Corps, set out soon but had to march three miles before reaching the right flank of Logan's position. By then it was well past dark, and the fighting had long since ended. Moore constructed good breastworks and stayed during the night of July 28, returning to Johnson's division sector the next morning.[31]

It pleased Howard to tell a story related to him by his brother. After arranging for Moore's brigade to head south, Sherman told Charles that some stragglers had earlier fled north from the battlefield and spread rumors of pending disaster along the Fifteenth Corps line. "Everything is lost," they told Sherman, "the troops are missing McPherson; if you don't at once take care of that flank you will be defeated!" Sherman asked them, "Is General Howard there?" When he found out that Howard was indeed on duty and in charge, Sherman replied, "Then I shall wait for his report." Howard liked this story because it reassured him that "Sherman sustained and trusted me, and I was content."[32]

But Sherman was concerned because Howard had so repeatedly asked for support. The dispatch of Charles Howard seemed to convince Sherman that he ought to find more men than Moore's lone brigade to substitute for Morgan's missing division. Brig. Gen. William T. Ward's Third Division of the Twentieth Corps had been pulled out of the line on July 27 to rest. Ward received an order at 5:00 P.M. to move toward Howard's far right, and he set his men on the road as soon as possible. At least one brigade in the division left a regiment behind to act as reserve for the Twentieth Corps position. The fighting at Ezra Church ended by about 5:00 or 6:00 P.M., however, and it soon became apparent that Ward was not needed. Sherman canceled the movement when various units of the division had marched anywhere from one to four miles toward Logan's flank. The men stopped and returned to their former position.[33]

The fierce Confederate attacks had started about noon and lasted for at least five hours. In that time, different parts of Logan's line had been hit from four to six times. While not all Rebel assaults were pressed home vigorously, some of them had come close to breaking or flanking the Union position. It was not by any means an easy victory, as testified by the dispatch of eleven regiments from the Sixteenth and Seventeenth Corps, a brigade from the Fourteenth Corps, and an entire division from the Twentieth Corps, not counting Morgan's errant Fourteenth Corps division.[34]

Howard had endured his first battle as commander of the Army of the Tennessee, and he had contributed mightily to its success that day. As the firing died down, he walked along the line "to make a better acquaintance with my forces." By now it was obvious that the Federals had survived the day without disaster and had inflicted heavy losses on the enemy. The men cheered their new one-armed commander as he passed by. Howard "felt proud and happy to be intrusted with such brave and efficient soldiers," as he put it in one of his many postwar accounts of the battle at Ezra Church. "Our troops here exhibited nerve and persistency."[35]

It is probably true that most of the men would have preferred Logan as their permanent commander, but the success of July 28 satisfied them that Sherman had made no mistake in choosing Howard. Their new chief's "soldierly bearing impressed the soldiers," recalled W. J. Shelton of the 70th Ohio. As he walked toward the right, each regiment gave Howard three cheers, and Howard stopped now and then to chat with the troops. "Well, boys, I thought I had seen fighting before; but I never saw anything like this," he told members of the 55th Illinois. Upon noticing a wounded Confederate sergeant who had crawled close to the breastwork, he chided the men by saying, "You didn't let them get as near as this, did you?" He also noticed a line of Rebel dead and wounded in the swale that fronted the Union position and joked that "there's a line of battle in your front." When the men became alarmed, he cautioned them not to worry, for "it seems to be a very harmless line now."[36]

Howard made his way to the far right where members of the 32nd Ohio recalled his interactions with them. Will McLain of Company B reported that they had been instructed at the start of the action not to "leave the rifle-pits for ANY cause, while life lasts." Howard asked them, "'Boys, do you know what orders I sent you, this morning?' 'Aye, sir,' 'Well, have you left the pit?' 'Nary time!' 'Well,' said he, 'if this is the way the Army of the Tennessee fights, I don't wonder McPherson called you heroes; and I am well satisfied with my command.' We gave him three cheers, and he bowed and retired."[37]

In the immediate wake of his victory, and with the cheers of his men ringing in his ears, Howard got the idea to take the offensive. He later confessed that "my ambition stimulated me to put in fresh troops in order to sweep the field and make a bold and strong effort to capture Atlanta." But upon cooler reflection he realized that Logan's men were exhausted and the rest of his army had endured a stressful day. He had no truly fresh troops and knew the Atlanta defenses were very strong. Howard's "cooler judgment said, Let well enough alone." He merely instructed Logan to double his skirmishers and press the enemy as far away "as practicable, and then give to the commands rest and quiet for the night."[38]

Soon after the firing stopped, a few Federals were tempted to cross the breastwork and see the sights of the battlefield. They got more than they expected. The field of Ezra Church, freshly littered with thousands of dead and wounded, presented nothing but a feast of visual horror to the observer that evening. William Royal Oake, an English-born member of the 26th Iowa, essayed a tour of the field with his friend P. J. Potter. The pair counted twenty dead lying on a space of ground only twenty feet square and found five bodies lined up behind "an upturned stump of a tree." Oake also noticed a man frozen in instantaneous rigor mortis. He was "in a crouching position his shoulder resting against a small tree, his eyes wide open, but still in death." In his old age, Oake recalled vividly what he saw upon further investigation. "Old gray-haired men and boys in thirteens lie on every side while gaping wounds and bloated forms with blood and froth oozing from mouth and nose which were covered by thousands of flies was a sight that time can never efface."[39]

Most of Logan's men did not have the opportunity of touring the battlefield. They were busy improving their breastworks, serving on skirmish lines, or resting after the hot, frenzied work of the afternoon. More tools now became available, and the Federals put them to good use in digging earth and piling it onto the rails. They also now had the chance to go forward and cut brush directly in front of the line along Wangelin's sector, clearing a space at least fifty yards deep to provide an observable field of fire for the troops. Confederate artillery continued to throw rounds onto Howard's formations as supply wagons brought forward rations under the cover of dusk.[40]

A short distance south of Logan's position, Lee tried to put his exhausted troops into a defensive position. Featherston moved Loring's Division forward a short distance to better secure the Lick Skillet Road and instructed his brigade commanders to make breastworks. Brown, Clayton, and Quarles (who led Walthall's Division) formed to the right and left of Featherston. The Confederates remained there until dark, skirmishing with the Federals. Featherston reported that the blue-clad skirmishers made a serious attempt to advance on his division but were repulsed.[41]

There was only a little time now to retrieve as many wounded as possible from the field, but that opportunity was severely constricted by the aggressive Union skirmishing. Shoup instructed the Army of Tennessee's medical director to transport the injured "to the rear as rapidly as possible to-night." John H. Bass, a regimental surgeon in Gibson's Brigade, worked himself to a point of exhaustion in getting as many wounded off the field as possible before he "laid down completely worn out" at 1:00 A.M. Pioneer Hiram Smith Williams of Baker's Brigade in Clayton's Division was astonished by the number of movable and walking wounded he encountered near Lick

Skillet Road. "I can truthfully say that I never saw so many wounded men in the same length of time before."[42]

A good many of those wounded troops received treatment at medical posts located just off the battlefield. Chaplain James H. McNeilly of Quarles's Brigade assisted the surgeons at an aid station located "in a slight depression" and near some water. He had to kneel in order to avoid the stray bullets that sometimes sailed overhead. The purpose of this aid station was to patch up the wounded well enough to be transported to proper field hospitals. "One of the Junior Surgeons was examining a wounded man when a shot struck the man and killed him right under the physician's hands," McNeilly recalled. "With perfect coolness the doctor crawled a few steps to another sufferer and bound up his wounds." Some of the injured men still had their wits about them. When a surgeon McNeilly thought was six feet six inches tall appeared to help, "His efforts to squat low enough to escape the flying missiles were greeted even by the wounded with chaff. 'Pull that lightning rod down, he'll draw the lightning to us. Don't you hear the thunder?'"[43]

By dark, Hood gave up hope of implementing his plan to hold the Lick Skillet Road on July 28 and launch a flanking movement against Howard the next day. Lee's frenzied attacks had nullified the possibility of such a strike. Hood told Lee to evacuate his defensive position along Lick Skillet Road and take position at the Atlanta City Line late that night. Hood had in mind to extend that line down to East Point to protect the vital rail link between Atlanta and Macon. Beginning about 10:00 P.M., the Confederates pulled away from the vicinity of the battlefield. Featherston placed Loring's Division inside the Atlanta defenses where the Lick Skillet Road crossed the earthworks, and the other divisions established a new line heading toward the southwest and some distance from the railroad. The last Confederates did not retire from the Lick Skillet Road until about 3:00 A.M. of July 29.[44]

The night of July 28–29 produced some alarms for the Federals. With Rebel details collecting wounded, some Union skirmishers worried that an attack rather than an errand of mercy was under way. There were periodic outbursts of musketry that soon died down but led to disturbed rest for everyone, even if they did not kill or injure people. A man of the 55th Illinois was mortally wounded because he was walking from the skirmish line back to the main position on the ridge when such an outburst of firing took place. It was little more than "a foolish scare" according to the regimental historian. Even on parts of the line where these alarms did not occur, many Unionists could hear the entreaties of enemy wounded who were in areas inaccessible to Confederate details. "The night was dark and dreary, and it was everything else but pleasant to hear the groans and cries of the wounded and dying on the field," wrote Thomas Connelly of the 70th Ohio. Many Federals went out to bring in the badly wounded Confederates, often to see them die before morning.[45]

On the right of the Fifteenth Corps line, Charles E. Smith of the 32nd Ohio settled down for the night. He was told to sleep with his weapon handy. No fires were allowed. Smith ate "raw meat and cracker." His clothes had become soaked with sweat because of the heat and humidity of the afternoon. "Laid down and slept on the ground with wet clothes," Smith recalled. "We were tired and hungry and sleep was sweet."[46]

It was now time for preliminary reports of the battle to be circulated. Howard wrote to Sherman, giving Logan credit for bearing "the brunt of the battle." He seemed to be aware of the need to mollify Logan's bruised ego. "The assaults were pertinaciously kept up for four hours with scarcely any intermission," Howard continued, "and were invariably repulsed. The enemy's dead lie thickly on our front." Howard credited the slim breastwork for the fact that Logan lost so few men. Sherman relayed the bare facts to Halleck in Washington that night. He was unable to offer casualty figures but hoped to do so soon. All he could say was that Federal losses were small and Confederate casualties reportedly were large.[47]

But Sherman also mused on the larger implications of the day's action concerning his overall plans to enter Atlanta. The Rebel attacks had been handsomely repulsed, but they had indeed stopped his progress toward the railroad at East Point. The attacks indicated continued resolve to bar his southward progress, and the ground south of Logan's position was only dimly known to the Federals. Moreover, Sherman's big cavalry raid on that rail system had only just begun. Time alone would tell whether McCook and Stoneman might be able to snip the trail link between Macon and Atlanta. Sherman ordered Thomas to fire a couple of guns every fifteen minutes into Atlanta during the night, "partly for effect and partly as signal to our cavalry."[48]

CHAPTER NINE

The Bloody Effects of That Half Day's Work
The Battlefield

The morning of July 29 began with cool air and a clear, blue sky. It did not remain pleasant for long. By midmorning the temperature rose, and the sun began to burn brightly, making life in the field uncomfortable. Intermittent showers, typical of the South in midsummer, arrived by the afternoon.[1]

Most Federals had ample time and opportunity to walk across the field of battle and see the sights. Although the Confederates had removed many of their wounded, the ground was still littered with the fallen on the morning of July 29. They lay thicker between the Union skirmish line and Logan's main position on the ridge, for the Rebels had no opportunity to retrieve them from that area.

The historian of the 55th Illinois in Smith's division remembered with a chill the sights of the battlefield. Bits of abandoned clothing littered the ground and "dark spots of clotted blood" marked the places where men had bled for some time before crawling away. Wherever there was a stump, one or two bodies lay behind it, the remains of men who had vainly sought shelter from the rain of balls. "Along the fence the rebels lay in a windrow, in some places two or three piled across each other," continued the historian. The small stream across the field named Dead Brook by newspaper correspondents was discolored by blood. It was the only source of water for many wounded men who could not make it to the rear, and some died as they drank, their bodies still lining the banks. Elsewhere on the field the dead often seemed to have been shot down almost at the same time, for they were piled up and in rows. George Hildt of the 30th Ohio found a Confederate "who had his head cut open by a saber, a long distance in front of the works." His comrades concluded the man had attempted to run away and was killed by an angry officer.[2]

When members of Harrow's division ventured beyond the breastworks, they also saw remarkable sights. The pine trees in front of their position were scarred by hundreds of bullets, and the smaller ones were literally cut down by the musketry. Reuben Williams found a private monument that a local farmer had erected in memory of his son, who had been killed at the battle of First Manassas. "The monument was bespattered by the marks of bullets from both sides," he noted. The dead lay in windrows along Harrow's front, as they did along the right flank of Woods's division. Abraham J. Seay of the 32nd Missouri walked across the field that morning and encountered "the most fearful slaughter I ever witnessed. The enemy lay dead in solid lines, many in a shooting posture."[3]

Charles Dana Miller of the 76th Ohio found the sights on the field to be "perfectly awful." He stood on one spot and counted 42 bodies; upon moving to a second spot, 103 bodies were visible, including that of Lieut. Col. Thomas Shields of the 30th Louisiana. The growth of underbrush fronting the angle in Logan's line was "perfectly riddled with bullets," according to Miller. A good deal of sassafras grew in the area, and bullets had so nicked and scarred it that the smell issuing from the bark mixed with the odor of decaying flesh to produce "a sickening sensation that I shall never forget." Spent balls littered the battlefield. Bodies were lined up along the fence held by Clayton's Division after its repulse, and blood seemed to spot the battlefield almost everywhere. William Royal Oake of the 26th Iowa found some cattle trails across the open ground. Shallow depressions in those ruts were filled with human blood.[4]

Sixteenth and Seventeenth Corps troops discovered similar sights when they wandered south to see the battlefield. "In some places it looked like a line just wilted down," commented Ephraim L. Girdner of the 66th Indiana when he saw the dead lying in rows. Morgan's Fourteenth Corps men awoke in the swamp after their long, tedious march of the day before to walk across the field as well. They were struck by the number of dead, the destruction to the vegetation, and the immensity of the firing that had wrought such havoc on men and the environment. It was a sickening sight, "the most awful slaughter I ever saw or heard tell of," wrote Albert L. Slack of the 121st Ohio.[5]

Ward moved his division from the Twentieth Corps sector north of Atlanta toward Logan's right flank on July 29. Upon arrival, his men gained an opportunity to view the field before it was cleaned up. They saw a good many graves already finished by late afternoon, but still more bodies littering the ground. The sight of dead lying in rows saddened many, even though they were mortal enemies, but Asst. Surgeon George Martin Trowbridge of the 19th Michigan wasted no sentiments on them. "It did me good to see some [Confederates] who could give no more trouble to us."[6]

By late afternoon, the dead presented a worse appearance than early in the morning. Flies now swarmed around the decaying flesh, and maggots began to appear on the bodies. Philo Beecher Buckingham, who commanded the 20th Connecticut in Ward's division, spared nothing in describing the view to his wife. He initially encountered 400 bodies lined up in two rows before burial, "with their faces all turned black & fly blown, . . . and it was the most disgusting & horrible sight I ever saw. I then passed over the fields & through the woods where they had advanced and found a great many dead that had not yet been gathered up & some wounded. Over the fields were strewn muskets, cartridge boxes, blankets, knapsacks, haversacks, coats all bloody as they were taken off their wounded owners, almost innumerable." Buckingham found the site of a Confederate field hospital, and "it looked as if it had been a Slaughter house," with a row of graves nearby to indicate how many had died.[7]

Generals and staff members could not resist the temptation to see the field before it was cleared of dead, wounded, and battle debris. George H. Thomas had a good excuse for doing so, given that one of his divisions was near the field and another was on its way there. He admired the defensive position Howard had assumed and saw the burial process underway. Clerks and staff officers from Sherman's, Corse's, and Blair's headquarters visited the field and reported their stunned reactions. Lieut. Col. John W. Barlow, an engineer officer on the Seventeenth Corps staff, believed he could have walked along a line of dead Rebels lying so close to each other that his foot would not have touched the ground. "Oh God! It was awful to see that 'line of battle,' dead," wrote John J. Safely who served on a brigade level staff in Blair's corps.[8]

Even though he rode his horse across the field on the morning of July 29, James A. Connolly of Baird's division staff found that the dead were beginning to decompose. "I rode over a space about 400 yards long by about 75 yards in width," Connolly informed his wife, "and in that area scanned the faces of 225 dead rebels, and then had not seen more than one-third of those who lay there." Death had reduced everyone to the same rank,

Connolly observed upon seeing the large number of colonels, majors, and captains lying on the ground.[9]

A few civilians were present to share the sights of the battlefield with combatants. William Salter, a U.S. Christian Commission worker, accompanied Corse when the division leader visited the field. Salter thought the place presented a "revolting scene." He counted about thirty bodies "lying close to each other & within 40 feet of our works. They had literally been mowed down." A minister named Washington L. Midler, who worked with officers recruiting black troops in the Western Theater, happened to be with the armies during the Atlanta campaign. He "walked among the slain and the bullet mowed bushes and torn trees and beheld the awful scene of yesterdays conflict with feelings of sadness[.] Saw rows of dead rebels rotting in the sun some of them quite black already."[10]

Q.P.F., who wrote for the *Cincinnati Commercial*, provided a poignant description of the battlefield. He wanted to see "the bloody effects of that half day's work" and passed by the rivulet where many had crawled for water and died in the stream. He counted ten bodies behind the fence that lay within a space only five yards wide and deep. One Confederate clutched "a bunch of dry leaves" in his hand with which he had vainly tried to stop the flow of blood from his open wound. All across the gory field Q.P.F. saw the faces of the dead. They exhibited "all the attitudes of fierce despair, of agony, or placid repose, and some, even, with a pleasant smile upon their upturned faces."[11]

The Federals had a huge task in cleaning up the battlefield. They began to bury the dead early on July 29, using the pioneers who were attached to every brigade and division in Sherman's army group. While many of those pioneers were troops detached from regiments, many others were black men hired by the government. The pioneers performed a wide variety of labor in camp and on the march to facilitate the operations of the army, and that included burial of the dead.[12]

The fact that much of the burial duty was performed by African Americans seemed appropriate to some Federals. Judson Austin noted with satisfaction that they were "covering up a lot of their dead masters." But observers also noted that the blacks tended to do a quick and imperfect job of it. "The nigs just shoveled the dirt onto them wherever they found one," continued Austin, "& that saved diging holes. Whare they lay dead clost together the nigs would roll one over into the hole that he dug to cover the first one & keep on diging in that way. I tell you Sarah these southern states are getting to be one vast burreing ground." Even when digging one large burial trench the blacks tended to pile in the bodies until they were "considerably above ground," according to Reuben Williams. The brigade commander thought it was fortunate that Sherman had a number of black workers available because whites could not stand such heavy labor in hot, humid conditions.[13]

But white soldiers detailed to the burial squads also tried to do a quick job of their work. It was understandable given the large number of bodies and the overpowering stench of rotting flesh. On some parts of the field, that meant they spent little effort to inter their fallen enemy. Samuel Black of the 1st Iowa Battery claimed that the pioneers merely lined up the bodies in rows and then threw "a light covering of dirt" over them. This soon was washed away, "leaving a gruesome and horrid sight." Black thought it was wrong of his comrades to deal with the task in such a "slighting manner."[14]

As Black indicated, some burial details decided that a quick covering to reduce the stench was better than nothing at all. Many other observers, however, reported that other burial details took the time and effort to properly inter the Confederate dead. They decided to dig mass graves, given the number of bodies that lay close together on a comparatively small battlefield. These mass graves were dug only about three feet deep, but they were wide enough to admit of two bodies side by side. This method allowed the Federals to avoid deep digging and yet have a hole large enough to accommodate many of the dead that lay nearby.[15]

Thomas Connelly of the 70th Ohio claimed that up to 300 bodies were buried in one mass grave, but many other observers and participants in the burial process reported the number in each grave as much lower. On the sector controlled by Martin's brigade of Smith's division, two graves were dug; 52 bodies were placed in one, while 57 were laid in the other. William Royal Oake of the 26th Iowa helped to bury 75 Rebels in one hole and 36 in another grave. Discounting Connelly's dubious estimate of 300 bodies, the highest number of men interred in one spot was 90.[16]

For some of the Federals, massing the remains of their enemy in shallow holes seemed poor respect for the bravery displayed by Lee's troops. "It looked hard to bury these soldiers—friend or foe—just like we bury animals, but this was all we could do," wrote Thomas Connelly. The increasingly bad condition of the bodies surely buffered sensibilities and made the burial details look upon their task as one to finish quickly. By the afternoon the appearance of the corpses and the odor emanating from them became "horrible in the extreme," reported Chaplain M. D. Gage of the 12th Indiana. He recalled for the rest of his life "the blackened and bloated forms of officers, of all ranks," arranged in rows awaiting their turn to be rolled into the pit. William Martin of the 11th Iowa, a Seventeenth Corps regiment, wasted no sentiment on the fallen enemy. He wrote of burying the dead at Ezra Church with the callous phrase, "we covered them like cabbage."[17]

But at least one fallen enemy received special treatment. James Connolly noticed that the lid of a hardtack box served as the head board to mark the grave of a Confederate officer who had been shot near the Union line. On it, written in pencil, were the words "Capt. Sharp, 10th Miss., Buried by the 35th N.J. Vols. I know that he will arise again." Also appearing on the cracker lid was a penciled representation of "the Masonic 'square and compass.'"[18]

Given the large number of dead on the field, many Federals were keen to know how many lay along the front of their units. On the sector held by the 116th Illinois of Martin's brigade, the number was 85, while 86 bodies were counted in front of the 70th Ohio and 31 before the 99th Indiana, both of Harrow's division. Williams's brigade gathered up 169 bodies along its line, and Wangelin reported the burial of 72 Confederates along the right wing of his brigade in Woods's division. The estimates of dead lying along Morgan L. Smith's division sector ranged from 230 to 320.[19]

Despite exaggerated reports that more than 2,400 bodies were buried on July 29, the true number was large enough. Logan told Howard's headquarters that his men had interred 565 Confederates by the end of the day, and they estimated that about 200 were left. Sherman pointed out that some bodies were buried by men not belonging to the detailed burial squads and thus were not counted. Some Federals took the time to examine the dead before placing them in graves and counted upwards of forty bullet marks on some. These were Rebels shot near the Union line; their bodies were hit numerous times in the hail of bullets issuing from the breastworks.[20]

There were far fewer Union dead to be interred on July 29. They also were buried on the field, although very little information is available to indicate where and how that was done. Capt. J. F. Summers of the 70th Ohio, mortally wounded in the fight, was buried "on the field" when he passed away. After the war, family members removed his body to Ohio.[21]

Some of the Confederate dead were in friendly hands and received loving burial. Philip Daingerfield Stephenson, a gunner in the Fifth Company of the Washington Artillery, lost a friend and schoolmate in Lieut. Ashton Johnson, who was killed on July 28 while serving on Quarles's staff. His body was recovered and taken well to the rear of the Confederate position late on the night of July 28–29. Stephenson took personal charge of the burial, selecting a site 100 yards behind his battery and "just behind a little out house of a large brick house." He erected a headboard and a rail fence around the grave. It was easy for Johnson's parents to locate the grave after the war, and "they never ceased to express their gratitude to me for years after for having done this simple thing."[22]

But for the overwhelming majority of the Rebel dead, there was no opportunity for loving parents, wives, or friends to grieve over the burial plot. They were placed in massed graves where their identity was rolled into that of every other Rebel killed at Ezra Church. All that could be done was to inform the family of their fate. John A. Harris of the 19th Louisiana in Gibson's Brigade left behind a wife who never knew where her husband's body lay. A friend and comrade of Harris informed her of his death; the letter today is so badly fragmented and deteriorated that is impossible even to decipher his name. Harris was shot and then passed away "a very few moments" later, the friend informed Rebecca. "Your husband died a true patriot and good soldier. And angels have caught up his Spirit and carried it to a land of rest where there is no war nor troubles to molest."[23]

Perhaps the unidentified friend was right; the dead had no more troubles. But those who were wounded at Ezra Church faced an uncertain future of pain, worry, and suffering. Logan's medical director, Surg. John Moore, reported handling 540 wounded Federals at Fifteenth Corps division hospitals. Those hospitals were initially located within a half mile of the Union line but later were moved farther north to escape Confederate artillery fire. On July 31, Moore moved the wounded to corps hospitals located at Marietta. They had to be transported by ambulance twenty-eight miles, one trip after another, wearing out teams and drivers alike. Ambulance driver George P. Metz of the 99th Indiana thought the wounded fared well. Most of them seemed to have relatively slight injuries, although some of them lost limbs because of their wounds.[24]

Those Federals who were badly injured had to be left behind in the field hospitals near the battlefield when the rest were transported to Marietta. Washington L. Midler organized medical supplies from three different agencies (the Western Sanitary Commission, the Indiana Sanitary Medical Purveyor's Office, and the U.S. Christian Commission) and loaded them into three ambulances. He took the material south and found the men in uncomfortable conditions on July 30. Rain had made a sloppy mess of the ground in and around the field hospitals. Midler's supplies were inadequate to meet the needs of these men, so he volunteered to go back to Marietta for more. Midler had also discovered an old friend among the wounded at the field hospital, Capt. Frank Farrell of the 48th Illinois, who had been injured in the arm. He took Farrell along with him to Marietta where he placed him comfortably in a house controlled by the U.S. Christian Commission. Mary Ann Bickerdyke, among other volunteers, was there to help the wounded housed in the building.[25]

When Midler returned to the field hospitals near Ezra Church on August 1, he found the wounded even more uncomfortable. They were "now lying on the ground and badly wounded and amputated cases on sticks and boards on leaves and blankets under them." Thomas Connelly reported that two men of the 70th Ohio who had been shot in the face and mouth lingered in the field hospitals until "maggots were found to be working in their mouths." They were among the last to be removed to Marietta before the field hospitals were completely dismantled.[26]

Soon after the war Surgeon Moore shared his medical records with the U.S. Sanitary Commission, and they provide a wealth of information about the treatment of wounded Fifteenth Corps troops at Ezra Church. According to his revised accounting, Moore treated 322 men for miscellaneous wounds. That was nearly as many as he treated for wounds suffered in the big battle of July 22 east of Atlanta, where Fifteenth Corps hospitals accommodated 381 men. Of the Ezra Church wounded, 208 out of 322 (or 64.5 percent) were wounded in the upper part of the body, probably due to the fact that the Federals fought from behind breastworks. A total of 272 of the wounded received simple dressings for their injuries, indicating that for 85 percent of the wounded their battlefield wounds were comparatively slight. Twenty-four men endured amputation of limbs or fingers, amounting to only .07 percent of the wounded. Surgeons extracted balls from only 17 men, or .05 percent of the wounded, and a complex dressing was administered to only 1 man out of the 320 whose dressings were reported.[27]

Moore's surgeons also reported the type of missile or weapon that caused these injuries. Conoidal balls accounted for 301 (or 95.2 percent) of the wounds. Artillery shelling caused 8 of the wounds, and the surgeons found only 1 man injured by a bayonet. That fact, however, indicates that some hand-to-hand combat took place at Ezra Church. Pvt. Allen Dodd of the 70th Ohio suffered the bayonet wound on the "left side face, front of ear." Pvt. John Shaw of the 90th Illinois was injured when his rifle musket barrel burst, probably due to fouling by powder residue. It lacerated his hand, and Shaw was lucky that the injury was not more severe.[28]

Three men suffered tears in the palm of their hand from ramming down the ramrod too vigorously. This injury testified to the frenzied, rapid firing some Federals engaged in when the Confederates pressed dangerously close to their line. These three Unionists were Pvt. Patrick Judge of the 26th Illinois, Pvt. John Hampton of the 57th Ohio, and Serg. Erastus Laphan of the 111th Illinois. The surgeon typically described the injuries as puncture wounds of the right hand, or "slight wd. palm of hand" in Judge's case. One man, Pvt. Phillip Kensler of the 47th Ohio, suffered an injury from canister, and another, Pvt. William M. Smith of the 53rd Ohio, from buckshot. The former probably was on the skirmish line close enough to a Rebel battery to make canister fire dangerous. The latter injury indicates that someone in gray must have been armed with a shotgun, perhaps one of Armstrong's cavalrymen during the skirmishing phase of the battle on July 28.[29]

Surgeon Moore reported the case of one man who refused to have his leg amputated. Pvt. John Driskell of the 90th Illinois suffered badly when a ball smashed into his right knee. It literally opened up the knee joint and fractured bones, but Driskell resisted amputation. Nelson Hempleman of the 70th Ohio allowed surgeons to take off his leg; in fact, the stump was further reduced in a second operation, but Hempleman died under the knife.[30]

Climatic conditions also produced casualties at Ezra Church. Several Federal soldiers succumbed to heat exhaustion, and reportedly a handful of them died as a result. Thomas Connelly identified John McMillen of Company B, 70th Ohio, as one such victim. According to Connelly, McMillen was overcome by the heat and humidity during the battle and "died instantly."[31]

Ezra Church was an impressive victory for the Federals, and they suffered comparatively light casualties, but the deaths of loved ones and friends hit home sharply. Capt. Albert Affleck of the 12th Missouri was shot through both thighs and died August 4, only nine days before he was due to be mustered out at the end of the regiment's three-year service. His relatives in Belleville, Illinois, were uncertain of his fate until the newspapers confirmed his death on August 19. The body was shipped home for services, arriving six days later. Belleville honored Affleck's sacrifice by placing his remains in state in the county courthouse before interment.[32]

Affleck's death greatly affected his friend and fellow officer, Capt. Henry A. Kircher, who was still recuperating from losing an arm and a leg at the battle of Ringgold, Georgia, on November 27, 1863. The last letter Affleck wrote to Kircher was dated July 26, only two days before the battle at Ezra Church. "I shall be glad to get home as soon as possible after this

Campaign is over," Affleck admitted, "for I feel worn out and tired[.] I need rest and good living for a time, and then I shall be ready to go into service again if I am needed." When the twenty-two-year-old Kircher learned of his friend's death, he scribbled a note on the back of Affleck's letter. "So one by one all my friends are droping off to live in a better world than this, O Will we ever mete again?"[33]

Maj. Philip H. Murphy of the 29th Missouri had been badly wounded at the height of Toulmin's attack on the angle, but he lived for some time with his terrible injury. He was shot through the chest, the bullet passing through his lungs and exiting from his back. Despite the horrible damage, Murphy seemed to be "doing very well" on July 30. David Allan visited the officer and "found him resting easy." The wound caused great pain, but Murphy bore it and kept up a brave front. He was discharged from the army and returned to St. Louis where he had a wife and two young sons. Murphy fathered three more children before he died because of the lingering effects of his Ezra Church wound on June 28, 1872. His wife Anastatia passed away owing to "effusion of the brain" three years later, leaving his three sons and two daughters orphans.[34]

Like Murphy, the Federal wounded received generally good care in the aftermath of Ezra Church, but Federal surgeons also helped Confederate wounded who were left behind on the field. Ambulance drivers transported them to Marietta when Fifteenth Corps field hospitals were dismantled near Ezra Church. Moore reported treating eighty Confederates in his hospital system by midnight of July 28, representing 44.6 percent of the total number of prisoners that Logan took as a result of the battle. It was not true that "our Hospitals are filled with the Reble wounded five to our one," as a member of the 57th Ohio reported home, but the presence of gray-clad patients in these hospitals must have impressed Federal observers. A few of them were high-ranking regimental officers.[35]

An unidentified member of the 31st Iowa was detailed to bring in the wounded Rebels who littered the field on July 29. He also wandered about a field hospital located at a small house where these captives were treated. "Saw five legs on One pile and other pile close to [it] four legs and 3 arms," the Missourian reported. When he walked onto the porch of the house, the Federal surgeon "was trying to Opperate on a poor fellows leg that had been shattered by a musket ball the Dr wanted me to hold it could not see it." He later helped to carry wounded Confederates under the shade of trees. "They say they could not avoid the Shot they came so close," the unidentified Yankee reported.[36]

Confederate surgeons had thousands of their own wounded men to care for, and their individual stories told volumes about the experience of being wounded at Ezra Church. Lieut. Col. C. Irvine Walker of the 10th South Carolina had been shot in the neck "severely but not dangerously" soon after he had taken the regimental flag away from Stephen Lee. Shot at about 4:00 P.M., Walker was transported from the field and to the railroad station at Atlanta along with many other wounded Rebels. He was sent to Vineville, a suburb of Macon, for several days before his wound allowed him to go home to Columbia, South Carolina.[37]

At Clayton's division hospital, close to the battlefield, staff officer Taylor Beatty saw what happened to his former comrades of the 1st Louisiana (Regulars) in Gibson's Brigade. "Found [Capt. Charles H.] Tew & [Capt. James C.] Stafford badly wounded in side—[Maj. S. S.] Batchelor in groin. . . . [Lieut. Louis] West is wounded in shoulder but has gone off. Poor [Lieut. M. C.] Gladden was dead when I got there—had just died—he was shot through both legs." Beatty took on the responsibility of burying Gladden in "a good coffin" that evening.[38]

Lieut. Emmett Ross of the 20th Louisiana in Gibson's Brigade was "very severely wounded" on July 28. "I was struck in the left Knee by a minie ball causing a very painful and ugly wound," he informed his fiancée. Ross's men carried him to the division hospital, where the wound was dressed. Attendants then transported him to the railroad depot by wagon on the night of July 28. The McCook-Stoneman raid against Hood's rail line disrupted Confederate logistics. When Ross set out in the cars for Macon, the train had to return to Atlanta because of the Federal cavalry. He and hundreds of other wounded men were compelled to stay on the cars "all day in the hot sun and suffered a great deal" on July 29, even though the local relief committee was "very kind to us."[39]

Ross and the others in his group were able to leave Atlanta on July 30. They again "stuck" at Jonesboro only a few miles south because the track had been torn up below that place. "This little town is crowded with wounded soldiers," Ross told Mary, "I never saw the like before." The women of Jonesboro did everything they could to help the suffering men. When he was taken to the hotel in Jonesboro, Ross still carried the Federal bullet that had wrecked his knee. Here a local physician treated his wound without charge and procured a pair of crutches for the ailing lieutenant.[40]

Finally, the train of wounded men left Jonesboro early on the morning of August 1 and reached Macon late that evening, where Ross took a bed in the City Hall Hospital. His wound continued to pain him a great deal after the ball was extracted, but the ladies of Macon visited the hospital with refreshments to ease the suffering of the troops. Joseph E. Johnston had lived with his wife in Macon since being relieved from command of the Army of Tennessee and he visited the hospital on the afternoon of August 2. According to Ross, Johnston "conversed with each wounded man" while there. It was not until August 3 that Ross had a chance to have his dirty and bloodied clothes washed, and he applied for a furlough as well. He left Macon on August 5 and was transported home where his wound began to improve.[41]

Of course, wounded officers had many advantages over injured enlisted men. Both Walker and Ross went home to recuperate, and attending physicians tended to devote a bit more attention to officers when making their rounds. For the enlisted men shot down on the field of Ezra Church (and they, of course, represented the overwhelming majority of Rebel wounded), medical care tended to be more quick and harried. Their individual experiences were submerged in the sea of commonality, and they became a name on a scribbled chart or a number buried within a report.

Orderly Sergeant James Marston of the 4th Louisiana rose above the commonality a bit because his wound happened to be particularly interesting to assistant surgeon Joseph M. Craig. Marston received a bullet on July 28 that literally created a hole in his forehead. Even so, Marston could walk, so Craig sent him to the field hospital. Marston eventually was transported to West Point, Georgia, and Craig found him there a few days later, "in a decided epileptic fit. I gave chloroform and reduced the convulsion, and he wrote on a paper asking me if he was always to be unable to talk. I assured him he would get over it." Whether Marston really recovered the ability to speak was not reported, but he received a medical discharge from the Confederate army and died four years later after carrying the bullet in his head for the rest of his life.[42]

Both Union and Confederate commanders wrestled with the sometimes difficult task of tabulating troop strength and casualties soon after the battle ended. The number of Federals engaged in the battle has been estimated by historians as 11,000 to more than 13,000. My own estimate is based on the fact that six Fifteenth Corps brigades were involved in repelling the attack, and an additional number of regiments arrived from the Sixteenth and Seventeenth Corps to amount to two brigades. Toulmin reported that Johnston's Brigade of Brown's Division took 1,143 troops into action on July 28. If that is about average for the ten Confederate brigades that took part in the battle of Ezra Church, then Lee and Stewart had

11,430 men in action. The historian of the 55th Illinois reported after the war that 180 men fought in the ranks of that regiment at Ezra Church. If we use that as an average, Martin's brigade of Morgan L. Smith's division had 1,080 men in action, and there were 8,640 Yankees in the battle. But if we use the same average indicated for Toulmin's Confederate brigade (1,143 men), the total number of Federals engaged at Ezra Church amounted to 9,144.[43]

Logan reported losing 562 men on July 28 (50 killed, 439 wounded, and 73 missing). About 70 men from the Sixteenth and Seventeenth Corps troops involved in the battle were lost as well, bringing total Union casualties to 632 or 6.9 percent of those engaged.[44]

Circulars went out to unit commanders in Lee's and Stewart's Corps on July 30 to report losses, but not all officers followed through with that directive. Inadequate data hampers the historian's effort to pin down Confederate losses. While the total has been variously reported as high as 5,000, the most authoritative estimate places Confederate casualties at 3,000 or 26.2 percent of the number engaged. Brown reported losing 807 men, while Walthall placed the losses in his division at 1,152 troops, well over one-third of the number engaged. Jacob Sharp listed 214 losses out of 1,020 men engaged, or a loss ratio of 20.9 percent. With 269 casualties, the loss ratio in Johnston's Brigade reached 23.5 percent. Manigault lost 170 men while Quarles suffered 514 casualties. Losses among the Confederate cavalrymen who skirmished with Logan during the morning of July 28 amounted to about 50 or 60 men.[45]

The Federals took in a relatively small number of Confederate prisoners. Sherman reported that "a few of the rebel officers and men reached our line of rail piles only to be killed or hauled over as prisoners." Logan's report bore that out. He counted 106 prisoners of war in addition to 73 wounded Confederates who were picked up off the battlefield after the engagement. According to Thomas Connelly of the 70th Ohio, many of those prisoners were afraid of the Yankees. They pleaded for their lives and told their captors that "they had been led to believe that the Yankees had no regard for the rules of civilized warfare, and would murder them as soon as captured." According to Connelly, this view went so far that some of the more ignorant Southerners believed the Northerners wore horns and "belonged to some part of the animal kingdom." These men were surprised to find their counterparts in blue treated them decently and "walked and talked just like they did."[46]

Abandoned equipment littered the field after the battle. Logan's men picked up between 1,500 and 2,000 small arms from the bloodied ground, dropped not only by killed and wounded Confederates but to some degree by men who had scampered away from danger. Members of the 116th Illinois found 185 guns on their sector of the battlefield.[47]

Harrow's division secured five Confederate flags, abandoned by disabled Rebel color-bearers. As a writer for the *New York Daily Tribune* put it, some of the enemy standards were "manufactured of elegant silk, with the name of the regiment beautifully wrought in colors."[48]

Union soldiers who wandered about the field on July 29 picked up souvenirs as well as replacement equipment, shoes, and clothing from the dead. Samuel Black of the 1st Iowa Battery "cut a little hickory stick to carry home as a relic to my father for a walking cane or staff." The stick had marks of eighteen bullets on it, according to Black. Capt. J. F. Wintrode of the 76th Ohio needed a different pair of boots desperately enough to scavenge the field before all Rebel dead were buried. He found a pair of decent boots near a Confederate officer and wondered why they were off his feet. When Wintrode showed the boots to acquaintances in the regiment, a Federal private recognized them. He had already taken the Confederate officer's boots and left his own behind. "It was a good joke on Wintrode," recalled Charles Dana Miller, "yet he was satisfied with the exchange."[49]

Three Union soldiers received the Medal of Honor for deeds performed at Ezra Church. Pvt. Harry Davis of the 46th Ohio retrieved the flag of the 30th Louisiana and was recognized for bringing it in. Serg. Ernst Torgler of the 37th Ohio rescued a wounded officer, and Musician Robinson B. Murphy of the 127th Illinois led two regiments to the line as reinforcement, having his horse shot from under him in the process. Murphy had been detailed as an orderly and thus had an opportunity to do this task. He reportedly was only fifteen years old at the time.[50]

Enough for One or Two More Killings
Evaluating Ezra Church

For some time following the battle of Ezra Church, participants and observers tried to make sense of it. They evaluated their own conduct, assessed the actions of their enemy, and judged how well their commanders had conducted themselves. They also spread rumors and listened to official reports issued by the generals that contained accurate news of the engagement. Ezra Church was the third effort by Hood to stop Sherman's attempt to snip Confederate rail lines into the city. After ten days, it was time to evaluate his performance and wonder about his future prospects.

Federal generals reacted to the battle near the Lick Skillet Road with unrestrained praise for their officers and the rank and file. "I never saw better conduct in battle," wrote Oliver Otis Howard on July 29. Logan praised his Fifteenth Corps troops by noting that the desperate battle took place with little in the way of fieldworks and what he perceived as fewer troops than the attacking Confederates. Yet his officers and men "could not have displayed more courage nor determination not to yield. Had they shown less, they would have been driven from their position." William Harrow had seen a lot of action in the East. His division of the Second Corps of the Army of the Potomac had helped to repel Pickett's Charge at Gettysburg. Yet he highly praised his Fourth Division of the Fifteenth Corps for what the men did on July 28. It was "the most distinguished exhibition of courage that I have witnessed during three years of active service," he wrote. For the fight at Ezra Church alone, Harrow believed the men of the Fifteenth Corps deserved "the lasting gratitude of their country."[1]

Brigade and regimental officers were even more effusive in their praise for the rank and file. George Hildt pointed out that the slim pile of rails offered scant protection; many men were hit as low as the knee, indicating that for some regiments the breastworks were so low as to be less significant in repelling the enemy than determination and stubbornness. "Officers and men seemed to have but one thought," wrote Lieut. Col. Frederick S. Hutchinson of the 15th Michigan, "to die before falling back." Capt. Louis Love wrote the ultimate encomium for the 70th Ohio, which had been one of the most hard-pressed Union regiments on the field. "I would like to mention every man who distinguished himself on that day, but it would be too lengthy; it embraces the muster-rolls of the entire regiment."[2]

The enlisted men of Logan's corps felt the heady sense of victory in the days following the battle. They often expressed it with immense pride in their outfit. Stories circulated that Rebel prisoners were surprised and mortified to find that they had been trying to shove the Fifteenth Corps off that shallow ridge, for Sherman's old command from the days of Vicksburg seemed to be everywhere and unmovable. According to the historian of the 55th Illinois, one Confederate prisoner spread the story that his general "told us the Fifteenth Corps had bragged long enough that they had never been whipped, and that today he would drive you to the river or hell before supper." Whether such stories were true is less important than that they were readily believed by the Federals. The stories added spice to the obvious victory Fifteenth Corps troops had achieved that afternoon. It was easy to understand why one of Logan's men felt "proud to say that he belonged to the old 15th Corps."[3]

Of all the stories that circulated through Federal ranks, none caught the imagination of the victors more readily than that expressed by the quote "Enough for one or two more killings." Some Federals insisted that this comment was made by a captured Confederate soldier, but others indicated that Rebel pickets made it in conversations with their Yankee counterparts. In fact, Fourteenth Corps division commander Richard W. Johnson claimed that he personally heard a Union picket call out to the other side, "'Johnnie, how many men have you got left?' He replied, 'Enough for one or two more killings.'" Capt. Hartwell Osborn of the 55th Ohio in the Twentieth Corps also claimed to have personally heard a Rebel picket make this comment. James Miller Wysor of the 54th Virginia in Stevenson's Division of Lee's Corps reported that the men of Brown's Division were the ones who started the saying, based on their heavy losses at Ezra Church. Grenville Dodge heard that John C. Brown himself started it by calling Ezra Church "a killing instead of a battle."[4]

In fact, this telling comment on the futility of Hood's aggressive tactics was made by many Confederate soldiers along the lines at Atlanta. "This was a severe judgment on the reckless efforts of their new commander," wrote Henry Aten of the 85th Illinois, "and especially severe when coming from men whose fighting qualities were unexcelled." The Confederates were aware that "these charges don't pay," as Capt. Jay Butler of the 101st Ohio put it. In fact, Sixteenth Corps brigade commander Robert Adams described the killing on July 28 in terms commensurate with the Confederate view of the affair, writing that the Rebels "were cut down like sheep in a slaughter pen." The demoralization of Confederate troops, as interpreted by the Federals, was exemplified by Henry H. Maley of the 84th Illinois, who told his parents that "the dezerters say there is Just enough left to make a nother charge and when the officers git drunk a gain they will mak a nother and then muck under."[5]

Most Confederates clearly recognized the magnitude of their defeat at Ezra Church, a battle that proved to be pivotal in Howard's career as a soldier. It was his first engagement as commander of the Army of the Tennessee. Howard had to take over an army of strangers while it was on the move into dangerous territory, deploy it in a way to be ready for battle, and react to whatever developed. He did so with consummate ability and laid the foundation for the defensive victory his men achieved on July 28. Howard offered immense praise for his men and felt sorry for the Confederates who had been "rushed into the fight without mercy" and who now lay "in great numbers in our front," as he told his wife on July 29. Yet, despite the thrill of this "exciting day," Howard admitted that "I had my fill of battle that day."[6]

Howard was keenly aware that his appointment deeply affected Logan, and he went out of his way to praise the commander of the Fifteenth Corps for the victory of July 28. Although "ill and much worn," Logan perked up when the fighting started. His old energy and spirit returned. Howard endorsed Logan's initial report of the battle by claiming that "the success of the day is as much attributable to him as to any one man." In this Howard was not being overly generous, for Logan really did play an important role in inspiring his men to fight, shifting reinforcements where needed, and maintaining his line against great pressure all afternoon. Howard also gave Logan full credit when he wrote his official report of the campaign in September, but Logan pointedly refused to mention Howard in his own reports, holding a grudge against both Howard and Sherman for the rest of his life. Instead, Logan praised Dodge and Blair for sending reinforcements to his aid at opportune moments, ignoring the fact that those Sixteenth and Seventeenth Corps units came to him as a result of Howard's orders, not his own.[7]

The success on July 28 sealed Howard's future as commander of Grant's and Sherman's old army. If anyone had any doubt about his ability to fill McPherson's shoes, they gave them up by the time the fighting ended at Ezra Church. "Major Genl Howard is rapidly becoming a great favorite with his command," wrote Mortimer D. Leggett, one of Blair's division commanders. "He almost excels McPherson in his kind, gentlemanly, affable manner, and his skill and personal bravery manifested in the battle of the 28th ult won the admiration of all who saw him." Robert Adams in the Sixteenth Corps fully agreed with Leggett's assessment.[8]

Sherman had every reason to rejoice that Howard was received well by his new command, for he had encountered significant trouble in choosing him to replace McPherson. "Yesterday's work justified my choice," Sherman told his wife on July 29, "for Howards dispositions and manner Elicited the shouts of my old Corps, and he at once stepped into the Shoes of McPherson and myself." In writing to Schofield, or to Washington, or in his memoirs, Sherman repeated the story of Howard's walk along the line near the end of the battle to show his men their new commander and bond with them under fire. The fact that the troops responded well to his presence confirmed that all was well with the Army of the Tennessee and its new general. "I have now Thomas, Schofield & Howard," Sherman concluded in his letter to Ellen, "all tried & approved soldiers."[9]

Two days after the battle of Ezra Church, the War Department in Washington issued General Orders No. 238, officially assigning Howard to command the Department and Army of the Tennessee. It also assigned Henry W. Slocum to replace Hooker as commander of the Twentieth Corps and named David S. Stanley to replace Howard as commander of the Fourth Corps.[10]

"I did not seek the field-command which McPherson had vacated," Howard told the Society of the Army of the Tennessee in 1894. "No friends pressed my name upon General Sherman and so it was, is, and ever will be a special gratification to my military pride that I was selected for the high position." Howard had felt pressure ever since he took over the army on July 27. McPherson's friends did not believe he could fill the great man's shoes. Logan's friends were bitter, and there was a certain degree of prejudice against West Pointers in the Army of the Tennessee. That army had no professional soldiers at the corps level and comparatively few on the division and brigade levels. To an extent there was prejudice against officers who had previously served in the Army of the Potomac as well. "The personal gossip of mischief-makers came in here to make me a great deal of trouble at first," Howard recalled, but Sherman's "frank, genuine support . . . soon gave me the footing I needed." By August 5, Howard told his wife that he felt fully comfortable in his new position, directing a total of 140,000 men in a department located along the Mississippi River and with a mobile field force operating in Georgia.[11]

Howard had learned an important lesson at Chancellorsville. There, as commander of the Eleventh Corps, he had relied too heavily on reports that the Confederates were retreating and thereby neglected to protect the right flank of Hooker's Army of the Potomac with a well-refused line, proper earthworks, or proper scouts and picket lines to give early warning of an enemy approach. Stonewall Jackson's attack on the evening of May 2, 1863, crippled the corps and nearly spelled disaster for the army before it was stalled in the darkness of the Wilderness, and Jackson was accidentally shot by his own men. With Hooker's support, Howard survived that disaster and kept his command. At Ezra Church, he did everything possible to make sure his troops were not surprised again.[12]

The care and foresight with which Howard conducted the deployment of his army on July 27–28 prevented Lee from successfully attacking the Union flank. As Sherman expressed it, the enemy advance "was magnificent, but founded on an error that cost him sadly, for our men coolly and deliberately cut down his men." Sherman told his brother three days after the battle that the Rebels "got dreadfully whipped." He saw Johnston as a cagey adversary, and took pride in pushing him from Dalton down to the Chattahoochee River. But Sherman viewed Hood as "a new man and a fighter" who "must be watched closer, as he is reckless of the lives of his Men." Sherman also interpreted the battle of Ezra Church as an unusual event in the morale of his troops. The Federals had maintained high spirits throughout the campaign, but what happened on July 28 revealed "that we could compel Hood to come out from behind his fortified lines to attack us at a disadvantage." Of course, the Confederates did not repeat Ezra Church after July 28, making the battle along the Lick Skillet Road the end of a short phase in the Atlanta campaign, a phase marked by vigorous but unsuccessful efforts by Hood to take the tactical offensive against his more numerous opponent.[13]

The comparative vigor of Lee's assaults produced awe in the minds of many Federals. Rather than an easy victory, they considered it one of the hardest-fought engagements of the war, producing a heavy toll of human debris. Capt. Louis Love of the 70th Ohio called it "a terrible battle." Observers and participants alike recognized that the Confederates pressed hard on some parts of the line and nearly broke through, taking Logan's men perilously near the "edge of disaster." Some Federals lumped July 22 with Ezra Church. "The scenes witnessed on these two battlefields before Atlanta surpassed all that we had previously witnessed," argued Chaplain M. D. Gage of the 12th Indiana, "and nothing was afterward seen to compare with them in sickening details." But many others thought that what had happened at Ezra Church was a memorable experience by itself. "I have seen a good many fights," wrote William McCulloch Newell of the 57th Ohio, "but I never before saw such fighting, so destructive, neither do I wish to see such again." In fact, many men of the Fifteenth Corps thought Ezra Church was "the most stubbornly contested and bloodiest battle-field of the campaign," as William Harrow phrased it. "We all think that the last battle is by far the most brilliant of the campaign," wrote Charles Wills about Ezra Church.[14]

The Federals realized that Lee's fierce effort bore on the Fifteenth Corps because it was the point in Sherman's thrust to cut the railroad linking Atlanta with the South. But they also realized that Lee's tactics played so well into Federal hands that the campaign would end much sooner if the Confederates continued along the same course. "The quickest way that they can youse up their armey is to charge our brest works," commented James F. Sawyer of the 21st Wisconsin; "it will not hurt us so mutch to have them charge our brest works 6 times as it would to charge thairs onse." Morale in Logan's ranks, already high before Ezra Church, soared to new levels after July 28. "We have the greatest of confidence in (Corpl Billy) Gen'l Sherman," David Allan assured his mother. "Rest assured he will take no backward steps."[15]

Many Unionists also made a point of praising their gray-clad opponents at Ezra Church. They described the attacks as conducted with a great deal of bravery and consistency. "I rode over this bloody field," wrote Clifford Stickney, a signal officer with Blair's Seventeenth Corps, "and could not but admire the bravery of these poor misguided men, laying mangled and torn behind fences trees stumps and in the open field."[16]

While the Federals admired the rank and file of the Army of Tennessee, they unloaded nothing but contempt for the new commander of that army. After three unsuccessful attacks on Sherman since July 20, Hood's policy seemed doomed to failure, and the Federals recognized the awful effect on his men. James A. Connally of Baird's staff referred to Hood hurling his troops into bloody battles "with all the fury of a maniac. Reason seems dethroned, and Despair alone seems to rule the counsels within the walls of Atlanta." Hood appeared to be willing to sacrifice his army in desperate bids for tactical and strategic success. Some Federals such as Lieut. Col. Samuel Merrill of the 70th Indiana admitted that Johnston probably would have evacuated Atlanta long before this point, but they also wondered if the Army of Tennessee would be used up before long. Of course, this thought pleased the Federals. They gloated in letters home that Atlanta would be in Sherman's hands very quickly if Hood continued his pattern. Shooting down thousands of Confederates making frontal attacks against their positions was preferable to chasing a retreating Rebel army deeper into Georgia. "Hood is the best General for us," concluded Mendal C. Churchill of the 27th Ohio, while Chaplain Gage of the 12th Indiana counted Hood among the world's greatest military leaders if generalship was based merely on rashness, adding the telling comment, "But the rebel army will know best how to appreciate a commander who immolates them by thousands."[17]

For a handful of Union soldiers, the flow of events brought not only hope for a speedy end to the campaign but a sense of pity for the Confederate soldier. Samuel Merrill complained that Rebel officers hardly exerted themselves to recover their wounded enlisted men or to properly bury their dead, leaving the grim task of cleaning up one battlefield after another to the advancing Federals. Right after the fight at Ezra Church, Merrill admitted that he had begun to be "touched with pity for our deluded enemies. It is very sad to read letters by men just before they died, or to see a corpse deserted by everyone except a howling dog," he wrote. Daniel Griffin of the 38th Indiana saw Ezra Church in much the same light and prayed "that the poor deluded people [of the Confederacy] would drop the scales from their eyes and open them to a true realization of their position and their crimes."[18]

Many of the Federals who commented on the results and significance of the fight at Ezra Church had not participated in repelling Lee's furious attacks. The rumor mill as well as official communications spread the word of this fight along the Federal line and elicited commentary from many men. "We learn that Howard gave the Rebs a severe whipping on the right," reported John Law Marshall to his sister in New York. The verbal reports tended to be surprisingly accurate in their details, and they ran the entire line all the way to Schofield's Twenty-third Corps, now holding the far left of Sherman's position. The few prisoners taken by the Yankees at Ezra

Church tended to be talkative, giving Union officers accurate information about which Confederate generals were wounded in the battle along with wholly inaccurate information about other issues. A report circulated that a lieutenant of the 10th South Carolina deserted on the morning of July 29 and fed a good deal of information about conditions in Confederate ranks to the Unionists. J. C. Moore, a Federal soldier sent behind Confederate lines on July 26, returned to his Fourth Corps division commander three days later to report that the Rebels claimed casualties of up to 9,000 men at Ezra Church. Moore also confirmed that Confederate soldiers were demoralized over Johnston's removal and the results of Hood's tactics.[19]

The most authoritative way to spread news about Ezra Church was the reading of official orders to the troops. Many thinking soldiers knew full well that rumors and verbal reports normally were unreliable, but official statements from various commanders were about as close as one could come to the truth in the army. Howard's short report about the battle was read to nearly every unit along Sherman's line on July 29. Perhaps never before in a Civil War battle was reliable information about what happened in an engagement spread so widely or so quickly in the victorious camp as in the aftermath of the fight at Ezra Church.[20]

The civilian population of the North had to wait some time for full reports of the battle to appear in newspapers. The lag time typically was about one or two weeks before eager readers in Chicago, St. Louis, or New York had the chance to read halfway reliable reports about what happened in the bloody swale of ground fronting Logan's position. It took a full month for the illustrated newspapers to print pictures depicting the battle, and they tended to be rather generic scenes of combat only vaguely cued in to some specific aspects of the battle. *Harper's Weekly* appeared on August 27, 1864, with three scenes of the fight at Ezra Church sketched by field artist Theodore R. Davis. A short editorial piece accompanied the scenes, which gave an estimate of losses on both sides in the battle.[21]

Civilians who could not wait for the newspapers bombarded their relatives serving in units of Sherman's army group for news. Mary Royse wrote her cousin W. H. Thompson in the 66th Indiana that she had heard there was "an awful Battel at Atlanta," prompting Thompson to inform her that they actually had three awful battles lately and all of them were victories. But a rumor that the Federals buried 1,000 Confederates in one grave after Ezra Church "is all a mistake."[22]

For Andrew Evans of Brown County, Ohio, the news that the 70th Ohio suffered heavy casualties while holding down Harrow's left flank struck home. He and his family knew many men who served in that regiment, and Andrew reported the deaths and injuries suffered by them to his son, who served in the 59th U.S. Colored Troops in Mississippi. The father worried that the 70th Ohio "lost its best stuff" at Ezra Church.[23]

Getting information about loved ones, about the course of the engagement on July 28, and about casualties on that bloody day was comparatively easy. But trying to estimate Confederate losses was an entirely different matter. The Unionists debated among themselves exactly how many Rebel troops they had taken out of action on July 28 as a way to measure the extent of their defensive victory. They often added those losses to those Hood suffered at Peach Tree Creek and on July 22 to make the calculation even more meaningful to their sense of progress in the campaign. Estimates ranged across the spectrum, often resting at 20,000 for the combined Rebel losses in the three battles, but going as high as 32,000. "There is no shadow of gas in this," Charles W. Wills told his relatives in Illinois, "as you would know if you could see an unsuccessful charge on works." But the estimates were far too high if modern historians have been able to obtain a handle on the difficult task of determining battle losses. The best conclusion is that Hood lost a combined total of 11,000 men on July 20, 22, and 28.[24]

While the basic news of what happened on July 28 could be circulated through orders and official reports, no one could control Dame Rumor when it came to unsubstantiated stories about the battle near Ezra Church. None of these stories were given such confidence as the one that the Confederates were drunk when they madly charged Logan's corps. "Tis reported & believed," reported George Martin Trowbridge of the 19th Michigan, that the Rebels "charged up like insane men to be slaughtered by hundreds. Reb ladies had passed the cup freely before the brave defenders of Southern Rights came out to fight." According to some rumors Confederate prisoners confirmed the notion that Rebel officers freely provided strong drink to the men just before the attack. "General Hood had ordered barrels of whiskey, with the head knocked in, placed along the lines where the men in forming over the rise of ground dipped their tin cups in and drank as they passed along." The prisoners remained drunk even the next day, according to some stories, indicating the whiskey must have been pretty strong.[25]

There is no evidence of any kind to indicate that the Confederates were issued whiskey before the attack on July 28. But the rumor played into Federal prejudices about the nature of their opponent and helped to explain why the Rebels conducted uncoordinated but fierce attacks on Logan's position. The next day, when the faces of many dead Confederates began to blacken, the Unionists saw it as proof that they had imbibed whiskey on the day of battle. Daniel Griffin of the 38th Indiana was not sure if the rumor was true, but he admitted that strong drink would give a soldier "extreme daring." He shuddered at the thought of the Union army using it as freely as the Confederates seemed to do. "Tis a point at which I never want to see our Army arrive, nor do I think it will ever reach it."[26]

Other rumors about the Confederates also shed light on how the Federals viewed their enemy. One such story had it that 500 blacks armed "with picks and shovels" had been captured on July 28. Obviously the Rebels were planning to use them to construct fortifications as they had done under Johnston's command north of the Chattahoochee River. A persistent rumor also had it that a woman was found dressed in a Confederate uniform lying dead on the battlefield near Ezra Church. This story played into the Unionists' hope that the Confederates were desperately short of manpower. "I think that is going a little to far," wrote Henry H. Maley of the 84th Illinois to his parents; "all that sticks them selvs up for a mark aught to be shot[;] it is not a womans place in a fight."[27]

Reuben Williams recalled in his postwar reminiscences that a good friend of his, Dr. J. K. Leedy of the 74th Indiana, examined the field of dead and came up with a rather curious idea about the fighting ability of the enemy. Leedy thought there were many more sandy-haired and light-complexioned men among the killed than those with dark complexions. In fact he placed the relative proportion at four to one. Leedy's explanation for this "fact" led him to assume that a lighter-skinned man had a "sanguine temperament," while darker-skinned men possessed a "phlegmatic nature." Williams did not truly believe the good doctor's theory, advising each of his readers to "judge for himself."[28]

The Confederates also spread reports and rumors about the fight at Ezra Church along their extended line protecting Atlanta. Many of the reports had it that Lee drove the enemy, based on the fact that the Confederates did push Logan's skirmishers back to their main line. But a second report usually conveyed the accurate news that the attacks then stalled.[29]

Lee put the best spin he could on the battle he had created and ineptly led. Seven months later, when writing his official report, he blamed the lack of resolve among some units for his failure. "I am convinced that if all the troops had displayed equal spirit we would have been successful, as the enemy's works were slight, and besides they had scarcely gotten into position when we made the attack." Of course a lot had happened in the intervening seven months between the battle and the writing of Lee's report. Lee's men had certainly displayed a decided lack of spirit in their attack on Sherman's troops during the first day of the battle at Jonesboro on August 31. They had been badly handled in their attack on Schofield's position at Franklin on November 30, and they had collapsed and fled the field at Nashville on December 16. Lee may well have been thinking more of those later conflicts than of Ezra Church when he penned this ungenerous comment on the rank and file.[30]

Confederate soldiers in many different units commented on Lee's first battle with the Army of Tennessee. Some of them praised the new corps commander, but they tended to be men who had no personal experience in the battle at Ezra Church. Lieut. F. Halsey Wigfall, son of a Confederate senator from Texas and a member of Hood's staff, admired Lee's personal conduct during the battle. He "behaved in the most gallant and almost over-reckless manner, seizing colors and rallying his men and exposing himself continually." Halsey probably reflected the attitude at Hood's headquarters when he wrote that everyone liked Lee. "They would doubtless have preferred a commander with whom they were acquainted but he is too good an officer not to soon overcome any feeling of that sort."[31]

After the war, Hood himself had nothing but praise for Lee. Despite the fact that Lee wrecked Hood's plan to set up a flank attack on Howard, the army commander strongly supported his corps commander's hasty decision to attack on the afternoon of July 28. As Hood put it, Lee "unexpectedly" found the enemy that afternoon and "a spirited engagement ensued." He accepted Lee's report that the Federals already possessed part of the ground that Hood had told him to secure. Hood admitted that Lee failed to drive the enemy, but he accepted the results of Ezra Church as at least a partial victory. Moreover, Hood devoted little time to discussing the engagement in his postwar writings, preferring to focus on the smashing of Sherman's cavalry raids that were launched simultaneously with Howard's move to the west of Atlanta. The personal relationship between the two remained strong and supportive after the war. Hood's surviving letters to Lee are warm, friendly, and confiding. He believed that the Confederates would have saved their railroad link if Lee instead of Hardee had been in charge of operations at Jonesboro.[32]

Those men who fought under Lee on July 28 generally had a far less generous attitude toward the new corps leader. It is also possible that Lee himself suffered enormous emotional trauma when he realized the heavy losses and comparative lack of success that resulted from the fight. Samuel Wragg Ferguson, who commanded a cavalry brigade in Hood's army, recalled seeing Lee on the night of the battle. Ferguson witnessed "the agony he endured on account of the slaughter of his men that day." If Ferguson can be relied upon (he believed this incident occurred on the night of July 22, not July 28), it is an indication that in the first flush of reality Lee fully realized his failure and the immense human cost of his decision.[33]

The majority of soldiers under Lee's direction that day were critical of his actions. "It was one of the many miserable exhibitions of generalship, this whole affair, which was characteristic of the officers of the Army of Tennessee," wrote Arthur Manigault after the war, "and one of the numerous instances of which I was a witness and a sufferer." While he did not name Lee specifically, Manigault implied that he was the chief culprit. "The mismanagement in this affair was so patent to the dullest spectator or combatant, that the men lost all confidence in their leaders, and were much dispirited in consequence." John H. Marshall of the 41st Mississippi in Sharp's Brigade of Brown's Division supported Manigault's view. He reported that many of his comrades deserted in the days following Ezra Church and conveyed his opinion that "Mr. Lee don't fight to please me he fights by detail and all may w[e]ll get whipped."[34]

Historians have uniformly criticized Lee for starting the battle in the first place and for conducting it in piecemeal fashion. They cite his tender age and comparative lack of experience at high command. They also note that he failed to understand from the first round of attacks that these efforts were useless. Lee should have stopped the battle long before he did rather than press forward every available unit as it arrived on the field, duplicating failure the whole afternoon.[35]

If Lee was distraught on the evening of July 28, as Ferguson contended, he soon regained his composure. Three days following the battle of Ezra Church, he issued a circular instructing his men how better to conduct themselves under fire. Lee noted several things about their behavior on July 28 that disturbed him. First, he wanted his officers not to urge the men forward too fast when attacking. They should instead maintain a slow but steady pace "until they become well engaged with the enemy before they are commanded to charge." This would maintain unit cohesion and not fatigue the men until their utmost energy was needed. Lee also urged the troops to recognize the importance of quickly rallying after a failed attack. Officers were to select points at which they could reform ranks as quickly as possible.[36]

This circular, with its sound tactical advice, did not criticize the men. But Lee developed an ever more negative opinion of his troops on the basis of subsequent battles. As mentioned earlier, he was disgusted with their performance at Jonesboro and made a point to give talks to them about it. The men uniformly disliked what he had to say. When Lee ordered Brown's Division into formation on September 6 for his lecture, Jesse L. Henderson of the 41st Mississippi complained that "I had as soon hear most any person else." He was reprieved because a hard rain came up and soaked Lee to the skin, causing the general to postpone the talk. Lee managed to give the lecture to Brown's Division three days later. While Jonesboro was the key in turning Lee's opinion of his corps toward the carping and the negative attitude that it became, Ezra Church played a role in that development as the start of a critical view of the efficiency of his units.[37]

It was obvious to all Confederates who fought at Ezra Church that Lee gained little if anything from the bloody effort. "We lost a great many men for mity little gain," concluded Thomas Warrick of the 34th Alabama. Arthur Manigault was greatly pained to see "how uselessly and foolishly" his men "had been butchered." Comments such as these indicate that the depression following Ezra Church was accentuated by the energy and desperation with which many Confederates attempted to drive the Federals back. After such an exertion, to lose so many troops and gain nothing was too much for many to bear. "This Battle Discouraged our men Badly," wrote Capt. John W. Lavender of the 4th Arkansas, "as they could never understand why they Should have been Sent in to such a Death Trap to be Butchered up with no hope of gaining any thing." They fell back after the fight "in a terrible shattered and Demoralized Condition." Hearing the news, H. L. G. Whitaker of the 29th Georgia was disheartened, even though he had not participated in the battle. "O dear friends," he wrote home, "I don't See eny chance for Eny of us to Ever Escape for we had a fite hear yesterday and lost 2000 men. you may not under stand them figers. the lose on our Syd too thousand, the yankes not none yet."[38]

Henry Clayton admitted that his men's spirits were very depressed after July 28, but they began to pick up after the passage of about ten days. When Sherman evacuated his lines fronting Atlanta on August 26 to conduct his flank march toward Jonesboro, Confederate spirits rose again. News of the Northern Democratic Party's peace platform, adopted at about the same time, also boosted Rebel morale. In short, the depression attendant on the bloody repulse at Ezra Church was not permanent in Confederate ranks.[39]

While most Rebels thought ill of the results, a handful of them saw the battle of Ezra Church as a success. It is true that Lee's attacks temporarily stopped Sherman's effort to reach the railroad linking Atlanta with

Macon. "The Yanks have not got Atlanta yet," exulted Grant Taylor of the 40th Alabama in Baker's Brigade. It was even easier for men who did not participate in the battle to see its positive results. "Gen. Hood watches his flanks closely and has twice shipped the flanking columns out," commented Andrew Jackson Neal in Hardee's Corps. But very few soldiers went as far as Surgeon James Madison Brannock of the 4th and 5th Tennessee in Cheatham's Division when he told his wife that any apprehension about Hood had evaporated in the Army of Tennessee. "Since Genl' Hood has fought the enemy so successfully he has gained the entire confidence almost to as great an extent as Johnston had done."[40]

Brannock was among a minority. Stephen Cowley of Quarles's staff condemned the removal of Johnston as casting "a gloom over the veterans of this Army which will as long as the Army exists show in their war worn faces." Hiram Smith Williams of Baker's Brigade penned similar comments in his diary. "This day's work has done more to demoralize our army than 3 months under Genl Johnston." After the war, Philip Daingerfield Stephenson of the Fifth Company, Washington Artillery, wrote a damning comment on Hood's generalship. "This last battle swept away every trace of any lingering defense of Hood in our army, or of confidence in him as a commander," he asserted. Many men "looked upon Hood with a sort of dread, as though he was almost a madman." Stephenson felt that many of the more ignorant troops came to fear Hood more than the Yankees. The general "had broken the spirits of his men in less than two weeks after assuming command."[41]

While opinion varied somewhat in the Confederate ranks, there is no doubt that many more Rebels were demoralized than inspirited by the battle of Ezra Church. Many more were critical of Hood than had confidence in his leadership. Many more looked on the fight as a defeat than as a success. It is also apparent that the authorities at Richmond had little if any awareness that the engagement had depressed the morale of most men engaged in the fight. Hood's official pronouncements implied that Ezra Church was at least a partial success. "The two recent engagements [July 22 and Ezra Church] have checked his extension on both flanks," he informed Richmond of Sherman's moves on July 30. Hood's new chief of staff, Francis Shoup, reported in the journal he kept at headquarters that Lee fulfilled his mission to keep the enemy off the Lick Skillet Road. Hood argued that same point in his official report, dated February 15, 1865. Thomas L. Clayton, who had served as Hood's engineer officer on the corps level, admitted in private letters that Lee suffered very heavy losses "without much result." But the ever-loyal Halsey Wigfall supported Hood's view of the battle in letters to his family.[42]

Historians have been very critical of Hood. Jacob Cox, who both commanded a division in the Twenty-third Corps and wrote an admirable history of the campaign, blasted Hood for "passing over this battle" in his memoirs. The Confederate general treated it as a chance encounter rather than as the disruption of a major effort to duplicate July 22 west of Atlanta. Cox dismissed Hood's assertion that Confederate morale had been depressed by Johnston's Fabian tactics while campaigning north of the Chattahoochee River. He noted the vigor with which Lee's men conducted the attack at Ezra Church, and he emphasized the consequent depression that followed the battle to make his point that Hood's aggressive policy severely depressed morale in the Army of Tennessee.[43]

Hood devoted a great deal of effort in his memoirs to shift the blame for losing Atlanta on his predecessor. He argued that Johnston's reluctance to offer battle during the course of the campaign before reaching the Chattahoochee River had sapped the offensive spirit of the troops. Judging Johnston by the standard established by Robert E. Lee in Virginia, Hood complained that the "continued use of breastworks during a campaign, renders troops timid in pitched battle." Lee relied on earthworks only as a last resort rather than a mode of operations. When Hood took control of the Army of Tennessee and called on the men to take spirited offensive action, they failed him. Hood solicited supporting testimony from Stephen D. Lee, who readily complied. Lee testified that a "general who resorts to entrenchments, when there is any chance of success in engaging in the open field, commits a great error."[44]

Twentieth-century historians have roundly criticized Hood for staying at his headquarters rather than presenting himself at the scene of action to guide his new and somewhat unsteady corps commander. It is true that Hood and his headquarters were preoccupied with the important task of dealing with Sherman's cavalry raid. Yet he bypassed his most experienced corps leader because he had developed a distrust of Hardee arising from the battles of Peach Tree Creek and July 22. He assigned his least experienced corps leader to perform the holding maneuver while letting Stewart (his second best corps commander) take on the heavier responsibility of mounting the flank attack on July 29. To a degree, Hood could be allowed the privilege of deciding that the cavalry raid was more important at the moment than contending with the enemy flank movement, and he had every reason to expect that Lee would obey his orders. But Lee did much more than he was supposed to do, and much more than Hood expected. It would be unfair to place the major blame for Ezra Church on Hood's shoulders.[45]

Would Hardee have done better handling the operations west of Atlanta on July 28? Judging by his prior record, it is virtually certain that he would have taken a more cautious approach to the task and avoided rash attacks. Yet Hood had already made an enemy of Hardee before July 28. The two had not gotten on well during the Atlanta campaign, and Hardee was miffed that Hood was elevated above him on July 18. He did not conduct the attack at Peach Tree Creek with much vigor. His flank movement on July 22 was well done under difficult circumstances, but his corps attack that afternoon was as disjointed as was Lee's at Ezra Church. In his official report, Hood slammed Hardee for the failures on July 20 and July 22. Hardee was stunned by Hood's "astonishing statements and insinuations." He told Samuel Cooper, the Confederate adjutant general, that Hood glossed over the results of Ezra Church in his report so as "to leave an impression of its success, but it was well known throughout the army that so great was the loss in men, organization, and morale in that engagement that no action of the campaign probably did so much to demoralize and dishearten the troops engaged in it." Furthermore, as Hardee pointed out, if Hood had so little faith in his ability, why did he call on Hardee to take charge at Ezra Church when disturbing reports of the battle began to filter into army headquarters? Joseph Johnston asked the same question after he read Hood's report, criticizing Hood for not taking personal charge of affairs on the battlefield.[46]

All three of Hood's battles north, east, and west of Atlanta during the last two weeks of July were filled with mistakes and miscues, providing fodder for rethinking events after the fact. Hood was responsible for many of these blunders, but his fellow officers, including Lee, bore the responsibility for others. To the rank and file who survived what happened on that bloody afternoon, a lifetime of making sense of Ezra Church was in store.

CHAPTER ELEVEN

Our True Move

July 29 to August 3

The point behind moving Howard's Army of the Tennessee from east of Atlanta to the west of the city was to cut the last rail link supplying Hood's army. Despite the enormous bloodletting, Lee's attacks at Ezra Church stopped that movement temporarily. Sherman had hoped that Howard could reach the railroad in one movement, but that proved to be optimistic. The Federals resumed efforts to extend south on July 29, banking mostly on Howard's men supplemented by a couple of divisions from Thomas's Army of the Cumberland. They would continue to make these efforts until August 2, when Sherman shifted Schofield's Army of the Ohio from his extreme left to his extreme right. From that point on, Schofield was in charge of the flanking effort.

Sherman was motivated to move on July 29 not only by a desire to continue extending southward but even more by a desire to help the cavalry columns he had sent to strike the rail system. Early that morning, Sherman wrote Thomas that he wanted Morgan's division and a division from the Twentieth Corps to move out from Howard's right flank and head toward East Point to divert Confederate attention from the cavalry. "Don't form a line but move so as to occupy or threaten the railroad," he specified. Sherman did not want to extend the line that day, but he wanted the Federals to "operate in the nature of a strong reconnaissance toward East Point." Sherman also informed Howard that this movement would give him an opportunity to advance his skirmish line toward White Hall and collect more of the Confederate dead on the battlefield.[1]

Before the movement started, and while Logan's men were already collecting the dead between their skirmish line and their main position, Howard received a report that Hardee's entire corps was endeavoring to reach a point between his right flank and Turner's Ferry on the Chatta-hoochee River. The source of this information was never reported, but if it was true, Hardee represented a major threat. Sherman did not readily believe the report. He told Howard someone must have seen a small group of Confederate infantrymen who were positioned to intercept McCook's column of mounted men as it tried to return to its starting point on the Chattahoochee. He did not worry about McCook, for the column was not supposed to return the same way it had gone out. Instead, Sherman saw an opportunity. If it was true that Hardee's Corps was maneuvering so far from Atlanta, Howard and Thomas could cut it off. Word of Hardee's supposed effort to flank Howard spread through the ranks and prompted many members of the Army of the Tennessee to expect another battle on July 29. At some point in the day, Howard's scouts finally confirmed that there was no sizable force of enemy troops between his flank and Turner's Ferry. Fears of an immediate attack now eased.[2]

Morgan's division of the Fourteenth Corps was on the move even before the tension created by erroneous reports of Hardee's maneuver subsided. On the morning of July 29, the division formed line and moved about half a mile from its swampy bivouac area of the night before to align to the right of Howard's flank. This was the same flank that had nearly been crushed in the heavy fighting of the previous day. There Morgan's men stopped to draw rations and rest.[3]

Thomas once again designated his only reserve, Ward's Third Division of the Twentieth Corps, as the force to help Howard. Ward's men had started for the battlefield the previous afternoon but were recalled when it became obvious they were not needed. Now the troops awoke at 2:00 A.M., ate breakfast two hours later, and left their position near the right flank of Williams's Twentieth Corps line at 8:30 A.M. They moved six to eight miles in increasing heat.[4]

Ward's division arrived near Howard's right flank and rested a bit. Now they had a good opportunity to see the battlefield and talk with Howard's troops. Corpses still dotted the countryside, and trees were barked and mangled by the heavy musketry. Members of the 129th Illinois marveled at the nonchalance of Logan's men who "were in the best humor, standing and sitting, jesting and laughing between wounded and dead rebels, talk-ing of the events of the day just passed." From Logan's troops, Ward's men learned that the battle "was a serious affair."[5]

After a while, the two divisions moved forward about a mile and pushed Confederate skirmishers back. Morgan's men secured the Lick Skillet

Road. Formed in two lines, Morgan's command dug in for the night. For the first time, Federal troops were in undisputed possession of the road that Hood had wanted to use in Stewart's planned flank attack, which was supposed to have taken place that day. The Fourteenth Corps troops found at least fifty-seven dead bodies and some wounded Rebels in their march across the edge of the battlefield. Abandoned guns and bits of clothing also littered the area.[6]

Ward moved forward behind Morgan when the Fourteenth Corps men started. He extended Morgan's fortified line as it ran just south of the Lick Skillet Road and positioned part of his division at a right angle to the line, refusing the flank in case the enemy tried to turn it. Teamsters brought rations for Ward's men, who occupied what one of them called "a commanding position." Morgan sent his skirmish line forward to clear the area between his new post and the main Confederate position, an extension of the City Line of Atlanta that stretched southwestward toward East Point. Many of Morgan's men worked well past dark, using torches to help them construct breastworks. Troops on the far right of Ward's line constructed a redoubt, enclosed on all four sides, to better protect the flank. Thomas personally inspected the position of the two divisions and was satisfied that they were in no danger.[7]

Howard's command spent July 29 adjusting its position and cleaning up the battlefield, while Morgan and Ward advanced the colors. Logan's artillery chief, Maj. Thomas Davies Maurice, was busy planting his guns along the Fifteenth Corps line that day. He had to break up the large concentration of artillery ordered by Howard the previous afternoon to support Logan's flank and parcel the guns out on any available ground the battery commanders could find along the narrow ridge, necessitating a great deal of digging and timber cutting. From here, the Union gunners caught glimpses of Rebel works 3,500 yards away near Atlanta. During the course of the day, all of the Sixteenth and Seventeenth Corps regiments that had rushed to Logan's assistance during the battle returned to their parent units.[8]

Men of Iowa were honored by the sudden appearance of their governor on July 29. William M. Stone had commanded the 22nd Iowa during the arduous campaign and siege of Vicksburg before running for elected office. Stone gave a speech to every Iowa regiment he could find in Howard's force that evening, telling the men of Lincoln's plans to raise more troops for the Union army. Charles Berry Senior of the 7th Iowa was on picket duty that evening, but he could hear "a good deal of cheering & thought there must be some good news."[9]

Thomas was busy along his part of the line fronting Atlanta on July 29. In addition to inspecting the position of Morgan and Ward, he urged Palmer and Williams to conduct a reconnaissance against the Rebel line. Johnson's and Baird's divisions of the Fourteenth Corps pushed heavy skirmish lines forward and reported the possibility that the Rebels had withdrawn most of their troops, holding the trenches only with skirmishers. Thomas ordered further activity that night to see if that supposition was true. Williams's division of the Twentieth Corps, now commanded by Brig. Gen. Joseph F. Knipe, captured a section of the Rebel skirmish line and 115 troops. This allowed the Federals to shorten their line and obtain a better view of the remaining ground between the opposing positions.[10]

Schofield also contributed to Federal activity on July 29. He sent a brigade to demonstrate toward the Confederate line and then move out as far as Decatur. The main purpose was to distract Rebel attention from the McCook-Stoneman raid. Jacob Cox sent a brigade commanded by Brig. Gen. James W. Reilly for this mission. Reilly drove Confederate cavalry and militia away only to discover a brigade of infantrymen holding the Rebel entrenchments. Despite Reilly's discovery, Sherman relayed to Schofield Thomas's tantalizing idea that the Confederates might have evacuated their lines and were holding them only with skirmishers. He wanted Schofield to feel the lines strongly that night to see if it was true.[11]

Sherman's hopes for the large cavalry raid he had unleashed on July 27 proved false. There was initial success; Edward McCook's men tore up some track near Palmetto Station on July 28 as the battle raged at Ezra Church. But then the two Union columns failed to coordinate their efforts. With Sherman's prior approval, George Stoneman decided not to join McCook at Lovejoy's Station as planned but instead headed off for Macon and ultimately Andersonville in an effort to free Union prisoners of war. The two columns were now on their own, and by this time Hood had sent sizable mounted forces after them. McCook reached Lovejoy's Station on July 29 but had to fight his way back to the Chattahoochee River. Later that day, at Brown's Mill near Newnan, Confederate forces cornered him. McCook was compelled to tell his men to save themselves any way they could. Most of his troopers managed to escape, but 600 Union cavalrymen were lost in the near catastrophe. Stoneman reached the vicinity of Macon on July 29 but could not cross the Ocmulgee River and enter the town. As he headed north, three brigades of Confederate cavalrymen attacked Stoneman's column near Sunshine Church on July 30. Stoneman and 700 of his men fought a delaying action to allow the rest to escape, and then they surrendered. All in all the large cavalry raid was a disaster that not only failed to cut Hood's logistics but cost Sherman much of his available mounted force.[12]

Hood and his staff were preoccupied with the Union cavalry strike from July 27 to 29, as evidenced by the dispatches issued from Army of Tennessee headquarters and by Shoup's journal. When he had time to think of other matters, Hood assigned Benjamin Cheatham to temporarily command Stewart's Corps while Stewart recuperated from his Ezra Church wound. Samuel G. French was angry when he learned the news. As next in line behind Stewart and Loring, he assumed he would take over the corps until Stewart recovered. Upon finding his assumption wrong, French wrote a letter of protest to the army commander. "Hood's act was in keeping with the intriguing so ruinous to this army," French wrote after the war, "and I asked to be relieved from serving in it any longer." Hood did not comply with French's request, and the frustrated division leader continued to soldier on in the Army of Tennessee for several more months.[13]

Maj. Gen. James Patton Anderson reported to Hood for duty and was assigned to command Hindman's old division, which had been led by John C. Brown at Ezra Church. Brown reported to Hood for other assignment; the army commander wanted him to take over Loring's Division, but that was not approved. Brown later commanded a brigade in Hardee's Corps at the end of the Atlanta campaign.[14]

Hood had no interest in regaining control of the Lick Skillet Road. Instead Confederate troops spent the day adjusting lines and digging earthworks to extend the Rebel position southwest from the City Line to block Yankee access to the railroad near East Point. This was the beginning of the East Point Line, which was created in reaction to Sherman's movement west of the city. Hood was compelled to thin his troops holding the rest of the Atlanta works to construct this new position. He counted on his engineers and the ingenuity of the rank and file to make the defenses everywhere along the line so strong that they could be held with fewer men. Shoup asked Hardee to send out scouts and discover if Sherman was shifting any more troops from his extreme left, located east of Atlanta, to the west. He also cautioned Hardee that available supplies of small-arms ammunition were running low, with uncertain prospects for replenishment. The word was out to control unnecessary firing and husband the rounds the troops had left.[15]

As Union movements ground to a halt on the night of July 29, Thomas urged Sherman to continue the effort the next day. He suggested that Howard thin his line so as to extend his right flank in a southerly direction. Then he could order Morgan and Ward to move forward and extend Howard's line even farther south, hoping to "overlap the enemy." Howard was willing to do so, and Sherman supported the plan. "I think we can draw the enemy out of Atlanta," he told Howard, "or force him to the attack, which is to be desired." Howard ordered Dodge and Blair to reduce their two lines into one and hold no more than one brigade as a reserve for each corps. He also told Logan to get ready to shift his east-facing line southward at 8:00 A.M. on July 30, while Dodge and Blair extended their line to keep pace with that shift. All hopes that the enemy had evacuated Atlanta had vanished, Sherman told Halleck that night, yet optimism ran high in the Union camp that the next day might bring decisive results.[16]

Saturday, July 30, produced heavy showers and an atmosphere that one observer described as dense. Everyone agreed it was "awful hot" despite the rain. But Logan set out at 8:00 A.M. as planned, advancing the Fifteenth Corps southward in line across the polluted battlefield of July 28 until he occupied the ridge from which the Confederates had launched their attacks. That ridge ran roughly north of the Lick Skillet Road. Logan connected with Morgan and Ward to his right and relieved them with Morgan L. Smith's division. This freed up Morgan's and Ward's troops for a further advance southward. Blair and Dodge extended their lines to support Logan. Seventeenth Corps troops took over the position formerly held by Woods's division of the Fifteenth Corps at the angle of Howard's line.[17]

Soon after Logan settled down in his new position, Morgan and Ward continued advancing southeast toward the important railroad at about noon of July 30. They marched from half a mile to a mile before establishing a new position on advantageous ground well short of the track. Again, on Thomas's order, Ward established a refused line to Morgan's right. Both divisions constructed fortifications that evening. Many units of Ward's division, located on the extreme right of the formation, again constructed a fully enclosed redoubt to anchor the right flank, even though there were no concentrations of enemy troops nearby. In fact, Charles Laforest Dunham of the 129th Illinois in Ward's division thought the area was "the quietest . . . of any place we hav ben for the last three months." But Lee's attack on July 28 had made everyone a bit more cautious.[18]

When Blair's men shifted southward that day, they moved across the edge of the Ezra Church battlefield. It was littered with burial mounds and badly scarred trees. Some of Blair's units aligned to the left of Logan's corps on the ridge used by the Confederates to launch their attacks, facing southward. Charles E. Smith of the 32nd Ohio was impressed by the fact that his brigade "camped on the battlefield where hundreds of Confederate soldiers fell, bled and died and were buried by our troops." His comrades could not think about it too long because it was imperative that they throw up "strong earthworks on the ridge" in case the enemy made a comeback.[19]

The fact that the Union movements on July 30 were unopposed even by Confederate skirmishers, and erroneous reports that Stoneman had broken the railroad at Jonesboro, spurred renewed hopes that Hood had evacuated Atlanta. Sherman ignored those hopes, assuming that he would have to take the city by movement and fighting. He was not pleased with the progress on July 30, for the Federals had advanced only a short distance and were still not in position to seriously threaten the railroad. Sherman also had no word yet on the disaster that was befalling his cavalry columns.[20]

By the evening of July 30, Sherman began to think in terms of shifting Schofield's Army of the Ohio from the far left to the far right. Schofield had already led efforts to flank the Confederates out of strongly fortified lines during the campaign, most notably at Kennesaw Mountain, and now Sherman hoped he could lead the effort west of Atlanta. He planned to ride to the left and consult with Schofield on July 31, urging Thomas to mount "a bold reconnaissance over toward East Point" with Morgan's division that day as well. At Fourth Corps headquarters, David S. Stanley made plans to strengthen the obstructions in front of his earthworks as Sherman ordered engineer Poe to select a new refused line extending back from Stanley's left flank to be held by Fourth Corps troops after Schofield's withdrawal.[21]

There was comparatively little activity at Army of Tennessee headquarters on July 30. The minor Union advance across the battlefield of Ezra Church worried no one. Hood was satisfied that his new East Point Line was long enough, at least for the time being, to check these tentative moves by Howard and Thomas. Shoup told Lee that the commanding general did not "consider it necessary to extend the line any farther to the left."[22]

The morning of July 31 introduced a new element in the weather. It began to rain and hardly stopped all day. The downpour, combined with intermittent Rebel artillery fire, compelled most Union troops to stay in their works even though the trenches often filled with water and mud; "we were wet, cold and uncomfortable all day," remembered H. I. Smith of the 7th Iowa in Dodge's command.[23]

The heavy weather made Union troop movements more difficult but not impossible. By 9:30 A.M., however, Thomas complained to Sherman that Howard had not fulfilled his part of the plan for July 31. Instead of moving his line forward to align with the position occupied by Morgan and Ward, Logan had merely sent out reconnoitering parties. Sherman was responsible for this miscue. Early on the morning of July 31 he had instructed Howard to have his men examine the ground forward to see if a line of approach toward the railroad between White Hall and East Point could be mapped out. The previous plan to have the Army of the Tennessee move its line forward to align with Thomas's two divisions was ignored. Logan's skirmishers went ahead and encountered Confederate skirmishers about a mile in front of the East Point Line. The Rebel works appeared to be strong and well manned. Federal scouts, however, reported that the enemy had only cavalry pickets southeast of Morgan's and Ward's position. This ended Howard's activity for the day.[24]

Thomas was frustrated that so little had been done to support his two divisions. The sense of frustration filtered down to the corps level as well. Sherman had been urging the two divisions to move forward even farther on July 31, and those instructions were routed through Thomas's and Palmer's headquarters. They went through Jefferson C. Davis's headquarters as well, even though Davis was not yet well enough to take the field personally. Davis could not exactly understand what his division was supposed to do. He sent a message to Palmer expressing his confusion and concern. "If he advances it amounts to an assault upon the enemy's position. If he withdraws with a view to passing to General Ward's rear he leaves a gap." Palmer added his own complaint when passing this information on to Thomas, writing that Sherman had sent numerous orders "imposing special duties upon Davis' division away from his corps."[25]

The confusion was cleared up with subsequent communications, and Morgan's division moved forward with Ward supporting it late on July 31. The Federals advanced three-quarters of a mile in heavy rain before encountering Rebel skirmishers. They did not press the contest but stopped on the nearest defensible ground and started to make breastworks. Thomas rode out to see the new position and was worried that the troops were exposed so far from supporting units. Yet he did not want to give up the small gain of territory, so he ordered Ward's division to return to its position of the night before. In this way the area between Morgan and Howard could be better covered to prevent a Rebel attempt to cut off Morgan, and Ward would still be within supporting distance of the Fourteenth Corps division.[26]

Despite the minimal achievements of the day, Thomas wrote optimistically to Sherman about the prospects. He thought that if Schofield could be shifted to the right flank, the Twenty-third Corps "will surely reach" the railroad. Morgan and Ward could guard Schofield's flank as he moved forward and support the Twenty-third Corps if trouble developed.[27]

Sherman agreed with Thomas, calling the plan to rely on the Army of the Ohio "our true move." He told Schofield to expect him at 10:00 A.M. on August 1 to go over the details of the movement. The first problem was to figure out how to secure the left flank northeast of Atlanta after the Army of the Ohio evacuated its position. To that end, Stanley was directed to construct the new refused line Poe had already laid out along Pea Vine Creek, extending back from the left flank of the Fourth Corps.[28]

By the evening of July 31, Sherman had firmly set the outline of his next move. Schofield would evacuate his position on the night of August 1–2. Col. Israel Garrard's cavalry brigade would place skirmishers in Schofield's vacated trenches to serve as an advanced line for Stanley's new refused left flank. When the Twenty-third Corps neared the Federal right flank, Howard was to straighten and advance his line so as to extend it as far south as possible. Then Schofield would extend it even farther, relying on Morgan and Ward to cover his flank. Referring to the enemy, Sherman told Howard, "I think we can make him quit Atlanta, or so weaken his lines that we can break through somewhere, the same as our Kenesaw move." By now the Federals were well aware of the Confederate East Point Line, but Sherman hoped there might be a weak spot in the curtain linking White Hall and East Point that could be exploited, even if Schofield was unable to turn the Rebel flank. Schofield was busy on July 31 with preparations for the move.[29]

The Confederates were also busy, observing their enemy and moving troops on both flanks of their extended line. Confederate cavalrymen noted activity in the Federal camp and reported the Yankees were moving troops away from their position northeast of Atlanta, anticipating Schofield's move by many hours. Hardee ordered his division leaders to send out scouts and discover what was going on. Hood's headquarters also instructed the cavalry commander on that flank to be more active in obtaining information to verify the movement of Federal troops from the area. The only conclusion to make was that Schofield was on the way to the west of Atlanta. This prompted a further extension of the East Point Line on July 31, making the success of Sherman's next move more problematic.[30]

Nevertheless, there was a good deal of Federal activity on August 1. Howard had suggested he adjust and straighten his existing lines before Schofield arrived to make the job of extending southward easier, and Sherman approved. The result was heavy skirmishing along Howard's line and the capture of some Rebel troops. To the south, Confederate skirmishers advanced close to Ward's division to determine where it was located. Ward's men feared an attack and improved their redoubt for better defense, but nothing serious resulted.[31]

On the far Union left, Schofield's wagon trains left the area at 3:00 P.M. on August 1. After dusk, Garrard's cavalry relieved the Twenty-third Corps, and the infantry left the area at 9:00 P.M. The men moved slowly in the darkness until resting about three miles away at midnight. They resumed the march at 6:00 A.M. The day was cooler than usual; the recent rain had settled the dust, and the marching went smoothly. They stopped to eat a meal at 11:00 A.M. and then moved on until reaching Howard's right flank late on August 2.[32]

Sherman preferred to keep the divisions of a single corps together, so he took Schofield's arrival as an opportunity to send Ward back to the Twentieth Corps line north of Atlanta. Morgan remained where he had been located since July 31, but Sherman now shifted the rest of Palmer's Fourteenth Corps to join him. Ward relieved Richard W. Johnson's First Division and Absalom Baird's Third Division. Both Johnson and Baird marched south on August 3 to help Schofield extend southward.[33]

Logan finally made a move to get away from the Ezra Church battle-field and align his corps north to south on August 3. His men conducted a left wheel, traversing the area south of the Lick Skillet Road and bring-ing themselves to face east instead of south, skirmishing along the way. Woods's division continued to hold the left of the corps position, Harrow's division the center, and Morgan L. Smith's division the right. Once in their new position, heavy skirmishing erupted on different parts of the line as the Federals tried to advance a bit more and place their skirmishers on advantageous ground. Harrow's division advanced a heavy skirmish line forward, with Smith's skirmishers to the right supporting the move. A fight that was "severe but of short duration" occurred. The Federals captured a ridge, took 140 Rebel prisoners, and lost 95 men in the process. Maj. Wil-liam B. Brown of the 70th Ohio had survived the dangers of Ezra Church but was mortally wounded in the skirmishing on August 3. According to Thomas Connelly, he had a premonition that he would be killed. "Say to General Harrow I died like a soldier doing his duty," he reportedly asked of friends before he expired at 9 o'clock that evening.[34]

By the time of Brown's death, the Union line west of Atlanta had finally been straightened and was now aimed generally toward the railroad be-tween Atlanta and East Point. Lee's attack at Ezra Church caused a delay

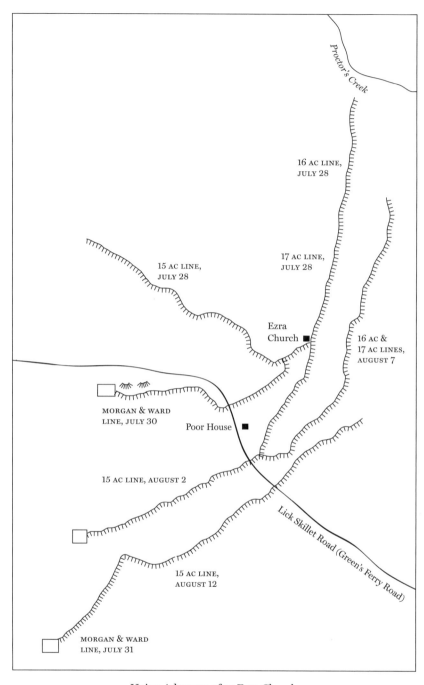

Union Advances after Ezra Church
(Earl J. Hess and Pratibha A. Dabholkar)

of six days in Sherman's efforts to reach the track. The mincing movements conducted by the Federals from July 29 to August 3 indicated that those Confederate attacks had imposed an emotional strain on the Unionists. Sherman's commanders had moved with excessive caution against nothing but skirmishers. Yet by August 3, with more than a corps of additional troops on the extreme right, the Federals were ready to press farther. Whatever benefit the Confederates gained from the loss of 3,000 troops on July 28 was ephemeral.

Sherman's new alignment would remain stable for the next three weeks. The Fourth Corps continued to hold the extreme left northeast of Atlanta, while the Twentieth Corps occupied the trenches north of the city. The Sixteenth Corps and then the Seventeenth and Fifteenth Corps continued the line northwest of Atlanta. South of Logan's position, Baird, Davis, and then Johnson held the Fourteenth Corps sector. Farther south, and connecting to Johnson's right, Schofield's Twenty-third Corps troops extended the line still farther south.[35]

Now the entire battlefield of Ezra Church was fully behind the Union position and easily available to visitors. The 1st Minnesota Battery was positioned in the Seventeenth Corps line, and Thomas D. Christie was shocked by the "awful" sight of the field, "the long mounds of red dirt that show where the Rebel dead are buried, in trenches containing 30, 40, 50 and in one trench 240 bodies." Christie refrained from describing more so as not to shock his sister. With a bit more time on their hands after August 3, more details scoured the field to throw additional dirt over the hasty burials as rain had washed away some of the covering.[36]

Sherman's hope that Schofield could turn the Rebel flank or force the Confederates out of their trenches failed to materialize. Hood acted strictly on the defensive after Ezra Church, urged to do so by a direct suggestion from Jefferson Davis on August 5. As Howard put it in his report of the campaign, "The enemy seemed satisfied to stand on the defensive as long as he held Atlanta." Schofield made cautious moves to find and turn the Confederate flank, but Hood continued to extend the East Point Line to block his efforts. When trying to cross the Sandtown Road near Utoy Creek, the Federals found William B. Bate's Division fortified on high ground south of the roadway and at a right angle to the East Point Line. Reilly's brigade of the Twenty-third Corps attacked Bate on August 6 and lost 306 men out of 1,500 engaged while inflicting very little damage on the Confederates. Two other Union brigades then sought and turned Bate's left flank, compelling his division to retire to the East Point Line that night. The battle of Utoy

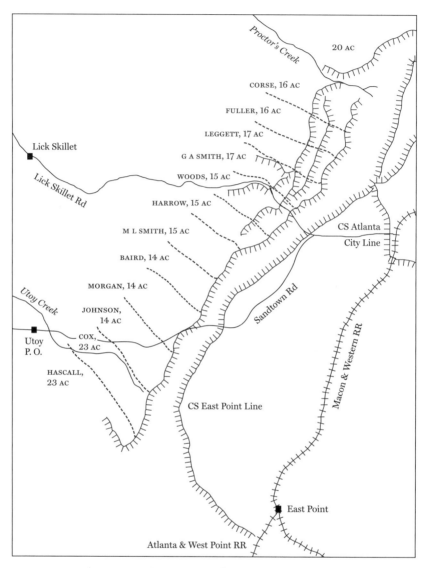

20 AC

CORSE, 16 AC

FULLER, 16 AC

LEGGETT, 17 AC

G A SMITH, 17 AC

WOODS, 15 AC

HARROW, 15 AC

M L SMITH, 15 AC

BAIRD, 14 AC

MORGAN, 14 AC

JOHNSON, 14 AC

COX, 23 AC

HASCALL, 23 AC

Proctor's Creek

Lick Skillet

Lick Skillet Rd

Utoy Creek

Utoy P. O.

CS Atlanta
City Line

Sandtown Rd

Macon & Western RR

CS East Point Line

East Point

Atlanta & West Point RR

Union Line in Mid-August, 1864
(Earl J. Hess and Pratibha A. Dabholkar)

Creek demonstrated the potential of Hood's new defensive policy to delay and damage the Federal army in its effort to extend south.[37]

Sherman was frustrated and impatient. It was dangerous to stretch his manpower any further in a continuous line, and he came to the conclusion that a drastic change in tactics was needed to reach the railroad. Two months earlier, Sherman had temporarily cut his connection with his supply line at Kennesaw Mountain in order to flank a long Confederate line. Now that plan seemed to offer the best chance of success. Sherman could temporarily march away from the Western and Atlantic Railroad with most of his army group and move south in a freewheeling march to cut the railroad between Atlanta and Macon.[38]

A great deal of preparation was necessary to implement this move. Sherman planned to shift the Fourth Corps from the extreme left to the area west of Atlanta to participate in the flanking march, while the Twentieth Corps would evacuate its trenches north of the city and fall back to the railroad crossing of the Chattahoochee River. There Williams's men would protect Sherman's link with Chattanooga. The shifting of Williams's corps would expose the left flank of Howard's Army of the Tennessee. To cover that flank, Sherman told Poe to select a place to dig a refused line stretching back from the rear of Howard's position toward the west. The object was to place the parapet on the north side of the trench so troops could hold it against a threat from the north. Poe assigned that task to Howard's chief engineer, Capt. Chauncey B. Reese, and Reese chose the very same ridge that Logan had used to fight the battle of Ezra Church. Reese made his decision on August 23 and troops began digging that trench the next day. Units from all three corps, including the 15th Iowa, 63rd Ohio, and 26th Illinois, contributed to the digging. On the far left of this new line (the western end), the Federals curved the trench round to face northwest and then west to provide flank protection for the new position. By August 25, the new work was finished. It is ironic that this low, irregular ridge provided the venue for Logan's men to defend themselves from heavy attacks coming from the south and now would provide the scene for Howard's army to defend itself in case Confederate attacks came from the north.[39]

Stanley pulled the Fourth Corps away from the far Union left on the night of August 25. By dawn the next day, he reached positions near Proctor's Creek and the hill that Davis's division had held before Howard brought the Army of the Tennessee to the west of Atlanta. The Twentieth Corps had already evacuated its position by then and had fallen back to the Chattahoochee River. Resting in this new position, now exposed to

Confederate skirmishers, some light fighting developed for Stanley's men. Howard waited until Stanley resumed his march to a point west of the Fifteenth Corps, and then he swung the Sixteenth Corps and Leggett's division of the Seventeenth Corps back to hold the new refused line facing north by the evening of August 26. Capt. Oscar L. Jackson of the 63rd Ohio arrived in the line at 1:00 A.M. with his men. Despite the darkness, he noticed the land south of the ridge was dotted with burial mounds, some of them quite large in size. Many still had only shallow coverings. Jackson saw a shoe and foot sticking out of one mound when he went close enough to examine it in the dark.[40]

Most of Howard's men held this line on the battlefield only a few hours before setting off to join Sherman's flanking movement on August 26. Some Sixteenth Corps troops remained behind to serve as skirmishers, protecting the rear of Sherman's columns for another day. They engaged in fairly heavy skirmishing from about 10:00 A.M. until dusk but held the Rebel skirmishers back. All Federals evacuated the ridgeline during the night of August 26–27 to join Sherman.[41]

The scarred battlefield of Ezra Church had finally witnessed its last fighting. It now was open to the Confederates, who had not been able to see the field since the evening of July 28. Many Southerners merely wandered about, but some of them had a special purpose. Capt. H. W. Henry and a party of friends took shovels and began to look for the grave of Col. Benjamin R. Hart of their regiment, the 22nd Alabama. Hart had been among those who were killed on July 28. In some unexplained way the party located the grave not only of Hart but of other regimental members. "The bodies had been thrown into a shallow gully in the valley near their intrenchments and covered lightly with brush and earth." Henry and his comrades made an effort to retrieve the remains but gave it up. "It was a hot day in August," Henry recalled after the war, "and the sight and odor proved so sickening that we soon had to desist."[42]

Henry found at least two graves that the Federals had marked with some kind of identification. One of them was the grave of Captain Sharp, 10th Mississippi, with the inscription, "buried with the honors of his brother Masons of the 35th New Jersey Regiment." Another grave bore a telling inscription. "Here lies a hero, the color bearer of the 19th Alabama Regiment, who planted his colors within this intrenchment."[43]

The Confederates had access to the battlefield for only about six days. Sherman's flanking movement succeeded in grand fashion, cutting the Atlanta and West Point Railroad about fifteen miles southwest of East Point.

By the time the Federals marched to the Macon and Western Railroad at Jonesboro, Hood had shifted Hardee and Lee to that town. The Confederates attacked on August 31 and were repulsed rather easily. Then Hood shifted Lee away because he received reports of other Union troops nearing the railroad north of Jonesboro. Hardee was now isolated and heavily outnumbered. The Federals attacked him on September 1 and drove his corps from Jonesboro. There was nothing left for Hood to do but evacuate Atlanta on the night of September 1–2. After four months of grueling operations, the Atlanta campaign came to an end.[44]

Conclusion

The battle that Lee started west of Atlanta came to be known to its participants by different names. While the Federals mostly referred to it as the battle of Ezra Church, they also called it the battle of Ezra Chapel. The Confederates often used either of these terms, but they also referred to the engagement as the battle of July 28, or the battle of the Lick Skillet Road, or the battle of the Poor House. To historians of the Civil War, however, it is best known as the battle of Ezra Church.[1]

Sherman initiated an idea about this engagement that has resonated among historians ever since. He talked with some of Logan's men after the fight and recalled that they "spoke of the affair of the 28th as the easiest thing in the world; that, in fact, it was a common slaughter of the enemy." He observed the position of Confederate dead before the burial details had cleared the field. It appeared as if the enemy had halted his battle lines "within easy musket-range of our men" to produce this victory. Another observer supported Sherman's contention. Henry Aten of the 85th Illinois in Morgan's division also spoke to some of Logan's men and came away with the same impression. They told him "that to repulse the enemy was as easy as lying."[2]

Historians have had a tendency to characterize the result of the fight at Ezra Church as a foregone conclusion. They tend to dismiss it as a lost cause from the Confederate standpoint because the odds were too heavily stacked against them. The defending Federals merely had to aim and shoot to win the battle. The large disparity of losses between victor and vanquished tends to support that interpretation.[3]

But for most of the Federals Ezra Church did not appear to be an easy victory. "This was an afternoon of desperate fighting," asserted Joseph

Saunier of the 47th Ohio, while Henry Wright of the 6th Iowa argued that Ezra Church "was the most stubbornly contested and bloodiest battlefield of the campaign." Although detailed as a teamster, George P. Metz of the 99th Indiana hovered near the battlefield during the engagement and saw the bloody results. "This is another day to be remembered," he confided to his diary, "of hard fighting and great man Slaughter. This was decidedly the hardest fighting I ever saw, our men held their position with a Small loss the Rebs Suffered terable. The ground is covered with dead Rebs." Many other Federals agreed with Metz. Only "superior fighting & Northern pluck" saved the day, according to George Hildt.[4]

Having already seen many battles, Howard offered cogent analysis of the tactical situation at Ezra Church. While the "slight cover of rails and logs was a great protection," the real key to Logan's defense was that veteran troops calmly fired their muskets in measured ways to sustain a defense against repeated attacks for five or six hours. "It was as severe a musketry engagement as it was my fortune to see during the war," Howard wrote many years later. His men held their position with determination. "They fired low, and ceased firing when the enemy was driven back, thus keeping cool and self-possessed."[5]

In short, Ezra Church was not an easy victory for the Federals despite what a handful of them told Sherman and Aten. The overwhelming majority of Logan's troops, and those Sixteenth and Seventeenth Corps men who came to help them, considered it a very difficult battle. Lee's men nearly overwhelmed Logan's right flank. In fact, Brantley's Brigade actually captured the ridgetop that lay west of the West Ravine and held it for a short while. Other Confederates engaged in hand-to-hand combat across the Union breastwork in Logan's center. Still other Rebels pressed Logan's left so hard that the Federals had to stack several regiments one behind another to hold the angle in Howard's line. Despite the disjointed nature of Lee's attacks, the Confederates mostly conducted the battle with a good deal of spirit and came closer to success than one had a right to expect.

In fact most Federals tended to respect their opponent for what the Rebels did on July 28. John Arbuckle of the 4th Iowa thought that Lee's troops deserved similar credit as George Pickett's men for attacking the Union center at Gettysburg on July 3, 1863.[6]

But Lee opened himself to criticism by ordering the attacks at Ezra Church. The Federals were not fully in control of the Lick Skillet Road. Instead of attacking, Lee could have deployed a heavy skirmish line and pushed the Federal skirmishers away from the road. Then his infantry could have established a line along or just north of the road and dug in. This would have fulfilled Hood's overall plan with the loss of a few dozen instead of 3,000 men. Whether Stewart's projected flank attack on July 29 would have worked is an open question. The Federals were alert to such a move, and Howard particularly was keen to avoid another Chancellorsville. But even if Stewart's flank movement had failed, Lee would have suffered few casualties while stopping Sherman's effort to move toward the railroad.

Historians generally agree with this interpretation of Lee's actions. They also correctly point out that his conduct of affairs at Ezra Church eerily duplicated his action at Tupelo two weeks before. "Both times," as Lee biographer Herman Hattaway has put it, "strategic pressures had goaded him into fighting on unfavorable ground against protected defenders." Such mistakes played to Sherman's advantage.[7]

From Lee's perspective, the Federals seemed already to have gained control of the Lick Skillet Road. The situation demanded action immediately, there was no time to wait and prepare. He needed to strike before the enemy consolidated its position with earthworks. The wisdom of that assessment is highly questionable, but given that Lee accepted it, there was nothing he could do except throw every unit into the attack as it arrived on the field. Thus the Confederate assaults that afternoon were foredoomed to take place in unsupported waves, a mode of operations that normally ended in failure.

Despite Lee's hope that his men could push the enemy back before they consolidated their hold on the Lick Skillet Road, the Federals barely had enough time to establish their position on the ridge with at least a minimal amount of fortifying. Howard and Logan were aware of the vulnerable right flank and other weak spots in the Fifteenth Corps line. Fortunately for the Union cause, both officers called up sufficient reinforcements in time to bolster those weak points.

A well-planned and coordinated effort by the Confederates was needed to deal with this Union position, but Lee felt he had no time to organize one. As it turned out, the best efforts were conducted by Brantley's Brigade against the Union right, by Gibson's Brigade against the angle in the line, and by Quarles's Brigade against the right. Three regiments of Johnston's Brigade also conducted their second attack with impressive zeal. While O'Neal's Brigade made the worst effort, the other Confederate units involved in the fight at Ezra Church tried in commendable ways to achieve Lee's purpose. Taken together, these attacks failed to achieve the level of planning and coordination necessary to have a good chance of success against Howard's command.

Most experienced commanders probably would have opted for the safer course of skirmishing rather than the uncertainties inherent in piecemeal attacks against an enemy whose strength and position were largely unknown. Lee never indicated that he considered skirmishing as an option on July 28. But it is true that the Army of Tennessee often failed to skirmish properly during the course of the Atlanta campaign. Hood himself had ordered a major attack at Kolb's Farm on June 22, during the Kennesaw Mountain phase of the campaign, rather than send out heavy skirmish lines. As a result, his assault was conducted with woefully inadequate information about the Union position and the terrain. When the Federals captured a portion of Baker's Brigade skirmish line on August 3, Lee blamed want of energy on the part of officers for the result. He was pleased, however, with the defensive stamina of his corps skirmishers in subsequent actions on August 7 and praised them in general orders as a way to encourage his troops to skirmish more aggressively. It is possible that, even if Lee had ordered out a heavy skirmish line rather than major attacks on July 28, his men might not have been able to deal with the Federal skirmishers.[8]

Historians have also blamed Hood to a limited degree for what happened at Ezra Church. Although he put together a viable plan to stop Sherman's movement, he remained at headquarters under the assumption that Lee and Stewart could handle their assignments. But Richard McMurry has pointed out that Lee and Stewart were the least experienced of Hood's corps leaders, and they commanded between them two-thirds of Hood's available infantry. According to McMurry, Hood should have tried to exert more personal direction on the movements taking place west of Atlanta on July 28, or should have assigned Hardee to conduct them as he tried to do late in the afternoon after signs of trouble began to filter in to army headquarters.[9]

After the war, Howard argued that the Confederates were almost compelled to attack his Army of the Tennessee on July 28 because if unopposed he could have advanced all the way to the railroad. "Certainly our movement would have forced even Johnston to have attacked us as Hood did," Howard commented. But the cost obviously was too high. The fact that Hood acted on the defensive after July 28 indicated that he came to believe Johnston's tactics were not so wrong after all.[10]

An unusual amount of attention was devoted to estimating Confederate losses at Ezra Church, probably because of the startling disparity of casualties. This disparity in turn tended to make people think Ezra Church was an easy Union victory. Logan believed the Rebels suffered 6,000 to 7,000 casualties. Howard more conservatively estimated the loss at about 5,000 on July 29. Influenced by Logan, he later placed it at 7,000 when writing his official report of the campaign in September. Sherman took seriously the conservative estimates that ranged from 3,300 to 5,000. Federal losses, only 632 men, were far easier to verify.[11]

The disparity in casualties made an impression on everyone from the lowest private to the most recent historian. As signal officer Clifford Stickney put it in a letter home, the Federals suffered "slight loss compared to the magnitude of the attack." Such a discrepancy was unprecedented, and soldiers assumed the home front would find it strange, but they assured correspondents that it was true. "The great difference in numbers may seem [inexplicable]," surgeon George Martin Trowbridge of the 19th Michigan told his wife, "but from position of forces, obstinacy of enemy & rapid firing of our forces it is not strange."[12]

The nature of the Union position contributed to the disparity of losses suffered at Ezra Church. Logan's men aligned along the top of a ridge that was anything but straight in its configuration, with many twists and turns. This enabled them to obtain crossfires on the approaching enemy, who advanced in piecemeal fashion exposing their flanks to these crossfires. On many parts of the Union line troops were massed in ways to deliver heavy fire on vulnerable Confederate flanks.

The Federals had the advantage of terrain, and Lee's attacks were disjointed, but an important factor in the disparity of losses lay in the efficient way most Unionists handled their rifle muskets. Chaplain M. D. Gage of the 12th Indiana reported that the 26th Illinois fired 40,000 rounds during the course of the battle. If that is a guide, then the forty-three Union regiments at Ezra Church fired a total of 1,720,000 rounds of small arms ammunition in about five hours. That amounted to 344,000 rounds per hour. If 9,144 Federals were engaged, they fired on average 188 rounds per man in five hours. Each Yankee fired on average 37.6 rounds per hour, or about one round every two minutes. This is a ratio consistent with exceptionally heavy firing in other major battles of the Civil War.[13]

A point of comparison lies in a detailed report of how many rounds of small arms ammunition were expended by the Confederate Army of Mississippi from June 18 to 23, during the Kennesaw Mountain phase of the Atlanta campaign. The three divisions of the army (later designated Stewart's

Corps) fired almost 200,000 rounds in six days, and this was considered excessive because the army was not engaged in major fighting during this time period. In contrast, the Federals would have exhausted those 200,000 rounds in a little more than half an hour of firing at Ezra Church.[14]

If one compares the firing rates of Logan's men at Ezra Church and that of Loring's Army of Mississippi at Kennesaw Mountain with the expenditure of Thomas C. Hindman's Division at Chickamauga, it becomes more apparent that the drive toward Atlanta was unusual in the grand sweep of the Civil War. Hindman started the battle of September 20, 1863, with 6,122 men in his division (which later, with the addition of Brantley's Brigade, was commanded by John C. Brown at Ezra Church). The troops fought almost continuously for nine hours that day and expended 217,080 rounds of small arms ammunition. That amounted to 24,120 rounds per hour; each man on average firing nearly 4 rounds every hour of the engagement that day. The Federal rate of fire at Ezra Church dwarfed the expenditure of rounds by Hindman's command at Chickamauga by a wide margin.[15]

In fact, it is possible that the rate of Union rifle fire at Ezra Church dwarfed that of nearly every other battle in the Civil War. At Gettysburg, for example, the First Corps of the Army of the Potomac fired 241,000 rounds of small arms ammunition. That amounted to about two-thirds the volume of rounds expended by the equivalent of a corps at Ezra Church. About 30,000 members of the Army of the Cumberland expended 2 million rounds in one and a half days of fighting at Stones River. In only five hours, 9,144 Union troops expended a total amounting to 86 percent of that number of rounds at Ezra Church. While 56,000 Unionists fired 2.65 million rounds in two days at Chickamauga, the Federals at Ezra Church expended the equivalent of 64.9 percent of the same number of rounds.[16]

Personal accounts and official reports far too often fail to provide statistics on volume and rate of fire in Civil War battles. But the evidence available supports the contention that Ezra Church witnessed the most intense and sustained musketry of any engagement in the Civil War.

Logan tried to place the battle of July 28 within the context of losses inflicted on the enemy and casualties suffered during the entire Atlanta campaign. He believed that the Fifteenth Corps killed and wounded 18,000 Confederates from early May to early September, 1864, 36.1 percent of them at Ezra Church alone (a figure based on his overly high estimate of 6,500 Confederates losses on July 28). The corps lost only 13 percent of its campaign casualties at Ezra Church. Forty-five percent of the Rebel flags captured by the corps during the campaign were picked up from the Ezra Church battlefield, and more than one-third of the enemy small arms retrieved from battlefields during the campaign were taken on July 28. The conclusion was clear. The battle of Ezra Church had been a major episode of the Fifteenth Corps experience during the important campaign toward Atlanta.[17]

Chaplain Gage of the 12th Indiana wrote one of the best assessments of the battle when he penned the history of his unit. "Perhaps no severer engagement, with mere musketry—duration of conflict and numbers engaged in the defense considered—occurred during the war than at Ezra Church."[18]

The fact that these muskets were rifled rather than smoothbore was not the key to understanding what happened at Ezra Church. The older interpretation of the rifle musket's impact on Civil War military operations has been undercut by recent scholarship. Rather than accounting for horrendous casualties, making frontal attacks ineffective, and prolonging the war unnecessarily because it rendered battles indecisive, all the evidence indicates that battles like Ezra Church were not bloodbaths because troops engaged were using a weapon that could fire 500 yards instead of only 100 yards. There were many factors that influenced how battles were fought, and the technical capability of weapons was only one of them. Terrain, lack of coordination of the Confederate attacks, and the experience and grit of the defending Federals were more important in determining the outcome of the fight at Ezra Church than the range of small arms. The letters, reports, and diaries of soldiers North and South indicate that most men preferred to fire at short ranges, that they actually opened fire when the enemy was about 100 yards or less away, and that this kind of short-range fighting was very effective. While rifle fire was responsible for a loss of 26 percent of the Confederate soldiers on July 28, smoothbore musketry caused the loss of 47 percent of British forces at the battle of Bunker Hill in 1775.[19]

The range of engagement at Ezra Church supports the idea that the long range of the rifle musket failed to alter the nature of infantry combat during the Civil War. In their first attack, Brantley's men actually captured the Union position for a short while, and during their second assault they surged on until only sixty yards from the Federals. Sharp's first advance did not end until the men were fifty yards from its objective. Johnston's Brigade came within thirty paces of the defender, and elements of the brigade actually fought hand to hand with the enemy in their second advance. Gibson, Baker, Manigault, and Quarles also made it to within thirty paces of the Yankee line before their brigades were stopped. Reynolds's Brigade received enemy fire at a distance of 300 yards, much farther than the effective range of a smoothbore musket, but this fire failed to stop the troops. They continued moving until only thirty yards away from the Federals. Overall, the short range at which attacks ground to a halt because of musketry on July 28 was very consistent with smoothbore battles of the eighteenth century. There is no evidence that the rifle musket had an appreciable effect on the nature of main-line fighting at Ezra Church.

The rifle musket did affect the character of skirmishing in the Civil War. In fact, that conflict can be said to have witnessed the apogee of skirmishing in Western military history, and no other campaign of the Civil War saw such effective skirmishing as Sherman's drive toward Atlanta. But that effective skirmishing was largely done by the Federals, who usually dominated the skirmish line throughout the campaign.

Ezra Church provided a good case study. Logan's skirmishers decisively won their struggle with Armstrong's cavalrymen before the battle began. This may well have happened because the Rebel troopers were outnumbered and armed with short barrel weapons, but the success of Fifteenth Corps skirmishers greatly facilitated Logan's ability to secure the ridge where he established his line. They also went on to closely threaten and in some cases stand on the Lick Skillet Road. This was the key to Lee's decision to launch his uncoordinated attacks, bringing on the battle. The Confederates could have countered this threat by deploying a large infantry force as skirmishers, but they failed to do so.

Even when the battle took place, Union skirmishers played a far more significant role in events than Confederate skirmishers. They severely punished Johnston's Brigade, wounding Johnston and his successor, and killing the third man who took command of the brigade. Federal skirmishers held up Johnston's command for twenty to forty-five minutes before falling back to their main line. Moreover, Union officers sent their skirmishers out after nearly every repulse of a Rebel assault during the course of this long afternoon. Near the end of the battle, Yankee skirmishers closed in on Loring's Division as it was taking position and delivered a terribly annoying fire. They wounded Stewart and Loring in the process. Overall the battle of Ezra Church witnessed impressive skirmishing by the Federals. They took out of action half of the Confederate corps commanders, one-fourth of the division leaders, and three of the fourteen officers who held brigade command on the field. To a large degree, they were able to do this because the Confederates failed to skirmish well during the course of the battle.

In many ways, the short movement of Howard's Army of the Tennessee to the west of Atlanta and the resulting battle of Ezra Church represented a significant and instructive phase of the Atlanta campaign. It was the next step in Sherman's major effort to cut the rail lines that kept the Army of Tennessee in the city, and it represented Hood's third attempt to stop the Federals from neutralizing his supply network. Despite Lee's unwise decision to launch major attacks on Howard, the fight at Ezra Church temporarily stopped the Union drive toward the railroad south of Atlanta. Although they lost far fewer men, the Federals continued their move after July 28 with a great deal of caution.

Hood had taken command of the Army of Tennessee with a mandate to attack, and he did so with a will. At Peach Tree Creek on July 20 and east of Atlanta on July 22, the Confederates found their opponents only partially prepared to receive them. The center of Thomas's line, held by Hooker's Twentieth Corps, was not fully in position when Hardee and Stewart started their assault at Peach Tree Creek. McPherson had taken far too long to secure his vulnerable left flank on July 22 and paid for it with a near disaster and the loss of his own life. On July 28, the Federals were almost fully ready for the Confederate attack, and they owed that mostly to their new commander, Oliver O. Howard. Hood's men enjoyed more advantages at Ezra Church than at either of the previous two battles. They had parity of troop strength with Logan's corps and were near a vulnerable flank and a sharp angle in the Union line.

Lee failed to capitalize on his advantages because of the almost complete lack of coordination that characterized the assaults on July 28. On one level, the Army of Tennessee had a long history of uncoordinated tactical offensives, probably more than any other field army in the Civil War. The causes of this problem deserve an entirely different study than this book can afford. But it is notable that at Ezra Church Brown's Division and Walthall's Division began their advance with all brigades starting at the same time. At some point before they heavily engaged the enemy, the brigades lost contact along the way. There is no indication in the reports that they maintained connected flanks across the shallow valley or hit the enemy at exactly the same time. Much the same was true of Hood's two previous battles north and east of Atlanta, and one can see similar lack of coordination at Chickamauga, Murfreesboro, Perryville, and Shiloh.

Lee could not be held responsible for the institutional problems of his corps, given that he had taken command of it only the day before the battle. But Lee played a large role in neutralizing Clayton's ability to advance his division in a coordinated fashion. Desperate to keep the attacks rolling, he sent staff member Ed. H. Cunningham to hurry Clayton along. Cunningham unwisely ordered Gibson's Brigade to attack, even though Gibson was nowhere to be found. Leon von Zinken unwisely obeyed Cunningham instead of informing Gibson. The result was that the Louisiana brigade went forward unsupported on either flank and without its commander. Clayton had to order another brigade forward unsupported, but he decided to spare his third brigade. His division wasted most of its strength and power because of Lee's and Cunningham's interference.

In the end, even if one adopts the most conservative number of Confederate casualties, Lee suffered far more losses than could be justified by the slim and fleeting advantages he gained at Ezra Church. The battle is significant for finally convincing Hood that his policy of bold tactical advances had better end. He acted almost strictly on the defensive from July 29 to the end of the campaign, except for the attack that Hardee conducted on the first day at Jonesboro. Hood never admitted it, but he adopted Joseph Johnston's defensive policy of merely blocking Union moves behind Confederate earthworks to save manpower. At least 11,000 Confederate troops had paid the price in three battles for proving that uncoordinated attacks could not stop Sherman's men.

This point brings us to another factor in the failure of Hood's triple offensive against Sherman. On each day of battle, Union soldiers fought with courage, determination, and coordination. John Newton's division of the Fourth Corps and William Ward's division of the Twentieth Corps largely won the battle of Peach Tree Creek for the Federals. Dodge's Left Wing of the Sixteenth Corps and Blair's Seventeenth Corps largely won the battle of July 22. And Logan's Fifteenth Corps bore the brunt of the successful defensive battle on July 28. Federal success thus far in the campaign had built up Union morale to an impressive height. Most men in Sherman's army group had complete confidence that they could handle anything Hood threw their way.

At most, the Confederates won limited gains in all three battles, mostly in the way of temporarily halting Sherman's effort to snip lines of communication into Atlanta. But that was inadequate to tip the balance in favor of Southern fortunes. Howell Cobb, the politician turned general who held a district command in Macon, paid close attention to news coming from Atlanta in the heady days of late July. Cobb was encouraged by initial reports but noted that limited success would do little more than add false hope to a gloomy situation. "No battle will amount to anything of importance that does not drive the enemy to the other side of the Chattahoochee," he told his wife.[20]

To prove Cobb's point, the Ezra Church phase of the campaign gave rise to the next phase, with continued efforts to reach the railroad by relying on Schofield's Army of the Ohio to lead the way. Howard's role in this was merely to hold his sector of the line and support efforts to extend south. The result was a small but bloody repulse of one of Schofield's brigades at Utoy Creek on August 6 and futile moves to reach the railroad before the Confederates could extend the East Point Line to block those moves. Eventually Sherman adopted a major flanking maneuver, temporarily moving most of his command from its supply line, to cut the Rebel railroad at Jonesboro by early September. Ezra Church contributed in its own way, just as every other phase of the campaign, to the eventual Union occupation of Atlanta on September 3, 1864.

The war's end only nine months after the battle of Ezra Church ushered in a long period of healing and reconciliation. This process, in which millions of Americans were involved, can be seen in capsule form when looking at the relationship between the opposing commanders at Ezra Church. Howard and Lee had known each other since their West Point days; more than old army colleagues, they were friends. Lee applied to President Andrew Johnson for a pardon in mid-July 1865 and tried to enlist Howard's support in the effort. "I take the liberty of an old class mate and friend," he told Howard. Lee seemed to be completely unaware that Howard had commanded the Federal forces at Ezra Church and did not know that his correspondent had lost an arm early in the conflict. The Confederate general reported that he had "escaped through the terrible war with one slight wound. I am glad you are unhurt." Lee also expressed his hope that "the war has not changed your feelings toward me personally."[21]

Lee was stunned by Howard's reply. "I do not doubt your sincerity," Howard wrote as he promised to help Lee obtain a pardon as long as it did not conflict with his duty. "I should not have predicted that you would have turned against the Union," he continued, "and hope you may yet be a true and earnest friend of the government, that we once loved alike, which nurtured and educated us together."[22]

This mild rebuke was enough to make an enemy of Lee. "Your letter is a studied effort to wound my feelings," he retorted, "it is neither civil or generous. I had hoped if there were no other reasons that the terrible scenes you have witnessed in this war, the great sacrifice of life, treasure & property by the Southern people, at least would have made you charitable enough to consider them as sincere and actuated by pure motives."[23]

Hurting Lee was far from Howard's motive. "You completely misunderstand the spirit of my letter to you," he hurriedly wrote back. "I did not intend it as official but as a truthful answer." Howard explained that he had been forced to dictate the letter because of the loss of his right arm. "God forbid I should insult you or attempt to wound your feelings," he concluded, but Lee never responded to his letter.[24]

For thirty-eight years Howard and Lee were estranged from each other. Both men lived busy, fruitful lives, but it was not until Wharton J. Green of Fayetteville, North Carolina, a mutual acquaintance, wrote to Lee that the estrangement broke. Green had conversed with Howard when both men visited the battlefield at Gettysburg. The old Union general "spoke most feelingly of a slight misunderstanding" between himself and Lee. Green felt that Howard was open to a reconciliation and asked Lee if he could bring himself to do likewise. Lee wrote to Howard in October 1903 about it. "Yes General we are too near the end of our lives to harbor ill feeling or misunderstanding . . . and here is my hand. There is no feeling now, and I salute you as my classmate & friend." With this antagonism laid aside, Lee passed away in May 1908, and Howard died one and a half years later in October 1909.[25]

The battlefield of Ezra Church suffered the same fate as most other fields of the Atlanta campaign. Kennesaw Mountain became the object of intense preservation efforts by Union veterans, which eventually resulted in the creation of a national military park. Pickett's Mill was preserved in a state park in the late twentieth century. But the rest of the campaign's sacred ground has largely remained in private hands, and most signs of the war have been obliterated.[26]

Atlanta civic leaders made efforts to memorialize the battle of Ezra Church for a time. As the city began to expand westward onto the ground, they named topographic features in memory of the fight. The area where Logan's right flank rested became known as Battle Hill, and a new street that ran between the opposing lines was designated Battle Hill Avenue. In 1895 the Atlanta Camp of the United Confederate Veterans published a pamphlet about the various battles fought around the city that was designed to encourage Civil War tourism. It identified the location of Ezra Church and the "County Alms House." The home of Dr. Hiram Mozley was located near the site of the church. When the city created a recreational park that encompassed the area around the angle in Howard's line, it was named after the doctor.[27]

Some impetus in favor of preserving the battlefield at Ezra Church sprang up by the turn of the century. Union and Confederate veterans lobbied for the creation of a national park to encompass the battlefields of Peach Tree Creek, July 22, and Ezra Church, and by 1906 the Atlanta City Council and the local Chamber of Commerce strongly supported the idea. Decades went by with no success. Another wave in the effort to create a national park surfaced in 1931 when Col. H. J. Landus of the Army War College targeted small segments of each battlefield for preservation. These included six acres at Peach Tree Creek, two acres of the July 22 battle site, and forty acres at Ezra Church. A civic group headed by local historian Wilbur G. Kurtz cooperated with Landus and continued to urge the federal government to act on the park concept.[28]

But nothing came of this latest effort even though prominent Atlantans continued to be interested in preserving the city's Civil War battlefields. "They have been neglected for sixty years" complained businessman Ivan Allen Sr. in 1939. Allen referred to a proposed "Alms House Site Park," but it apparently never materialized. There was more focus that year on preserving a portion of the Peach Tree Creek battlefield, which also fizzled after a while.[29]

No preservation of any kind took place on the battlefield of July 28. Today the Ezra Church area is covered with suburban neighborhoods, and only a few historical markers erected by the state of Georgia indicate that a bloody battle took place. The old village of Lick Skillet is now called Adamsville, and it has been engulfed by the larger Atlanta metro area. The Lick Skillet Road has been replaced by a jumble of modern highways and streets running through the general area of the battlefield. Sherman's headquarters at the White House on Peach Tree Road, where Howard replaced Logan as commander of the Army of the Tennessee, is today near the Brookwood Station of the Atlanta public transit system on Peachtree Street.[30]

A great deal of the ridge that the Confederates used to launch their attacks on July 28 was destroyed by the construction of Interstate 20. Battle Hill Sanitarium for the treatment of tuberculosis occupied the ground held by the 83rd Indiana east of the West Ravine until replaced by the Sadie G. Mays Memorial Nursing Home. Ezra Church has long since disappeared, but it was located in what is now the southeast corner of Mozley

Park. The Sixteenth and Seventeenth Corps line ran roughly along what is today called Chappell Road. The name of this modern street apparently is a corruption of Chapel Road, a reference to the fact that it ran directly toward Ezra Church in 1864. The hill occupied by Davis's division of the Fourteenth Corps before the arrival of Howard's Army of the Tennessee is today called Davis Hill. It is located near the junction of Bankhead Highway and Chappell Road.[31]

On the Confederate side of the battlefield, the huge Westview Cemetery took up much of the ground just south of the old Lick Skillet Road that was used by various units to form line before advancing. The cemetery was founded in 1884, and a Confederate memorial statue and many graves of Rebel veterans were added over the years. The Fulton County Alms House, or Poor House, was located near the main gateway of the cemetery. A. P. Stewart was wounded near the modern junction of Gordon Terrace and Cowley Avenue.[32]

Evidence of combat surfaced periodically on the Ezra Church battlefield. Workers digging the foundation of the Frank L. Stanton School uncovered bones of Civil War soldiers in 1927. The school was located on top of the ridge held by Logan's command, just west of the East Ravine. As late as the 1970s it was still possible to discern the faint remnants of earthworks at some isolated parts of the Ezra Church battlefield. None of these works existed at the time of the battle but represent various digging efforts during the month following the engagement of July 28.[33]

The fate of the Ezra Church battlefield was shared by that of Peach Tree Creek and July 22. Battlefields engulfed by city development lose most of their value to students and historians of armed conflict, but the lay of the land largely remains intact. If one can imagine the houses gone, search for views along the cleared lanes created by streets, and examine topographic maps of the area, it is possible to catch a glimpse of history and understand the essential terrain features that guided the action. The fury of Ezra Church continues to live in the remaining personal accounts and reports that document the event, even if the physical environment of battle is scarred by postwar marks of material culture.

Order of Battle
Ezra Church, July 28, 1864

FEDERAL FORCES

9,144 engaged, lost 632 (6.9 percent)

Military Division of the Mississippi: Maj. Gen. William T. Sherman

ARMY OF THE TENNESSEE: MAJ. GEN. OLIVER O. HOWARD

Fifteenth Corps: Maj. Gen. John A. Logan

FIRST DIVISION: BRIG. GEN. CHARLES R. WOODS

First Brigade: Col. Milo Smith
26th Iowa: Lieut. Col. Thomas G. Ferreby
30th Iowa: Lieut. Col. Aurelius Roberts
27th Missouri: Col. Thomas Curly
76th Ohio: Col. William B. Woods

Second Brigade: Col. James A. Williamson
4th Iowa: Capt. Randolph Sry
9th Iowa: Col. David Carskaddon (wounded); Maj. George Granger
25th Iowa: Col. George A. Stone
31st Iowa: Col. William Smyth

Third Brigade: Col. Hugo Wangelin
3rd Missouri: Col. Theodore Meumann
12th Missouri: Lieut. Col. Jacob Kaercher (wounded);
    Maj. Frederick T. Ledergerber
17th Missouri (Battalion): Maj. Francis Romer
29th Missouri: Lieut. Col. Joseph S. Gage
31st Missouri: Lieut. Col. Samuel P. Simpson
32nd Missouri: Maj. Abraham J. Seay

SECOND DIVISION: BRIG. GEN. MORGAN L. SMITH

First Brigade: Col. James S. Martin
55th Illinois: Capt. Francis H. Shaw
111th Illinois: Col. James S. Martin (no information available
as to his replacement)
116th Illinois: Capt. John S. Windsor
127th Illinois: Lieut. Col. Frank S. Curtiss
6th Missouri: Lieut. Col. Delos Van Deusen
57th Ohio: Lieut. Col. Samuel R. Mott

Second Brigade: Brig. Gen. Joseph A. J. Lightburn
83rd Indiana: Capt. George H. Scott
30th Ohio: Col. Theodore Jones
37th Ohio: Maj. Charles Hipp (wounded); Capt. Carl Moritz
47th Ohio: Maj. Thomas T. Taylor
53rd Ohio: Col. Wells S. Jones
54th Ohio: Lieut. Col. Robert Williams Jr.

FOURTH DIVISION: BRIG. GEN. WILLIAM HARROW

First Brigade: Col. Reuben Williams
26th Illinois: Lieut. Col. Robert A. Gillmore
90th Illinois: Lieut. Col. Owen Stuart
12th Indiana: Lieut. Col. James Goodnow
100th Indiana: Lieut. Col. Albert Heath

Second Brigade: Brig. Gen. Charles C. Walcutt
40th Illinois: Maj. Hiram W. Hall (wounded); Capt. Michael Galvin
103rd Illinois: Capt. Franklin C. Post
97th Indiana: Lieut. Col. Aden G. Cavins
6th Iowa: Maj. Thomas J. Ennis (mortally wounded); Capt. William H. Clune
46th Ohio: Lieut. Col. Isaac N. Alexander

Third Brigade: Col. John M. Oliver
48th Illinois: Maj. Edward Adams
99th Indiana: Lieut. Col. John M. Berkey
15th Michigan: Lieut. Col. Frederick S. Hutchinson
70th Ohio: Maj. William B. Brown

Left Wing, Sixteenth Corps: Maj. Gen. Grenville M. Dodge
SECOND DIVISION: BRIG. GEN. JOHN M. CORSE

Second Brigade: Lieut. Col. Jesse J. Phillips
12th Illinois: Lieut. Col. Henry Van Sellar
66th Illinois: Capt. William S. Boyd
81st Ohio: Lieut. Col. Robert N. Adams

FOURTH DIVISION: BRIG. GEN. JOHN W. FULLER

First Brigade: Lieut. Col. Henry T. McDowell
64th Illinois: Col. John Morrill

Second Brigade: Brig. Gen. John W. Sprague
35th New Jersey: Col. John J. Cladek

Seventeenth Corps: Maj. Gen. Frank P. Blair Jr.

THIRD DIVISION: BRIG. GEN. MORTIMER D. LEGGETT

First Brigade: Col. George E. Bryant
31st Illinois: Lieut. Col. Robert N. Pearson
12th Wisconsin: Col. George E. Bryant

FOURTH DIVISION: BRIG. GEN. GILES A. SMITH

First Brigade: Col. Benjamin F. Potts
3rd Iowa (3 companies): Lieut. Lewis T. Linnell
32nd Ohio: Lieut. Col. Jeff. J. Hibbets

Third Brigade: Col. John Shane
13th Iowa: Maj. William A. Walker
15th Iowa: Col. William W. Belknap

CONFEDERATE FORCES
11,430 engaged, lost 3,000 (26.2 percent)
ARMY OF TENNESSEE: GEN. JOHN B. HOOD

Lee's Corps: Lieut. Gen. Stephen D. Lee

BROWN'S DIVISION: BRIG. GEN. JOHN C. BROWN

Johnston's Brigade: Brig. Gen. George D. Johnston (wounded);
Col. John G. Coltart (wounded); Col. Benjamin R. Hart (killed);
Lieut. Col. Harry T. Toulmin
19th Alabama: Lieut. Col. George R. Kimbrough
22nd Alabama: Col. Benjamin R. Hart (replaced Coltart);
    Capt. Isaac M. Whitney
25th Alabama: Capt. Napoleon B. Rouse
39th Alabama: Capt. Thomas J. Brannon
50th Alabama: Col. John G. Coltart (replaced Johnston);
    Capt. George W. Arnold (wounded); Capt. Archibald D. Ray
17th Alabama Battalion Sharpshooters: Capt. James F. Nabers

Sharp's Brigade: Col. Jacob H. Sharp
7th Mississippi: Col. William H. Bishop
9th Mississippi: Lieut. Col. Benjamin F. Johns
10th Mississippi: Lieut. Col. George B. Myers
41st Mississippi: Col. J. Byrd Williams
44th Mississippi: Lieut. Col. R. G. Kelsey
9th Mississippi Battalion Sharpshooters: Lieut. J. B. Downing

Manigault's Brigade: Brig. Gen. Arthur M. Manigault
24th Alabama: Capt. Starke H. Oliver
28th Alabama: Lieut. Col. William L. Butler
34th Alabama: Maj. John N. Slaughter
10th South Carolina: Lieut. Col. C. Irvine Walker (wounded)
19th South Carolina: Capt. Thomas W. Getzen (wounded);
    Capt. Elijah W. Horne (wounded); Adjutant James O. Ferrell

Brantley's Brigade: Col. William F. Brantley
24th and 27th Mississippi: Col. Robert P. McKelvaine (wounded);
    Lieut. Col. William L. Lyles
29th and 30th Mississippi: Lieut. Col. James M. Johnson
34th Mississippi: Capt. T. S. Hubbard

CLAYTON'S DIVISION: MAJ. GEN. HENRY D. CLAYTON

Baker's Brigade: Brig. Gen. Alpheus Baker
37th Alabama: Lieut. Col. Alexander A. Greene
40th Alabama: Col. John H. Higley
42nd Alabama: Capt. R. K. Wells
54th Alabama: Lieut. Col. John A. Minter

Gibson's Brigade: Brig. Gen. Randall L. Gibson
1st Louisiana (Regulars): Capt. W. H. Sparks
4th Louisiana: Col. S. E. Hunter
13th Louisiana: Lieut. Col. Francis L. Campbell
16th and 25th Louisiana: Lieut. Col. Robert H. Lindsay
19th Louisiana: Col. Richard W. Turner
20th Louisiana: Col. Leon von Zinken
30th Louisiana: Lieut. Col. Thomas Shields (killed)
4th Louisiana Battalion: Maj. Duncan Buie
Austin's Louisiana Battalion Sharpshooters: Maj. John E. Austin

Holtzclaw's Brigade: Brig. Gen. James T. Holtzclaw
18th Alabama: Lieut. Col. Peter F. Hunley
32nd and 58th Alabama: Col. Bushrod Jones
36th Alabama: Lieut. Col. Thomas H. Herndon
38th Alabama: Maj. Shep. Ruffin

Stewart's Corps: Lieut. Gen. Alexander P. Stewart (wounded);
Maj. Gen. Edward C. Walthall

WALTHALL'S DIVISION: MAJ. GEN. EDWARD C. WALTHALL;
BRIG. GEN. WILLIAM A. QUARLES

Quarles's Brigade: Brig. Gen. William A. Quarles; Col. Robert A. Owens
1st Alabama: Maj. Samuel L. Knox (wounded)
42nd Tennessee: Col. Isaac N. Hulme
46th and 55th Tennessee: Col. Robert A. Owens
48th Tennessee: Lieut. Col. Aaron S. Godwin
49th Tennessee: Col. William F. Young (wounded)
53rd Tennessee: Col. John R. White (killed); Maj. William C. Richardson
   (mortally wounded)

Cantey's Brigade: Col. Edward A. O'Neal
17th Alabama: Maj. Thomas J. Burnett (wounded); Capt. John A. Foster
26th Alabama; Maj. David F. Bryan
29th Alabama: Capt. John A. Foster
37th Mississippi: Maj. Samuel H. Terral
Sharpshooter Battalion: Capt. A. L. O'Brien

Reynolds's Brigade: Brig. Gen. Daniel H. Reynolds
1st Arkansas Mounted Rifles (dismounted): Lieut. Col. Morton G. Galloway
   (wounded)
2nd Arkansas Mounted Rifles (dismounted): Lieut. Col. James T. Smith (killed)
4th Arkansas: Col. Henry G. Bunn (wounded)
9th Arkansas: Col. Isaac L. Dunlop
25th Arkansas: Lieut. Col. Eli Hufstedler (killed)
Gholson's Brigade (attached to Reynolds's Brigade): Col. John McGuirk
Youngblood's Battalion (attached to Reynolds's Brigade): Maj. Youngblood

Cavalry Corps: Maj. Gen. Joseph Wheeler

JACKSON'S DIVISION: BRIG. GEN. WILLIAM H. JACKSON

Armstrong's Brigade: Brig. Gen. Frank C. Armstrong
1st Mississippi Cavalry: Lieut. Col. Frank A. Montgomery
2nd Mississippi Cavalry: Maj. John J. Perry
28th Mississippi Cavalry: Col. Peter B. Starke
Ballentine's Mississippi Regiment: Lieut. Col. William L. Maxwell

Notes

AAS   American Antiquarian Society, Worcester, Massachusetts
ADAH   Alabama Department of Archives and History, Montgomery
AHC   Atlanta History Center, Atlanta, Georgia
ALPL   Abraham Lincoln Presidential Library, Springfield, Illinois
AM   Archives of Michigan, Lansing
BC   Bowdoin College, Special Collections, Brunswick, Maine
BHL-UM   University of Michigan, Bentley Historical Library, Ann Arbor
CHM   Chicago History Museum, Chicago, Illinois
CHS   Connecticut Historical Society, New Haven
CU   Cornell University, Division of Rare and Manuscript Collections,
            Ithaca, New York
CWM   College of William and Mary, Special Collections, Williamsburg,
            Virginia
DU   Duke University, Rubenstein Rare Book and Manuscript Library,
            Durham, North Carolina
EU   Emory University, Manuscript, Archives, and Rare Book Library,
            Atlanta Georgia
FHS   Filson Historical Society, Louisville, Kentucky
GLIAH   Gilder Lehrman Institute of American History, New York,
            New York
HU   Harvard University, Houghton Library, Cambridge, Massachusetts
IHS   Indiana Historical Society, Indianapolis
ISL   Indiana State Library, Indianapolis
ISU   Iowa State University, Special Collections, Iowa City
LC   Library of Congress, Manuscript Division, Washington, D.C.
LMU   Lincoln Memorial University, Abraham Lincoln Library and
            Museum, Harrogate, Tennessee
LSU   Louisiana State University, Louisiana and Lower Mississippi Valley
            Collection, Special Collections, Baton Rouge
MassHS   Massachusetts Historical Society, Boston
MDAH   Mississippi Department of Archives and History, Jackson
MHM   Missouri History Museum, St. Louis
MHS   Minnesota Historical Society, St. Paul

MOC	Museum of the Confederacy, Richmond, Virginia
MSU	Mississippi State University, Special Collections, Starkville
MU	Miami University, Special Collections, Oxford, Ohio
NARA	National Archives and Records Administration, Washington, D.C.
NC	Navarro College, Pearce Civil War Collection, Corsicana, Texas
N-YHS	New-York Historical Society, New York
NYPL	New York Public Library, Rare Books and Manuscripts, New York
OHS	Ohio Historical Society, Archives/Library, Columbus
OR	*The War of the Rebellion: A Compilation of the Official Records of the Union and Confederate Armies.* 70 Vols. in 128. Washington, D.C.: Government Printing Office, 1880–1901. *OR* citations take the following form: volume number(part number):page number(s)— e.g., *OR* 38(3):66–67. Unless otherwise cited, all references are to series 1.
SCHS	South Carolina Historical Society, Charleston
SHSI	State Historical Society of Iowa, Des Moines
SHSM-RCC	State Historical Society of Missouri, Research Center Columbia
SHSM-RCSL	State Historical Society of Missouri, Research Center St. Louis
SOR	*Supplement to the Official Records of the Union and Confederate Armies.* 100 Vols. Wilmington, NC: Broadfoot, 1993–2000. *SOR* citations take the following form: part number, volume number: page number(s)—e.g., *SOR*, Pt. 2, 12:588.
SU	Syracuse University, Special Collections Research Center, Syracuse, New York
TSLA	Tennessee State Library and Archives, Nashville
UA	University of Alabama, W. Stanley Hoole Special Collections Library, Tuscaloosa
UAF	University of Arkansas, Special Collections, Fayetteville
UG	University of Georgia, Hargrett Rare Book and Manuscript Library, Athens
UI	University of Iowa, Special Collections, Iowa City
UM	University of Mississippi, Archives and Special Collections, Oxford
UNC	University of North Carolina, Southern History Collection, Chapel Hill
UND	University of Notre Dame, Rare Books and Special Collections, South Bend, Indiana
UO	University of Oklahoma, Western History Collections, Norman
USAMHI	U.S. Army Military History Institute, Carlisle, Pennsylvania
USC	University of South Carolina, South Caroliniana Library, Columbia
USM	University of Southern Mississippi, McCain Library and Archives, Hattiesburg
UTA	University of Texas, Dolph Briscoe Center for American History, Austin
UTC	University of Tennessee, Special Collections, Chattanooga

UTK	University of Tennessee, Special Collections, Knoxville
UV	University of Virginia, Electronic Text Center, Charlottesville
UW	University of Washington, Special Collections, Seattle
UWY	University of Wyoming, American Heritage Center, Laramie
VHS	Virginia Historical Society, Richmond
WHS	Wisconsin Historical Society, Madison
WCL-UM	University of Michigan, William L. Clements Library, Ann Arbor

CHAPTER ONE

1. Castel, *Decision in the West*, 121–344; estimate of losses of both Union and Confederate forces can be found in ibid., 261–62.

2. Sherman to Ellen, June 30, 1864, Simpson and Berlin, *Sherman's Civil War*, 660; Sherman to Halleck, *OR* 38(5):66.

3. Castel, *Decision in the West*, 213–21; Hess, *Kennesaw Mountain*, 188–200.

4. Sears, *Gates of Richmond*, 65–86; Bearss, *Siege of Jackson*, 55–105.

5. Castel, *Decision in the West*, 462–71.

6. Ibid., 347–69.

7. Ibid., 352–65; McMurry, *John Bell Hood*, 116–24.

8. Castel, *Decision in the West*, 365–83.

9. Sherman to Thomas, July 20, 1864, *OR* 38(5):198.

10. Howard to Schofield, July 21, 1864, *OR* 38(5):218; Castel, *Decision in the West*, 383–88.

11. Sherman to Thomas, July 22, 1864, *OR* 38(5):223.

12. Castel, *Decision in the West*, 384–414.

13. Poe to [Delafield], October 8, 1865, *OR* 38(1):132–33; Reese to Poe, September 14, 1864, *OR* 38(3):66–67; Special Field Orders No. 42, Headquarters, Military Division of the Mississippi, July 25, 1864, *OR* 38(5):255; diary, July 24, 1864, Orlando Metcalfe Poe Papers, LC; Henry Schmidt to Kate, July 30, 1864, Schmidt Family Papers, FHS. A newspaper correspondent obtained and published accurate information about the fortification plan to cover Sherman's left flank after the Army of the Tennessee left it in Q.P.F. to *Cincinnati Commercial*, July 29, 1864, published in *St. Louis Daily Missouri Democrat*, August 8, 1864.

14. Castel, *Tom Taylor's Civil War*, 151–52; Bell, *Tramps and Triumphs*, 20–21; John C. Brown Diary, July 25, 1864, UI; William F. Graham Diary, July 23, 1864, ALPL; Allen to parents, July 25 and 26, 1864, Edward W. Allen Papers, UNC.

15. Allen to parents, July 25 and 26, 1864, Edward W. Allen Papers, UNC.

16. Diary, July 24, 1864, Orlando Metcalfe Poe Papers, LC; Michael Houck Diary, July 24, 1864, UTK; Stanley to Fullerton, September 1864, *OR* 38(1):226; Bauer, *Soldiering*, 154; Holzhucter, "William Wallace's Civil War Letters," 102–3; Dunlap, "*Your Affectionate Husband*," 332; Kirkup to Creigh, September 9, 1864, *OR* 38(2):175–76; Sherman to Halleck, July 26, 1864, *OR* 38(5):260.

17. Sherman to Logan, July 23, 1864, and Special Field Orders No. 76, Headquarters, Army of the Tennessee, July 23, 1864, *OR* 38(5):238–40; Dodge to Clark, No-

vember 25, 1864, *OR* 38(3):385; diary, July 24, 1864, David James Palmer Papers, UI; John C. Brown Diary, July 24, 1864, UI; Sherman to Halleck, September 15, 1864, *OR* 38(1):75.

18. W. W. Black, "Marching with Sherman," 324; Moore to Howard, September 28, 1864, *OR* 38(3):54; diary, July 22–23, 25, 1864, George W. Modil Papers, MDAH.

19. Sherman to Logan, July 24, 1864, *OR* 38(5):243.

20. Logan to Sherman, July 24, 1864, and Sherman to Logan, July 24, 1864, *OR* 38(5):242–43.

21. Sherman to Schofield, July 23, 1864; Sherman to Halleck, July 24, 1864; Sherman to Logan, July 24, 1864; Special Field Orders No. 45, Headquarters, Left Wing, Sixteenth Corps, July 24, 1864; Sherman to Thomas, July 25, 1864; and Sherman to Garrard, July 25, 1864, *OR* 38(5):237–38, 240, 243, 247, 248, 251; Castel, *Decision in the West*, 417.

22. Sherman to Logan, July 24, 1864, *OR* 38(5):243.

23. Special Field Orders No. 42, Headquarters, Military Division of the Mississippi, July 25, 1864, *OR* 38(5):255–256.

24. Sherman to Grant, July 25, 1864; Van Duzer to Eckert, July 25, 1864; and Special Field Orders No. 42, Headquarters, Military Division of the Mississippi, July 25, 1864, *OR* 38(5):247, 254, 255.

25. Sherman to Halleck, September 15, 1864, *OR* 38(1):75–76; Sherman to Garrard, July 25, 1864, *OR* 38(5):251; Sherman to Halleck, July 26, 1864; Stoneman to Sherman, July 26, 1864; and Sherman to Stoneman, July 26, 1864, *OR* 38(5):260–61, 264–65.

26. Organization of the Confederate Forces, *OR* 38(3):664.

27. Hale, *Third Texas Cavalry*, 233; Crabb, *All Afire to Fight*, 231–32; Ross to Jackson, July 22, 1864, 1:00 P.M. and 9:11 P.M., and Ross to Jackson, July 24, 1864, 8:00 A.M., *OR* 38(5):901–2, 907.

28. Sherman to Thomas, July 25, 1864; Sherman to McCook, July 25, 1864; Sherman to Thomas, July 26, 1864; and Ross to Jackson, July 26, 1864, 10:45 A.M., *OR* 38(5):249, 250, 261, 911.

29. Sherman to Halleck, July 24, 1864, *OR* 38(5):240.

30. "Personal Biography of Major General Grenville Mellen Dodge 1831–1870," 1:258, Grenville Mellen Dodge Papers, SHSI.

31. The standard biography of Howard is Carpenter, *Sword and Olive Branch*, but Howard's *Autobiography* contains a full narrative of the general's life as well. For Chancellorsville, see Keller, *Chancellorsville and the Germans*; for Pickett's Mill, see Dean, "Forgotten 'Hell Hole.'"

32. Howard, "Battles about Atlanta," 395.

33. Grant to Stanton, July 26, 1864, 2:00 P.M., and Halleck to Sherman, July 26, 1864, 4:00 P.M., *OR* 38(5):260.

34. Howard, "Battle of Ezra Chapel," 3, and Howard to wife, July 23, 1864, O. O. Howard Papers, BC.

35. The standard biography of Logan is Jones, *Black Jack*; Sherman, *Memoirs*, 2:86.

36. Sherman, *Memoirs*, 2:85–86.

37. Sherman to Thomas, July 26, 1864; Sherman to Howard, July 26, 1864, received 10:00 P.M.; Special Field Orders No. 44, Headquarters, Military Division of the Mississippi, July 26, 1864; and Howard to the Fourth Army Corps, July 26, 1864, *OR* 38(5):261, 266, 267; Howard to Dayton, September 17, 1864, *OR* 38(3):40.

38. Hood to Seddon, July 19, 1864, *OR* 38(5):892.

39. Hattaway, *General Stephen D. Lee*, 3, 10, 13, 46–55, 62–77, 90–98, 111; Howard, *Autobiography*, 2:21.

40. Hattaway, *General Stephen D. Lee*, 120–21, 123–24; Castel, *Decision in the West*, 416–17.

41. Hattaway, *General Stephen D. Lee*, 125.

42. Hess, *Kennesaw Mountain*, 28–46; Bragg to Davis, July 25, 1864, *OR* 38(5):908; J. Davis, *Rise and Fall*, 2:557–60.

43. McMurry, *John Bell Hood*, 86–92.

44. Diary, July 23, 25, 1864, Emmett Ross Papers, MSU; Venet, *Sam Richards's Civil War Diary*, 228.

45. Throne, "History of Company D," 64; Reese to Poe, September 14, 1864, *OR* 38(3):67.

46. Special Field Orders No. 79, Headquarters, Army of the Tennessee, July 26, 1864; Special Field Orders No. 62, Headquarters, Fifteenth Corps, July 26, 1864; and Special Field Orders No. 47, Headquarters, Left Wing, Sixteenth Corps, July 26, 1864, *OR* 38(5):268–69, 270. Logan's Special Field Orders No. 79 can also be found in John Alexander Logan Papers, LC.

47. Sherman to Thomas and Schofield, July 26, 1864, *OR* 38(5):261–62.

48. Howard to Whipple, July 26, 1864; Fullerton to Stanley, July 26, 1864; Cox to Cameron, July 26, 1864; and Special Field Orders No. 62, Headquarters, Army of the Ohio, July 26, 1864, *OR* 38(5):263, 267–68.

49. Sherman to Halleck, July 26, 1864, *OR* 38(5):260; Sherman to Ellen, July 26, 1864, Simpson and Berlin, *Sherman's Civil War*, 672.

50. Special Field Orders No. 56, Headquarters, Army of Tennessee, July 24, 1864; Hood to Cooper, July 26, 1864; Hood to Seddon, July 26, 1864; Bragg to Sale, July 26, 1864; and Special Field Orders No. 58, Headquarters, Army of Tennessee, July 26, 1864, *OR* 38(5):907, 910, 911, 912.

51. General Field Orders No. 7, Headquarters, Army of Tennessee, July 25, 1864, *OR* 38(5):909.

CHAPTER TWO

1. J. S. Gage, "In the Front Line at Ezra Chapel," *National Tribune*, August 1, 1895; W. W. Black, "Marching with Sherman," 324; Blodgett to Morrison, September 5, 1864, *OR* 38(3):472.

2. Corse to Barnes, September 8, 1864, and Bowen to Morrison, September 6, 1864, *OR* 38(3):408–9, 431; Bell, *Tramps and Triumphs*, 21; Castel, *Decision in the West*, 418–19.

3. Dodge to Clark, November 25, 1864, and Jenkins to Boggis, September 7, 1864, *OR* 38(3):385, 502; C. H. Smith, *Fuller's Ohio Brigade*, 173.

4. Morning Reports and Records, July 26, 1864, Minnesota Light Battery, 1st Company, MHS; Martin, *"Out and Forward,"* 38; H. Smith, *Brother of Mine*, 244; William Graham Diary, July 26, 1864, DU; Throne, "History of Company D," 64; Blair to Clark, September 12, 1864, *OR* 38(3):554.

5. L. D. Hord, "Forcing a Hard Campaign: The Battle of July 28, 1864, as Told of By a 32d Ohio Comrade—Incidents of a Trying Time," *National Tribune*, July 6, 1899.

6. Cryder and Miller, *A View from the Ranks*, 420.

7. Logan to Clark, [September 13, 1864]; Hildt to McAuley, September 9, 1864; Martin to Fisk, September 9, 1864; Gillmore to Upton, September 12, 1864; Williams to Wilkinson, August 3, 1864; Adams to Philips, August 8, 1864; and Berkey to Philips, August 6, 1864, *OR* 38(3):104, 210, 235, 288, 294, 348, 351; William H. Lynch Diaries, July 27, 1864, SHSM-RCC; Goodnow to wife, August 1, 1864, James Harrison Goodnow Papers, LC; "War Diary," 389; *Story of the Fifty-Fifth*, 344; Wills, *Army Life*, 286; diary, July 26, 1864, David James Palmer Papers, UI; W. W. Black, "Marching with Sherman," 324; Saunier, *History of the Forty-Seventh*, 296.

8. Jackson, *Colonel's Diary*, 141; Logan, *Volunteer Soldier*, 690; William Henry Harlow Diary, July 26–27, 1864, ALPL; Sherman to Halleck, September 15, 1864, *OR* 38(1):77.

9. C.A.L. note, Logan, *Volunteer Soldier*, 690n; General Field Orders No. 5, Headquarters, Department and Army of the Tennessee, July 27, 1864, *OR* 38(5):277.

10. "Personal Biography of Major General Grenville Mellen Dodge 1831–1870," 1:257, Grenville Mellen Dodge Papers, SHSI.

11. Ibid.

12. Howard, *Autobiography*, 2:17.

13. Sherman to Logan, July 27, 1864, Simpson and Berlin, *Sherman's Civil War*, 675.

14. Sherman to Halleck, July 27, 1864, 8:30 P.M., *OR* 38(5):272.

15. James P. Snell Diary, July 26, 1864, ALPL; Chamberlin, *History of the Eighty-First Regiment*, 137; Ackley to wife, July 28–29, 1864, Charles Thomas Ackley Civil War Letters, UI; George Lemon Childress Diary, July 27, 1864, ALPL; C. Wright, *A Corporal's Story*, 136; Corse to Barnes, September 8, 1864, *OR* 38(3):409.

16. Cryder and Miller, *A View from the Ranks*, 421; William Graham Diary, July 26–27, 1864, DU; Levi H. Nickel Diary, July 27, 1864, WHS; Throne, "History of Company D," 64; H. Smith, *Brother of Mine*, 244; L. D. Hord, "Forcing a Hard Campaign: The Battle of July 28, 1864, as Told of By a 32d Ohio Comrade—Incidents of a Trying Time," *National Tribune*, July 6, 1899; diary, July 27, 1864, John Wesley Marshall Papers, OHS; George A. Cooley Civil War Diary, July 27, 1864, WHS; Bennett and Tillery, *Struggle*, 190; W. W. Black, "Marching with Sherman," 324.

17. Diary, July 27, 1864, Abraham J. Seay Collection, UO; T. W. Connelly, *Seventieth Ohio*, 97; Cryder and Miller, *A View from the Ranks*, 421; William H. Lynch Diaries, July 27, 1864, SHSM-RCC; Logan, *Volunteer Soldier*, 691; Lucas, *New History*, 116; diary, July 27, 1864, George W. Modil Papers, MDAH; Throne, "History of Company D," 64; William Henry Harlow Diary, July 27, 1864, ALPL.

18. Aten, *History of the Eighty-Fifth Regiment, Illinois*, 209; Sherman, *Memoirs*, 2:87; Sherman to Schofield, July 27, 1864, *OR* 38(5):274–75; Sherman to Halleck, Sep-

tember 15, 1864, *OR* 38(1):77; Howard to Dayton, September 17, 1864, *OR* 38(3):40; Howard, *Autobiography*, 2:18.

19. Howard to Dayton, September 17, 1864, *OR* 38(3):40; Howard, *Autobiography*, 2:18.

20. Howard, *Autobiography*, 2:18.

21. Ibid.; "Battle of Ezra Chapel," 4, O. O. Howard Papers, BC; Howard, "Battles about Atlanta," 396.

22. "Battle of Ezra Chapel," 5, O. O. Howard Papers, BC; Howard, *Autobiography*, 2:19; Samuel Edge to Logan, September 12, 1864, *OR* 38(3):122.

23. Philip R. Ward Diary, July 27, 1864, Charles S. Harris Collection, UTC; Lusk to not stated, September 6, 1864, *OR* 38(3):532–33; Ellison, *On to Atlanta*, 68; Jamison, *Recollections*, 256–57.

24. Howard to Dayton, September 17, 1864; Dodge to Clark, November 25, 1864; Corse to Barnes, September 8, 1864; Bowen to Morrison, September 6, 1864; Mahon to Morrison, September 5, 1864; and Boyd to Ellis, September 6, 1864, *OR* 38(3):40, 385–86, 409, 431, 445, 459; George Lemon Childress Diary, July 27, 1864, ALPL; H. I. Smith, *History of the Seventh Iowa*, 162; Chamberlin, *History of the Eighty-First Regiment*, 137; Ackley to wife, July 28–29, 1864, Charles Thomas Ackley Civil War Letters, UI; "Battle of Ezra Chapel," 4, O. O. Howard Papers, BC; Howard, *Autobiography*, 2:18.

25. Howard to Dayton, September 17, 1864, *OR* 38(3):40; "Personal Biography of Major General Grenville Mellen Dodge 1831–1870," 1:257, Grenville Mellen Dodge Papers, SHSI.

26. Howard to Dayton, September 17, 1864; Corse to Barnes, September 8, 1864; Fuller to Barnes, September 12, 1864; Manning to not stated, n.d.; Fouts to Fenner, September 5, 1864; and Rusk to Williams, September 8, 1864, *OR* 38(3):40, 409, 486, 495, 520, 525; record of events, 64th Illinois, July 27, 1864, *SOR*, Pt. 2, 12:588; Howard, *Autobiography*, 2:19; C. H. Smith, *History of Fuller's Ohio Brigade*, 173.

27. Blair to Clark, July 27, 1864, *OR* 38(5):275–76; Howard to Dayton, September 17, 1864, *OR* 38(3):40; "Battle of Ezra Chapel," 4, O. O. Howard Papers, BC; Abernethy, *Private Elisha Stockwell*, 93; Howard, *Autobiography*, 2:19; Throne, "History of Company D," 64; H. Smith, *Brother of Mine*, 244.

28. Bennett and Tillery, *Struggle*, 190; *Story of the Fifty-Fifth*, 344; T. W. Connelly, *Seventieth Ohio*, 97; Nugen to sister, July 29, 1864, William H. Nugen Letters, DU.

29. Howard, *Autobiography*, 2:19; diary, July 27, 1864, David James Palmer Papers, UI; Jones to [Lofland], September 10, 1864, *OR* 38(3):198; Maurice to not stated, September 9, 1864, *SOR*, Pt. 1, 7:50; Woods to Townes, August 5, 1864; Williamson to Gordon, September 5, 1864; Lofland to Townes, September 10, 1864; Van Deusen to McAuley, September 10, 1864; Williams to Wilkinson, August 3, 1864; Walcutt to Wilkinson, August 10, 1864; and Oliver to Wilkinson, August 4, 1864, *OR* 38(3):140, 157, 189, 206, 288, 319, 343; H. H. Wright, *History of the Sixth Iowa*, 308; Allen, *On the Skirmish Line*, 237; John C. Brown Diary, July 27, 1864, UI; "War Diary," 389.

30. Hooker to Whipple, July 27, 1864, *OR* 38(5):273.

31. Balloch to Jennie, August 2, 1864, George Williamson Balloch Papers, DU.

32. Hess, *Kennesaw Mountain*, 28–49.

33. Sherman to Thomas, July 27, 1864, and Special Field Orders No. 205, Head-quarters, Department of the Cumberland, July 27, 1864, *OR* 38(5):273; Sherman, *Memoirs*, 2:86.

34. Sherman to Halleck, July 27, 1864, 8:30 P.M. and 11:00 P.M., *OR* 38(5):272.

35. Comfort to father, August 13, 1864, and Comfort to sister, August 13, 1864, John R. Comfort Papers, WCL-UM; Roberts to father, July 28, 1864, John H. Roberts Letters, WHS.

36. Miller to Crawford, September 9, 1864, *OR* 38(2):407–8.

37. Sherman to Halleck, July 27, 1864, 8:30 P.M., and Sherman to Schofield, July 27, 1864, *OR* 38(5):271–72, 275.

38. Special Field Orders No. 63, Headquarters, Army of the Ohio, July 27, 1864, *OR* 38(5):277; Sherman, *Memoirs*, 2:88.

39. Smith to Townes, August 1, 1864, *SOR*, Pt. 1, 7:57; Special Field Orders No. 63, Headquarters, Fifteenth Corps, July 27, 1864, *OR* 38(5):278.

40. C. H. Smith, *History of Fuller's Ohio Brigade*, 173; Boyd to Ellis, September 6, 1864, *OR* 38(3):459; L. D. Hord, "Forcing a Hard Campaign: The Battle of July 28, 1864, as Told of By a 32d Ohio Comrade—Incidents of a Trying Time," *National Tribune*, July 6, 1899; Saunier, *History of the Forty-Seventh*, 296; W. W. Black, "March-ing with Sherman," 324; John H. Puck speech, *Ninth Reunion of the 37th Regiment O.V.V.I.*, 52; J. S. Gage, "In the Front Line at Ezra Chapel," *National Tribune*, August 1, 1895; diary, July 27, 1864, Abraham J. Seay Collection, UO; J. R. Tisdale, "Ezra Chapel: How the Fifteenth Corps Withstood the Rebel Charges," *National Tribune*, May 10, 1888; Cryder and Miller, *A View from the Ranks*, 421.

41. Howard to Dayton, September 17, 1864, *OR* 38(3):40; "Battle of Ezra Chapel," 4–5, O. O. Howard Papers, BC.

42. Hood to Seddon, July 27, 1864; Smith to Wheeler, July 27, 1864, 4:15 A.M. and 11:00 A.M.; Shoup to Wheeler, July 27, 1864, 1:30 P.M., 5:40 P.M., 9:00 P.M., and 9:30 P.M.; and [Shoup] to Jackson, July 28, 2:00 P.M., *OR* 38(5):912–15, 923; Dodson, *Cam-paigns of Wheeler*, 217–19; Castel, *Decision in the West*, 425; McMurry, *Atlanta*, 156.

43. General Orders No. 58, Headquarters, Hood's Corps, July 27, 1864, *OR* 38(5):917; Lee to Mason, January 30, 1865, *OR* 38(3):762; Russell, "Col. E. L. Rus-sell," 315–16.

44. Shoup to Lee, July 27, 1864, 1:30 P.M., *OR* 38(5):916.

45. Lee to Mason, January 30, 1865; Brown to Ratchford, July 31, 1864; Miller to Williams, August 2, 1864; Manigault to Cheney, August 6, 1864; and Sharp to Cheney, August 1, 1864, *OR* 38(3):762, 767, 780–81, 789; Thomas B. Mackall journal, July 26, 1864 (McMurry transcript), Joseph E. Johnston Papers, CWM; Jesse L. Henderson Civil War Diary, July 27, 1864, UM; Tower, *A Carolinian Goes to War*, 230; narrative, 8, Henry DeLamar Clayton Sr. Papers, UA; E. D. Willett Diary, July 27, 1864, ADAH; "History of Company B," 208; diary, July 27, 1864, Emmett Ross Papers, MSU; Cate, *Two Soldiers*, 102; Castel, *Decision in the West*, 426.

46. Shoup to Stewart, July 27, 1864, 1:30 P.M.; [Shoup] to Stewart, July 27, 1864, 4:00 P.M.; [Shoup] to Beckham, July 27, 1864, 4:15 P.M.; and [Shoup] to Lee, July 27, 1864, 5:10 P.M., *OR* 38(5):915, 916.

47. Daniel Harris Reynolds Diary, July 25–28, 1864, UAF; S. Davis, *Atlanta Will*

Fall, 163; Walthall to Gale, January 14, 1865, and Reynolds to Barksdale, August 2, 1864, *OR* 38(3):926, 939; McGuirk to Goodman, October 16, 1863, *OR* 30(2):763; J. F. Butler to Darling Mol, June 5, 1864, Burton-Butler Papers, UM.

48. Hood, "Defense of Atlanta," 341; [Shoup] to Stewart, July 27, 1864, 6:40 P.M., and [Hood] to Lee, July 27, 1864, 6:45 P.M., *OR* 38(5):916–17; T. L. Connelly, *Autumn of Glory,* 453; Castel, *Decision in the West,* 426.

49. Hood, "Defense of Atlanta," 341; McMurry, *John Bell Hood,* 133; McMurry, *Atlanta,* 156; T. L. Connelly, *Autumn of Glory,* 453; Cox, *Atlanta,* 183; Castel, *Decision in the West,* 426.

50. Hardee to Cooper, April 5, 1865, *OR* 38(3):697–99.

CHAPTER THREE

1. King to Charles L. Keck, July 28, 1864, Josiah Edmond King Papers, WCL-UM; Bennett and Tillery, *Struggle,* 190; Goodloe, *Some Rebel Relics,* 309; Lucas, *New History,* 116; Q.P.F. to *Cincinnati Commercial,* July 29, 1864, in *St. Louis Daily Missouri Democrat,* August 8, 1864; "History of Company B," 208; diary, July 28, 1864, George W. Modil Papers, MDAH.

2. Howard to Dayton, September 17, 1864; Fuller to Barnes, September 12, 1864; Fouts to Fenner, September 5, 1864; Rusk to Williams, September 8, 1864; and Wiles to Douglass, September 13, 1864, *OR* 38(3):40, 486, 520, 525, 573; C. H. Smith, *History of Fuller's Ohio Brigade,* 174; record of events, 64th Illinois, July 28, 1864, *SOR,* Pt. 2, 12:588; Chamberlin, *History of the Eighty-First Regiment,* 137; Howard, *Autobiography,* 2:19; Abernethy, *Private Elisha Stockwell,* 93–94; Levi H. Nickel Diary, July 28, 1864, WHS; William Graham Diary, July 28, 1864, DU; Throne, "History of Company D," 64–65; L. D. Hord, "Forcing a Hard Campaign: The Battle of July 28, 1864, as Told of By a 32d Ohio Comrade—Incidents of a Trying Time," *National Tribune,* July 6, 1899; William F. Graham Diary, July 28, 1864, ALPL.

3. Logan to Clark, [September 13, 1864]; Woods to Townes, August 5, 1864; Smith to Gordon, August 5, 1864; Williamson to Gordon, September 5, 1864; and Wangelin to Gordon, August 5, 1864, *OR* 38(3):104, 140, 148, 157, 167; James P. Snell Diary, July 28, 1864, ALPL; Allen, *On the Skirmish Line,* 237; Bennett and Tillery, *Struggle,* 190; diary, July 28, 1864, David James Palmer Papers, UI; diary, July 28, 1864, Abraham J. Seay Collection, UO.

4. Wangelin to Gordon, August 5, 1864; Oliver to Wilkinson, August 4, 1864; and Brown to not stated, July 30, 1864, *OR* 38(3):167, 343, 358–59.

5. Van Deusen to McAuley, September 10, 1864; Williams to Wilkinson, August 3, 1864; Gillmore to Upton, September 12, 1864; and Stuart to Williams, August 6, 1864, *OR* 38(3):206, 288, 294, 299; W. W. Black, "Marching with Sherman," 324; Lucas, *New History,* 116; George Samuel Neel Civil War Diary, July 28, 1864, ISU; Goodnow to wife, August 1, 1864, James Harrison Goodnow Papers, LC.

6. Lofland to Townes, September 10, 1864; Martin to Lofland, July 29, 1864; Browne to McAuley, September 5, 1864; Hildt to McAuley, September 9, 1864; and Jones to Lofland, September 12, 1864, *OR* 38(3):189, 196, 202, 210, 228–29; Smith to Townes, August 1, 1864, *SOR,* Pt. 1, 7:57; *Story of the Fifty-Fifth,* 345; Saunier, *History*

of the Forty-Seventh, 297; Hildt to parents, August 15, 1864, George H. Hildt Letters and Diary, OHS; Castel, *Decision in the West*, 428.

7. "Battle of Ezra Chapel," 8–9, O. O. Howard Papers, BC; Howard, *Autobiography*, 2:19–21; Howard, "Struggle for Atlanta," 319; Howard to Dayton, September 17, 1864, *OR* 38(3):40–41.

8. Sherman to Schofield, July 28, 1864, *OR* 38(5):283; James P. Snell Diary, July 28, 1864, ALPL; Sherman, *Memoirs*, 2:88–89; Sherman to Halleck, September 15, 1864, *OR* 38(1):77.

9. Sherman to Halleck, September 15, 1864, *OR* 38(1):177; Sherman, *Memoirs*, 2:89; Howard, *Autobiography*, 2:20–21.

10. *Story of the Fifty-Fifth*, 345; Gould and Kennedy, *Memoirs of a Dutch Mudsill*, 273.

11. Cox, *Atlanta*, 182–83; Cox to Campbell, September 10, 1864, *OR* 38(2):690. The Confederates called the Lick Skillet Road by many other names, apparently out of honest misinformation about its true designation. It was called the Sandtown Road, the Buck Head Road, and the Taylor's Ferry Road. See Slaughter to Enholm, July 28, 1864; Kelsey to Richards, July 30, 1864; and Downing to Richards, July 30, 1864, *OR* 38(3):785, 793–94.

12. Sherman to Halleck, September 15, 1864, *OR* 38(1):77; Smith to Gordon, August 5, 1864; Wangelin to Gordon, August 5, 1864; and Oliver to Wilkinson, August 4, 1864, *OR* 38(3):148, 167, 343; H. M. Brandle, "At Ezra Chapel: Reminiscences of a Missouri Soldier," *National Tribune*, December 22, 1887; J. S. Gage, "In the Front Line at Ezra Chapel," *National Tribune*, August 1, 1895; Charles A. Booth Journal, July 30, 1864, WHS; James P. Snell Diary, July 28, 1864, ALPL.

13. Logan to Clark, [September 13, 1864], *OR* 38(3):104; Poe to [Delafield], October 8, 1865, *OR* 38(1):133; James P. Snell Diary, July 28, 1864, ALPL.

14. Howard, *Autobiography*, 2:20; Howard, "Battles about Atlanta," 396–97; Dodge to Clark, November 25, 1864, *OR* 38(3):386; L. D. Hord, "Forcing a Hard Campaign: The Battle of July 28, 1864, as Told of By a 32d Ohio Comrade—Incidents of a Trying Time," *National Tribune*, July 6, 1899; Cryder and Miller, *A View from the Ranks*, 421.

15. Woods to Townes, August 5, 1864, and Williamson to Gordon, September 5, 1864, *OR* 38(3):140, 157; Bennett and Tillery, *Struggle*, 191; John C. Brown Diary, July 28, 1864, UI.

16. Wangelin to Gordon, August 5, 1864, *OR* 38(3):167; J. R. Tisdale, "Ezra Chapel: How the Fifteenth Corps Withstood the Rebel Charges," *National Tribune*, May 10, 1888; J. S. Gage, "In the Front Line at Ezra Chapel," *National Tribune*, August 1, 1895; Allan to mother, July 30, 1864, David Allan Jr. Collection, MHM; Bek, "Civil War Diary," Pt. 2, 524–25; Kuck to wife, July 31, 1864, Henry Kuck Letters, SHSM-RCSL.

17. Gillmore to Upton, September 12, 1864; Oliver to Wilkinson, August 4, 1864; Berkey to Philips, August 6, 1864; and Love to Philips, August 6, 1864, *OR* 38(3):294, 343, 351, 359; T. W. Connelly, *Seventieth Ohio*, 98; Goodnow to wife, August 1, 1864, James Harrison Goodnow Papers, LC; W. W. Black, "Marching With Sherman," 324; Lucas, *New History*, 116.

18. Williams to Wilkinson, August 3, 1864, and Oliver to Wilkinson, August 4, 1864, *OR* 38(3):288, 343.

19. Mott to assistant adjutant general, First Brigade, Second Division, Fifteenth Corps, September 9, 1964, *OR* 38(3):218; "Battle of Ezra Chapel," 9, O. O. Howard Papers, BC; Howard, *Autobiography*, 2:21; Howard, "Struggle for Atlanta," 319.

20. Grant, *Personal Memoirs*, 2:506; Sherman to Halleck, September 15, 1864, *OR* 38(1):77.

21. Hess, *Rifle Musket*, 145–46, 156–63; Hess, *Kennesaw Mountain*, 76–78, 88–95.

22. Castel, *Decision in the West*, 434; Brown to Ratchford, July 31, 1864, *OR* 38(3):767.

23. F. A. Montgomery, *Reminiscences*, 190–91; Deupree, "Noxubee Squadron," 102.

24. F. A. Montgomery, *Reminiscences*, 192; Deupree, "Noxubee Squadron," 102; E. W. Smith, "Battle of Ezra Church," *National Tribune*, July 5, 1888.

25. W. C. Smith, *Private in Gray*, 105–6; J. A. Bigger Memoir, July 28, 1864, UM.

26. Smith to Townes, August 1, 1864, *SOR*, Pt. 1, 7:58; Sherman, *Memoirs*, 2:88–89; Sherman to Halleck, September 15, 1864, *OR* 38(1):77.

27. Warner, *Generals in Blue*, 279–80.

28. Howard to Dayton, September 17, 1864; Jones to Lofland, September 12, 1864; Moritz to Thomas, July 29, 1864; and Taylor to Fisk, September 10, 1864, *OR* 38(3):41, 229, 238, 247; Duke, *History of the Fifty-Third*, 150–51; Saunier, *History of the Forty-Seventh*, 297.

29. *Story of the Fifty-Fifth*, 345; Maurice to not stated, September 9, 1864, *SOR*, Pt. 1, 7:50; Landgraeber to Gordon, August 5, 1864, *OR* 38(3):104.

30. Henry Schmidt to wife, August 6, 1864, Schmidt Family Papers, FHS; W. C. Smith, *Private in Gray*, 106; Angus M. Martin to father, July 29, 1864, Martin Family Papers, NC.

31. W. C. Smith, *Private in Gray*, 107; F. A. Montgomery, *Reminiscences*, 193; Deupree, "Noxubee Squadron," 102.

32. Duke, *History of the Fifty-Third*, 151; Fulton to [Fisk], September 8, 1864, and Moore to Fisk, September 12, 1864, *OR* 38(3):254, 260; Castel, *Tom Taylor's Civil War*, 154; Woodworth, *Nothing but Victory*, 572.

33. F. A. Montgomery, *Reminiscences*, 193; Angus M. Martin to father, July 29, 1864, Martin Family Papers, NC.

34. Tapert, *Brother's War*, 208; Oliver to Wilkinson, August 4, 1864; Adams to Philips, August 8, 1864; and Hutchinson to Philips, August 8, 1864, *OR* 38(3):343, 348, 353–54; T. W. Connelly, *Seventieth Ohio*, 97–98; Goodnow to wife, August 1, 1864, James Harrison Goodnow Papers, LC.

35. J. S. Gage, "In the Front Line at Ezra Chapel," *National Tribune*, August 1, 1895.

36. Moore to Fisk, September 12, 1864, *OR* 38(3):260; Duke, *History of the Fifty-Third*, 151; E. W. Smith, "Battle of Ezra Church," *National Tribune*, July 5, 1888.

37. [Shoup] to Hardee, July 28, 1864, 9:00 A.M. and 10:30 A.M., and [Shoup] to Jackson, July 28, 1864, 9:30 A.M., *OR* 38(5):918, 923.

38. Lee to Mason, January 30, 1865, *OR* 38(3):762; [Shoup] to Hardee, July 28, 1864, 12:30 P.M., *OR* 38(5):919.

39. Brown to Ratchford, July 31, 1864, *OR* 38(3):767; Warner, *Generals in Gray*, 35–36.

40. Isaac Gaillard Foster Diary, July 28, 1864, James Foster and Family Correspondence, LSU; Johnson to Harrison, July 30, 1864, *OR* 38(3):807.

41. Warner, *Generals in Gray*, 52–53; Clayton to Ratchford, September 16, 1864, *OR* 38(3):821; Narrative, 8, Henry DeLamar Clayton Sr. Papers, UA.

42. Lee to Mason, January 30, 1865, *OR* 38(3):762–63.

43. Hattaway, *General Stephen D. Lee*, 128; McMurry, *Atlanta*, 156–57; T. L. Connelly, *Autumn of Glory*, 454; McMurry, *John Bell Hood*, 133.

44. [Shoup] to Lee, July 28, 1864, 12:00 M., *OR* 38(5):919.

45. Thomas B. Roy to William J. Hardee, July 28, 1864, and Thomas B. Roy to Patrick R. Cleburne, July 28, 1864, Letter Book, Irving Buck Papers, MOC.

46. Edge to Logan, September 12, 1864, *OR* 38(3):122; Q.P.F. to *Cincinnati Commercial*, July 29, 1864, in *St. Louis Daily Missouri Democrat*, August 8, 1864.

47. Tower, *A Carolinian Goes to War*, 236; Toulmin to Cheney, August 2, 1864, *OR* 38(3):777. Historians' estimates of troop strength at the battle of Ezra Church include 18,450 Confederates and 13,226 Federals (McCarley, "'Atlanta is Ours,'" 69); 18,000 Confederates and 13,000 Federals (Haughton, *Training, Tactics and Leadership*, 231n); 9,000 Confederates and 11,000 Federals (S. Davis, "Hood Fights Desperately," 33).

CHAPTER FOUR

1. Brown to Ratchford, July 31, 1864, *OR* 38(3):767.

2. Warner, *Generals in Gray*, 32–33.

3. Brantley to Cheney, July 31, 1864; Lyles to Harrison, July 30, 1864; and Johnson to Harrison, July 30, 1864, *OR* 38(3):799, 802–3, 807.

4. Sources indicating the battle started at noon include W. B. Corbitt Diary, July 28, 1864, EU; W. W. Black, "Marching with Sherman," 324; Wills, *Army Life*, 287; Woods to Townes, August 5, 1864; Martin to Lofland, July 29, 1864; and Berkey to Philips, August 6, 1864, *OR* 38(3):140, 196, 351; record of events, Company C, 83rd Indiana, July 28, 1864, *SOR*, Pt. 2, 18:216. Sources that indicate differing times for the start of the attack include George Samuel Neel Civil War Diary, July 28, 1864, ISU; diary, July 28, 1864, Brigham Foster Papers, USAMHI; Smith to Townes, August 1, 1864, *SOR*, Pt. 1, 7:58; H. H. Wright, *History of the Sixth Iowa*, 309; Sherman, *Memoirs*, 2:89; Howard to wife, July 29, 1864, O. O. Howard Papers, BC; Howard to Sherman, July 28, 1864, *OR* 38(5):282; Logan to Clark, July 29, 1864; Brantley to Cheney, July 31, 1864; and Lyles to Harrison, July 30, 1864, *OR* 38(3):86, 799, 803; Castel, *Decision in the West*, 428.

5. Brantley to Cheney, July 31, 1864; Lyles to Harrison, July 30, 1864; Johnson to Harrison, July 30, 1864; and Hubbard to Harrison, July 31, 1864, *OR* 38(3):799, 803, 807, 810; Smith to Townes, August 1, 1864, *SOR*, Pt. 1, 7:58; Saunier, *History of the Forty-Seventh*, 298.

6. Moore to Fisk, September 12, 1864; Brantley to Cheney, July 31, 1864; and Hubbard to Harrison, July 31, 1864, *OR* 38(3):260, 799, 810; Castel, *Tom Taylor's Civil War*, 154; E. W. Smith, "Battle of Ezra Church," *National Tribune*, July 5, 1888; E.S. to editor, July 29, 1864, in *New York Daily Tribune*, August 8, 1864; A. B. Crummel, "Ezra Chapel," *National Tribune*, April 26, 1888.

7. Taylor to Fisk, September 10, 1864, *OR* 38(3):247; Castel, *Tom Taylor's Civil*

War, 154–55; Woodworth, *Nothing but Victory*, 573; E. W. Smith, "Battle of Ezra Church," *National Tribune*, July 5, 1888; Saunier, *History of the Forty-Seventh*, 198–99.

8. Duke, *History of the Fifty-Third*, 151; Taylor to Fish, September 10, 1864, *OR* 38(3):247; Castel, *Decision in the West*, 428; Brown to Ratchford, July 31, 1864; Lyles to Harrison, July 30, 1864; and Johnson to Harrison, July 30, 1864, *OR* 38(3):767, 803, 807–8.

9. Moritz to Thomas, July 29, 1864, and Moritz to not stated, September 5, 1864, *OR* 38(3):238, 241; Henry Schmidt to wife, July 30, August 6, 1864, Schmidt Family Papers, FHS; Howard, *Autobiography*, 2:22–23; Duke, *History of the Fifty-Third*, 151; John H. Puck address, *Ninth Reunion of the 37th Regiment O.V.V.I.*, 52. Hipp's left arm was amputated in the Fifteenth Corps field hospital two hours after he was wounded. "Miscellaneous Wounds," Ezra Church, folder 23, series 1, reel 1, United States Sanitary Commission Records, NYPL.

10. Howard, *Autobiography*, 2:23; Woodworth, *Nothing but Victory*, 572–73; Moore to Fisk, September 12, 1864, *OR* 38(3):260; A. B. Crummel, "Ezra Chapel," *National Tribune*, April 26, 1888.

11. W. C. Smith, *Private in Gray*, 107.

12. Cryder and Miller, *A View from the Ranks*, 422.

13. Howard to wife, July 29, 1864, and "Battle of Ezra Chapel," 9, O. O. Howard Papers, BC; Carpenter, *Sword and Olive Branch*, 70; "Sherman," 30, folder 4, box 5, Oliver Otis Howard Papers, LMU; Howard to Dayton, September 17, 1864, *OR* 38(3):41; Howard, "Struggle for Atlanta," 319; Howard, *Autobiography*, 2:21.

14. Oliver Otis Howard to Samuel A. Christie, October 14, 1887, Frederick M. Dearborn Collection, HU; Howard, "Struggle for Atlanta," 319; "Battle of Ezra Chapel," 9, O. O. Howard Papers, BC.

15. Bennett and Tillery, *Struggle*, 191; Allen, *On the Skirmish Line*, 238; E.S. to editor, July 29, 1864, in *New York Daily Tribune*, August 8, 1864.

16. Howard, "Battles about Atlanta," 397; Howard, *Autobiography*, 2:25; E. W. Smith, "Battle of Ezra Church," *National Tribune*, July 5, 1888; White and Runion, *Great Things*, 136; F. Halsey Wigfall to Mama, August 7, 1864, Louis Trezevant Wigfall Family Papers, LC.

17. "Battle of Ezra Chapel," 9, O. O. Howard Papers, BC; "Sherman," 30, folder 4, box 5, Oliver Otis Howard Papers, LMU; Howard to Dayton, September 17, 1864; Reese to Poe, September 14, 1864; and Logan to Clark, [September 13, 1864], *OR* 38(3):41, 67, 105; Smith to Townes, August 1, 1864, *SOR*, Pt. 1, 7:58.

18. Bryant to Douglass, September 10, 1864, *OR* 38(3):569; Mortimer D. Leggett to Force, August 2, 1864, M. F. Force Papers, UW; [Rood], *Story of the Service of Company E*, 323.

19. Taylor to Fisk, September 10, 1864, *OR* 38(3):248; Saunier, *History of the Forty-Seventh*, 299.

20. Hildt to McAuley, September 9, 1864, *OR* 38(3):211; record of events, Company C, 83rd Indiana, July 28, 1864, *SOR*, Pt. 2, 18:216; diary, July 28, 1864, Wayne Johnson Jacobs Diaries and Lists, LSU.

21. Moritz to Thomas, July 29, 1864, and Taylor to Fisk, September 10, 1864, *OR* 38(3):238, 248; Saunier, *History of the Forty-Seventh*, 299.

22. A. B. Crummel, "Ezra Chapel," *National Tribune*, April 26, 1888.

23. Ibid.; Howard to Dayton, September 17, 1864, and Bryant to Douglass, September 10, 1864, *OR* 38(3):41, 569–70; Howard, "Battles about Atlanta," 397; Howard, *Autobiography*, 2:23; Mortimer D. Leggett to Force, August 2, 1864, M. F. Force Papers, UW; diary, July 28, 1864, Alonzo Miller Papers, WHS.

24. Walcutt to Wilkinson, August 10, 1864, and Miller to Upton, September 7, 1864, *OR* 38(3):319, 332–33; H. H. Wright, *History of the Sixth Iowa*, 309–10.

25. H. H. Wright, *History of the Sixth Iowa*, 310; Smith to Townes, August 1, 1864, *SOR*, Pt. 1, 7:58; Miller to Upton, September 7, 1864, *OR* 38(3):333.

26. James P. Snell Diary, July 28, 1864, ALPL; P. D. Jordan, "Forty Days," 144; *Medical and Surgical History*, 9:182; Walcutt to Wilkinson, August 10, 1864, and Miller to Upton, September 7, 1864, *OR* 38(3):319, 333–34.

27. Castel, *Tom Taylor's Civil War*, 155; Moritz to Thomas, July 29, 1864; Taylor to Fisk, September 10, 1864; and Miller to Upton, September 7, 1864, *OR* 38(3):238, 248, 333; Saunier, *History of the Forty-Seventh*, 299; Duke, *History of the Fifty-Third*, 151.

28. Howard to wife, July 29, 1864, O. O. Howard Papers, BC; Brown to Ratchford, July 31, 1864, *OR* 38(3):767.

29. Brown to Ratchford, July 31, 1864; Lyles to Harrison, July 30, 1864; Johnson to Harrison, July 30, 1864; and Hubbard to Harrison, July 31, 1864, *OR* 38(3):768, 803, 807, 810.

30. Lyles to Harrison, July 30, 1864, *OR* 38(3):803.

31. Brantley to Cheney, July 31, 1864, and Hubbard to Harrison, July 31, 1864, *OR* 38(3):799–800, 810.

32. Brown to Ratchford, July 31, 1864; Brantley to Cheney, July 31, 1864; Lyles to Harrison, July 30, 1864; Johnson to Harrison, July 30, 1864; and Hubbard to Harrison, July 31, 1864, *OR* 38(3):768, 800, 803, 807, 810; Castel, *Decision in the West*, 432; Castel, *Tom Taylor's Civil War*, 156.

33. Brown to Ratchford, July 31, 1864, and Brantley to Cheney, July 31, 1864, *OR* 38(1):768, 800.

34. Brown to Ratchford, July 31, 1864; Lyles to Harrison, July 30, 1864; and Hubbard to Harrison, July 31, 1864, *OR* 38(3):768, 803, 810.

35. "Report of Casualties in Brantley's Brigade, Hindman's Div &c. in the engagement on the 28th inst.," MOC; Brantley to Cheney, July 31, 1864; Lyles to Harrison, July 30, 1864; and Johnson to Harrison, July 30, 1864, *OR* 38(3):800, 803, 808; Ashley and Ashley, *Oh for Dixie!*, 46; Capt. William Van Davis Diary, July 28, 1864, USM.

36. R. A. Jarman, "The History of Company K, 27th Mississippi Infantry, and Its First and Last Muster Rolls," MDAH; E. L. Mitchell, "Civil War Letters," 79.

37. Brantley to Cheney, July 31, 1864, *OR* 38(3):800.

38. Logan to Clark, [September 13, 1864]; Landgraeber to Gordon, August 5, 1864; and Echte to Lofland, September 6, 1864, *OR* 38(3):104, 174–75, 263; Castel, *Decision in the West*, 434; Maurice to not stated, September 9, 1864, *SOR*, Pt. 1, 7:50; Howard, *Autobiography*, 2:20.

39. Maurice to not stated, September 9, 1864, *SOR*, Pt. 1, 7:50; J. S. Gage, "In the Front Line at Ezra Chapel," *National Tribune*, August 1, 1895; Q.P.F. to *Cincinnati*

Commercial, July 29, 1864, in *St. Louis Daily Missouri Democrat*, August 8, 1864; Howard, *Autobiography*, 2:21.

40. Howard, *Autobiography*, 2:23–24; Howard, "Battles about Atlanta," 397; Reese to Poe, September 14, 1864, *OR* 38(3):67; Woodworth, *Nothing but Victory*, 573–74; Maurice to not stated, September 9, 1864, *SOR*, Pt. 1, 7:50.

41. Smith to Townes, August 1, 1864, *SOR*, Pt. 1, 7:58.

42. Angle, *Three Years*, 248.

CHAPTER FIVE

1. Warner, *Generals in Gray*, 273.

2. Sharp to Cheney, August 1, 1864, and Downing to Richards, July 30, 1864, *OR* 38(3):789, 794.

3. Sharp to Cheney, August 1, 1864, and Downing to Richards, July 30, 1864, *OR* 38(3):789, 794.

4. Johns to Richards, July 30, 1864, and Williams to [Richards], July 30, 1864, *OR* 38(3):791–92.

5. Tapert, *Brothers' War*, 208.

6. Landgraeber to Gordon, August 5, 1864, *OR* 38(3):174–75; Howard, *Autobiography*, 2:20–21; E.S. to editor, July 29, 1864, in *New York Daily Tribune*, August 8, 1864; Maurice to not stated, September 9, 1864, *SOR*, Pt. 1, 7:50; A. B. Crummel, "Ezra Chapel," *National Tribune*, April 26, 1888.

7. Sharp to Cheney, August 1, 1864, and Williams to [Richards], July 30, 1864, *OR* 38(3):789, 792; Jesse L. Henderson Civil War Diary, July 28, 1864, UM.

8. Kelsey to Richards, July 30, 1864, *OR* 38(3):793.

9. *Story of the Fifty-Fifth*, 345.

10. E. Coombe, "The 28th of July Before Atlanta," *National Tribune*, February 7, 1884; Newell to Kate, August 2, 1864, William McCulloch Newell Papers, NC.

11. *Story of the Fifty-Fifth*, 346; Tapert, *Brothers' War*, 208; E.S. to editor, July 29, 1864, in *New York Daily Tribune*, August 8, 1864; Newell to Kate, August 2, 1864, William McCulloch Newell Papers, NC.

12. Sharp to Cheney, August 1, 1864; Johns to Richards, July 30, 1864; and Williams to [Richards], July 30, 1864, *OR* 38(3):789, 791–92.

13. Sharp to Cheney, August 1, 1864, and Bishop to Richards, July 30, 1864, *OR* 38(3):789–90.

14. Warner, *Generals in Gray*, 160–61; George D. Johnston to Jones, March 8, 1872, Charles Colcock Jones Papers, DU.

15. Adams to Philips, August 8, 1864; Toulmin to Cheney, August 2, 1864; and Miller to Williams, August 2, 1864, *OR* 38(3):348, 775–76, 780.

16. Brown to Ratchford, July 31, 1864; Toulmin to Cheney, August 2, 1864; and Whitney to [Williams], July 30, 1864, *OR* 38(3):767–68, 776–77.

17. Welsh, *Medical Histories of Confederate Generals*, 119; F. Halsey Wigfall to Mama, July 31, 1864, Louis Trezevant Wigfall Family Papers, LC; "Sketches of the Confederate War," 8, Thomas T. Smith Papers, MDAH.

18. Toulmin to Cheney, August 2, 1864; Whitney to [Williams], July 30, 1864; Rouse to Williams, August 1, 1864; and Miller to Williams, August 2, 1864, *OR* 38(3):776–77, 779–80.

19. Harrow to Townes, September 9, 1864, and Gillmore to Upton, September 12, 1864, *OR* 38(3):281, 294; H. H. Wright, *History of the Sixth Iowa*, 309.

20. M. D. Gage to editor, August 1, 1864, in *Indianapolis Daily Journal*, August 9, 1864; Lucas, *New History*, 116; Goodnow to Nelson, August 3, 1864, *OR* 38(3):305; Goodnow to wife, August 1, 1864, James Harrison Goodnow Papers, LC.

21. T. W. Connelly, *Seventieth Ohio*, 98; Oliver to Wilkinson, August 4, 1864, and Hutchinson to Philips, August 8, 1864, *OR* 38(3):343–44, 354; W. J. Shelton, "Ezra Chapel: How Gen. Howard Impressed Troops in Battle," *National Tribune*, January 5, 1888.

22. Wangelin to Gordon, August 5, 1864, *OR* 38(3):167; J. R. Tisdale, "Ezra Chapel: How the Fifteenth Corps Withstood the Rebel Charges," *National Tribune*, May 10, 1888.

23. Hess, "Twelfth Missouri Infantry," 149, 153; Hess, *German in the Yankee Fatherland*, 7, 147; Woods to Townes, August 5, 1864, and Wangelin to Gordon, August 5, 1864, *OR* 38(3):140, 167; Allan to mother, July 30, 1864, David Allan Jr. Letters, MHM; J. R. Tisdale, "Ezra Chapel: How the Fifteenth Corps Withstood the Rebel Charges," *National Tribune*, May 10, 1888; J. S. Gage, "In the Front Line at Ezra Chapel," *National Tribune*, August 1, 1895; Bek, "Civil War Diary," Pt. 2, 525.

24. Charles G. Ward Diary, July 28, 1864, USC; John C. Brown Diary, July 28, 1864, UI; Williamson to Gordon, September 5, 1864, *OR* 38(3):157; Arbuckle, *Civil War Experiences*, 76–78.

25. Goodnow to wife, August 1, 1864, James Harrison Goodnow Papers, LC; Lucas, *New History*, 116; J. S. Gage, "In the Front Line at Ezra Chapel," *National Tribune*, August 1, 1895.

26. Tapert, *Brothers' War*, 208; *Story of the Fifty-Fifth*, 346, 349.

27. T. W. Connelly, *Seventieth Ohio*, 98.

28. Sharp to Cheney, August 1, 1864; Bishop to Richards, July 30, 1864; Johns to Richards, July 30, 1864; and Williams to [Richards], July 30, 1864, *OR* 38(3):790–93; Jesse L. Henderson Civil War Diary, July 28, 1864, UM; Isaac Gaillard Foster diary, July 28, 1864, James Foster and Family Correspondence, LSU; *Story of the Fifty-Fifth*, 346.

29. Toulmin to Cheney, August 2, 1864, and Miller to Williams, August 2, 1864, *OR* 38(3):776, 780; E.S. to editor, July 29, 1864, in *New York Daily Tribune*, August 8, 1864.

30. Toulmin to Cheney, August 2, 1864, and Ray to Williams, July 30, 1864, *OR* 38(3):776, 781.

31. Williams to Wilkinson, August 3, 1864, and Goodnow to Nelson, August 3, 1864, *OR* 38(3):288, 305; Hogan, *General Reub Williams's Memories*, 188; Goodnow to wife, August 1, 1864, James Harrison Goodnow Papers, LC; Q.P.F. to *Cincinnati Commercial*, July 29, 1864, in *St. Louis Daily Missouri Democrat*, August 8, 1864.

32. William H. Odell to nephew, August 3, 1864, Jonathan Blair Papers, ALPL; Oliver to Wilkinson, August 4, 1864, *OR* 38(3):344.

33. Love to Philips, August 6, 1864, *OR* 38(3):359.

34. Warner, *Generals in Blue*, 534–35; Walcutt to Wilkinson, August 10, 1864; Alexander to not stated, September 12, 1864; and Love to Philips, August 6, 1864, *OR* 38(3):319, 338, 359; H. H. Wright, *History of the Sixth Iowa*, 309–10.

35. Willison to Upton, September 9, 1864; Alexander to not stated, September 12, 1864; and Love to Philips, August 6, 1864, *OR* 38(3):327, 338, 359.

36. Alexander to not stated, September 12, 1864, *OR* 38(3):338.

37. Post, *Soldiers' Letters*, 407; Cryder and Miller, *A View from the Ranks*, 422; J. S. Gage, "In the Front Line at Ezra Chapel," *National Tribune*, August 1, 1895; Love to Philips, August 6, 1864, *OR* 38(3):359.

38. J. S. Gage, "In the Front Line at Ezra Chapel," *National Tribune*, August 1, 1895; Wangelin to Gordon, August 5, 1864, *OR* 38(3):167.

39. J. S. Gage, "In the Front Line at Ezra Chapel," *National Tribune*, August 1, 1895; J. R. Tisdale, "Ezra Chapel: How the Fifteenth Corps Withstood the Rebel Charges," *National Tribune*, May 10, 1888; casualty sheet; medical certificates dated October 19, November 28, and December 17, 1864; James Peckham to Capt. Eno, October 24, 1864; and General Orders No. 10, Headquarters, First Division, Fifteenth Corps, April 22, 1863, Philip H. Murphy service record, 29th Missouri (US), M405, NARA; Allan to mother, July 30, 1864, David Allan Jr. Letters, MHM.

40. Russell, "Col. E. L. Russell," 316; Toulmin to Cheney, August 2, 1864; Whitney to [Williams], July 30, 1864; and Sharp to Cheney, August 1, 1864, *OR* 38(3):776–78, 790.

41. Brown to Ratchford, July 31, 1864, and Kelsey to Richards, July 30, 1864, *OR* 38(3):768, 793.

42. Isaac Gaillard Foster diary, July 28, 1864, James Foster and Family Correspondence, LSU; Johns to Richards, July 30, 1864, *OR* 38(3):792; index cards, George W. Braden service record, 9th Mississippi, M269, NARA; index cards and Johnson to Samuel Cooper, January 23, 1864, Cyrus A. Johnson service record, 9th Mississippi, M269, NARA.

43. Whitney to [Williams], July 30, 1864, *OR* 38(3):778.

44. Williams to Wilkinson, August 3, 1864; Stuart to Williams, August 6, 1864, and Oliver to Wilkinson, August 4, 1864, *OR* 38(3):288, 299, 344; William H. Odell to nephew, August 3, 1864, Jonathan Blair Papers, ALPL; T. W. Connelly, *Seventieth Ohio*, 98.

45. Lee to Mason, January 30, 1865, *OR* 38(3):763, 765; Welsh, *Medical Histories of Confederate Generals*, 29.

46. William F. Graham Diary, July 28, 1864, ALPL; "War Diary," 389; W. W. Black, "Marching with Sherman," 324–25.

47. "Battle of Ezra Chapel," 10, O. O. Howard Papers, BC; Cox, *Atlanta*, 185.

48. Q.P.F. to *Cincinnati Commercial*, July 29, 1864, in *St. Louis Daily Missouri Democrat*, August 8, 1864.

CHAPTER SIX

1. Diary, July 28, 1864, Emmett Ross Papers, MSU; Wooster, "Four Years," 36–37; narrative, 8, Henry DeLamar Clayton Sr. Papers, UA; Wynne and Taylor, *This War So*

Horrible, 107; record of events, July 28, 1864, Company A, 4th Louisiana, *SOR*, Pt. 2, 23:782; Castel, *Decision in the West*, 430.

2. Warner, *Generals in Gray*, 104; McBride and McLaurin, *Randall Lee Gibson*, 7–63; Wooster, "Four Years," 37; Salling, *Louisianians in the Western Confederacy*, 183; Gibson to Macon, September 16, 1864, *OR* 38(3):856.

3. Clayton to Ratchford, September 16, 1864, and Gibson to Macon, September 16, 1864, *OR* 38(3):821, 856; Castel, *Decision in the West*, 430.

4. Woods to Townes, August 5, 1864, and Gibson to Macon, September 16, 1864, *OR* 38(3):140, 856–57; Castel, *Decision in the West*, 429–30; Salling, *Louisianians in the Western Confederacy*, 185; Clarke, "With Sherman in Georgia," 364; Wooster, "Four Years," 37.

5. Narrative, 8, Henry DeLamar Clayton Sr. Papers, UA; Wooster, "Four Years," 37; Ross to Mary, July 31, 1864, Emmett Ross Papers, MSU; Leumas to editor, n.d., in *Mobile Register and Advertiser*, August 18, 1864.

6. Oliver to Wilkinson, August 4, 1864, *OR* 38(3):344; E.S. to editor, July 29, 1864, in *New York Daily Tribune*, August 8, 1864; T. W. Connelly, *Seventieth Ohio*, 98; Salling, *Louisianians in the Western Confederacy*, 186–88; J. S. Gage, "In the Front Line at Ezra Chapel," *National Tribune*, August 1, 1895.

7. Gibson to Macon, September 16, 1864, *OR* 38(3):856–57; narrative, 8, Henry DeLamar Clayton Sr. Papers, UA.

8. Oliver to Wilkinson, August 4, 1864, and Gibson to Macon, September 16, 1864, *OR* 38(3):344, 857; E.S. to editor, July 29, 1864, in *New York Daily Tribune*, August 8, 1864; Wooster, "Four Years," 37; Leumas to editor, n.d., in *Mobile Register and Advertiser*, August 18, 1864.

9. Gibson to Macon, September 16, 1864, *OR* 38(3):857; Q.P.F. to *Cincinnati Commercial*, July 29, 1864, in *St. Louis Daily Missouri Democrat*, August 8, 1864; Stephen Cowley to Minor, August 6, 1864, Hubbard T. Minor Papers, USAMHI; T. W. Connelly, *Seventieth Ohio*, 99.

10. Diary, July 28, 1864, and Ross to Mary, July 31, 1864, Emmett Ross Papers, MSU.

11. Kendall, "Recollections," 1177–78.

12. Kennedy to father, August 15, 1864, Hyder A. Kennedy File, Lewis Leigh Collection, USAMHI.

13. Clipping of poem "Charge of the Louisiana Brigade, July 28th, 1864," originally published in *Mobile Register and Advertiser*, in Kent-Amacker Family Papers, LSU; Fahs, *Imagined Civil War*, 30, 33, 63–68, 91–92.

14. Walcutt to Wilkinson, August 10, 1864; Alexander to not stated, September 12, 1864; Love to Philips, August 6, 1864; and "Medals of Honor awarded for distinguished services," *OR* 38(3):319, 338, 359, 612.

15. Q.P.F. to *Cincinnati Commercial*, July 29, 1864, in *St. Louis Daily Missouri Democrat*, August 8, 1864; Salling, *Louisianians in the Western Confederacy*, 189–90.

16. J. S. Gage, "In the Front Line at Ezra Chapel," *National Tribune*, August 1, 1895.

17. Arbuckle, *Civil War Experiences*, 77; H. M. Brandle, "At Ezra Chapel: Reminiscences of a Missouri Soldier," *National Tribune*, December 22, 1887; Stuart, *Iowa Colonels and Regiments*, 212; diary, July 28, 1864, David James Palmer Papers, UI.

18. Clayton to Ratchford, September 16, 1864, *OR* 38(3):821; Castel, *Decision in the West*, 429–30; Gibson to Macon, September 16, 1864, *OR* 38(3):857.

19. L. R. Smith and Quist, *Cush*, 121.

20. J. S. Gage, "In the Front Line at Ezra Chapel," *National Tribune*, August 1, 1895; T. W. Connelly, *Seventieth Ohio*, 99.

21. E. D. Willett Diary, July 28, 1864, ADAH; narrative, 8, Henry DeLamar Clayton Sr. Papers, UA; Blomquist and Taylor, *This Cruel War*, 269.

22. Clayton to Ratchford, September 16, 1864, Gibson to Macon, September 16, 1864, *OR* 38(3):821, 857; narrative, 8–9, Henry DeLamar Clayton Sr. Papers, UA; Castel, *Decision in the West*, 430.

23. "History of Company B," 208.

24. Wooster, "Four Years," 37; Salling, *Louisianians in the Western Confederacy*, 188; Kendall, "Recollections," 1177; Thomas B. Mackall Journal (McMurry transcript), July 28, 1864, Joseph E. Johnston Papers, CWM; narrative, 9, Henry DeLamar Clayton Sr. Papers, UA.

25. Allan to mother, July 30, 1864, David Allan Jr. Collection, MHM.

26. J. R. Tisdale, "Ezra Chapel: How the Fifteenth Corps Withstood the Rebel Charges," *National Tribune*, May 10, 1888.

27. Diary, July 28, 1864, Abraham J. Seay Collection, UO; Bek, "Civil War Diary," Pt. 2, 525; Wangelin to Gordon, August 5, 1864, *OR* 38(3):168.

28. Diary, July 28, 1864, Abraham J. Seay Collection, UO; William H. Lynch Diaries, July 28, 1864, SHSM-RCC; Kuck to wife, July 31, 1864, Henry Kuck Letters, SHSM-RCSL; Albert Hiffman reminiscences, 13, Hiffman Family Papers, MHM; Hess, "Twelfth Missouri Infantry," 153; "Miscellaneous Wounds," Ezra Church, series 1, folder 23, United States Sanitary Commission Records, NYPL.

29. Smith to Gordon, August 5, 1864, *OR* 38(3):148; Bennett and Tillery, *Struggle*, 191; Samuel Fetters, "Calls Up Memories: The Ezra Chapel Story Reminds a Comrade of His Experience," *National Tribune*, August 29, 1895; Fowler and Miller, *History of the Thirtieth Iowa*, 62; Allen, *On the Skirmish Line*, 238; Baugh to parents, July 31, 1864, William G. Baugh Letters, EU.

30. Bennett and Tillery, *Struggle*, 191–92; Baugh to parents, July 31, 1864, William G. Baugh Letters, EU; Allen, *On the Skirmish Line*, 237–38; H. M. Brandle, "At Ezra Chapel: Reminiscences of a Missouri Soldier," *National Tribune*, December 22, 1887.

31. Hogan, *General Reub Williams's Memories*, 188.

32. William Charles Pfeffer Diary, July 28, 1864, MHM.

33. J. R. Tisdale, "Ezra Chapel: How the Fifteenth Corps Withstood the Rebel Charges," *National Tribune*, May 10, 1888; H. M. Brandle, "At Ezra Chapel: Reminiscences of a Missouri Soldier," *National Tribune*, December 22, 1887.

34. Clayton to Ratchford, September 16, 1864, *OR* 38(3):821; J. W. Williamson to Mattie, August 1, 1864, Confederate Miscellany Collection, Series 1, EU.

35. Castel, *Decision in the West*, 430; Warner, *Generals in Gray*, 210–11; Tower, *A Carolinian Goes to War*, ix–x.

36. Manigault to Cheney, August 6, 1864; Slaughter to Enholm, July 28, 1864; and

Horne to Manigault, August 1, 1864, *OR* 38(3):781, 785, 788; Tower, *A Carolinian Goes to War*, 231–32.

37. Tower, *A Carolinian Goes to War*, 232.

38. Ibid., 232–33.

39. Manigault to Cheney, August 6, 1864; Slaughter to Enholm, July 28, 1864; and Horne to Manigault, August 1, 1864, *OR* 38(3):781, 785, 788; Tower, *A Carolinian Goes to War*, 233.

40. Manigault to Cheney, August 6, 1864, and Slaughter to Enholm, July 28, 1864, *OR* 38(3):782, 785; White and Runion, *Great Things*, 135–36.

41. Tower, *A Carolinian Goes to War*, 233; Oliver to Enholm, August 2, 1864; Butler to Enholm, n.d.; Slaughter to Enholm, July 28, 1864; and Horne to Manigault, August 1, 1864, *OR* 38(3):783–85, 788.

42. Slaughter to Enholm, July 28, 1864, and Horne to Manigault, August 1, 1864, *OR* 38(3):785, 788.

43. White and Runion, *Great Things*, 136.

44. Ibid.; W. A. Montgomery, "Memorial Address," 318.

45. Tower, *A Carolinian Goes to War*, 234; Manigault to Cheney, August 6, 1864; Butler to Enholm, n.d.; Slaughter to Enholm, July 28, 1864; and Horne to Manigault, August 1, 1864, *OR* 38(3):782, 784–85, 788.

46. Tower, *A Carolinian Goes to War*, 234.

47. Ibid.

48. Ibid., 234–35; Manigault to Cheney, August 6, 1864, *OR* 38(3):782; Castel, *Decision in the West*, 430.

49. Manigault to Cheney, August 6, 1864; Oliver to Enholm, August 2, 1864; Butler to Enholm, n.d.; Slaughter to Enholm, July 28, 1864; and Horne to Manigault, August 1, 1864, *OR* 38(3):782–84, 786, 788.

50. Brown to Ratchford, July 31, 1864, and Slaughter to Enholm, July 28, 1864, *OR* 38(3):768, 786; Tower, *A Carolinian Goes to War*, 237.

51. Manigault to Cheney, August 6, 1864, *OR* 38(3):782.

52. Slaughter to Enholm, July 28, 1864, *OR* 38(3):786.

CHAPTER SEVEN

1. Stewart to Mason, January 12, 1865, *OR* 38(3):872.

2. Johnston to Cooper, October 20, 1864, *OR* 38(3):617; Elliott, *Soldier of Tennessee*, 4–32; Warner, *Generals in Gray*, 293–94.

3. Lee to Mason, January 30, 1865, and Stewart to Mason, January 12, 1865, *OR* 38(3):763, 872; Castel, *Decision in the West*, 431.

4. Warner, *Generals in Gray*, 183, 294; Bragg to Davis, July 15, 1864, *OR* 39(2):713; Elliott, *Soldier of Tennessee*, 213–14, 303.

5. Walthall to Gale, January 14, 1865; Reynolds to Barksdale, August 2, 1864; and O'Neal to Barksdale, August 22, 1864, *OR* 38(3):926–97, 939, 942; Daniel Harris Reynolds Diary, July 28, 1864, UAF; Warner, *Generals in Gray*, 325–26; Castel, *Decision in the West*, 432.

6. Toulmin to Cheney, August 2, 1864, and Brantley to Cheney, July 31, 1864, *OR* 38(3):776, 800.

7. Walthall to Gale, January 14, 1865, *OR* 38(3):927; Castel, *Decision in the West*, 432–33; Warner, *Generals in Gray*, 226.

8. O'Neal to Barksdale, August 22, 1864, *OR* 38(3):942–43.

9. Ibid., 943.

10. Castel, *Decision in the West*, 432–33.

11. Dodge to Clark, November 25, 1864; Fuller to Barnes, September 12, 1864; and Sprague to Cadle, September 3, 1864, *OR* 38(3):386, 486, 507; "Personal Biography of Major General Grenville Mellen Dodge 1831–1870," 1:259, Grenville Mellen Dodge Papers, SHSI; C. H. Smith, *History of Fuller's Ohio Brigade*, 174; Woodworth, *Nothing but Victory*, 573.

12. Reynolds to Barksdale, August 2, 1864, *OR* 38(3):939; Daniel Harris Reynolds Diary, July 28, 1864, UAF.

13. Reynolds to Barksdale, August 2, 1864, *OR* 38(3):939; Worley, *War Memoirs*, 97–98.

14. Reynolds to Barksdale, August 2, 1864, *OR* 38(3):939; Daniel Harris Reynolds Diary, July 28, 1864, UAF.

15. Williams to Wilkinson, August 3, 1864, and Gillmore to Upton, September 12, 1864, *OR* 38(3):288, 294; Goodnow to wife, August 1, 1864, James Harrison Goodnow Papers, LC; M. D. Gage, *From Vicksburg to Raleigh*, 226.

16. William H. Odell to nephew, August 3, 1864, Jonathan Blair Papers, ALPL; W. J. Shelton, "Ezra Chapel: How Gen. Howard Impressed Troops in Battle," *National Tribune*, January 5, 1888; Oliver to Wilkinson, August 4, 1864, and Hutchinson to Philips, August 6, 1864, *OR* 38(3):344, 354; Q.P.F. to *Cincinnati Commercial*, July 29, 1864, in *St. Louis Daily Missouri Democrat*, August 8, 1864; T. W. Connelly, *Seventieth Ohio*, 99–100.

17. T. W. Connelly, *Seventieth Ohio*, 99–100.

18. Ibid., 99.

19. Howard, *Autobiography*, 2:24; Blair to Clark, September 12, 1864, *OR* 38(3):554.

20. Giles A. Smith to Alexander, September 10, 1864, and Shane to Cadle, August 8, 1864, *OR* 38(3):585, 603–4.

21. Oliver to Wilkinson, August 4, 1864, and Love to Philips, August 6, 1864, *OR* 38(3):344, 358–60; T. W. Connelly, *Seventieth Ohio*, 99.

22. Walthall to Gale, January 14, 1865, and Reynolds to Barksdale, August 2, 1864, *OR* 38(3):927, 939; Daniel Harris Reynolds Diary, July 28, 1864, UAF.

23. Daniel Harris Reynolds Diary, July 28, 1864, UAF; Leeper, *Rebels Valiant*, 243; Worley, *War Memoirs*, 98; Dacus, *Reminiscences*, not paginated; Reynolds to Barksdale, August 2, 1864, *OR* 38(3):939.

24. Daniel Harris Reynolds Diary, July 29, 1864, UAF.

25. W. J. Watson Diary, July 28, 1864, UNC; Warner, *Generals in Gray*, 248–49; Walthall to Gale, January 14, 1865, Quarles to Barksdale, August 6, 1864, *OR* 38(3):927, 931.

26. Walthall to Gale, January 14, 1865, and Quarles to Barksdale, August 6, 1864,

OR 38(3):927, 931; Love, "Forty-Eighth Tennessee," 548; P. G. Johnson, "Forty-Ninth Tennessee," 554–55; Castel, *Decision in the West*, 432.

27. Quarles to Barksdale, August 6, 1864, *OR* 38(3):932; Stephen Cowley to Minor, August 6, 1864, Hubbard T. Minor Papers, USAMHI.

28. Quarles to Barksdale, August 6, 1864, and O'Neal to Barksdale, August 22, 1864, *OR* 38(3):931, 942–43; Stephen Cowley to Minor, August 6, 1864, Hubbard T. Minor Papers, USAMHI; W. J. Watson Diary, July 28, 1864, UNC; Castel, *Decision in the West*, 432.

29. Stephen Cowley to Minor, August 6, 1864, Hubbard T. Minor Papers, USAMHI; E. W. Mebane to George Mebane, date obscured, TSLA.

30. Lofland to Townes, September 10, 1864, *OR* 38(3):189; Hildt to parents, July 31, 1864, George H. Hildt Letters and Diary, OHS; A. B. Crummel, "Ezra Chapel," *National Tribune*, April 26, 1888.

31. Castel, *Tom Taylor's Civil War*, 156, 158; Hildt to parents, July 31, 1864, George H. Hildt Letters and Diary, OHS; Saunier, *History of the Forty-Seventh*, 299; E. W. Smith, "Battle of Ezra Church," *National Tribune*, July 5, 1888.

32. [Rood], *Story of the Service of Company E*, 323.

33. Lofland to Townes, September 10, 1864, *OR* 38(3):189.

34. Record of events, 64th Illinois, July 28, 1864, *SOR*, Pt. 2, 12:588; Howard to Dayton, September 17, 1864, Manning to not stated, n.d., Belknap to Cadle, July 29, 1864, *OR* 38(3):41, 495, 607; Howard, "Battles about Atlanta," 397.

35. Manning to not stated, n.d., and Henry to Williams, September 9, 1864, *OR* 38(3):495, 512; record of events, 35th New Jersey, July 28, 1864, *SOR*, Pt. 2, 40:726; Howard, "Battles about Atlanta," 397; "Personal Recollections: Strategy and battles of Sherman & Johnston illustrated in active campaigns," not paginated, folder 3, box 5, Oliver Otis Howard Papers, LMU; Howard, "Struggle for Atlanta," 319; Howard, *Autobiography*, 2:24; G. W. Shrum, "Atlanta and Ezra Chapel," *National Tribune*, February 16, 1888; Allen to Mary, August 5, 1864, Edward W. Allen Papers, UNC; George Lemon Childress Diary, July 28, 1864, ALPL.

36. Chamberlin, *History of the Eighty-First Regiment*, 137–38; Hildt to McAuley, September 9, 1864; Corse to Barnes, September 8, 1864; Adams to Everts, September 10, 1864; and Henry to Ellis, September 5, 1864, *OR* 38(3):211, 409, 449, 462; James P. Snell Diary, July 28, 1864, ALPL; C. Wright, *A Corporal's Story*, 136–37.

37. Diary, July 28, 1864, Wayne Johnson Jacobs Diaries and Lists, LSU.

38. Saunier, *History of the Forty-Seventh*, 299–300; A. B. Crummel, "Ezra Chapel," *National Tribune*, April 26, 1888; Castel, *Tom Taylor's Civil War*, 156; Hildt to parents, July 31, 1864, George H. Hildt Letters and Diary, OHS; A. B. Crummel, "Ezra Chapel," *National Tribune*, April 26, 1888; Hildt to McAuley, September 9, 1864, *OR* 38(3):210.

39. Blair to Clark, September 12, 1864; Giles A. Smith to Alexander, September 10, 1864; Potts to Ware, September 10, 1864; and Belknap to Cadle, July 29, 1864, *OR* 38(3):554, 585, 590, 607.

40. Belknap to Cadle, July 29, 1864, *OR* 38(3):607; Cryder and Miller, *A View from the Ranks*, 422; L. D. Hord, "Forcing a Hard Campaign: The Battle of July 28, 1864, as Told of By a 32d Ohio Comrade—Incidents of a Trying Time," *National Tribune*, July 6, 1899.

41. Miller to Upton, September 7, 1864, *OR* 38(3):333.

42. Blair to Clark, September 12, 1864, and Lofland to Giles A. Smith, July 29, 1864, *OR* 38(3):554, 608; Woodworth, *Nothing but Victory*, 576.

43. E. Coombe, "The 28th of July Before Atlanta," *National Tribune*, February 7, 1884; Martin to Lofland, July 29, 1864, and Mott to assistant adjutant general, First Brigade, Second Division, Fifteenth Corps, September 9, 1864, *OR* 38(3):196, 218.

44. Quarles to Barksdale, August 6, 1864, *OR* 38(3):931–32.

45. Stewart to Mason, January 12, 1865, and Walthall to Gale, January 14, 1865, *OR* 38(3):872, 927.

46. Orlando S. Holland to Hood, n.d., John B. Hood Papers, NARA; Purifoy, "Washington Bryan Crumpton," 378.

47. P. G. Johnson, "Forty-Ninth Tennessee," 554–55; Love, "Forty-Eighth Tennessee," 547; Stephen Cowley to Minor, August 6, 1864, Hubbard T. Minor Papers, USAMHI.

48. Stephen Cowley to Minor, August 6, 1864, Hubbard T. Minor Papers, USAMHI; Quarles to Barksdale, August 6, 1864, *OR* 38(3):933.

49. Quarles to Barksdale, August 6, 1864, *OR* 38(3):932; W. J. Watson Diary, July 28, 1864, UNC.

50. E. W. Mebane to George Mebane, date obscured, TSLA.

51. Love, "Forty-Eighth Tennessee," 547; P. G. Johnson, "Forty-Ninth Tennessee," 554; Quarles to Barksdale, August 6, 1864, *OR* 38(3):932; Brannock to wife, July 29, 1864, James Madison Brannock Papers, VHS.

52. Quarles to Barksdale, August 6, 1864, *OR* 38(3):933.

CHAPTER EIGHT

1. French to Gale, December 6, 1864, *OR* 38(3):904; Warner, *Generals in Gray*, 193–94; Welsh, *Medical Histories of Confederate Generals*, 144; Winfield S. Featherston to Hood, December 18, 1866, John B. Hood Papers, NARA.

2. Stewart to Mason, January 12, 1865, *OR* 38(3):872; Featherston to William D. Gale, April 25, 1865, Winfield Scott Featherston Collection, UM; Winfield S. Featherston to Hood, December 18, 1866, John B. Hood Papers, NARA; Cannon, *Inside of Rebeldom*, 241; Noyes, "E. T. Eggleston," 348; Welsh, *Medical Histories of Confederate Generals*, 144; Whitehead to Irene Cowan, July 28, 1864, Dr. P. F. Whitehead Letters, USM.

3. Stewart to Mason, January 12, 1865, *OR* 38(3):872; Elliott, *Soldier of Tennessee*, 212; French, *Two Wars*, 219; Welsh, *Medical Histories of Confederate Generals*, 206; Whitehead to Irene Cowan, July 28 and August 6, 1864, Dr. P. F. Whitehead Letters, USM; "Tributes to Gen. A. P. Stewart," 595; Wingfield, *General A. P. Stewart*, 178–79; Castel, *Decision in the West*, 433.

4. Walthall to Gale, January 14, 1865; Quarles to Barksdale, August 6, 1864; and O'Neal to Barksdale, August 22, 1864, *OR* 38(3):927, 932, 943.

5. Featherston to William D. Gale, April 25, 1865, Winfield Scott Featherston Collection, UM; Goodloe, *Some Rebel Relics*, 309; Goodloe, *Confederate Echoes*, 431; "Sketches of the Confederate War," 8, Thomas T. Smith Papers, MDAH; Noyes, "E. T. Eggleston," 348; diary, July 28, 1864, John Wharton Papers, MHM.

6. W. T. Jordan, "Mathew Andrew Dunn Letters," 123.

7. [Shoup] to Lee, July 28, 2:20 P.M. and 4:00 P.M.; [Shoup] to Lee, July 28, 1864, 3:25 P.M.; and [Shoup] to Smith, July 28, 1864, 3:30 P.M., *OR* 38(5):919–20, 924; S. Davis, *Atlanta Will Fall*, 154.

8. French, *Two Wars*, 219; French to Gale, December 6, 1864, and Young to Sanders, September 17, 1864, *OR* 38(3):904, 910; [Shoup] to Walthall, July 28, 1864, 5:00 P.M., and Wade to [Walthall], July 28, 1864, 3:35 P.M., *OR* 38(5):921; W. L. Truman Memoir, July 28, 1864, www.cedarcroft.com.

9. T. L. Connelly, *Autumn of Glory*, 455; Roy, "General Hardee," 369–70; Hardee to Cooper, April 5, 1865, *OR* 38(3):699; "Sketch of Lieut. [Gen.] W. J. Hardee," 31, Hardee Family Papers, ADAH; [Shoup] to Cheatham, July 28, 1864, 5:00 P.M., *OR* 38(5):920.

10. Hood to Seddon, July 28, 1864, *OR* 38(5):917.

11. A. T. Holliday to Lizzie, July 28, 29, 1864, A. T. and Elizabeth Holliday Civil War Correspondence, AHC; Brannock to wife, July 28, 1864, James Madison Brannock Papers, VHS; Howard, "Struggle for Atlanta," 319; Stickney to Rose, August 5, 1864, Clifford Stickney Collection, CHM; Reese to Poe, September 14, 1864; and Bryant to Douglass, September 10, 1864, *OR* 38(3):67, 570; Throne, "History of Company D," 65; diary, July 28, 1864, James M. Randall Diary and Letters, www.ehistory.com; Allen to parents, July 25–26, 1864, Edward W. Allen Papers, UNC; Bennett and Tillery, *Struggle*, 191; Mathis, *In the Land of the Living*, 106; Nicodemus to Stanton, October 31, 1864, *OR*, Ser. 3, 4:823; Abernethy, *Private Elisha Stockwell*, 94.

12. Ackley to wife, July 28–29, 1864, Charles Thomas Ackley Civil War Letters, UI; Bowen to Morrison, September 6, 1864; Blodgett to Morrison, September 5, 1864; Sheldon to assistant adjutant general, First Brigade, Fourth Division, Sixteenth Corps, September 12, 1864; Jenkins to Boggis, September 7, 1864; and Rusk to Williams, September 8, 1864, *OR* 38(3):431, 472, 498, 502, 525; James P. Snell Diary, July 28–29, 1864, ALPL; Churchill to wife, July 30, 1864, Mendal C. Churchill Papers, UWY; Jackson, *Colonel's Diary*, 141; Morning Reports and Records, July 28, 1864, Minnesota Light Battery, 1st Company, MHS.

13. Sherman, *Memoirs*, 2:91; Douglas Hapeman Diaries, July 28, 1864, ALPL; Marshall to Mary, July 29, 1864, and Marshall to mother, July 30, 1864, John Law Marshall Correspondence, N-YHS; diary, July 28, 1864, Albert M. Cook Papers, SU; Stanley to Whipple, July 28, 1864, *OR* 38(5):280–81; Wood to Fullerton, August 14, 1864, *OR* 38(1):388; Longacre and Haas, *To Battle for God and the Right*, 204.

14. Cameron to Cox, July 28, 1864, 10:30 A.M.; Cox to Cameron, July 28, 1864, 11:30 A.M.; and Cameron to Wells, July 28, 1864, *OR* 38(5):286–88; Welton to parents, July 31, 1864, Chauncey Brunson Welton Papers, UNC; reminiscences, July 28, 1864, Thomas Doak Edington Papers, UTK; diary, July 28, 1864, and Watkins to Sarah, July 31, 1864, John Watkins Papers, UTK; Michael Houck Diary, July 28, 1864, UTK.

15. Sherman to Schofield, July 28, 1864; Schofield to Sherman, July 28, 1864; and Schofield to Thomas, July 28, 1864, *OR* 38(5):283–84.

16. Sherman to Schofield, July 28, 1864, and Schofield to Sherman, July 28, 1864, 9:00 P.M., *OR* 38(5):284–85.

17. Sherman to Thomas, July 28, 1864, *OR* 38(5):279n; "Battle of Ezra Chapel," 5,

O. O. Howard Papers, BC; Dodge to Clark, November 25, 1864, *OR* 38(3):386; Sherman to Halleck, September 15, 1864, *OR* 38(1):77–78.

18. Davis to Palmer, July 28, 1864, *OR* 38(5):281; Davis to McClurg, September, 1864, and Morgan to Morrison, August 23, 1864, *OR* 38(1):635, 650.

19. Sherman, *Memoirs*, 2:89; Castel, *Decision in the West*, 431; Sherman to Halleck, September 15, 1864, *OR* 38(1):78; Jamison, *Recollections*, 353.

20. Ellison, *On to Atlanta*, 68–69; Davis to McClurg, September 1864; Morgan to Morrison, August 23, 1864; and Holmes to Swift, September 7, 1864, *OR* 38(1):635, 650, 730; Jamison, *Recollections*, 257.

21. Kerr, *Fighting with Ross' Texas Cavalry*, 160; Ross to Sykes, August 1, 1864, *OR* 38(3):963; Hale, *Third Texas Cavalry*, 234; Ross to Jackson, July 28, 1864, *OR* 38(5):923; Morgan to Morrison, August 23, 1864, *OR* 38(1):650.

22. Aten, *History of the Eighty-Fifth*, 211; Ellison, *On to Atlanta*, 69; Mitchell to Wiseman, September 4, 1864; Vernon to Wilson, September 5, 1864; and Fahnestock to Swift, September 7, 1864, *OR* 38(1):681, 689, 721–22; Philip R. Ward Diary, July 28, 1864, Charles S. Harris Collection, UTC; Brown et al., *Behind the Guns*, 102–3; Barron, *Lone Star Defenders*, 199.

23. Howard, "Battles about Atlanta," 398; Howard to Dayton, September 17, 1864, *OR* 38(3):41; Howard, *Autobiography*, 2:24; Sherman to Halleck, September 15, 1864, *OR* 38(1):78; Palmer to Whipple, July 28, 1865, 1:45 P.M., *OR* 38(5):281; Cryder and Miller, *A View from the Ranks*, 423.

24. Morgan to Morrison, August 23, 1864, *OR* 38(1):650; Jamison, *Recollections*, 257–58.

25. Morgan to Morrison, August 23, 1864, *OR* 38(1):650; Brown et al., *Behind the Guns*, 103; Ellison, *On to Atlanta*, 69; Aten, *History of the Eighty-Fifth*, 211.

26. Lusk to Wiseman, September 13, 1864; Lum to Wiseman, August 8, 1864; and Banning to Wilson, September 9, 1864, *OR* 38(1):658, 671, 705; Jamison, *Recollections*, 258; Aten, *History of the Eighty-Fifth*, 211; Lusk to not stated, September 6, 1864, *OR* 38(3):533; Brown et al., *Behind the Guns*, 103.

27. Sherman to Thomas, July 28, 1864, *OR* 38(5):280; Sherman to Halleck, September 15, 1864, *OR* 38(1):78; Howard, "Struggle for Atlanta," 319; Sherman, *Memoirs*, 2:91; Hogan, *General Reub Williams's Memories*, 189.

28. Jamison, *Recollections*, 258; Brown et al., *Behind the Guns*, 102; Morgan to Morrison, August 23, 1864, *OR* 38(1):650.

29. Jamison, *Recollections*, 258–59, 353; Aten, *History of the Eighty-Fifth*, 211–12.

30. Jamison, *Recollections*, 354.

31. Howard, *Autobiography*, 2:24; Howard to Dayton, September 17, 1864, *OR* 38(3):41; Moore to Smith, September 8, 1864, *OR* 38(1):603; Griffin to wife, July 30, 1864, Daniel F. Griffin Papers, ISL.

32. Howard, "Battles about Atlanta," 398; Howard, "Struggle for Atlanta," 319–20.

33. Ward to Perkins, September 7, 1864, and Coburn to Speed, September 12, 1864, *OR* 38(2):329, 391; Charles A. Booth Journal, July 28, 1864, WHS; Grunert, *History*, 89; diary, July 28, 1864, Andrew Jackson Johnson Papers, IHS; Bohrnstedt, *Soldiering with Sherman*, 128; Daniel W. Sheahan Diary, July 28, 1864, ALPL; Harrow to

Townes, September 9, 1864, *OR* 38(3):281; Sherman to Thomas, July 28, 1864, *OR* 38(5):279–80.

34. Logan to Clark, July 29, 1864; Logan to Clark, [September 13, 1864]; Lofland to Townes, September 10, 1864; Van Deusen to McAuley, September 10, 1864; and Hutchinson to Philips, August 6, 1864, *OR* 38(3):86, 104, 189, 206, 354; Wills, *Army Life*, 287; Sherman to Halleck, September 15, 1864, *OR* 38(1):78; John C. Brown Diary, July 28, 1864, UI; Bennett and Tillery, *Struggle*, 191–92; H. H. Wright, *History of the Sixth Iowa*, 312; Q.P.F. to *Cincinnati Commercial*, July 29, 1864, in *St. Louis Daily Missouri Democrat*, August 8, 1864.

35. Howard, "Battles about Atlanta," 397–98; Howard, "Struggle for Atlanta," 319.

36. W. J. Shelton, "Ezra Chapel: How Gen. Howard Impressed Troops in Battle," *National Tribune*, January 5, 1888; Cryder and Miller, *A View From the Ranks*, 422; *Story of the Fifty-Fifth*, 347.

37. Post, *Soldiers' Letters*, 406–7.

38. Howard, *Autobiography*, 2:25; Howard, "Battles about Atlanta," 398.

39. Allen, *On the Skirmish Line*, 238.

40. Logan to Clark, [September 13, 1864]; Wangelin to Gordon, August 5, 1864; Taylor to Fisk, September 10, 1864; Moore to Fisk, September 12, 1864; and Stuart to Williams, August 6, 1864, *OR* 38(3):105, 167–68, 248, 261, 299; Bek, "Civil War Diary," Pt. 2, 525; Maurice to not stated, September 9, 1864, *SOR*, Pt. 1, 7:50; Morris, *History, 31st Regiment Illinois*, 117; J. S. Gage, "In the Front Line at Ezra Chapel," *National Tribune*, August 1, 1895; William Henry Harlow Diary, July 28, 1864, ALPL.

41. Winfield S. Featherston to William D. Gale, April 25, 1865, Winfield Scott Featherston Collection, UM; Toulmin to Cheney, August 2, 1864; Miller to Williams, August 2, 1864; Ray to Williams, July 30, 1864; Walthall to Gale, January 14, 1865; and O'Neal to Barksdale, August 22, 1864, *OR* 38(3):776, 780–81, 928, 943; narrative, 9, Henry DeLamar Clayton Sr. Papers, UA.

42. [Shoup] to Foard, July 28, 1864, *OR* 38(5):924; John H. Bass Diary, July 28, 1864, LSU; Wynne and Taylor, *This War So Horrible*, 107; Goodloe, *Confederate Echoes*, 431–32; Goodloe, *Some Rebel Relics*, 309; Logan to Clark, [September 13, 1864], *OR* 38(3):105.

43. McNeilly, "Recollections," 417–18.

44. Logan to Clark, July 29, 1864; Lee to Mason, January 30, 1865; Brown to Ratchford, July 31, 1864; Toulmin to Cheney, August 2, 1864; Johnson to Harrison, July 30, 1864; Clayton to Ratchford, September 16, 1864; Walthall to Gale, January 14, 1865; and Reynolds to Barksdale, August 2, 1864, *OR* 38(3):86, 763, 768, 776, 807, 821, 928, 939; [Shoup] to Lee, July 28, 1864, 7:00 P.M., *OR* 38(5):920; Cannon, *Inside of Rebeldom*, 241; Winfield S. Featherston to William D. Gale, April 25, 1865, Winfield Scott Featherston Collection, UM; Winfield S. Featherston to Hood, December 18, 1866, John B. Hood Papers, NARA; W. J. Watson Diary, July 28, 1864, UNC; E. D. Willett Diary, July 28, 1864, ADAH; diary, July 28, 1864, John Wharton Papers, MHM; Lucas, *New History*, 116.

45. Q.P.F. to *Cincinnati Commercial*, July 29, 1864, in *St. Louis Daily Missouri Democrat*, August 8, 1864; T. W. Connelly, *Seventieth Ohio*, 100–101; *Story of the Fifty-Fifth*, 349.

46. Cryder and Miller, *A View From the Ranks*, 423.

47. Sherman to Halleck, July 28, 1864, and Howard to Sherman, July 28, 1864, *OR* 38(5):279, 282–83.

48. Sherman to Halleck, July 28, 1864, *OR* 38(5):279.

CHAPTER NINE

1. Bek, "Civil War Diary," Pt. 2, 525; Levi H. Nickel Diary, July 29, 1864, WHS; diary, July 29, 1864, David James Palmer Papers, UI; Philip R. Ward Diary, July 29, 1864, Charles S. Harris Collection, UTC; P. D. Jordan, "Forty Days," 145.

2. *Story of the Fifty-Fifth*, 348; Morgan L. Smith to Townes, August 1, 1864, *SOR*, Pt. 1, 7:58; Saunier, *History of the Forty-Seventh*, 301; Henry Schmidt to wife, July 30, 1864, Schmidt Family Papers, FHS; Hildt to parents, July 31, 1864, George H. Hildt Letters and Diary, OHS.

3. M. D. Gage to editor, August 1, 1864, in *Indianapolis Daily Journal*, August 9, 1864; M. D. Gage, *From Vicksburg to Raleigh*, 226; Hogan, *General Reub Williams's Memories*, 191; Wills, *Army Life*, 287; Baugh to parents, July 31, 1864, William G. Baugh Letters, EU; diary, July 29, 1864, Abraham J. Seay Collection, UO; Seay to Gray, August 5, 1864, *OR* 38(3):171; Fowler and Miller, *History of the Thirtieth Iowa*, 62.

4. Bennett and Tillery, *Struggle*, 192; Allen, *On the Skirmish Line*, 239.

5. Churchill to wife, July 30, 1864, Mendal C. Churchill Papers, UWY; Edwin Witherby Brown, "Under a Poncho with Grant and Sherman," 95, MU; Girdner to Mollie, July 31, 1864, Ephraim L. Girdner Letters, EU; Stickney to Rose, August 5, 1864, Clifford Stickney Collection, CHM; William F. Graham Diary, July 30, 1864, ALPL; H. Smith, *Brother of Mine*, 245; Kinnear, *Eighty-Sixth Regiment*, 65; Aten, *History of the Eighty-Fifth Regiment Illinois*, 121; Jamison, *Recollections*, 259; Ellison, *On to Atlanta*, 70; John J. Mercer Diary, July 29, 1864, Antebellum and Civil War Collection, AHC; diary, July 29, 1864, and Ayers to wife, July 29, 1964, Alexander Miller Ayers Papers, EU; Slack to father and mother, August 1, 1864, Albert L. Slack Letters, EU.

6. Charles A. Booth Journal, July 30, 1864, WHS; Hurst, *Journal-History*, 144; Trowbridge to wife and baby, July 29, 1864, George Martin Trowbridge Papers, WCL-UM.

7. Daniel W. Sheahan Diary, July 29, 1864, ALPL; Buckingham to wife, August 2, 1864, Philo Beecher Buckingham Papers, AAS.

8. Thomas to Sherman, July 29, 1864, *OR* 38(5):291; Clarke, "With Sherman in Georgia," 364–65; Barlow, "Personal Reminiscences," 118; John J. Safely to Mary, July 31, 1864, McEwen Family Papers, MHM.

9. Angle, *Three Years*, 246–47.

10. P. D. Jordan, "Forty Days," 145; Washington L. Midler Diary, July 29, 1864, AAS.

11. Q.P.F. to *Cincinnati Commercial*, July 29, 1864, in *St. Louis Daily Missouri Democrat*, August 8, 1864.

12. John C. Brown Diary, July 29, 1864, UI.

13. Austin to wife, July 31, 1864, Judson L. Austin Papers, BHL-UM; Hogan, *General Reub Williams's Memories*, 190.

14. M. D. Gage, *From Vicksburg to Raleigh*, 228; Hitchcock to parents, August 2,

1864, Watson C. Hitchcock Papers, CHS; S. Black, *Soldier's Recollections*, 86; Daniel W. Sheahan Diary, July 29, 1864, ALPL.

15. T. W. Connelly, *Seventieth Ohio*, 101.

16. Ibid., 101; *Story of the Fifty-Fifth*, 348; Francis Fuller to Friend William, July 29, 1864, Gordon Smith Collection, AM; Hogan, *General Reub Williams's Memories*, 190; Allen, *On the Skirmish Line*, 238; M. D. Gage, *From Vicksburg to Raleigh*, 228.

17. T. W. Connelly, *Seventieth Ohio*, 101; M. D. Gage, *From Vicksburg to Raleigh*, 228; Martin, "*Out and Forward*," 39.

18. Angle, *Three Years*, 247.

19. Wangelin to Gordon, August 5, 1864; Lofland to Townes, September 10, 1864; Martin to Lofland, July 29, 1864; Windsor to McAuley, September 9, 1864; and Berkey to Philips, August 6, 1864, *OR* 38(3):168, 189, 196, 203, 351; W. J. Shelton, "Ezra Chapel: How Gen. Howard Impressed Troops in Battle," *National Tribune*, January 5, 1888; M. D. Gage to editor, August 1, 1864, in *Indianapolis Daily Journal*, August 9, 1864; Hildt to parents, July 31, 1864, George H. Hildt Letters and Diary, OHS.

20. William H. Odell to nephew, August 3, 1864, Jonathan Blair Papers, ALPL; Sherman to Halleck, September 15, 1864; Logan to Clark, July 29, 1864; and Logan to Clark, [September 13, 1864], *OR* 38(3):78, 86, 105; Van Duzer to Eckert, July 29, 1864, *OR* 38(5):299; Bennett and Tillery, *Struggle*, 192; Park to J. S. McBeth, August 2, 1864, Horace Park Letters, UG; Saunier, *History of the Forty-Seventh*, 301. Rumors of a burial truce filtered through the ranks, but there is no evidence to support them. See Ellison, *On to Atlanta*, 70, and Isaac Gaillard Foster diary, July 30, 1864, James Foster and Family Correspondence, LSU.

21. T. W. Connelly, *Seventieth Ohio*, 103.

22. Hughes, *Civil War Memoir*, 225.

23. Letter to Rebecca Harris, July 30, 1864, John A. Harris Papers, EU.

24. Moore to Howard, September 28, 1864, *OR* 38(3):54; diary, July 31–August 3, 1864, George P. Metz Papers, DU.

25. Washington L. Midler Diary, July 30, 1864, AAS.

26. Ibid., August 1, 1864; T. W. Connelly, *Seventieth Ohio*, 103.

27. "Miscellaneous Wounds," Ezra Church, United States Sanitary Commission Records, series 1: Medical Committee Activities, 1861–1865, folder 23, and "Atlanta, July 22, Wounds," series 1, folder 453, NYPL.

28. "Miscellaneous Wounds," Ezra Church, United States Sanitary Commission Records, series 1: Medical Committee Activities, 1861–1865, folder 23, NYPL.

29. Ibid.

30. Ibid.; T. W. Connelly, *Seventieth Ohio*, 103.

31. T. W. Connelly, *Seventieth Ohio*, 100.

32. Hess, *German in the Yankee Fatherland*, 157.

33. Ibid., 158.

34. Allan to mother, July 30, 1864, and Allan to Jim, August 6, 1864, David Allan Jr. Letters, MHM; Widow's Claim for Pension, December 19, 1872; Declaration for Minor Children, November 6, 1875; and Cemetery Certificate, undated, Philip H. Murphy Pension Record, NARA.

35. Ellison, *On to Atlanta*, 70; diary, July 29, 1864, George P. Metz Papers, DU;

Park to J. S. McBeth, August 2, 1864, Horace Park Letters, UG; Moore to Howard, September 28, 1864, and Logan to Clark, [September 13, 1864], *OR* 38(3):54, 105; E.S. to editor, July 29, 1864, in *New York Daily Tribune*, August 8, 1864; Newell to Kate, August 2, 1864, William McCulloch Newell Papers, NC; M. D. Gage, *From Vicksburg to Raleigh*, 233.

36. Diary of Unidentified Soldier of 31st Iowa, July 29, 1864, MHM.

37. White and Runion, *Great Things*, 135–36.

38. Taylor Beatty Diary, July 28, 1864, UNC.

39. Ross to Mary, July 31, 1864, and diary, July 29, 1864, Emmett Ross Papers, MSU.

40. Diary, July 30–31, 1864, Emmett Ross Papers, MSU.

41. Diary, August 1–2, 1864, Emmett Ross Papers, MSU.

42. "Report of the Proceedings," 461–62.

43. Davis, "Hood Fights Desperately," 33; McCarley, "'Atlanta is Ours,'" 69; Haughton, *Training, Tactics and Leadership*, 169, 231n; Tower, *A Carolinian Goes to War*, 236; Toulmin to Cheney, August 2, 1864, *OR* 38(3):777; *Story of the Fifty-Fifth*, 349.

44. Logan to Clark, July 29, 1864, *OR* 38(3):86; Castel, *Decision in the West*, 434. For other estimates of Union losses, see Howard to Dayton, September 17, 1864, *OR* 38(3):42; Sherman to Halleck, September 15, 1864, *OR* 38(1):78; Sherman, "Grand Strategy," 254; Van Duzer to Eckert, July 28, 1864, *OR* 38(5):288.

45. Circular, Headquarters, Loring's Division, July 30, 1864, Featherston Order Book, Winfield Scott Featherston Collection, UM; Castel, *Decision in the West*, 434; McCarley, "'Atlanta is Ours,'" 69; Haughton, *Training, Tactics and Leadership*, 169, 231n; Brown to Ratchford, July 31, 1864; Patton Anderson to Ratchford, February 9, 1865; Toulmin to Cheney, August 2, 1864; Whitney to [Williams], July 30, 1864; Rouse to Williams, August 1, 1864; Miller to Williams, August 2, 1864; Manigault to Cheney, August 6, 1864; Horne to Manigault, August 1, 1864; Sharp to Cheney, August 1, 1864; Walthall to Gale, January 14, 1865; and Quarles to Barksdale, August 6, 1864, *OR* 38(3):768–69, 777, 778–80, 783, 789–90, 927, 932; Sherman to Halleck, September 15, 1864, *OR* 38(1):78; Wooster, "Four Years," 37; Ross to Mary, July 31, 1864, Emmett Ross Papers, MSU; Isaac G. Foster to sister, July 30, 1864, James Foster and Family Correspondence, LSU; J. W. Williamson to cousin Mattie, August 1, 1864, Confederate Miscellany Collection, Series 1, EU; F. A. Montgomery, *Reminiscences*, 193.

46. Sherman to Halleck, September 15, 1864, *OR* 38(1):78; Logan to Clark, July 29, 1864, *OR* 38(3):86; T. W. Connelly, *Seventieth Ohio*, 100. Other data on Confederate prisoners in Union hands include Howard to Dayton, September 17, 1864, and Berkey to Philips, August 6, 1864 *OR* 38(3):42, 351; Q.P.F. to *Cincinnati Commercial*, July 29, 1864, in *St. Louis Daily Missouri Democrat*, August 8, 1864.

47. Howard to Dayton, September 17, 1864; Logan to Clark, July 29, 1864; and Windsor to McAuley, September 9, 1864, *OR* 38(3):42, 86, 203; Howard, *Autobiography*, 2:25; E.S. to editor, July 29, 1864, in *New York Daily Tribune*, August 8, 1864; Q.P.F. to *Cincinnati Commercial*, July 29, 1864, in *St. Louis Daily Missouri Democrat*, August 8, 1864.

48. Logan to Clark, July 29, 1864, *OR* 38(3):86; E.S. to editor, July 29, 1864, in *New York Daily Tribune*, August 8, 1864; Sherman to Halleck, July 28, 1864, 9:00 P.M., *OR*

38(5):279; Howard to Dayton, September 17, 1864, *OR* 38(3):42; Q.P.F. to *Cincinnati Commercial*, July 29, 1864, in *St. Louis Daily Missouri Democrat*, August 8, 1864.

49. S. Black, *Soldier's Recollections*, 86; Bennett and Tillery, *Struggle*, 192–93.

50. S. Davis, "Hood Fights Desperately," 37; J. B. Mitchell, *Badge of Gallantry*, 102.

CHAPTER TEN

1. Howard endorsement dated July 29, 1864, on Logan to Clark, July 29, 1864; Logan to Clark, [September 13, 1864]; and Harrow to Townes, September 9, 1864, *OR* 38(3):86, 104–5, 281–82; Logan, *Volunteer Soldier*, 691; Harrow to Officers and Soldiers of the Fourth Division, Fifteenth Corps, July 30, 1864, *OR* 52(1):571.

2. Martin to Fisk, September 9, 1864; Hutchinson to Philips, August 6, 1864; and Love to Philips, August 6, 1864, *OR* 38(3):235, 354, 360; Hildt to parents, August 15, 1864, George H. Hildt Letters and Diary, OHS.

3. Allan to mother, July 30, 1864, David Allan Jr. Letters, MHM; Diary of an Unidentified soldier of 31st Iowa, July 31, 1864, MHM; *Story of the Fifty-Fifth*, 346, 348; "War Diary," 389.

4. Hildt to parents, July 31, 1864, George H. Hildt Letters and Diary, OHS; Castel, *Tom Taylor's Civil War*, 158; Trowbridge to wife and baby, July 31, 1864, George Martin Trowbridge Papers, WCL-UM; Griffin to wife, July 30, 1864, Daniel F. Griffin Papers, ISL; Q.P.F. to *Cincinnati Commercial*, July 29, 1864, in *St. Louis Daily Missouri Democrat*, August 8, 1864; Foster to Moses C. Morgan, August 23, 1864, William F. Morgan Papers, NC; C. Wright, *A Corporal's Story*, 137; Chamberlin, *History of the Eighty-First Regiment*, 138; M. D. Gage, *From Vicksburg to Raleigh*, 226–27; Park to J. S. McBeth, August 2, 1864, Horace Park Letters, UG; W. P. Thornton to editor, July 31, 1864, in *St. Louis Daily Missouri Democrat*, August 9, 1864; Cox, *Atlanta*, 186; R. W. Johnson, *Soldier's Reminiscences*, 282; Osborn, "Sherman's Atlanta Campaign," 133; Wysor to father, July 19 (and continued thereafter), 1864, James Miller Wysor Letters, VHS; "Personal Biography of Major General Grenville Mellen Dodge 1831–1870," 1:259, Grenville Mellen Dodge Papers, SHSI.

5. Aten, *History of the Eighty-Fifth Regiment Illinois*, 213; Butler, *Letters Home*, 140–41; Adams, "Battle and Capture of Atlanta," 160; Maley to father and mother, July 30, 1864, Henry H. Maley Letters, UND.

6. Howard to wife, July 29, 1864, "Battle of Ezra Chapel," 7, O. O. Howard Papers, BC; Howard to Dayton, September 17, 1864, *OR* 38(3):41; Howard, *Autobiography*, 2:24; "Personal Recollections: Strategy and battles of Sherman & Johnston illustrated in active campaigns," not paginated, folder 3, box 5, Oliver Otis Howard Papers, LMU.

7. Howard to Dayton, September 17, 1864; Howard endorsement, dated July 29, 1864, on Logan to Clark, July 29, 1864; and Logan to Clark, [September 13, 1864], *OR* 38(3):41–42, 86, 104–5.

8. Mortimer D. Leggett to Force, August 2, 1864, M. F. Force Papers, UW; Adams, "Battle and Capture of Atlanta," 161; R. W. Johnson, *Soldier's Reminiscences*, 283.

9. Sherman to Ellen, July 29, 1864, Simpson and Berlin, *Sherman's Civil War*, 676; Sherman to Schofield, July 28, 1864, *OR* 38(5):285; Sherman, *Memoirs*, 2:91.

10. General Orders No. 238, War Department, Adjutant General Office, July 30, 1864, *OR* 38(5):307.

11. "Battle of Ezra Chapel," 3, and Howard to wife, August 4, 5, 1864, O. O. Howard Papers, BC; Howard, "Battles about Atlanta," 396.

12. Carpenter, *Sword and Olive Branch*, 73–74.

13. Sherman to Halleck, September 15, 1864, and Special Field Orders No. 68, Headquarters, Military Division of the Mississippi, September 8, 1864, *OR* 38(1):78, 88; Sherman to brother, July 31, [1864], (misfiled as July 31, 1863), William T. Sherman Papers, LC; Sherman to Ellen, July 29, 1864, Simpson and Berlin, *Sherman's Civil War*, 676; Sherman, *Memoirs*, 2:91.

14. Martin to Lofland, July 29, 1864; Mott to assistant adjutant general, First Brigade, Second Division, Fifteenth Corps, September 9, 1864; Harrow to Townes, September 9, 1864; and Love to Philips, August 6, 1864, *OR* 38(3):196, 218, 281, 358; Smith to father, July 31, 1864, Charles M. Smith Papers, WHS; Edwin C. Obriham to sister, August 14, 1864, June and Gilbert Krueger Civil War Letters, CU; Q.P.F. to *Cincinnati Commercial*, July 29, 1864, in *St. Louis Daily Missouri Democrat*, August 8, 1864; Charles A. Booth Journal, July 30, 1864, WHS; M. D. Gage, *From Vicksburg to Raleigh*, 228; Newell to Kate, August 2, 1864, William McCulloch Newell Papers, NC; Wills, *Army Life*, 287.

15. Finley to Miss M.A.C., July 26, 1864, Robert Stuart Finley Papers, UNC; Longacre and Haas, *To Battle for God and the Right*, 204; Randall to wife, July 30, 1864, James M. Randall Diary and Letters, www.ehistory.com; Nugen to Mary, July 29, 1864, William H. Nugen Letters, DU; Mortimer D. Leggett to Force, August 2, 1864, M. F. Force Papers, UW; Sawyer to Nancy, July 29, 1864, James F. Sawyer Letters, WHS; Wills, *Army Life*, 287; Allan to mother, July 30, 1864, David Allan Jr. Letters, MHM.

16. Logan, *Volunteer Soldier*, 691; W. W. Belknap to Aaron, August 5, 1864, Belknap Family Papers, N-YHS; H. Smith, *Brother of Mine*, 244; S. Black, *Soldier's Recollections*, 86; Stickney to Rose, August 5, 1864, Clifford Stickney Collection, CHM.

17. Angle, *Three Years*, 247; Merrill to Emma, July 30, 1864, Samuel Merrill Papers, ISL; "War Diary," 390; Adams, "Battle and Capture of Atlanta," 160; Jackson, *Colonel's Diary*, 141; Naylor to Coz Sallie, August 3, 1864, James M. Naylor Papers, OHS; Hildt to parents, July 31, 1864, George H. Hildt Letters and Diary, OHS; Longacre and Haas, *To Battle for God and the Right*, 204; French to wife, July 29, 1864, Orlando L. French Civil War Letters, UTK; John J. Safely to Mary, July 31, 1864, McEwen Family Papers, MHM; Tuttle to not stated, late July, 1864, Miletus Tuttle Letters, UG; Churchill to wife, July 30, 1864, Mendal C. Churchill Papers, UWY; M. D. Gage to editor, August 1, 1864, in *Indianapolis Daily Journal*, August 9, 1864.

18. Volwiler, "Letters from a Civil War Officer," 521–22; H. Smith, *Brother of Mine*, 245; Merrill to Emma, July 30, 1864, Samuel Merrill Papers, ISL; Griffin to wife, July 30, 1864, Daniel F. Griffin Papers, ISL.

19. Marshall to sister Mary, July 29, 1864, John Law Marshall Correspondence, N-YHS; Morse to Robert, July 29, 1864, Charles F. Morse Papers, MassHS; reminiscences, July 29, 1864, Thomas Doak Edington Papers, UTK; Wood to Fullerton, July 29, 1864, Sherman to Halleck, July 29, 1864, *OR* 38(5):281–82, 289; John J. Safely to

Mary, July 31, 1864, McEwen Family Papers, MHM; Q.P.F. to *Cincinnati Commercial*, July 29, 1864, in *St. Louis Daily Missouri Democrat*, August 8, 1864; E.S. to editor, July 29, 1864, in *New York Daily Tribune*, August 8, 1864.

20. Watkins to Sarah, July 31, 1864, John Watkins Papers, UTK; Marshall diary, July 29, 1864, John Wesley Marshall Papers, OHS; Foster to Moses C. Morgan, August 23, 1864, William F. Morgan Papers, NC.

21. Q.P.F. to *Cincinnati Commercial*, July 29, 1864, in *St. Louis Daily Missouri Democrat*, August 8, 1864; E.S. to editor, July 29, 1864, in *New York Daily Tribune*, August 8, 1864; *Harper's Weekly*, August 27, 1864, 556–58.

22. W. H. Thompson to Mary Royse, August 5, 1864, John W. Royse Papers, DU.

23. Engs and Brooks, *Their Patriotic Duty*, 282.

24. Churchill to wife, July 30, 1864, Mendal C. Churchill Papers, UWY; Gardner to parents, July 29, 1864, Lyman Gardner Papers, WCL-UM; Allan to mother, July 30, 1864, David Allan Jr. Letters, MHM; Bohrnstedt, *Soldiering with Sherman*, 128; Wills, *Army Life*, 287; Special Field Orders No. 65, Headquarters, Army of the Ohio, July 29, 1864, *OR* 38(5):299; Castel, *Decision in the West*, 381, 411–12, 434.

25. Trowbridge to wife and baby, July 31, 1864, George Martin Trowbridge Papers, WCL-UM; Bennett and Tillery, *Struggle*, 192; Slack to father and mother, August 1, 1864, Albert L. Slack Letters, EU; Baugh to parents, July 31, 1864, William G. Baugh Letters, EU; Maley to father and mother, July 30, 1864, Henry H. Maley Letters, UND; Ackley to wife, July 28–29, 1864, Charles Thomas Ackley Civil War Letters, UI.

26. Bennett and Tillery, *Struggle*, 192; Baugh to parents, July 31, 1864, William G. Baugh Letters, EU; Adams, "Battle and Capture of Atlanta," 161; Griffin to wife, July 30, 1864, Daniel F. Griffin Papers, ISL.

27. Diary, July 29, 1864, Albert M. Cook Papers, SU; Throne, "History of Company D," 65; Maley to father and mother, July 30, 1864, Henry H. Maley Letters, UND.

28. Hogan, *General Reub Williams's Memories*, 190.

29. Whitehead to Irene Cowan, July 28, 1864, Dr. P. F. Whitehead Letters, USM; Holliday to Lizzie, July 29, 1864, A. T. and Elizabeth Holliday Civil War Correspondence, AHC; diary, July 29, 31, 1864, Edwin Hansford Rennolds Sr. Papers, UTK.

30. Lee to Mason, January 30, 1865, *OR* 38(3):763.

31. F. Halsey Wigfall to Mama, August 7, 1864, Louis Trezevant Wigfall Family Papers, LC.

32. Hood, "Defense of Atlanta," 341; Hood to Lee, January 15, November 29, 1865, Stephen D. Lee Papers, UNC.

33. Samuel Wragg Ferguson Memoirs, 1, SCHS.

34. Tower, *A Carolinian Goes to War*, 236; Marshall to Mrs. E. J. Marshall, August 11, 1864, John H. Marshall Letters, MSU; French, *Two Wars*, 219.

35. S. Davis, *Atlanta Will Fall*, 153; Hattaway, *General Stephen D. Lee*, 128; Castel, *Decision in the West*, 435.

36. Circular, Headquarters, Lee's Corps, July 31, 1864, *OR* 38(5):936.

37. Jesse L. Henderson Civil War Diary, September 6, 9, 1864, UM.

38. Angus M. Martin to Father, July 29, 1864, Martin Family Papers, NC; Worley, *War Memoirs*, 98–99; Warrick to wife, July 31, 1864, Thomas Warrick Papers, ADAH;

Tower, *A Carolinian Goes to War*, 237; Hynes to brother, July 29, 1864, William D. Hynes Papers, ISL; W. L. Truman Memoir, July 28, 1864, www.cedarcroft.com; Stephen Cowley to Minor, August 6, 1864, Hubbard T. Minor Papers, USAMHI; L. R. Smith and Quist, *Cush*, 121; H. L. G. Whitaker to friends, July 29, 1864, Charles A. James Martin Family Papers, UG.

39. Clayton to wife, August 24, 28, 1864, Henry Delamar Clayton Sr. Papers, UA.

40. McMurry, *John Bell Hood*, 134; McMurry, "Confederate Morale," 236; Blomquist and Taylor, *This Cruel War*, 270; Neal to Ella, August 4, 1864, Andrew Jackson Neal Letters, EU; Jim Huffman, comp., "Pre- & Civil War Letters of Lt. Col. Columbus Sykes 16th [*sic*] Regiment, Mississippi Infantry," 77, MDAH; Brannock to wife, July 28, 1864, James Madison Brannock Papers, VHS.

41. Clampitt, *Confederate Heartland*, 81–82; McMurry, "Confederate Morale," 232–33; McNeill, "Survey of Confederate Soldier Morale," 15; Stephen Cowley to Minor, August 6, 1864, Hubbard T. Minor Papers, USAMHI; Wynne and Taylor, *This War So Horrible*, 107; Hughes, *Civil War Memoir*, 225.

42. Hood to Cooper, February 15, 1865, and Shoup journal, July 28, 1864, *OR* 38(3):631–32, 688; Hood to Seddon, July 30, 1864, *OR* 38(5):930; Thomas L. Clayton to wife, July 31, 1864, Clayton Family Papers, UNC; F. Halsey Wigfall to Mama, July 31, 1864, Louis Trezevant Wigfall Family Papers, LC.

43. Cox, *Atlanta*, 184–86.

44. Hood, *Advance and Retreat*, 129, 134, 138.

45. S. Davis, *Atlanta Will Fall*, 153–54; McMurry, *John Bell Hood*, 133–34; Castel, *Decision in the West*, 435.

46. Hardee to Cooper, April 5, 1865, *OR* 38(3):697–99; Roy, "General Hardee," 370; Joseph E. Johnston to Wigfall, February 28, 1865, Louis Trezevant Wigfall Family Papers, LC.

CHAPTER ELEVEN

1. Sherman to Thomas, July 29, 1864; Thomas to Sherman, July 29, 1864; and Sherman to Howard, July 29, 1864, *OR* 38(5):290, 297.

2. Sherman to Thomas, July 29, 1864; Howard to Sherman, July 29, 1864; and Sherman to Howard, July 29, 1864, *OR* 38(5):290, 296–97; diary, July 29, 1864, David James Palmer Papers, UI; Allen to Dear Ones at Home, August 1, 1864, Dwight S. Allen Papers, WHS.

3. Morgan to Morrison, August 23, 1864, *OR* 38(1):650; Philip R. Ward Diary, July 29, 1864, Charles S. Harris Collection, UTC.

4. Diary, July 29, 1864, Curtis J. Judd Papers, CHM; diary, July 29, 1864, Andrew Jackson Johnson Papers, IHS; Bohrnstedt, *Soldiering with Sherman*, 128; Buckingham to wife, August 2, 1864, Philo Beecher Buckingham Papers, AAS; diary of unidentified soldier in 85th Indiana, July 29, 1864, Civil War Miscellany, UTA; Alfred H. Trego Diary, July 29, 1864, CHM; James A. Congleton Diary, July 29, 1864, LC.

5. Grunert, *History*, 90; Charles A. Booth Journal, July 29, 1864, WHS.

6. Morgan to Morrison, August 23, 1864, *OR* 38(1):650; Philip R. Ward Diary,

July 29, 1864, Charles S. Harris Collection, UTC; Lum to Wiseman, August 8, 1864; Banning to Wilson, September 9, 1864; and Holmes to Swift, September 7, 1864, *OR* 38(1):671, 705, 730; Jamison, *Recollections*, 259.

7. Hurst, *Journal-History*, 144; Charles A. Booth Journal, July 29, 1864, WHS; Buckingham to wife, August 2, 1864, Philo Beecher Buckingham Papers, AAS; Thomas to Sherman, July 29, 1864, *OR* 38(5):290–91; Ward to Perkins, September 7, 1864; Harrison to [Speed], September 14, 1864; Coburn to Speed, September 12, 1864; and Miller to Crawford, September 9, 1864, *OR* 38(2):329, 349, 391, 408; Byrne, *View from Headquarters*, 176; Ellison, *On to Atlanta*, 69; Jones to Wilson, September 10, 1864, *OR* 38(1):698; Jamison, *Recollections*, 259; Grunert, *History*, 90.

8. Berkey to Philips, August 6, 1864, and Belknap to Cadle, July 29, 1864, *OR* 38(3):351, 607; Washington L. Midler Diary, July 29, 1864, AAS; Maurice to not stated, September 9, 1864, *SOR*, Pt. 1, 7:50–51; diary, July 29, 1864, Alonzo Miller Papers, WHS; James P. Snell Diary, July 29, 1864, ALPL; record of events, 64th Illinois, July 29, 1864, *SOR*, Pt. 2, 12:588; Lofland to Giles A. Smith, July 29, 1864, *OR* 38(5):298.

9. Hudson, Bergman, and Horton, *Biographical Dictionary*, 493–94; H. M. Brandle, "At Ezra Chapel: Reminiscences of a Missouri Soldier," *National Tribune*, December 22, 1887; Charles G. Ward Diary, July 29, 1864, USC; diary, July 29, 1864, Alexander Miller Ayers Papers, EU; Nugen to sister, July 29, 1864, William H. Nugen Letters, DU; Charles Berry Senior to father, July 31, 1864, Electronic Text Center, UV.

10. Thomas to Sherman, July 29, 1864, *OR* 38(5):291.

11. Sherman to Schofield, July 29, 1864; Schofield to Sherman, July 29, 1864; Schofield to Cox, July 29, 1864; and Cox to Campbell, July 29, 1864, *OR* 38(5):293–94.

12. Evans, *Sherman's Horsemen*, 208–376.

13. Shoup journal, July 25–29, 1864, and Walthall to Gale, January 14, 1865, *OR* 38(3):688, 928; Special Field Orders No. 61, Headquarters, Army of Tennessee, July 29, 1864, *OR* 38(5):930; French, *Two Wars*, 219.

14. Hood to Davis, July 29, 1864; [Shoup] to Brown, July 29, 1864; and Special Field Orders No. 61, Headquarters, Army of Tennessee, July 29, 1864, *OR* 38(5):924–26, 930; Brown to Ratchford, July 31, 1864, and Anderson to Ratchford, February 9, 1865, *OR* 38(3):768–69; Isaac Gaillard Foster diary, July 29, 1864, James Foster and Family Correspondence, LSU.

15. [Shoup] to Cheatham, July 29, 1864; [Shoup] to Lee, July 29, 1864; and [Shoup] to Hardee, July 29, 1864, *OR* 38(5):925; E. D. Willett Diary, July 29, 1864, ADAH; Jesse L. Henderson Civil War Diary, July 29–30, 1864, UM; W. J. Watson Diary, July 29, 1864, UNC; Cannon, *Inside of Rebeldom*, 242; Brown to Ratchford, July 31, 1864, and Walthall to Gale, January 14, 1865, *OR* 38(3):768, 928; Capt. William Van Davis Diary, July 29, 1864, USM; Ashley and Ashley, *Oh for Dixie!*, 48.

16. Sherman to Halleck, July 29, 1864; Thomas to Sherman, July 29, 1864; Sherman to Thomas, July 29, 1864; Howard to Sherman, July 29, 1864; Sherman to Howard, July 29, 1864; and Special Field Orders No. 82, Headquarters, Army of the Tennessee, July 29, 1864, *OR* 38(5):289, 291, 297, 299–300.

17. P. D. Jordan, "Forty Days," 145; diary, July 30, 1864, George P. Metz Papers, DU; Lofland to Townes, September 10, 1864; Taylor to Fisk, September 10, 1864; and

Berkey to Philips, August 6, 1864, *OR* 38(3):189, 248, 351; Charles G. Ward Diary, July 30, 1864, USC; diary, July 30, 1864, David James Palmer Papers, UI; Jamison, *Recollections*, 259; Blair to Clark, July 30, 1864, and Special Field Orders No. 50, Headquarters, Left Wing, Sixteenth Corps, July 30, 1864, *OR* 38(5):305, 307; diary, July 30, 1864, Alonzo Miller Papers, WHS; Jackson, *Colonel's Diary*, 141.

18. Davis to McClurg, July 30, 1864, *OR* 38(5):302; Jamison, *Recollections*, 259; Philip R. Ward Diary, July 30, 1864, Charles S. Harris Collection, UTC; Holmes to Swift, September 7, 1864, *OR* 38(1):730; Charles A. Booth Journal, July 30, 1864, WHS; Ward to Perkins, September 7, 1864; Harrison to [Speed], September 14, 1864; Coburn to Speed, September 12, 1864; and Miller to Crawford, September 9, 1864, *OR* 38(2):329, 349, 391–92, 408; Alfred H. Trego Diary, July 30, 1864, CHM; Daniel W. Sheahan Diary, July 30, 1864, ALPL; diary, July 30, 1864, Andrew Jackson Johnson Papers, IHS; diary of unidentified soldier in 85th Indiana, July 30, 1864, Civil War Miscellany, UTA; diary, July 30, 1864, Curtis J. Judd Papers, CHM; Grunert, *History*, 90–91; DeRosier, *Through the South*, 135.

19. William Graham Diary, July 30, 1864, DU; Throne, "History of Company D," 65; Cryder and Miller, *A View from the Ranks*, 423.

20. Sherman to Thomas, July 30, 1864, and Van Duzer to Eckert, July 30, 1864, *OR* 38(5):301, 306–7.

21. Sherman to Thomas, July 30, 1864; Fullerton to Grose, July 30, 1864; and Sherman to Schofield, July 30, 1864, *OR* 38(5):301, 303.

22. [Shoup] to Lee, July 30, 1864, *OR* 38(5):931; Cannon, *Inside of Rebeldom*, 242.

23. H. I. Smith, *History of the Seventh Iowa*, 163.

24. Thomas to Sherman, July 31, 1864; Sherman to Howard, July 31, 1864; and Howard to Sherman, July 31, 1864, *OR* 38(5):308, 313–14.

25. Thomas to Sherman, July 31, 1864, and Palmer to Whipple, July 31, 1864, *OR* 38(5):309, 311.

26. Thomas to Sherman, July 31, 1864, *OR* 38(5):309; Grunert, *History*, 90–91; John J. Mercer diary, July 31, 1864, Antebellum and Civil War Collection, AHC; Buckingham to wife, August 2, 1864, Philo Beecher Buckingham Papers, AAS; Johnson to Folks at Home, August 1, 1864, Andrew Jackson Johnson Papers, IHS.

27. Thomas to Sherman, July 31, 1864, *OR* 38(5):309.

28. Sherman to Thomas, July 31, 1864, and Sherman to Schofield, July 31, 1864, *OR* 38(5):309, 311.

29. Sherman to Halleck, July 31, 1864; Sherman to Thomas and Howard, July 31, 1864; Sherman to Howard, July 31, 1864; and Special Field Orders No. 67, Headquarters, Army of the Ohio, July 31, 1864, *OR* 38(5):308, 310, 314–15; diary, August 1, 1864, George W. Gallup Papers, FHS.

30. Roy to Cleburne, July 31, 1864, and [Shoup] to Martin, July 31, 1864, *OR* 38(5):933; "History of Company B," 208–9.

31. Howard to Sherman, July 31, 1864, *OR* 38(5):313; Wills, *Army Life*, 288; Grunert, *History*, 91.

32. Reminiscences, August 1–2, 1864, Thomas Doak Edington Papers, UTK; journal, August 1, 1864, Tilghman Blazer Collection, UTK.

33. Grunert, *History*, 91; diary, August 2, 1864, Andrew Jackson Johnson Papers,

IHS; Byrne, *View from Headquarters*, 178; Johnson to McClurg, August 1864, and Baird to McClurg, September 7, 1864, *OR* 38(1):525, 744; Williams to Whipple, September 20, 1864, *OR* 38(2):18.

34. Logan to Clark, August 4 and [September 13, 1864], and Harrow to Townes, September 9, 1864, *OR* 38(3):87, 105–6, 282; T. W. Connelly, *Seventieth Ohio*, 102–3.

35. Logan to Clark, [September 13, 1864], *OR* 38(3):105; Davis to McClurg, September 1864, *OR* 38(1):635.

36. Thomas D. Christie to sister, August 5, 1864, Christie Family Letters, MHS; H. Smith, *Brother of Mine*, 254; diary, July 29, 1864, Brigham Foster Papers, USAMHI; Winther, *With Sherman to the Sea*, 122.

37. Davis to Hood, August 5, 1864, *OR* 38(5):946; Howard to Dayton, September 17, 1864, *OR* 38(3):42; Castel, *Decision in the West*, 459–60.

38. Castel, *Decision in the West*, 467–68.

39. Poe to [Delafield], October 8, 1865, *OR* 38(1):135; Reese to Poe, September 14, 1864, *OR* 38(3):67; *History of the Fifteenth Regiment*, 390–91; Jackson, *Colonel's Diary*, 145; W. W. Black, "Marching with Sherman," Pt. 1, 327–28.

40. Special Field Orders No. 108, Headquarters, Army of the Tennessee, August 24, 1864; Thomas to Howard, August 25, 1864; Howard to Thomas, August 25, 1864; and Stanley to Whipple, August 26, 1864, *OR* 38(5):661, 664, 669; Cryder and Miller, *A View From the Ranks*, 433–34; Jackson, *Colonel's Diary*, 145.

41. Jackson, *Colonel's Diary*, 146; Ellison, *On to Atlanta*, 79–81.

42. Henry, "Little War-Time Incidents," 306.

43. Ibid.

44. Castel, *Decision in the West*, 494–526.

CONCLUSION

1. W. Smith, *Private in Gray*, 108; E. D. Willett Diary, July 28, 1864, ADAH; "Battle of Ezra Chapel," O. O. Howard Papers, BC.

2. Sherman, *Memoirs*, 2:91–92; Aten, *History of the Eighty-Fifth Regiment, Illinois*, 212.

3. McMurry, *Atlanta*, 157; S. Davis, *Atlanta Will Fall*, 153; McPherson, *Battle Cry of Freedom*, 754–55.

4. Saunier, *History of the Forty-Seventh*, 299; H. H. Wright, *History of the Sixth Iowa*, 312; diary, July 28, 1864, George P. Metz Papers, DU; Tapert, *Brothers War*, 207; Hildt to parents, August 15, 1864, George H. Hildt Letters and Diary, OHS.

5. Howard, "Battles about Atlanta," 397; Howard, *Autobiography*, 2:24.

6. Arbuckle, *Civil War Experiences*, 78.

7. Castel, *Decision in the West*, 435; Hattaway, *General Stephen D. Lee*, 130; S. Davis, "Hood Fights Desperately," 34.

8. Ratchford to Clayton, August 9, 1864, General Orders No. 63, Headquarters, Lee's Corps, August 12, 1864, *OR* 38(3):766, 960–61.

9. Castel, *Decision in the West*, 435; McMurry, *John Bell Hood*, 134.

10. "Battle of Ezra Chapel," 8, O. O. Howard Papers, BC; Sherman, "Grand Strategy," 254.

11. Howard to Dayton, September 17, 1864, and Logan to Clark, July 29, 1864, and [September 13, 1864], *OR* 38(3):42, 86, 105; Sherman to Halleck, July 29, 1864, *OR* 38(5):289; Sherman to Halleck, September 15, 1864, *OR* 38(1):78; Sherman, "Grand Strategy," 254.

12. Stickney to Rose, August 5, 1864, Clifford Stickney Collection, CHM; Bennett and Tillery, *Struggle*, 192; Griffin to wife, July 30, 1864, Daniel F. Griffin Papers, ISL; Trowbridge to wife and baby, July 29, 1864, George Martin Trowbridge Papers, WCL-UM.

13. M. D. Gage to editor, August 1, 1864, in *Indianapolis Daily Journal*, August 9, 1864; Hogan, *General Reub Williams's Memories*, 188; Hess, *Rifle Musket*, 100–104.

14. Circular, Headquarters, Army of Mississippi, June 24, 1864, Featherston Order Book, Winfield Scott Featherston Collection, UM.

15. Riley to Oladowski, October 1, 1863, *OR* 30(2):303, 305–6, 314.

16. Rosengarten to Williams, July 19, 1863, *OR* 27(1):265; Rosecrans to [Lorenzo Thomas], [October 1863], OR, 30(1):62.

17. Logan to Clark, July 29, 1864, and [September 13, 1864], *OR* 38(3):86, 111.

18. M. D. Gage, *From Vicksburg to Raleigh*, 225–26.

19. McWhiney and Jamieson, *Attack and Die*, 3–40; Hess, *Rifle Musket*, 107–15, 202.

20. Phillips, *Correspondence*, 648–49.

21. Lee to Andrew Johnson, July 9, 1865, Stephen D. Lee Papers, UNC; Lee to Oliver O. Howard, July 12, 1865, Stephen D. Lee Letters, GLIAH.

22. Oliver O. Howard to Stephen D. Lee, July 25, 1865, O. O. Howard Papers, BC.

23. Lee to Howard, August 22, 1865, Stephen D. Lee Letters, GLIAH.

24. Howard to Lee, September 12, 1865, Stephen D. Lee Papers, UNC.

25. Lee to Oliver O. Howard, October 29, 1903, Stephen D. Lee Papers, UNC.

26. Hess, *Kennesaw Mountain*, 235–39.

27. *Battles of Atlanta*, 8, 20, 27.

28. "Chamber Favors National Park," *Atlanta Constitution*, March 10, 1906; "Wilbur Kurtz Explains Selection of U.S. Memorial Park Sites Here," *Atlanta Constitution*, November 14, 1931.

29. Allen to Troy Chastain, February 16, 1939, Ivan Allen Sr. Papers, AHC.

30. Erquitt, "Confederate Defeat," 21; *Georgia Civil War Historical Markers*, 90.

31. *Georgia Civil War Historical Markers*, 89–91; McCarley, "'Atlanta is Ours,'" 70–75; Erquitt, "Confederate Defeat," 24.

32. McCarley, "'Atlanta is Ours,'" 73, 76; *Georgia Civil War Historical Markers*, 89, 90–91; Erquitt, "Confederate Defeat," 23, 33.

33. Erquitt, "Confederate Defeat," 20, 23; "Driving Tour," 38, 68.

Bibliography

ARCHIVES

Abraham Lincoln Presidential Library, Springfield, Illinois
    Jonathan Blair Papers
    George Lemon Childress Diary
    William F. Graham Diary
    Douglas Hapeman Diaries
    William Henry Harlow Diary
    Daniel W. Sheahan Diary
    James P. Snell Diary
Alabama Department of Archives and History, Montgomery
    Hardee Family Papers
    Thomas Warrick Papers
    E. D. Willett Diary
American Antiquarian Society, Worcester, Massachusetts
    Philo Beecher Buckingham Papers
    Washington L. Midler Diary
Archives of Michigan, Lansing
    Francis Fuller Letters, Gordon Smith Collection
Atlanta History Center, Atlanta, Georgia
    Ivan Allen Sr. Papers
    A. T. and Elizabeth Holliday Civil War Correspondence
    John J. Mercer Diary, Antebellum and Civil War Collection
Bowdoin College, Special Collections and Archives, Brunswick, Maine
    O. O. Howard Papers
Chicago History Museum, Chicago, Illinois
    Curtis J. Judd Papers
    Clifford Stickney Collection
    Alfred H. Trego Diary
College of William and Mary, Special Collections, Williamsburg, Virginia
    Joseph E. Johnston Papers
Connecticut Historical Society, New Haven
    Watson C. Hitchcock Papers
Cornell University, Division of Rare and Manuscript Collections, Ithaca, New York
    Edwin C. Obriham Letters, June and Gilbert Krueger Civil War Letters

Duke University, Rubenstein Rare Book and Manuscript Library,
    Durham, North Carolina
  George Williamson Balloch Papers
  William Graham Diary
  Charles Colcock Jones Papers
  George P. Metz Papers
  William H. Nugen Letters
  John W. Royse Papers
Emory University, Manuscripts, Archives, and Rare Books Library,
    Atlanta, Georgia
  Alexander Miller Ayers Papers
  William G. Baugh Letters
  W. B. Corbitt Diary, Confederate Miscellany Collection, Series 1
  Ephraim L. Girdner Letters
  John A. Harris Papers
  Andrew Jackson Neal Letters
  Albert L. Slack Letters
  J. W. Williamson Letter, Confederate Miscellany Collection, Series 1
Filson Historical Society, Louisville, Kentucky
  George W. Gallup Papers
  Henry Schmidt Letters, Schmidt Family Papers
Gilder Lehrman Institute of American History, New York, New York
  Stephen D. Lee Letters
Harvard University, Houghton Library, Cambridge, Massachusetts
  Oliver Otis Howard Letters, Frederick M. Dearborn Collection
Indiana Historical Society, Indianapolis
  Andrew Jackson Johnson Papers
Indiana State Library, Indianapolis
  Daniel F. Griffin Papers
  William D. Hynes Papers
  Samuel Merrill Papers
Iowa State University, Special Collections, Iowa City
  George Samuel Neel Civil War Diary
Library of Congress, Manuscript Division, Washington, D.C.
  James A. Congleton Diary
  James Harrison Goodnow Papers
  John Alexander Logan Papers
  Orlando Metcalfe Poe Papers
  William T. Sherman Papers
  Louis Trezevant Wigfall Family Papers
Lincoln Memorial University, Abraham Lincoln Library and Museum,
    Harrogate, Tennessee
  Oliver Otis Howard Papers

Louisiana State University, Louisiana and Lower Mississippi Valley Collection,
     Baton Rouge
   John H. Bass Diary
   Isaac Gaillard Foster Diary and Letters, James Foster and Family
       Correspondence
   Wayne Johnson Jacobs Diaries and Lists
   Kent-Amacker Family Papers
Massachusetts Historical Society, Boston
   Charles F. Morse Papers
Miami University, Special Collections, Oxford, Ohio
   Edwin Witherby Brown. "Under a Poncho with Grant and Sherman."
Minnesota Historical Society, St. Paul
   Christie Family Letters
   Minnesota Light Battery, 1st Company, Morning Reports and Records,
       1861–1865
Mississippi Department of Archives and History, Jackson
   Jim Huffman, comp. "Pre– & Civil War Letters of Lt. Col. Columbus Sykes
       16th [sic] Regiment, Mississippi Infantry."
   R. A. Jarman. "The History of Company K, 27th Mississippi Infantry,
       and Its First and Last Muster Rolls."
   George W. Modil Papers
   Thomas T. Smith Papers
Mississippi State University, Special Collections, Starkville
   John H. Marshall Letters
   Emmett Ross Papers
Missouri History Museum, St. Louis
   David Allan Jr. Letters
   Diary of Unidentified Soldier of 31st Iowa
   Hiffman Family Papers
   William Charles Pfeffer Diary
   John J. Safely Letters, McEwen Family Papers
   John Wharton Papers
Museum of the Confederacy, Richmond, Virginia
   Irving Buck Papers
   "Report of Casualties in Brantley's Brigade, Hindman's Div &c. in the
       engagement on the 28th inst." Confederate Military Leaders Collection,
       Western Theatre Trans-Mississippi, Miscellaneous
National Archives and Records Administration, Washington, D.C., RG109,
       War Department Collection of Confederate Records
   John B. Hood Papers
   George W. Braden Service Record, 9th Mississippi, M269, Compiled Service
       Records of Confederate Soldiers Who Served in Organizations from the
       State of Mississippi

Cyrus A. Johnson Service Record, 9th Mississippi, M269, Compiled Service Records of Confederate Soldiers Who Served in Organizations from the State of Mississippi

Philip H. Murphy Pension Record, 29th Missouri (US)

Philip H. Murphy Service Record, 29th Missouri (US), M405, Compiled Service Records of Volunteer Union Soldiers Who Served in Organizations from the State of Missouri

Navarro College, Pearce Civil War Collection, Corsicana, Texas
Martin Family Papers
William F. Morgan Papers
William McCulloch Newell Papers

New-York Historical Society, New York
Belknap Family Papers
John Law Marshall Correspondence

New York Public Library, Rare Books and Manuscripts, New York, New York
United States Sanitary Commission Records

Ohio Historical Society, Archives/Library, Columbus
George H. Hildt Letters and Diary
John Wesley Marshall Papers
James M. Naylor Papers

South Carolina Historical Society, Charleston
Samuel Wragg Ferguson Memoirs

State Historical Society of Iowa, Des Moines
Grenville Mellen Dodge Papers

State Historical Society of Missouri, Research Center Columbia
William H. Lynch Diaries

State Historical Society of Missouri, Research Center St. Louis
Henry Kuck Letters

Syracuse University, Special Collections Research Center, Syracuse, New York
Albert M. Cook Papers

Tennessee State Library and Archives, Nashville
E. W. Mebane Letters, Civil War Collection

U.S. Army Military History Institute, Carlisle, Pennsylvania
Brigham Foster Papers
Hyder A. Kennedy File, box 5, book 19, file 81, Lewis Leigh Collection
Hubbard T. Minor Papers

University of Alabama, W. Stanley Hoole Special Collections Library, Tuscaloosa
Henry DeLamar Clayton Sr. Papers

University of Arkansas, Special Collections, Fayetteville
Daniel Harris Reynolds Diary

University of Georgia, Hargrett Rare Book and Manuscript Library, Athens
Charles A. James Martin Family Papers
Horace Park Letters
Miletus Tuttle Letters

University of Iowa, Special Collections, Iowa City
    Charles Thomas Ackley Civil War Letters
    John C. Brown Diary
    David James Palmer Papers
University of Michigan, Bentley Historical Library, Ann Arbor
    Judson L. Austin Papers
University of Michigan, William L. Clements Library, Ann Arbor
    John R. Comfort Papers, James M. Schoff Civil War Collections
    Lyman Gardner Papers, James M. Schoff Civil War Collections
    Josiah Edmond King Papers, James M. Schoff Civil War Collections
    George Martin Trowbridge Papers, James M. Schoff Civil War Collections
University of Mississippi, Archives and Special Collections, Oxford
    J. A. Bigger Memoir
    J. F. Butler Letters, Burton-Butler Papers
    Winfield Scott Featherston Collection
    Jesse L. Henderson Civil War Diary
University of North Carolina, Southern History Collection, Chapel Hill
    Edward W. Allen Papers
    Taylor Beatty Diary
    Clayton Family Papers
    Robert Stuart Finley Papers
    Stephen D. Lee Papers
    W. J. Watson Diary
    Chauncey Brunson Welton Papers
University of Notre Dame, Rare Books and Special Collections, South Bend,
    Indiana
    Henry H. Maley Letters
University of Oklahoma, Western History Collections, Norman
    Abraham J. Seay Collection
University of South Carolina, South Caroliniana Library, Columbia
    Charles G. Ward Diary
University of Southern Mississippi, McCain Library and Archives, Hattiesburg
    Capt. William Van Davis Diary
    Dr. P. F. Whitehead Letters
University of Tennessee, Special Collections, Chattanooga
    Philip R. Ward Diary, Charles S. Harris Collection
University of Tennessee, Special Collections, Knoxville
    Tilghman Blazer Collection
    Thomas Doak Edington Papers
    Orlando L. French Civil War Letters
    Michael Houck Diary
    Edwin Hansford Rennolds Sr. Papers
    John Watkins Papers
University of Texas, Dolph Briscoe Center for American History, Austin
    Unidentified Diary, Civil War Miscellany

University of Virginia, Electronic Text Center, Charlottesville
  Charles Berry Senior Letters
University of Washington, Special Collections, Seattle
  M. F. Force Papers
University of Wyoming, American Heritage Center, Laramie
  Mendal C. Churchill Papers
Virginia Historical Society, Richmond
  James Madison Brannock Papers
  James Miller Wysor Letters
Wisconsin Historical Society, Madison
  Dwight S. Allen Papers
  Charles A. Booth Journal
  George A. Cooley Civil War Diary
  Alonzo Miller Papers
  Levi H. Nickel Diary
  John H. Roberts Letters
  James F. Sawyer Letters
  Charles M. Smith Papers

NEWSPAPERS

Atlanta Constitution
Cincinnati Commercial
Frank Leslie's Illustrated Newspaper
Harper's Weekly
Indianapolis Daily Journal

Mobile Register and Advertiser
National Tribune
New York Daily Tribune
St. Louis Daily Missouri Democrat

WEBSITES

James M. Randall Diary and Letters, www.ehistory.com
W. L. Truman Memoir, www.cedarcroft.com

ARTICLES AND BOOKS

Abernethy, Byron R., ed. *Private Elisha Stockwell, Jr. Sees the Civil War*. Norman: University of Oklahoma Press, 1958.

Adams, Robert N. "The Battle and Capture of Atlanta." In *Glimpses of the Nation's Struggle, Fourth Series: Papers Read before the Minnesota Commandery of the Military Order of the Loyal Legion of the United States, 1892–1897*, 144–63. Wilmington, N.C.: Broadfoot Publishing, 1992.

Allen, Stacy Dale, ed. *On the Skirmish Line behind a Friendly Tree: The Civil War Memoirs of William Royal Oake, 26th Iowa Volunteers*. Helena, Mont.: Farcountry Press, 2006.

Angle, Paul M., ed. *Three Years in the Army of the Cumberland: The Letters and Diary of Major James A. Connolly*. Bloomington: Indiana University Press, 1959.

Arbuckle, John C. *Civil War Experiences of a Foot-Soldier Who Marched with Sherman*. Columbus, Ohio: n.p., 1930.

Ashley, Joe, and Lavon Ashley, eds. *Oh for Dixie! The Civil War Record and Diary of Capt. William V. Davis, 30th Mississippi Infantry, C.S.A.* Colorado Springs, Colo.: Standing Pine Press, 2001.

Aten, Henry J. *History of the Eighty-Fifth Regiment, Illinois Volunteer Infantry*. Hiawatha, Kans.: Henry J. Aten, 1901.

Barlow, John W. "Personal Reminiscences of the War." In *War Papers: Being Papers Read before the Commandery of the State of Wisconsin, Military Order of the Loyal Legion of the United States*, 1:106–19. Wilmington, N.C.: Broadfoot Publishing, 1993.

Barron, S. B. *The Lone Star Defenders: A Chronicle of the Third Texas Cavalry, Ross' Brigade*. New York: Neale, 1908.

Battles of Atlanta. Atlanta: n.p., 1895.

Bauer, K. Jack, ed. *Soldiering: The Civil War Diary of Rice C. Bull, 123rd New York Volunteer Infantry*. San Rafael, Calif.: Presidio Press, 1977.

Bearss, Edwin C. *The Siege of Jackson, July 10–17, 1863*. Baltimore: Gateway Press, 1981.

Bek, William G., trans. and ed. "The Civil War Diary of John T. Buegel, Union Soldier, Part Two." *Missouri Historical Review* 40, no. 4 (July 1946): 503–30.

Bell, John T. *Tramps and Triumphs of the Second Iowa Infantry*. Omaha: Gibson, Miller and Richardson, 1886.

Bennett, Stewart, and Barbara Tillery, eds. *The Struggle for the Life of the Republic: A Civil War Narrative by Brevet Major Charles Dana Miller, 76th Ohio Volunteer Infantry*. Kent, Ohio: Kent State University Press, 2004.

Black, Samuel. *A Soldier's Recollections of the Civil War*. Minco, Okla.: Minco Minstrel, 1912.

Black, Wilfred W., ed. "Marching with Sherman through Georgia and the Carolinas: Civil War Diary of Jesse L. Dozer." *Georgia Historical Quarterly* 52, no. 3 (September 1968): 308–31.

Blomquist, Ann K., and Robert A. Taylor, eds. *This Cruel War: The Civil War Letters of Grant and Malinda Taylor, 1862–1865*. Macon, Ga.: Mercer University Press, 2000.

Bohrnstedt, Jennifer Cain, ed. *Soldiering with Sherman: Civil War Letters of George F. Cram*. DeKalb: Northern Illinois University Press, 2000.

Brandle, H. M. "At Ezra Chapel: Reminiscences of a Missouri Soldier." *National Tribune*, December 22, 1887.

Brown, Thaddeus S. C., Samuel J. Murphy, and William G. Putney. *Behind the Guns: The History of Battery I, 2nd Regiment, Illinois Light Artillery*. Carbondale: Southern Illinois University Press, 1965.

Butler, Watson Hubbard, [ed.]. *Letters Home: Jay Caldwell Butler, Captain, 101st Ohio Volunteer Infantry*. N.p.: n.p., 1930.

Byrne, Frank L., ed. *The View from Headquarters: Civil War Letters of Harvey Reid*. Madison: State Historical Society of Wisconsin, 1965.

Cannon, J. P. *Inside of Rebeldom: The Daily Life of a Private in the Confederate Army*. Washington, D.C.: National Tribune, 1900.

Carpenter, John A. *Sword and Olive Branch: Oliver Otis Howard*. Pittsburgh, Pa.: University of Pittsburgh Press, 1964.

Castel, Albert. *Decision in the West: The Atlanta Campaign of 1864*. Lawrence: University Press of Kansas, 1992.

———. *Tom Taylor's Civil War*. Lawrence: University Press of Kansas, 2000.

Cate, Wirt Armistead, ed. *Two Soldiers: The Campaign Diaries of Thomas J. Key, C.S.A., and Robert J. Campbell, U.S.A.* Chapel Hill: University of North Carolina Press, 1938.

"Chamber Favors National Park." *Atlanta Constitution*, March 10, 1906.

Chamberlin, W. H. *History of the Eighty-First Regiment Ohio Infantry Volunteers during the War of the Rebellion*. Cincinnati: Gazette Steam Printing House, 1865.

Clampitt, Bradley R. *The Confederate Heartland: Military and Civilian Morale in the Western Confederacy*. Baton Rouge: Louisiana State University Press, 2011.

Clarke, John T. "With Sherman in Georgia." *Bulletin of the Missouri Historical Society* 8, no. 4 (July 1952): 356–70.

Connelly, Thomas Lawrence. *Autumn of Glory: The Army of Tennessee, 1862–1865*. Baton Rouge: Louisiana State University Press, 1971.

Connelly, Thomas W. *History of the Seventieth Ohio Regiment*. Cincinnati, Ohio: Peak Brothers, 1902.

Coombe, E. "The 28th of July Before Atlanta." *National Tribune*, February 7, 1884.

Cox, Jacob D. *Atlanta*. New York: Charles Scribner's Sons, 1882.

Crabb, Martha L. *All Afire to Fight: The Untold Tale of the Civil War's Ninth Texas Cavalry*. New York: Avon Books, 2000.

Crummel, A. B. "Ezra Chapel." *National Tribune*, April 26, 1888.

Cryder, George R., and Stanley R. Miller, comps. *A View From the Ranks: The Civil War Diaries of Charles E. Smith*. Delaware, Ohio: Delaware County Historical Society, 1999.

Dacus, Robert H. *Reminiscences of Company "H," First Arkansas Mounted Rifles*. Dayton, Ohio: Morningside Bookshop, 1972.

Davis, Jefferson. *The Rise and Fall of the Confederate Government*. 2 vols. New York: Thomas Yoseloff, 1958.

Davis, Stephen. *Atlanta Will Fall: Sherman, Joe Johnston, and the Yankee Heavy Battalions*. Wilmington, Del.: Scholarly Books, 2001.

———. "Hood Fights Desperately: The Battles for Atlanta." *Blue and Gray* 6, no. 6 (1989): 8–39, 45–62.

Dean, Jeffrey S. "The Forgotten 'Hell Hole': The Battle of Pickett's Mill." In *The Campaign for Atlanta and Sherman's March to the Sea*, vol. 2, edited by Theodore P. Savas and David A. Woodbury, 343–73. Campbell, Calif.: Savas Woodbury, 1994.

DeRosier, Arthur H., Jr., ed. *Through the South with a Union Soldier*. Johnson City: East Tennessee State University Research Advisory Council, 1969.

Deupree, J. G. "The Noxubee Squadron of the First Mississippi Cavalry, C.S.A.,

1861–1865." *Publications of the Mississippi Historical Society*, Centenary
Series, 2 (1918): 12–43.

Dodson, W. C., ed. *Campaigns of Wheeler and His Cavalry, 1862–1865*. Atlanta, Ga.:
Hudgins, 1899.

"A Driving Tour of Civil War Battlefields of Suburban Atlanta." *Brown's Guide to
Georgia*, August 1980: 37–38, 68–70, 72.

Duke, John K. *History of the Fifty-Third Regiment Ohio Volunteer Infantry, During
the War of the Rebellion, 1861 to 1865*. Portsmouth, Ohio: Blade Printing, 1900.

Dunlap, Leslie W., ed. *"Your Affectionate Husband, J. F. Culver": Letters Written
during the Civil War*. Iowa City: Friends of the University of Iowa Libraries,
1978.

Elliott, Sam Davis. *Soldier of Tennessee: General Alexander P. Stewart and the Civil
War in the West*. Baton Rouge: Louisiana State University Press, 1999.

Ellison, Janet Correll, ed. *On to Atlanta: The Civil War Diaries of John Hill
Ferguson, Illinois Tenth Regiment of Volunteers*. Lincoln: University of Nebraska
Press, 2001.

Engs, Robert F., and Corey M. Brooks, eds. *Their Patriotic Duty: The Civil War
Letters of the Evans Family of Brown County, Ohio*. New York: Fordham
University Press, 2007.

Erquitt, Bill. "Confederate Defeat at Ezra Church." *North South Trader* 5, no. 2
(January–February 1978): 20–26, 33.

Evans, David. *Sherman's Horsemen: Union Cavalry Operations in the Atlanta
Campaign*. Bloomington: Indiana University Press, 1996.

Fahs, Alice. *The Imagined Civil War: Popular Literature of the North & South,
1861–1865*. Chapel Hill: University of North Carolina Press, 2001.

Fetters, Samuel. "Calls Up Memories: The Ezra Chapel Story Reminds a Comrade
of His Experience." *National Tribune*, August 29, 1895.

Fowler, James, and Miles M. Miller. *History of the Thirtieth Iowa Infantry
Volunteers*. Mediapolis, Iowa: T. A. Merrill, 1908.

French, Samuel G. *Two Wars: An Autobiography*. Nashville, Tenn.: Confederate
Veteran, 1901.

Gage, J. S. "In the Front Line at Ezra Chapel." *National Tribune*. August 1, 1895.

Gage, M. D. *From Vicksburg to Raleigh: Or, A Complete History of the Twelfth
Regiment Indiana Volunteer Infantry*. Chicago: Clarke and Company, 1865.

Georgia Civil War Historical Markers. 2nd ed. Atlanta: Georgia Historical
Commission, 1982.

Goodloe, Albert Theodore. *Confederate Echoes: A Voice from the South in the Days
of Secession and of the Southern Confederacy*. Nashville, Tenn.: Smith and
Lamar, 1907.

———. *Some Rebel Relics from the Seat of War*. Nashville, Tenn.: Methodist
Episcopal Church, South, 1893.

Gould, David, and James B. Kennedy, eds. *Memoirs of a Dutch Mudsill: The 'War
Memories' of John Henry Otto, Captain, Company D, 21st Regiment Wisconsin
Volunteer Infantry*. Kent, Ohio: Kent State University Press, 2004.

Grant, Ulysses S. *Personal Memoirs of U. S. Grant*. New York: Viking, 1990.

Grunert, William. *History of the One Hundred and Twenty-Ninth Regiment Illinois Volunteer Infantry*. Winchester, Ill.: R. B. Dedman, 1866.

Hale, Douglas. *The Third Texas Cavalry in the Civil War*. Norman: University of Oklahoma Press, 1993.

Hattaway, Herman. *General Stephen D. Lee*. Jackson: University Press of Mississippi, 1976.

Haughton, Andrew. *Training, Tactics and Leadership in the Confederate Army of Tennessee: Seeds of Failure*. Portland, Ore.: Frank Cass, 2000.

Henry, H. W. "Little War-Time Incidents." *Confederate Veteran* 22 (1914): 306.

Hess, Earl J. *Kennesaw Mountain: Sherman, Johnston, and the Atlanta Campaign*. Chapel Hill: University of North Carolina Press, 2013.

———. *The Rifle Musket in Civil War Combat: Reality and Myth*. Lawrence: University Press of Kansas, 2008.

———. "The Twelfth Missouri Infantry: A Socio-Military Profile of a Union Regiment." In *A Rough Business: Fighting the Civil War in Missouri* edited by William Garrett Piston, 145–65. Columbia: State Historical Society of Missouri, 2012.

———, ed. *A German in the Yankee Fatherland: The Civil War Letters of Henry A. Kircher*. Kent, Ohio: Kent State University Press, 1983.

"A History of Company B, 40th Alabama Infantry, C.S.A." *Alabama Historical Quarterly* 17, no. 3 (Fall 1955): 159–222.

History of the Fifteenth Regiment, Iowa Veteran Volunteer Infantry From October, 1861, to August, 1865. Keokuk, Iowa: R. B. Ogden and Son, 1887.

Hogan, Sally Coplen, ed. *General Reub Williams's Memories of Civil War Times*. Westminster, Md.: Heritage Books, 2004.

Holzhueter, John O., ed. "William Wallace's Civil War Letters: The Atlanta Campaign." *Wisconsin Magazine of History* 57, no. 2 (Winter 1973-1974): 90–116.

Hood, J. B. *Advance and Retreat: Personal Experiences in the United States and Confederate States Armies*. New Orleans: Hood Orphan Memorial Fund, 1880.

———. "The Defense of Atlanta." In *Battles and Leaders of the Civil War*, vol. 4, edited by Robert Underwood Johnson and Clarence Clough Buel, 336–44. New York: Thomas Yoseloff, 1956.

Hord, L. D. "Forcing a Hard Campaign: The Battle of July 28, 1864, as Told of By a 32d Ohio Comrade—Incidents of a Trying Time." *National Tribune*, July 6, 1899.

Howard, Oliver Otis. *Autobiography*. 2 vols. New York: Baker and Taylor, 1907.

———. "The Battles about Atlanta." *Atlantic Monthly* 38, no. 228 (October 1876): 385–99.

———. "The Struggle for Atlanta." In *Battles and Leaders of the Civil War*, vol. 4, edited by Robert Underwood Johnson and Clarence Clough Buel, 293–325. New York: Thomas Yoseloff, 1956.

Hudson, David, Marvin Bergman, and Loren Horton. *The Biographical Dictionary of Iowa*. Iowa City: University of Iowa Press, 2009.

Hughes, Nathaniel Cheairs, Jr. *The Civil War Memoir of Philip Daingerfield Stephenson, D.D.* Conway: University of Central Arkansas Press, 1995.

Hurst, Samuel H. *Journal-History of the Seventy-Third Ohio Volunteer Infantry.* Chillicothe, Ohio: n.p., 1866.

Jackson, Oscar L. *The Colonel's Diary.* N.p.: n.p., n.d.

Jamison, Matthew H. *Recollections of Pioneer and Army Life.* Kansas City, Mo.: Hudson Fields, [1911].

Johnson, Polk G. "Forty-Ninth Tennessee Infantry." In *The Military Annals of Tennessee, Confederate,* edited by John Berrien Lindsley, 551–58. Spartanburg, S.C.: Reprint Company, 1974.

Johnson, R. W. *A Soldier's Reminiscences in Peace and War.* Philadelphia: J. B. Lippincott, 1886.

Johnson, Robert Underwood, and Clarence Clough Buel, eds. *Battles and Leaders of the Civil War.* 4 vols. New York: Thomas Yoseloff, 1956.

Jones, James P. *Black Jack: John A. Logan and Southern Illinois in the Civil War Era.* Tallahassee: Florida State University Press, 1967.

Jordan, Philip D., ed. "Forty Days with the Christian Commission: A Diary by William Salter." *Iowa Journal of History and Politics* 33, no. 2 (April 1935): 123–54.

Jordan, Weymouth T., ed. "Mathew Andrew Dunn Letters." *Journal of Mississippi History* 1 (1939): 110–27.

Keller, Christian B. *Chancellorsville and the Germans: Nativism, Ethnicity, and Civil War Memory.* New York: Fordham University Press, 2007.

Kendall, John Smith. "Recollections of a Confederate Officer." *Louisiana Historical Quarterly* 29 (1946): 1041–1228.

Kerr, Homer L., ed. *Fighting with Ross' Texas Cavalry Brigade, C.S.A.: The Diary of George L. Griscom, Adjutant, 9th Texas Cavalry Regiment.* Hillsboro, Tex.: Hill Junior College Press, 1976.

Kinnear, J. R. *History of the Eighty-Sixth Regiment Illinois Volunteer Infantry.* Chicago: Tribune, 1866.

Leeper, Wesley Thurman. *Rebels Valiant: Second Arkansas Mounted Rifles (Dismounted).* Little Rock, Ark.: Pioneer Press, 1964.

Logan, John A. *The Volunteer Soldier of America.* Chicago: R. S. Peale, 1887.

Longacre, Glenn V., and John E. Haas, eds. *To Battle for God and the Right: The Civil War Letterbooks of Emerson Opdycke.* Urbana: University of Illinois Press, 2003.

Love, Joseph. "Forty-Eighth Tennessee Infantry." In *The Military Annals of Tennessee, Confederate,* edited by John Berrien Lindsley, 546–49. Spartanburg, S.C.: Reprint Company, 1974.

Lucas, D. R. *New History of the 99th Indiana Infantry.* Rockford, Ill.: Horner Printing, 1900.

Martin, William. *"Out and Forward"; or, Recollections of the War of 1861 to 1865.* Manhattan, Kans.: Art Craft Printers, 1941.

Mathis, Ray, ed. *In the Land of the Living: Wartime Letters by Confederates from the Chattahoochee Valley of Alabama and Georgia.* Troy, Ala.: Troy State University Press, 1981.

McBride, Mary Gorton, and Ann Mathison McLaurin. *Randall Lee Gibson of Louisiana: Confederate General and New South Reformer.* Baton Rouge: Louisiana State University Press, 2007.

McCarley, J. Britt. "'Atlanta is Ours and Fairly Won': A Driving Tour of the Atlanta Area's Principal Civil War Battlefields." *Atlanta Historical Journal* 28, no. 3 (Fall 1984): 7–98.

McMurry, Richard M. *Atlanta, 1864: Last Chance for the Confederacy.* Lincoln: University of Nebraska Press, 2000.

———. "Confederate Morale in the Atlanta Campaign of 1864." *Georgia Historical Quarterly* 54 (1970): 226–43.

———. *John Bell Hood and the War for Southern Independence.* Lexington: University Press of Kentucky, 1982.

McNeill, William J. "A Survey of Confederate Soldier Morale during Sherman's Campaign through Georgia and the Carolinas." *Georgia Historical Quarterly* 55 (1971): 1–25.

McNeilly, James H. "Recollections From One, Who Though Not a Surgeon, Was With Them All the Time." *Southern Practitioner* 22, no. 9 (September 1900): 415–20.

McPherson, James M. *Battle Cry of Freedom: The Civil War Era.* New York: Ballantine, 1988.

McWhiney, Grady, and Perry D. Jamieson. *Attack and Die: Civil War Military Tactics and the Southern Heritage.* Tuscaloosa: University of Alabama Press, 1982.

The Medical and Surgical History of the Civil War. 12 vols. Wilmington, N.C.: Broadfoot Publishing, 1991.

Mitchell, Enoch L., ed. "The Civil War Letters of Thomas Jefferson Newberry." *Journal of Mississippi History* 19, no. 1 (January 1948): 44–80.

Mitchell, Joseph B. *The Badge of Gallantry: Recollections of Civil War Congressional Medal of Honor Winners.* New York: Macmillan, 1968.

Montgomery, Frank A. *Reminiscences of a Mississippian in Peace and War.* Cincinnati: Robert Clarke, 1901.

Montgomery, W. A. "Memorial Address on Gen. S. D. Lee." *Confederate Veteran* 16 (1908): 317–18.

Morris, William S. *History, 31st Regiment Illinois Volunteers.* Evansville, Ind.: Keller, 1902.

Ninth Reunion of the 37th Regiment O.V.V.I. Toledo, Ohio: Montgomery and Vrooman, 1890.

Noyes, Edward, ed. "Excerpts from the Civil War Diary of E. T. Eggleston." *Tennessee Historical Quarterly* 17, no. 4 (December 1958): 336–58.

Osborn, Hartwell. "Sherman's Atlanta Campaign." *Western Reserve University Bulletin* 14, no. 6 (November 1911): 116–38.

Phillips, Ulrich B., ed. *Correspondence of Robert Toombs, Alexander H. Stephens, and Howell Cobb: Annual Report of the American Historical Association for the Year 1911.* 2 vols. Washington, D.C.: Government Printing Office, 1913.

Post, Lydia Minturn, ed. *Soldiers' Letters From Camp, Battle-Field and Prison.* New York: Bunce and Huntington, 1865.

Purifoy, John. "Washington Bryan Crumpton, D.D., Chaplain General, Army of Tennessee Department, U.C.V." *Confederate Veteran* 34 (1926): 377–79.

"Report of the Proceedings of the Annual Meeting of the Association of Medical

Officers of the Army and Navy of the Confederacy, at New Orleans, May 19–22, 1903, Third Day, Thursday, May 23, 1903." *Southern Practitioner* 25, no. 8 (August 1903): 447–74.

[Rood, Hosea W.]. *Story of the Service of Company E, and of the Twelfth Wisconsin Regiment, Veteran Volunteer Infantry.* Milwaukee, Wisc.: Swain and Tate, 1893.

Roy, T. B. "General Hardee and the Military Operations around Atlanta." *Southern Historical Society Papers* 8 (1880): 337–87.

Russell, E. L. "Col. E. L. Russell, Orator of the Occasion." *Confederate Veteran* 16 (1908): 315–17.

Salling, Stuart. *Louisianians in the Western Confederacy: The Adams-Gibson Brigade in the Civil War.* Jefferson, N.C.: McFarland, 2010.

Saunier, Joseph A., ed. *A History of the Forty-Seventh Regiment Ohio Veteran Volunteer Infantry.* Hillsboro, Ohio Lyle Printing, [1903].

Sears, Stephen W. *To the Gates of Richmond: The Peninsula Campaign.* New York: Ticknor and Fields, 1992.

Shelton, W. J. "Ezra Chapel: How Gen. Howard Impressed Troops in Battle." *National Tribune*, January 5, 1888.

Sherman, William T. "The Grand Strategy of the Last Year of the War." In *Battles and Leaders of the Civil War*, vol. 4, edited by Robert Underwood Johnson and Clarence Clough Buel, 247–59. New York: Thomas Yoseloff, 1956.

———. *Memoirs.* 2 vols. New York: D. Appleton, 1875.

Shrum, G. W. "Atlanta and Ezra Chapel." *National Tribune*, February 16, 1888.

Simpson, Brooks D., and Jean V. Berlin, eds. *Sherman's Civil War: Selected Correspondence of William T. Sherman, 1860–1865.* Chapel Hill: University of North Carolina Press, 1999.

Smith, Charles H. *The History of Fuller's Ohio Brigade, 1861–1865.* Cleveland, Ohio: A. J. Watt, 1909.

Smith, Edwin W. "Battle of Ezra Church." *National Tribune*, July 5, 1888.

Smith, H. I. *History of the Seventh Iowa Veteran Volunteer Infantry during the Civil War.* Mason City, Iowa: E. Hitchcock, 1903.

Smith, Hampton, ed. *Brother of Mine: The Civil War Letters of Thomas and William Christie.* St. Paul: Minnesota Historical Society Press, 2011.

Smith, Louis R., Jr., and Andrew Quist, eds. *Cush: A Civil War Memoir.* Livingston, Ala.: Livingston Press, 1999.

Smith, W. C. *The Private in Gray.* N.p.: n.p., n.d.

Story of the Fifty-Fifth Regiment Illinois Volunteer Infantry in the Civil War, 1861–1865. Clinton, Mass.: W. J. Coulter, 1887.

Stuart, A. A. *Iowa Colonels and Regiments: Being a History of Iowa Regiments in the War of the Rebellion.* Des Moines, Iowa: Mills and Company, 1865.

Supplement to the Official Records of the Union and Confederate Armies. 100 vols. Wilmington, N.C.: Broadfoot Publishing, 1993–2000.

Tapert, Annette, ed. *The Brothers' War: Civil War Letters to Their Loved Ones from the Blue and Gray.* New York: Vintage Books, 1988.

Throne, Mildred, ed. "A History of Company D, Eleventh Iowa Infantry, 1861–1865." *Iowa Journal of History* 55, no. 1 (January 1957): 35–90.

Tisdale, J. R. "Ezra Chapel: How the Fifteenth Corps Withstood the Rebel Charges." *National Tribune*, May 10, 1888.

Tower, R. Lockwood, ed. *A Carolinian Goes to War: The Civil War Narrative of Arthur Middleton Manigault, Brigadier General, C.S.A.* Columbia: University of South Carolina Press, 1983.

"Tributes to Gen. A. P. Stewart." *Confederate Veteran* 16 (1908): 594–95.

Venet, Wendy Hamand, ed. *Sam Richards's Civil War Diary: A Chronicle of the Atlanta Home Front*. Athens: University of Georgia Press, 2009.

Volwiler, A. T., ed. "Letters from a Civil War Officer." *Mississippi Valley Historical Review* 14, no. 4 (March 1928): 508–29.

"War Diary of Thaddeus H. Capron, 1861–1865." *Journal of the Illinois State Historical Society* 12, no. 3 (October 1919): 330–406.

The War of the Rebellion: A Compilation of the Official Records of the Union and Confederate Armies. 70 vols. in 128. Washington, D.C.: Government Printing Office, 1880–1901.

Warner, Ezra J. *Generals in Gray: Lives of the Confederate Commanders*. Baton Rouge: Louisiana State University Press, 1959.

Welsh, Jack D. *Medical Histories of Confederate Generals*. Kent, Ohio: Kent State University Press, 1995.

White, William Lee, and Charles Denny Runion, eds. *Great Things Are Expected of Us: The Letters of Colonel C. Irvine Walker, 10th South Carolina Infantry, C.S.A.* Knoxville: University of Tennessee Press, 2009.

"Wilbur Kurtz Explains Selection of U.S. Memorial Park 'Sites Here.'" *Atlanta Constitution*, November 14, 1931.

Wills, Charles W. *Army Life of an Illinois Soldier, Including a Day By Day Record of Sherman's March to the Sea*. Washington, D.C.: Globe Printing, 1906.

Wingfield, Marshall. *General A. P. Stewart: His Life and Letters*. Memphis: West Tennessee Historical Society, 1954.

Winther, Oscar Osburn, ed. *With Sherman to the Sea: The Civil War Letters, Diaries, & Reminiscences of Theodore F. Upson*. New York: Kraus Reprint, 1969.

Woodworth, Steven E. *Nothing but Victory: The Army of the Tennessee, 1861–1865*. New York: Alfred A. Knopf, 2005.

Wooster, Ralph A., ed. "Four Years in the Confederate Infantry: The Civil War Letters of Private R. F. Eddins, 19th Louisiana Volunteers." *Texas Gulf Historical and Biographical Record* 7 (1971): 11–37.

Worley, Ted R., ed. *The War Memoirs of Captain John W. Lavender, C.S.A.* Pine Bluff, Ark.: Southern Press, 1956.

Wright, Charles. *A Corporal's Story: Experiences in the Ranks of Company C, 81st Ohio Vol. Infantry, During the War for the Maintenance of the Union, 1861–1864*. Philadelphia: James Beale, 1887.

Wright, Henry H. *A History of the Sixth Iowa Infantry*. Cedar Rapids, Iowa: Torch Press, 1923.

Wynne, Lewis N., and Robert A. Taylor, eds. *This War So Horrible: The Civil War Diary of Hiram Smith Williams*. Tuscaloosa: University of Alabama Press, 1993.

Index

Adams, Robert N., 127
Affleck, Albert, 105, 156–57
Alabama units
  17th, 117
  19th, 86–87
  22nd, 86, 91
  24th, 110, 112
  25th, 80, 86, 91
  28th, 110–12
  34th, 110–11, 113
  35th, 133
  39th, 80, 86, 91
  50th, 86
Alexander, Isaac N., 89
Allan, David, Jr., 83, 104, 157, 167
Allen, Edward W., 9
Allen, Ivan, Sr., 206
Arbuckle, John C., 83–84, 102, 195
Armstrong, Frank C., 49, 50–51, 55
Army of Tennessee, xiii–xiv, 22, 197, 202
Army of the Tennessee, 9, 23
Aten, Henry J., 139–41, 164, 194
Atlanta, battle of, xi, 8–9, 11, 202–3, 206–7
Atlanta and West Point Railroad, 6, 12
Atlanta campaign, xi–xiv, 1–28, 56
Austin, Judson, 151

Baker, Alpheus, 102–3
Balloch, George W., 34
Barlow, John W., 150
Bass, John H., 145
Beatty, Taylor, 158
Bell, Charles J., 98
Bickerdyke, Ann, 155

Black, Samuel, 152, 161
Blair, Francis P., Jr., 18, 33
Blair, Jonathan, 87
Boughton, Sam, 87
Braden, George W., 91
Bragg, Braxton, 24
Brandle, H. M., 102, 105–6
Brannock, James M., 131, 175
Brantley, William F., 58–59, 69–70
Brown, John C., 55, 58, 68–70, 91–92, 108–9, 112–13, 163, 182
Brown, William B., 187
Bryant, George E., 64
Buckingham, Philo B., 150
Buegel, John T., 48
Bumfoeder, Henry, 61
Bunn, Henry G., 122
Butler, Jay, 164
Butler, William L., 110

Cameron, Daniel, 136
Carskaddon, David, 102
Chancellorsville, battle of, 14, 195
Cheatham, Benjamin F., 19, 182
Chickamauga, battle of, 199, 202
Christie, Thomas D., 189
Churchill, Mendal C., 168
Clayton, Andrew J., 43
Clayton, Henry D., 55–56, 94, 96, 102, 106–8, 174, 203
Clayton, Thomas L., 175
Clement, James H., 64
Clune, William H., 67
Cobb, Howell, 203–4
Coltart, John G., 80

Comfort, John R., 36
Connelly, Thomas W., 34, 82, 121, 147, 152, 155–56, 160
Connolly, James A., 72, 150–51, 153, 168
Coomb, Elijah, 77, 129
Corse, John M., 26, 31–32, 67, 151
Cowley, Stephen, 123–24, 130, 175
Cox, G. Thomas, 123
Cox, Jacob, 45, 92, 176, 181
Craig, Joseph M., 159
Crummel, A. B., 65, 124
Crumpton, Washington B., 129–30
Cunningham, Ed. H., 96, 203
Curry, J. H., 103

Davis, Harry, 100, 161
Davis, Jefferson, 4, 21–22, 41
Davis, Jefferson C., 23, 32, 137–38, 140, 185, 207
DeGress, Francis, 51
Devall, David, 99
Dodd, Allen, 155
Dodge, Grenville M., 14, 18, 26, 28, 33, 117, 163
Downing, J. B., 73–74
Dozer, Jesse, 92
Driskell, John, 156
Duke, John K., 61
Dunham, Charles L., 183
Dunn, Matthew A., 133–34

Eddins, R. F., 94, 96
Elrick, Thomas J., 67
Evans, Andrew, 169–70
Evans, Eddie, 70
Ezra Church, 44–45, 47
Ezra Church, battle of, xi–xv, 56–57, 59, 65, 80–81, 134, 143, 162–77, 194–204; ammunition expended at, 105–6, 120, 124–27, 198–99; appearance of field at, 144–45, 149–51, 161, 183, 189, 192; artillery in, 71–72, 135; burial of dead at, 151–54, 242 (n. 20); entrenching tools at, 46, 48, 84; fieldworks at, 46–48, 85, 91–92, 162–63, 195; flags captured at, 100–101, 161; liquor at, 170–71; losses at, 70, 91, 99, 103–5, 112, 122, 130–31, 159–60, 198–200; Masons at, 153, 192; Medal of Honor at, 61, 100, 161; medical care at, 146, 154–59; poem about, 99–100; preservation efforts at, 205–7; prisoners at, 160, 243 (n. 46); range of engagement at, 200–201; reinforcements to Fifteenth Corps, 63–64, 117, 119, 121–22, 126–28, 143; rifle musket at, 200–201; skirmishing at, xiv, 48–54, 59, 68, 73–74, 79–80, 82, 122–23, 133, 136, 195, 197, 201; troop strength at, 57, 159–60, 226 (n. 47); vegetation at, 46, 67, 80, 96, 110; weather and, 31, 38, 42, 64, 70, 90, 106, 113, 156; women soldiers in, 171

Featherston, Winfield S., 132
Ferguson, John H., 140
Ferguson, Samuel W., 49, 172–73
Foster, Isaac Gaillard, 55
Frank Leslie's Illustrated Newspaper, 84–85
French, Samuel G., 134, 182
Fuller, John W., 26, 33
Fultz, William, 27

Gage, Joseph S., 90, 97, 102–3
Gage, M. D., 152–53, 167–68, 198, 200
Galvin, Michael, 67
Georgia Railroad, 2, 4, 6, 10–11
Gettysburg, battle of, 199
Gibson, Randall L., 94–99
Gilkey, Walter Mims, 103
Gillmore, Robert A., 48
Girdner, Ephraim L., 149
Goodnow, James H., 48, 53, 82, 84, 86
Grant, Ulysses S., xiv, 17, 48
Greathouse, Lucien, 53
Greene, Alexander A., 102

Griffin, Daniel, 168, 171

Hall, Hiram W., 67
Hamilton, Andrew J., 70
Hampton, John, 156
Hampton, Wade, 19
Hardee, William J., 6, 38–39, 41,
    134–35, 177, 182, 197
Harllee, Robert Z., 111
Harper's Weekly, 47, 76–77, 100–101,
    169
Harris, John A., 154
Harrow, William, 81–82, 162
Hart, Benjamin R., 80, 192
Hasty, Willis, 85
Hattaway, Herman, 196
Hempleman, Nelson, 156
Henderson, Jesse L., 174
Henry, H. W., 192
Hickenlooper, Andrew, 72
Hildt, George H., 64, 124, 148, 163, 195
Hipp, Charles, 61, 227 (n. 9)
Holtzclaw, James T., 103
Hood, John B., xi–xii, 4–5, 7–8, 19,
    21–22, 24, 38, 40–41, 54–56,
    134–35, 146, 166, 182, 168, 172,
    175–77, 189, 193, 197, 202–3
Hooker, Joseph, 6, 16, 34–37
Hord, L. D., 27, 128
Howard, Charles H., 142–43
Howard, Oliver O., xi–xii, 7, 13–19,
    28, 30–33, 43–44, 46, 48, 50–51,
    62–63, 68, 71–72, 117, 121, 127,
    139–44, 147, 162, 166, 183–86, 189,
    195, 197–98, 204–5
Humes, William Y. C., 138
Hurt, Joseph, 131
Hutchinson, Frederick S., 82, 163

Illinois units
    9th, 137–38
    12th, 117, 127
    26th, 87, 120, 191, 198
    31st, 64, 67
    40th, 67, 126

    48th, 53, 79, 87, 91
    55th, 77–78, 85
    64th, 117, 126
    65th, 136
    66th, 117, 126
    90th, 91
    103rd, 89
    111th, 62
    116th, 77, 129, 153
    127th, 53
    Battery A, 1st Light Artillery, 51–52
Indiana units
    12th, 86
    63rd, 136
    83rd, 62, 64, 206
    99th, 153
Innes, Thomas J., 67–68
Iowa units
    3rd, 121
    6th, 67–68, 126, 128
    13th, 121–22
    15th, 128, 191

Jackson, Oscar L., 27, 192
Jackson, William H., 13, 49, 54, 138
Jacobs, Wayne Johnson, 64
Jamison, Matthew, 141
Johnson, Ashton, 130, 153–54
Johnson, Cyrus A., 91
Johnson, Richard W., 163
Johnston, George D., 78–79
Johnston, Joseph E., 1–2, 4, 41, 159, 166,
    176–77, 203
Jones, Wells S., 51, 53, 61, 65
Judge, Patrick, 156

Kaercher, Jacob, 105
Kendall, John I., 104
Kennedy, Hyder A., 99
Kennesaw Mountain, battle of, 198–99,
    205
Kensler, Phillip, 156
Kentucky units
    24th, 136
Kircher, Henry A., 156–57

Knox, Samuel L., 130
Kolb's Farm, battle of, 21, 35, 197
Kurtz, Wilbur G., 206

Landus, H. J., 206
Laphan, Erastus, 156
Lavender, John, 119, 174
Leary, William R., 91
Lee, Stephen D., xi–xii, 19–22, 25,
    39–40, 54, 56–58, 63, 71, 92, 111,
    114–15, 134, 145, 171–74, 176,
    195–97, 202–5
Leeper, John W., 122
Leggett, Mortimer D., 165
Lick Skillet, Ga., 45, 206
Lick Skillet Road, 45, 49–50, 53–57, 59,
    133, 145, 182, 195–96, 206–7, 224
    (n. 11)
Lightburn, Joseph A. J., 50–51
Lofland, Gordon, 126
Logan, John A., 8, 10–11, 14, 17–18, 23,
    26–30, 37–38, 42–43, 50, 62–63,
    67, 147, 153, 162, 164–65, 183, 199
Loring, William W., 132
Louisiana units
    1st (Regulars), 158
    4th, 98, 104
    19th, 99
    20th, 104
    30th, 98, 100
Love, Joseph, 131
Love, Louis, 87, 100, 167
Loveless, Michael H., 99
Lovell, Mansfield, 19

Mackall, Thomas B., 103–4
Macon and Western Railroad, 6, 8
Maley, Henry H., 164, 171
Manigault, Arthur M., 57, 108–13,
    173–74
Marriott, Cary M., 106
Marshall, John H., 173
Marshall, John L., 168
Marston, James, 159
Martin, Angus, 53

Martin, John, 53
Martin, William, 153
Maurice, Thomas Davies, 71, 180
McCook, Edward M., 12–13, 181
McCormack, Andrew, 74
McGuirk, John, 40, 120
McLain, Will, 144
McMillen, John, 156
McMurry, Richard, 197
McNeilly, J. H., 131, 146
McPherson, James B., xi, 8, 17
Mebane, E. W., 124, 131
Merrill, Samuel, 168
Metz, George P., 154, 195
Michigan units
    15th, 53, 120
Midler, Washington L., 151, 154–55
Miller, Alonzo, 67
Miller, Charles Dana, 149, 161
Mississippi units
    1st Cavalry, 49, 51
    2nd Cavalry, 50
    7th, 76, 78
    9th, 76, 78
    9th (Battalion Sharpshooters), 73
    10th, 91
    24th, 69
    27th, 69
    28th Cavalry, 50, 53
    29th, 69
    30th, 69
    34th, 69
    37th, 129
    41st, 76, 78
    44th, 73, 76, 78
    Ballantine's Cavalry, 50
    Cowan's Battery, 133
    Yates's Battery, 123
Missouri units
    3rd (US), 90
    12th (US), 83, 90, 97, 103, 105, 156–57
    17th (Battalion, US), 43, 83
    29th (US), 43, 83, 90
    31st (US), 105
    32nd (US), 105

Guibor's Battery (CS), 134
Wade's Battery (CS), 133
Montgomery, Frank A., 49–50
Moore, J. C., 169
Moore, John, 10, 154–55, 157
Moore, Marshall F., 142–43
Morgan, James D., 137–40, 142, 180, 183, 187
Mortiz, Carl, 61–62
Mott, Samuel R., 48
Mozley, Hiram, 205–6
Murphy, Philip H., 90, 157
Murphy, Robinson B., 161

Neal, Andrew Jackson, 175
Newberry, Thomas J., 70
Newell, William M., 77–78, 167
New Jersey units
    35th, 117, 127, 153, 192

Oake, William R., 105, 145, 149, 152
Odell, William H., 91
Ohio units
    4th Battery, 51–52, 73–75
    30th, 62, 64, 127
    32nd, 27, 128
    37th, 51, 61–62, 65, 68, 127
    46th, 89, 97, 103
    47th, 51, 53, 60, 62, 65, 127
    53rd, 51, 53–54, 60–62, 65
    54th, 53–54, 60, 62, 65, 127
    57th, 77
    63rd, 191
    70th, 43, 53, 83, 89, 120, 122, 153, 155, 170
    76th, 105
    81st, 117, 127
    103rd, 136
Oliver, John, 97–98
Oliver, Starke H., 112
O'Neal, Edward A., 116–17
Osborn, Hartwell, 163
Owens, Robert A., 133

Palmer, John M., 142, 185

Palmer, Martin, 120
Peachtree Creek, battle of, xi, 6, 202–3, 206–7
Perryville, battle of, 202
Pfeffer, William C., 106
Phillips, Henry L., 121
Pickett's Mill, battle of, 16, 22, 205
Poe, Orlando M., 8–9, 191
Post, Franklin C., 89
Proctor's Creek, 45

Quarles, William A., 123, 129, 131, 133

Reese, Chauncey B., 8–9, 23, 191
Reynolds, Daniel H., 40, 119–20, 122–23
Richardson, William C., 130
Roberts, John H., 36
Ross, Emmett, 97–98, 158–59
Ross, Lawrence S., 13, 49, 138–39
Rouse, Napoleon B., 80

Safely, John J., 150
Salling, Stuart, 103–4
Salter, William, 151
Saunier, Joseph, 127, 195
Sawyer, James F., 167
Schmidt, Henry, 61
Schofield, John M., 23–24, 37, 136, 181, 184, 186, 189
Scott, George H., 64
Seay, Abraham J., 104, 149
Senior, Charles B., 180
Shane, John, 121–22
Sharp, Jacob H., 73, 108–9
Shaw, John, 155
Shelton, W. J., 144
Sherman, William T., xi–xii, 1–4, 6, 8, 10–11, 23, 28, 30–37, 44, 50, 56, 72, 117, 135–38, 140–43, 147, 153, 164–66, 194, 204; movements after battle of Ezra Church, 178–79, 183–87, 189, 191; selection of Howard, 13–18; use of cavalry, 11–12, 181–82
Shields, Thomas, 98, 149

Shiloh, battle of, 202
Shoup, Francis A., 24, 38, 54, 57,
    134, 145, 175, 182
Slack, Albert L., 149
Slaughter, John N., 110, 113
Slocum, Henry W., 36, 165
Smith, Charles E., 27, 30, 38, 62,
    147, 184
Smith, Edwin W., 54, 63
Smith, H. I., 184
Smith, Milo, 105
Smith, Morgan L., 34, 43–44, 50, 72
Smith, Thomas H., 130
Smith, Thomas T., 80, 133
Smith, W. C., 62
Smith, William M., 156
South Carolina units
    10th, 110
    19th, 111
Sprague, John W., 26
Sprott, William, 102
Stanley, David S., 36, 136, 165, 184
Stephenson, Philip D., 153–54, 175
Stevenson, Carter L., 54
Stewart, Alexander P., 6, 13, 40–41,
    55, 114–15, 129, 132–34, 197, 207
Stickney, Clifford, 167, 198
Stockwell, Elisha, 135
Stone, William M., 180
Stoneman, George, 12, 181–82
Stones River, battle of, 199, 202
Strong, William K., 126
Summers, James F., 121, 153
Sweeny, Thomas W., 26

Taylor, Grant, 103, 175
Taylor, Thomas T., 51, 53, 68–69,
    127
Tennessee units
    42nd, 123
    49th, 123
    53rd, 130
    55th, 131
Thomas, George H., 13, 35–36, 150,
    179, 181–82, 184–85

Thompson, W. H., 169
Tinsley, W. J., 112
Tisdale, J. R., 90, 104, 106
Titus, Daniel, 126
Torgler, Ernst, 61, 161
Toulmin, Harry T., 57, 80
Trowbridge, George M., 150, 170, 198
Tupelo, battle of, 21–22

Van Duzer, John C., 12

Walcutt, Charles C., 67, 87–89
Walker, C. Irvine, 110–11, 158
Walthall, Edward C., 116, 123, 129, 133
Wangelin, Hugo, 43, 47, 83, 90, 104
Ward, William, 183, 187
Warrick, Thomas, 174
Waters, David R., 138, 142
Weber, William, 124
Weirick, John H., 57
Western and Atlantic Railroad, 2, 6, 8
Wheeler, Joseph, 13, 38
Whitaker, H. L. G., 174
White, John R., 130
Whitehead, P. F., 132–33
Whitney, Isaac M., 80
Wigfall, F. Halsey, 172, 176
Willett, Elbert D., 103
Williams, Alpheus S., 36
Williams, Hiram Smith, 94, 145, 175
Williams, J. Byrd, 86
Williams, Reuben, 82, 106, 149, 171
Wills, Charles W., 170
Wintrode, J. F., 161
Wisconsin units
    12th, 64–65
Worley, Isaiah C., 57
Wright, Henry, 195
Wysor, James M., 163

Young, William F., 123, 131
Young, William H., 134
Youngblood, Major, 40

Zinken, Leon von, 96, 203